BEASTLY MODERNISMS

BEASTLY MODERNISMS

The Figure of the Animal in Modernist Literature and Culture

Edited by Saskia McCracken and
Alex Goody

EDINBURGH
University Press

Edinburgh University Press is one of the leading university presses in the UK. We publish academic books and journals in our selected subject areas across the humanities and social sciences, combining cutting-edge scholarship with high editorial and production values to produce academic works of lasting importance. For more information visit our website: edinburghuniversitypress.com

© editorial matter and organisation Saskia McCracken and Alex Goody 2023, 2024
© the chapters their several authors 2023, 2024

Edinburgh University Press Ltd
13 Infirmary Street
Edinburgh EH1 1LT

First published in hardback by Edinburgh University Press 2023

Typeset in 10/12.5 Adobe Sabon by
IDSUK (DataConnection) Ltd

A CIP record for this book is available from the British Library

ISBN 978 1 4744 9802 9 (hardback)
ISBN 978 1 4744 9803 6 (paperback)
ISBN 978 1 4744 9804 3 (webready PDF)
ISBN 978 1 4744 9805 0 (epub)

The right of Saskia McCracken and Alex Goody to be identified as the editor of this work has been asserted in accordance with the Copyright, Designs and Patents Act 1988, and the Copyright and Related Rights Regulations 2003 (SI No. 2498).

CONTENTS

List of Figures   vii
Acknowledgements   ix

   Introduction: Beastly Modernisms   1
   Saskia McCracken and Alex Goody

Part I: Companion Species
1. Metamodernist Beasts, or Flush's Future: Ceridwen Dovey's *Only the Animals* and Sigrid Nunez's *Mitz: The Marmoset of Bloomsbury*   23
   Derek Ryan
2. Can Flush Count?: Virginia Woolf, Animality and Numbers   38
   Jane Goldman
3. Canine Companions, Race and Affective Anthropomorphism in Florence Ayscough's *The Autobiography of a Chinese Dog* (1926) and Mary Gaunt's *A Broken Journey* (1919)   56
   Juanjuan Wu

Part II: Beastly Traces
4. Making an Impression Deeply: Authorising Animals in D. H. Lawrence   75
   Carrie Rohman
5. Following the Beast Familiar: Djuna Barnes's Family Dramas   91
   Peter Adkins

6. The Taxidermic Imaginary in Modernist Literature 107
   Paul Fagan

Part III: Animal, Nation, Empire
7. Species Cleansing: The Rhetoric of Rat Control in the People's Republic of Poland 1945–1956 125
   Gabriela Jarzębowska
8. The Barking Dog and Crying Bird in Partition Stories: Beastly Modernism and the Subaltern Animism of Manto, Rakesh and Anand 143
   Beerendra Pandey
9. Resistant Reindeers: Human–Animal Relations and Cultural Self-Appropriation in Sámi Art and Literature 159
   Katharina Alsen

Part IV: Intersections, Encounters
10. Animal–Human Entanglements in the Canadian Wild Animal Stories of Charles G. D. Roberts 181
    Lauren Cullen
11. Encountering Female Human Animal Becomings in Leonora Carrington's Surrealist Hybrid Tales 198
    Karen Eckersley
12. Modern Intersections: Reading Anita Scott Coleman's Animals 215
    Elizabeth Curry

Part V: Extinction, War, Proliferation
13. 1940s *Avian Noir* 231
    Laura Blomvall
14. Unhoming the Pigeon: Ahmed Ali's *Twilight in Delhi* 248
    Caroline Hovanec
15. The Modernist Jellyfish 263
    Rachel Murray

Afterword: The Animal in the Mirror 279
Kari Weil

Notes on Contributors 292
Index 297

FIGURES

7.1	Anon. Map. Courtesy of the Polish National Archive, Szczecin.	131
7.2	Bogdan Nowakowski. *Rozwój*. 1925. Courtesy of the Poster Museum, Wilanow. Public domain.	132
7.3	Anon. Szczury *tępi* Delicia. Undated [c.1940s]. Courtesy of the Polona Archive, Narodowa Library. Public domain. Available at: <https://polona.pl/search/?query=delicia&filters=public:1> (last accessed 7 July 2022).	133
7.4	Włodzimierz Zakrzewski. *Demokracja Buduje*. 1945. Courtesy of the Poster Museum, Wilanow.	135
9.1	Britta Marakatt-Labba. *Historjá (History)* (Detail). 2003–7. Embroidery, print, applications and wool on linen. 39 cm × 23.5 m. Oslo: KORO Public Art Norway. © Britta Marakatt-Labba / BONO, Oslo 2022. Photo: Cathrine Wang.	160
9.2	Britta Marakatt-Labba. *Historjá*. (Overview at UiT The Arctic University of Norway, Tromsø). 2003–7. © Britta Marakatt-Labba / BONO, Oslo 2022. Photo: Larissa Acharya.	161
9.3	Johan Turi. *Reindeer Corral in Autumn*. 1910. Ink drawing. Illustration from *Muittalus samid birra (An Account of the Sámi)*.	167
9.4	John Savio. *Mann med reinokse (Almei hergin / Man with Bull Reindeer)*. Between 1925 and 1938. Hand-coloured woodcut on paper. 26.5 cm × 22.5 cm. Oslo: National Museum of Art, Architecture and Design.	169

9.5 John Savio. *Pulkkjøring (Hærgevuodje* or *Heargevuoddji / Sleighride).* Undated. Woodcut on paper. 25.2 cm × 19.5 cm. Kirkenes: The Savio Museum. 170

9.6 John Savio. *Alene (Okto / Alone).* Between 1928 and 1934. Woodcut on paper. 28 cm × 32.5 cm. Oslo: National Museum of Art, Architecture and Design. 171

9.7 John Savio. *Gutter med lasso (Gánddat suohpaniin / Boys with Lasso).* Between 1928 and 1938. Woodcut on paper. 20.5 × 29 cm. Oslo: National Museum of Art, Architecture and Design. 174

ACKNOWLEDGEMENTS

First of all, we would like to thank the contributors to this volume for all their hard work, patience, research and excellent chapters. Thank you also to Jackie Jones, Susannah Butler and the team at Edinburgh University Press for the care with which they brought this volume to publication. We would like to thank Peter Adkins, Caitlin Stobie and Maria Sledmere, who helped co-organise the 2019 Beastly Modernisms conference at the University of Glasgow, as well as those who made the conference possible, including the university, volunteers and all the participants for sharing their research and inspiring us to put this volume together. Many of those participants have work included in the following pages. We would also like to thank Peter Adkins for his phrasing for the conference call for papers which shaped our editors' Introduction.

We would like to thank the Polish National Archive, Szczecin; the Poster Museum, Wilanow; the Polona Archive, Narodowa Library; KORO Public Art Norway; the National Musuem of Art, Oslo; and the Franz Marc estate for granting us to reproduce images from their archives.

Alex would also like to thank her colleagues Andrea Macrae and Antonia Mackay for their unstinting support and friendship and all the Willoughby-Goodys – Matthew, Jasmine, Imogen, Maverick and Indy – for their encouragement, love and care.

Saskia would also like to thank Jane Goldman and Nigel Leask for their supervisory support, which made this project possible. And Greg, as ever, for everything.

INTRODUCTION: 'BEASTLY MODERNISMS'

Saskia McCracken and Alex Goody

I still do not think La Somnambule the perfect title – Night Beast would be better except for that debased meaning now put on that nice word beast.
— Djuna Barnes to Emily Holmes Coleman

Nonhuman animals, both written and pictorial, form one of the many beastly connections between two singular modernists, Djuna Barnes and James Joyce. Joyce had moved to Paris from Zürich in July 1920, and in early 1922 Barnes was also visiting Paris, continuing her career as a journalist and working on the collection that would be published as *A Book* the following year. As a Greenwich Village expatriate, Barnes had a network of connections in Paris, and her first-hand knowledge of *Ulysses* (1922) and the recent *Little Review* obscenity trial gave her an entry to conversations with Joyce: she collated her early encounters with him into a piece entitled 'A Portrait of a Man Who Is, At Present, One of the More Significant Figures in Literature' and published in *Vanity Fair* in April 1922. Recalling their first meeting 'Sitting in the café of the Deux Magots, that faces the little church of St. Germain des Prés', Barnes's gaze alights on Joyce's waistcoat:

> the most delightful waistcoat it has ever been my happiness to see. Purple with alternate doe and dog heads. The does, tiny scarlet tongues hanging out over blond lower lips, downed in a light wool, and the dogs no more

> ferocious or on the scent than any good animal who adheres to his master through the seven cycles of change. (Barnes 1922: 65)

This hunting waistcoat was a family heirloom – originally belonging to his great-grandfather, James Joyce – and, in 'The Dead', Joyce attires Gabriel in a version of it, 'a waistcoat of purple tabinet, with little foxes' heads upon it, lined with brown satin and having round mulberry buttons' (Joyce 1993: 347). Joyce inherited the waistcoat from his father and wore it for special occasions (Jackson and Costello 1998: 17); it was presented to the James Joyce Museum at Sandycove by Samuel Beckett in the 1960s (Nicholson 2001: 295). The waistcoat is not the only nonhuman animal figure that mediates their exchanges in Barnes's article: 'We have talked of death, of rats, of horses, the sea; languages, climates and offerings,' Barnes relates (Barnes 1922: 65), suggesting something again of their shared interest in the lives and affects of the more-than-human world.

It is the detail of Joyce's waistcoat, on first meeting him, that generates delight and happiness for Barnes. The garment is thus in contrast to the 'sadness' and 'weariness' that her article otherwise attributes to Joyce. It is as if the animal abundance of the antique embroidered waistcoat agglomerates and externalises the inhuman and nonhuman energies that come to resonate with both Barnes's and Joyce's modernism and their conversations of 'death, of rats, of horses, the sea [. . .] climates and offerings' (Barnes 1922: 65). And Barnes sees, in the proliferating doe and dog heads of Joyce's purple waistcoat, not the carnage of blood sports but a suggestion of companion species relations, an adherence between or assemblage of 'master' and 'good animal' that extends in time through the 'seven cycles of change'. With this phrase Barnes alludes, not to Shakespeare's Seven Ages, but to Rudolf Steiner's Anthroposophy and his theory of human development; references to Theosophy, from which Steiner broke in 1912, run through *Ulysses* and Joyce owned a copy of Steiner's 1910 *Blut ist ein ganz besonderer Saft* (Morrison 2009: 512). In Steiner's anthroposophical ideas of evolution and of human nature, human life is connected to the life force of plants (the life or etheric body) and nonhuman animals (the astral body), a notable challenge to the absolute division between human and nonhuman that underpins the hierarchical binaries of humanism.

When Barnes resolves to identify 'what seemed to be the most characteristic pose of James Joyce', animal affinities surface again: 'the head; turned farther away than disgust and not so far as death, for the turn of displeasure is not so complete, yet the only thing at all like it, is the look in the throat of a stricken animal' (Barnes 1922: 65). In this complex figuration Joyce turns away from the human world, afflicted by and distanced from it, caught in the impossible gazing at, and gaze of, an alterity that is itself unutterable ('the look in the throat'). For Bonnie Kime Scott this is 'an extraordinary metaphor that imagines the mental attitude and represents the physical attribute of a hunted animal', serving to 'bring the complex artist in to the realm of the natural world, and primal desperation' (Scott 1991: 157). It opens the way for Scott to foreground 'Joyce and Barnes['s] shared [. . .] interest in the interface of human and animal' (158) and to explore how, through motifs of childbirth, the bovine, rape and hunting in their texts, they 'deal in the dark, primitive, sexual, bestial, under-texts of life and its continuation' (172). But Joyce is 'stricken' with a more than a primal desperation and mental orientation towards the natural world in Barnes's metaphor; his turning is not a recoiling from the human, but a turning in, an orbiting towards the void, 'the central emptiness, the hiatus that – within man – separates man and animal' (Agamben 2004: 92). This is the 'intimate cesura' that the philosopher Giorgio Agamben uncovers in the functioning of the 'anthropological machine' 'at work in our culture' (37). In categorising and placing human and nonhuman animals along vectors of inclusion and exclusion, the anthropological machine functions in a perpetual process of differentiation, essaying to establish the human by bracketing off human and nonhuman life within and outside man. What results is not 'the human' itself but a 'zone of indifference' at the core (37), an ontological hiatus that is 'perfectly empty' (38). To 'render inoperative' (33) this ceaseless process, to turn off the anthropological machine we could, Agamben proposes, 'risk ourselves in this emptiness, the suspension of the suspension' (92). Joyce takes this risk, as does Barnes, and, as the contributions to this volume illustrate, so do many other modernists.

Beastly Modernisms?

If modernism heralded a moment of socio-political, cultural and aesthetic transformation, it also instigated a refashioning of how we think about, encounter and live with animals. Recognising this correspondence raises crucial questions about human–nonhuman animal coexistence at the foundation of modernity. Beasts abound in modernism. Virginia Woolf's spaniel, Zora Neale Hurston's dog and mule, Langston Hughes and Leonora Carrington's cats, D. H. Lawrence's snake, Samuel Beckett's lobster and Mulk Raj Anand's cows all present prominent examples of animals and animality at the forefront of modernist innovation. At stake in such beastly figurations are not just matters of species relations but matters of the nonhuman animal in excess of capture by culture, language and representation. The attendant questions of human animality, nonhuman agency and the limits of humanism also open on to broader ideas of social relations, culture, race, sex, gender, empire, capitalism and religion, and motivate this volume of essays on *Beastly Modernisms*. We begin here with Barnes and Joyce, not because they are key to unlocking the figure of the animal in modernism, but because they help to illustrate the trajectories and affects of the new articulations of animal studies and modernist studies.

Explorations of the nonhuman, more-than-human and human–animal in Joyce have become central concerns in contemporary work on this canonical modernist figure, generating innovative readings of *Ulysses* and bringing a new attention to *Finnegan's Wake* (1939).[1] Whilst Joyce studies may have been enlivened by such animal encounters, refurbishing claims for Joyce's centrality to modernist studies, Barnes's 'improper modernism', resting in the canonical margins for much of the last four decades, has come to figure significantly in the animal turn of modernist studies. Following her earlier exploration of the bovine/childbirth in Barnes and Joyce, Scott devotes considerable space to Barnes's 'blurring of the distinctions' 'between the bestial and the human' in the second volume of *Refiguring Modernism* (Scott 1995: 73). Successive scholars have turned to the animal in Barnes's work, and she occupies a significant place in Carrie Rohman's *Stalking the Subject* (2009). *Nightwood*'s (1936) 'beast turning human' emerges as one focal motif for much work in modernist animal studies and, as Peter Adkins's contribution to this volume illustrates, new work on Barnes is moving the focus beyond *Nightwood* to examine the animal traces in her drama and short stories.

While Barnes appears in our list of contents, we have not given space to work on Joyce and the nonhuman animal in the contents of this volume; if there is a touchstone for the book it is Virginia Woolf, not Joyce. Woolf studies has also been enlivened by the animal and nonhuman turn in modernist scholarship (see Adkins 2022b, Alt 2010, Goldman 2016, Hovanec 2018, McCracken 2012, Ryan 2013, Scott 2012). But the recurrence of Woolf in the pages that follow is not an attempt to enshrine her, in Joyce's stead, as the exemplar of this new field; instead, it illustrates something that Kari Weil points out in *Thinking Animals* (2012) about the coincidence of feminism and animal studies. Thus, though it may be 'easier for many to contemplate animals as significant others than women', '[m]uch like the "women" in women's studies, the "animal" in animal studies must be placed under erasure' (Weil 2012: 24, 23). Moreover Woolf, as a queer, pacifist, woman modernist, signals how the recent animal turn in the humanities necessitates both new ways of thinking about the beasts that we find in modernist culture, and a final dethroning of the *man*kind of modernism. Animal studies indeed arrives at a point at which modernist studies is already in the process of redefining what modernism means.

Turning to modernism's animals and building on the foundational work on animals and modernism by Carrie Rohman, Margot Norris, Kari Weil, Derek Ryan and others, as this volume does, promises fresh ways of understanding its multispecies foundations. Signalling how modernist studies might intervene in contemporary debates around nonhuman animal life, this volume and its field also indicate the need to resist the centrifugal force of canonical modernism – how many more new readings of *Ulysses* do we need? That the animal turn is a particular opportunity to read modernism differently means not just decolonising modernism, turning to women modernists, reading queer modernists, including inter-, adjacent or late modernists, but also, as we have essayed with this volume, providing a welcome to different geographies and ontologies, to defiantly non-canonical texts, writers and forms. The beastly or brutish has powerful racial valencies and animalising rhetoric is often deployed, in modernist primitivism and elsewhere, for the purposes of racialising and depersonalising. Mel Y. Chen highlights how the 'figurative substitution of a human with an animal figure often accomplishes [. . .] and constitutes a displacement to lower levels of the animacy hierarchy', producing an 'objectification' that is 'above and beyond the possibility of dehumanization' (Chen 2012: 44, 45); our beastly modernisms are intended to confront the dynamics of this rhetoric and the racial hierarchies that it enshrines.

Beastly Modernisms focuses on the 'beastly' understood as the nonhuman other of modernity; the contiguous animality of contemporary human existence; the persistence of more-than-human life; the unknowable animal that is apprehended within the experiments of modernism. Our deployment of the term 'beastly' is strategic, and we offer it as a speculative frame for encountering the nonhuman knowledges and animal proximities that manifest in modernist literature and culture. Terminology is crucial in the field this volume contributes to – thus, although the contributors here do employ the terminology that prevails in the particular animal studies theoretical frameworks they utilise, this volume as a whole adheres to a language that is respectful of our relation to animals of other species, and fully acknowledges the role that linguistic designation has in the appropriations and violences enacted on nonhuman life. The term 'creatural' does significant work in recent animal studies, emphasising as it does the continuities of animal and human embodiment; as David Herman explains, the 'slight semantic shift from *creaturely* to *creatural*' indicates 'the status of being a creature, subject to the requirements of the surrounding environment, the vicissitudes of time, and the vulnerabilities of the body' (Herman 2016: 3). Donna Haraway's preference for the term 'critters' also points to the importance of the words and signs we use in our critical work on human–animal relations: 'the taint of "creatures" and "creation" does not stick to "critters"', she writes; 'if you see such a semiotic barnacle, scrape it off [. . .] "critters" refers promiscuously to microbes, plants, animals, humans and nonhumans, and sometimes even to machines' (Haraway 2016: 169, n1). Beastly is our idiom, however, our own way of coming to terms with those figures, those 'material-semiotic knots' (Haraway 2007: 4) that modernists generated in attempts to apprehend the nonhuman animal world. In the *Oxford English Dictionary* 'beastly', as an adjective, is defined as describing that which resembles a beast (irrational, brutish, inhuman) or that which is 'Unfit for human use or enjoyment; abominable; disgusting, or offensive, especially from dirtiness'. As an adverb its meaning is 'In a beastly manner, like a beast', and 'as an adjunct to an adjective: Brutishly, brutally, abominably, offensively (in society slang, often merely = Exceedingly)'. It is this slippage – from the brutish, animal and inhuman, offensive, abominable, to slang for 'exceedingly' – that we deploy in theorising the 'beastly' knowledges that emerge from the modernist appropriations and disavowals of, and coincidences with, the nonhuman animal. The animal, as we consider it here, is a living map of modernist taxonomic excess; the intemperate, superfluous and overdetermined, the trace that slips between aesthetic and ontological closure, the supplement that exposes the incompleteness of the project of modernism.

Beastly also shares an etymological root with *bestiary* (from *bestiarium vocablum*), the term for a book of real and imagined animals that had its roots in Near Eastern cultures. Medieval bestiaries, drawing on the Latin translation of the *Physiologus*, Pliny the Elder's *Historia naturalisai* and Isidore of Seville's *Etymologiae*, offer a sequential arrangement of images and texts that derive allegorical interpretation and symbolic relationships from the attributes of nonhuman animals. The anthropomorphic moral and spiritual guidance of the bestiary was always set against gorgeous, fantastical illustrations, and the aesthetics of the bestiary animals escaped from the covers of these manuscripts to populate tapestries, metalwork and stained glass. Bestiaries, though comprised of specific correlations of creature–attribute–moral, never contained a set number or order of entries and this heterogeneity, alongside the affects of the animal illuminations and the secular textual enjoyment the works provided, suggests something of the miscellaneous pleasures of the bestiary and its animal figures.

The influence of medieval bestiaries can be seen in the marginal animal illustrations of Djuna Barnes's *Ladies Almanack* (1928) and the posthumously published *Creatures in an Alphabet* (1982), while Guillaume Apollinaire, Pablo Neruda and Jorge Luis Borges all produced modernist versions of the bestiary. Borges's bestiary is one of 'Imaginary Beings' and it offers, against any claims to the bestiary as moral taxonomy or source of natural historical knowledge, what Melanie Nicholson describes as 'a glimpse into the human imagination as it confronts the unknown or imperfectly known' (2020: 138). Elsewhere Borges points out that 'there is no classification of the universe that is not arbitrary and conjectural' straight after enumerating an alternate animal taxonomy, that of the fantastical Chinese encyclopaedia *Celestial Emporium of Benevolent Knowledge*, where 'animals are divided into (a) belonging to the Emperor, (b) embalmed, (c) tame, (d) sucking pigs, (e) sirens, (f) fabulous, (g) stray dogs, (h) included in the present classification, (i) frenzied, (j) innumerable, (k) drawn with a very fine camelhair brush, (l) others, (m) having just broken a flower vase, (n) those that resemble flies from a long way off' (Borges 1993: 231). Michel Foucault responds to this taxonomic animal 'fable' in his Preface to *The Order of Things* (1966), with a 'laugh that shattered' a ludic recognition of the impossibility of our own systems of thought 'with which we are accustomed to tame the wild profusion of existing things'. For Foucault, such recognition 'threaten[s] with collapse our age-old distinction between the Same and the Other' (Foucault 1994: xv).

The beastly modernisms explored in this volume do not function within the allegorical tradition of the bestiary, but they do share in the heterogenous energies and delights of their more-than-human figures, and they turn our attention, as scholars and readers, to the wild profusions and manifold liveliness that cannot be trapped with the anthropocentric logic of Same and Other. In their 2019 *An Eclectic Bestiary*, Birgitte Spengler and Babette Tischleder suggest that the bestiary convention can be differently implemented, to 'redirect the attention of our readers to the diverse forms and rich more-than-human "cultures" of our multispecies world' (2019: 12). Tischleder thus suggests that the bestiary can 'invite thinking through and with plants and animals', and provides a 'means for imagining historical power relations and cultural hierarchies, as well as offering occasion to assess the role and place of humanity as species among species' (16). Antoinette Burton and Renisa Mawani also identify the disruptive potential of the bestiary, functioning as an 'unruly taxonomy' in their *Animalia: An Anti-Imperial Bestiary for Our Times* (2020: 13). Exposing the operations and limits of the biopolitical power of Empire, the 'bestiary form [...] offers a provocation to new ways of seeing and writing about empire and its biocultural creatures' (6). Our beastly modernisms offer different modes of thinking through the multispecies relations of modernism and its hierarchies of power, and of disclosing the brutish beauty of modernism's encounters with its own wildness.

Modernist Animals in History and Theory

Modernism's interest in the figure of the nonhuman animal speaks to the immense changes in animal life in the early twentieth century, a period when the reverberations of Darwinian theory were being felt in the new life sciences, as well as in emergent social theories that employed discourses of species, and when developing technologies, media and markets radically altered everyday human–nonhuman animal relations. It was also a period in which newly formed animal rights groups – such as the Royal Society for the Protection of Animals (RSPCA, established in 1824) and the Royal Society for the Protection of Birds (RSPB, established as the SPB in 1889) in the UK – were pushing for animal welfare legislation and drawing public attention to questions around human responsibilities towards animals. These contexts raised questions about how we think about and represent the (sometimes human) animal. Modernist artists and writers, along with these welfare groups, knew from Darwinism that humans descended from animals, 'that animals have some phenomenological experience' and that humans had caused numerous species extinctions (Hovanec 2018: 27). Questions of human animality, animal sentience and animal welfare intersected, furthermore, with the discourse on

British imperial identity. As Burton and Mawani explain, 'The British empire was entangled in animal life at every possible scale' and animals were used 'as imaginative resources, military vehicles, settler foodstuffs, status emblems, contested signs, or motors of capital' (2020: 1). Thousands of exotic birds were tortured and killed for the global feather fashion trade. When India legislated against exporting such plumage in 1902, and other countries such as Australia, Egypt and New Guinea followed suit, Britain rushed to catch up (Haynes 1983: 28). Maneesha Deckha observes that 'imperialism and the need to maintain a "civilized" identity vis-à-vis colonized peoples' led to the criminalisation of some forms of animal cruelty, which reinforced civilisational hierarchies and British claims 'to a more civilized and progressive "home" culture and nation' (2013: 521). Actual nonhuman animals, then, were central to the British colonial project and imperial discourse.

At the same time the 'cultivation of ideas of race, culture, gender, and species' under colonialism were 'interactive and mutually constitutive' (Deckha 2008: 252). The *figure* of the animal became a synonym for colonised, racialised, gendered humans. At the turn of the century, modernist writers and artists, not least those in colonised countries, were paying attention to, and subverting, these beastly tropes in the context of increased calls for independence from colonial rule. Between 1900 and 1945, for example, several countries gained this independence: Australia (1901), Afghanistan (1919), Egypt (1922), New Zealand (1931), Iraq (1932) and South Africa (1934), with Partition – and the associated deaths and displacements of millions – following in 1947. By 1950, Jordan (1946), India and Pakistan (1947), Israel, Myanmar and Sri Lanka (1948) were also independent. The figure of the anticolonial animal is under-discussed in modernist animal studies, and is the focus of chapters in this volume on Indian and Pakistani writing: Beerendra Pandey's work on dogs and birds in Saadat Hasan Manto's, Mohan Rakesh's and Mulk Raj Anand's partition stories, and Caroline Hovanec's 'Unhoming the Pigeon: Ahmed Ali's *Twilight in Delhi*'. Meanwhile, questions of race, nation and belonging are explored through animal figures in Gabriela Jarzębowska's work on (human and nonhuman) pests in Polish Stalinist propaganda, Katharina Alsen's exploration of reindeers in Sámi art and Elizabeth Curry's writing on animality, race and gender in the writing of African American Mexican modernist Anita Scott Coleman. Perhaps the most popular approach to the animal as a figure for the other is feminist animal studies, as we have observed above. This volume considers beastly women in the works of Virginia Woolf (in chapters by Jane Goldman and Kari Weil), Djuna Barnes (Peter Adkins), Leonora Carrington (Karen Eckersley) and more. The figure of the nonhuman animal often gestures towards the other more broadly (including the working classes and disabled people) but addressing the racialised colonial context in which modernists figured animals is central to our approach in this volume.

It is not surprising, given the above contexts, that, as Derek Ryan puts it, 'there is something specific to early twentieth-century modernity' that 'finds writers probing the boundaries between humans and other species' (2019: 321). Modernists not only recognised 'the proximity of human and non-human life' and analysed the 'discursive prejudices behind representations of these lives', but they also 'model[led] new agencies that reimagine the ontological and ethical relations between human and non-human' (Ryan 2019: 322). Many modernists were also part of a wider milieu concerned with animals and animality. Virginia Woolf, for example, knew biologist Julian Huxley, evolutionary scientist J. B. S. Haldane and philosopher Bertrand Russell, who were 'deeply invested in the question of how to represent animal subjectivity, and whose forays into animal worlds shaped their understanding of science and literature' (Hovanec 2018: 162, 3). Such modernist networks 'can be understood as responding to the same two questions – How should we understand animal life after Darwin? And how can we capture animals in words that are true to life?'– whilst recognising that any possible answers are 'speculative, provisional' (Hovanec 2018: 4–5, 3). The challenge, which Darwinism made possible, both to 'understand animals as subjects' and to know that 'one cannot know animals' subjective experience, drove many modernists to the very limits of literary scientific representation' (Hovanec 2018: 3) and animal figuration.

Animal studies scholarship on modernism is rich and recent, beginning in earnest with Carrie Rohman's *Stalking the Subject: Modernism and the Animal* (2009) and Kari Weil's *Thinking Animals* (2012). Rohman, discussing how Darwin's 'discourse of species' (13) destabilises notions of human subjectivity, observes that British modernist literature 'is marked by a certain crisis in the human vis-à-vis the animal' (21). Weil, drawing on the works of Woolf, Kafka and Thomas Mann, considers the personal, ethical and political implications of the boundaries which have so often been drawn between the human and the animal. Since these foundational works, modernist animal studies has developed substantially, and in the last few years Caroline Hovanec's *Animal Subjects: Literature, Zoology, and British Modernism* (2018) has considered animal subjectivity in British literary modernism; Cathryn Setz's *Primordial Modernism: Animals, Ideas, Transition 1927–1938* (2020) has explored primordial critters in the works of writers including James Joyce and Gottfried Benn; Cary Wolfe has offered a posthumanist theory of ecopoetics and used Wallace Steven's poetry as an illustration of meaning-making beyond the human in *Ecological Poetics, or Wallace Stevens's Birds* (2020); and Rachel Murray's *The Modernist Exoskeleton: Insects, War, Literary Form* (2020) has examined modernist insect imagery and literary form in the works of Wyndham Lewis, D. H. Lawrence, H.D. and Samuel Beckett. More recently, Peter Adkins's *The Modernist Anthropocene: Nonhuman Life and Planetary Change in James Joyce, Virginia Woolf and Djuna Barnes* (2022) frames modernist literary works in the context of climate change and extinction, while Hovanec and Murray's collection, *Modernism/modernity* Print Plus cluster *Reading Modernism in the Sixth Extinction* (2022), and Alberto Godioli's and Carmen van den Berg's *Crossing Borders: Transnational Modernism Beyond the Human* (forthcoming) share these international and environmental concerns. In 2019, Saskia McCracken, Peter Adkins, Caitlin Stobie and Maria Sledmere organised an international *Beastly Modernisms* conference at the University of Glasgow, bringing together established and emerging scholars, artists and poets from across Europe, Asia and North America to share new modernist animal studies work. The success of that conference inspired us to create this volume, to recreate the sense of a beastly modernist scholarly community begun in Glasgow and to share the fascinating research that arose during and following that event. Our volume builds on, and includes, the valuable work of many of the scholars listed above, and those at the conference, celebrating different animal studies approaches to a range of modernist literary and artistic works.

In *Animal Rites: American Culture, the Discourse of the Species, and Posthumanist Theory* (2003) Cary Wolfe examines the 'cross-articulation of speciesism and heteronormative gender' (141) in the work of the canonical, masculinist modernist Ernest Hemingway. For Wolfe, it is possible to read at once 'the transgressive possibilities of gender performativity' in Hemingway's texts (122) and the 'desperate humanism' that seeks to heal the 'internal rift' of the Enlightenment subject through violence and domination (141). Wolfe's concern in this reading of Hemingway, and across his volume, is to engage concurrently the 'unexamined framework of *speciesism*' (1) and the 'constitutive disavowals and self-constructing narratives enacted by that fantasy figure called "the human"' (6). Wolfe's work exemplifies how the interdisciplinary field of animal studies engages in a concerted interrogation of the species discourse of humanism informed by poststructuralist and, more recently, posthumanist and new materialist theoretical frames. So Donna Haraway's 'natureculture' (2003), Karen Barad's intra-action (2007) and Stacy Alaimo's 'transcorporeality' (2010) can be seen as contrasting conceptions of the inextricable entanglements and ontological intimacies between bodies and environments. In Jane Bennett's vital materiality affect extends far beyond the human, and thus 'organic and inorganic bodies, natural and cultural objects [. . .] all are affective' (xii); Bennett illustrates our enmeshment in the material world and surmises 'an ontological field without any unequivocal demarcations between human, animal, vegetable, or mineral' and where '*all* forces and flows (materialities) are or can become lively, affective, and signalling' (2010: 117). Of importance also, in thinking through the designation, regulation and control of liveliness, are Michel Foucault's biopower and biopolitics – that is, the governance of biological life (1994; 2003) – and Giorgio Agamben's theorisation of 'bare life' and *zoē* – the biological life that is excluded from the polis and from individuation (Agamben 1998).

Acknowledging the irreducible alterity and plurality of nonhuman life and the systems of thought that have sought to categorise and control it, contemporary animal theory seeks to decentre the human, develop a rigorous riposte to anthropocentrism and explore the ways that human and nonhuman life are entangled. But as our discussion in this Introduction and the contributions to this volume illustrate, modernist writers and artists were already querying the figure of the animal as antithesis or even straightforward counterpart to the human. It might be possible to locate, in Jakob von Uexküll's concept of animal *Umwelten* or 'environment-worlds' (first posited in *Umwelt und Innenwelt der Tiere* [*The Environment and Inner World of Animals*] in 1909), for example, an early twentieth-century understanding of the alterity of the phenomenological experiences of animals, and in the vitalist philosophy of Henri Bergson the roots of a vital materialist celebration of the multiplicities and intensities of life.

Multiplicity and intensity are central to the animal encounters that Gilles Deleuze and Félix Guattari theorise. Following in some senses from the non-anthropocentric thinking Friedrich Nietzsche undertakes through the animals of his *Thus Spoke Zarathustra* (1883–5), Deleuze and Guattari propose human–animal encounters where 'each deterritorializes the other' (1986: 22) and profoundly disturb the boundaries between human and nonhuman. Deleuze and Guattari's accounts, in *A Thousand Plateaus* (1980) and elsewhere, imagine assemblages of human and nonhuman animal, and intensive and affective proximities and encounters, that challenge the ontological foundations on which notions of stable subjects and categories of being are founded. Their 'becoming-animal' (1988: 233ff.) functions as an influential means for reconfiguring the fixed terms, positions and relations through which both 'human' and 'animal' have been defined. This becoming-animal is not about imitation or identity, but about affective assemblages and proximities of human and nonhuman that destabilise the privileged starting point of the human self.

Becoming with, and personal, everyday proximities with nonhuman animals, such as her canine companion, Cayenne, are foundational to Donna Haraway's work, particularly *The Companion Species Manifesto* (2003) and *When Species Meet* (2008). As she argues in the latter, 'nothing is passive to the action of another [. . .] the unfoldings can only occur in the fleshly detail of situated, material-semiotic beings' (263). Haraway's 'A Cyborg Manifesto' (1985) did much of the foundational work for (particularly feminist) posthumanism and animal theory. The implications of Haraway's 'cyborg' – who 'appears in myth precisely where the boundary between the human and animal is transgressed' – to 'signal disturbingly and pleasurably tight coupling' of 'human and other living creatures' (1991: 152) resonates through the work of others, such as Rosi Braidotti, and the lineage is clear through to Haraway's recent work. Thinking outside the 'prick tale' of the 'Anthropos' (2016: 39) and in the face of the sixth great extinction, Haraway urges that to 'think-with is to stay with the naturalcultural multispecies trouble on earth' (2016: 40). For her, 'becoming-with' also means encountering the human as humus and becoming-with the assemblages of symbiotic, sympoetic, compost communalities.

A discussion of philosophers who have shaped animal studies would be incomplete without mentioning Jacques Derrida; it is an encounter, naked, with a companion species (a cat) in *The Animal That Therefore I Am* that leads him to multiple questions about the human conceptualisation of animal life. The gaze of the cat opens, for Derrida, into a theoretical and textual deconstruction of the human/animal binary and a shift to thinking about animal perspectives and meanings, and to speculating on response, responsibility and ethics beyond the human realm. Derrida draws attention to the problems of thinking through the 'animal' as category with his neologism *animot*, and suggests that the 'abyssal ruptures' between human and nonhuman be acknowledged along with a realisation of the 'heterogeneities' of nonhuman animals in their alterity (2008: 30). Derrida's work in animal theory thus not only deconstructs the binaries that bind the animal, but also urges an ethics of 'responsibility with respect to the most dissimilar [. . .] the unrecognizable other' (2009: 108). Derrida's work still carries weight in animal studies, but it is contemporary postcolonial and critical race theorists who have asked the most significant questions about the politics and ethics of the human/nonhuman divide.

Vital in recent animal theory are critics who examine how the subjugation and othering of the nonhuman world is repeated in the logics of racial oppression and objectification. Maneesha Deckha appeals for a feminist postcolonial approach to animal studies that can consider 'how the social forces that code and privilege whiteness inform questions related to the human/animal divide' and an 'awareness of how colonial logics fortifying a reified Western/non-Western binary and civilisational discourses positioning Western culture as superior to non-Western cultures continue to be formative in current debates/ideas about human "nature" and human–animal relationships' (2012: 530). Bénédicte Boisseron, in revisiting the question of the animal and human dynamic, and the nonhuman in the history of the Black diaspora, emphasises 'interspecies connectedness' (Boisseron 2018: xix) and 'seeks to defy the construction of blacks and animals as *exclusively* connected through their comparable state of subjection and humiliation, and instead focus on interspecies alliances' (Boisseron 2018: 36). Alexander Weheliye, who is also concerned with resisting a reductive 'comparison between human and animal slavery [that] is brandished about in the field of animal studies', examines the 'racializing assemblages' at work in colonial modernity that construct a 'hierarchical ordering [. . .] into humans, not-quite-humans and nonhumans' (2014: 10, 3, 8). Crucial for Weheliye's analysis is the recognition of 'black studies as a mode of knowledge production' (19) – and the work of Hortense Spillers and Sylvia Wynter in particular – in confronting 'the barring of nonwhite subjects from the category of the human' (3). Bringing intersectionality into animal theory means that it is possible, as Yamini Narayanan does, to recognise 'anthropatriarchy': that is 'the human, gendered oppression, exploitation, and control of nonhuman animals *via* their sexual and reproductive systems' (Narayanan 2019: 196), and to think through, as Mel Y. Chen does, the 'insistent collisions of race, animality, sexuality, and ability' and the 'queerness of some human racialized animalities' (2012: 104). Challenging binary systems of difference using these various approaches, as several of our contributors do, enables us to reconsider the material and figurative politics of, and relations between, human and nonhuman animals; they help to illustrate how we might 'think differently if nonhuman animals [. . .] and even inanimate objects were to inch into the biopolitical fold' (Chen 2012: 6).

These intersecting and often contrasting theoretical and critical perspectives illustrate how strands of thought can and do diverge in animal theory; such variance is one of the key strengths of animal studies as a mode of analysis that resists closed debate. One way, perhaps, to approach the distinctive strands that characterise animal studies is to consider the contrast that critical animal studies (CAS) provides. Although CAS is not wholly distinct from the interdisciplinary fields of other forms of animal studies,[2] it is more firmly rooted in the questions of ethical responsibility, and the resistance to speciesism, that are inherited from Peter Singer's *Animal Liberation* (1975) and his subsequent work. Nik Taylor and Richard Twine point out that 'critical' is used as a way to express 'the urgency of our times' and to acknowledge that 'the twenty-first century represents a pivotal period in which ecology and animal life face unprecedented threats' (Taylor and Twine 2014: 2). The chapters in this volume are not predominantly concerned, as CAS is, with practical and activist responses to speciesism, but they do show, and Hovanec's chapter on 'Unhoming the Pigeon: Ahmed Ali's *Twilight in Delhi*' exemplifies, how the theory of animal studies is never separate from an ethics of life.

In this volume our contributors draw on the various theoretical currents in animal studies as they unearth and examine some of the key issues related to the animal turn in modernist studies. The chapters from leading figures in this field sit alongside those from new and emerging scholars, and together they delineate some significant dynamics and debates, and also decentre the canons and geographies of modernism. Grounded in interdisciplinary approaches, the chapters in *Beastly Modernisms* work with cultural history and theoretical frameworks to unearth the multispecies dynamics of twentieth-century literature and culture conceived in broad aesthetic, temporal and geographical terms. They are concerned with critical race studies, colonialism, and modernisms of the global south and marginalised modernists. Our contributors cover a diverse range of topics, from exploring dogs in Virginia Woolf to Republican China, from animals and gender in surrealist Mexican work to African American texts, from Sámi reindeers to Stalinist rat propaganda, from modernist jellyfish to metamodernist beasts, from 1940s poetry to Indian Partition stories. We aim to provide a more comprehensive and global vision of modernist animal studies than extant canonical scholarship, avoiding the pitfalls of Euro-American exclusivity, an over-emphasis on domestic or wild species, and extremes of capitulating to, or outright rejecting, canonicity. Just as importantly, the animal always already invokes the other, the marginalised. This other is racialised, gendered, queered, colonised and so on. It makes sense, therefore, to focus on writers who have been marginalised by canonisation, and who are othered in these ways, or are preoccupied with such othering.

That said, this volume is not a completely comprehensive survey of global modernist animal studies. Rather, it attempts to begin the process of broadening the scope of the discipline. Various geographical fields, including African, South American and Australasian modernist studies, are not included, and the focus leans heavily towards Anglophone writers and artists. Likewise, Indigenous and disability studies approaches are not represented as much as we would like. Our volume is limited by length (some omissions are inevitable) but this is counterbalanced by the diversity we do offer and the fact that the volume offers exciting work across the spectrum from canonical to emergent fields. Nonetheless, it is worth pointing readers to important literary animal studies scholars we have not included in this volume, such as Belinda Kleinhans on German animal studies, Kaori Nagai on literary animals and empire, Jade Munslow-Ong on African modernism, Maki Eguchi on sheep in Japanese literature, and Christopher Pexa on Native American and First Nation animal literature. We also recommend Stephanie Jenkins, Kelly Struthers Montford and Chloë Taylor's edited volume, *Disability and Animality: Crip Perspectives in Critical Animal Studies* (2020). These scholars and works have been invaluable to our own research and are making significant contributions to the field.

Volume Overview

This volume is divided into five sections: *Companion Species*; *Beastly Traces*; *Animal, Nation, Empire*; *Intersections, Encounters*; and *Extinction, War, Proliferation*, and concludes with an Afterword by founding literary animal studies scholar Kari Weil. Each section takes a different approach to the figure of the animal in modernist literature and culture. Our opening section, *Companion Species*, uses Donna Haraway's term, which offers a collaborative alternative to the hierarchical, possessive and patronising word 'pets'. This section considers modernist writers and their companion species – marmosets, tortoises and dogs – from Bloomsbury to China. Derek Ryan's chapter on 'Metamodernist Beasts' considers anthropomorphic language and narrative techniques in relation to nonhuman consciousness, imperialism, gender, sexuality, war and science in Sigrid Nunez's biography of Leonard Woolf's marmoset, *Mitz: The Marmoset of*

Bloomsbury (1998), Ceridwen Dovey's fictional memoir of Virginia Woolf's pet tortoise, *Only the Animals* (2014), and Woolf's canine narrative, *Flush: A Biography* (1933). In 'Can Flush Count? Virginia Woolf, Animality and Numbers' Jane Goldman considers canine counting and Woolf's suspicion of measuring as a patriarchal practice in relation to Derrida's dictum, 'Counting is a bad procedure'. Juanjuan Wu's chapter on women and dogs in China, which concludes this section, examines anthropomorphic configurations of cross-species and interracial relationships in Mary Gaunt's travel writing from China (1913–14) and Florence Ayscough's *The Autobiography of a Chinese Dog* (1926). These texts, Wu argues, respectively reinforce and call into question modernism's imperialist racialised binaries.

The second section of the volume, *Beastly Traces*, explores how animals authorise, contaminate or unsettle structures of signification and subjectification in the early twentieth century. Carrie Rohman's 'Making an Impression Deeply: Authorising Animals in D. H. Lawrence' asks, drawing on the work of Foucault and Derrida, how animals are represented or experienced as authorising and as 'authors' in literature of the modernist period. In 'Following the Beast Familiar: Djuna Barnes's Family Dramas' Peter Adkins identifies a beastly idiom across Barnes's 1924 work, *The Biography of Julie von Bartmann*, first published in 2020, *Ryder* (1928) and *The Antiphon* (1958), which runs through her fiction of the family unit. Paul Fagan's 'The Taxidermic Imaginary in Modernist Literature' follows the traces of a taxidermal imaginary from a realist Victorian writing, through early twentieth-century literature to late modernism. Each of these chapters draws on modernism's fascination and unease concerning animality.

Our third section – *Animal, Nation, Empire* – considers how the figure of the animal was central to discourses of modernity regarding national purity, belonging, empire and colonisation. In her chapter on species cleansing, Gabriela Jarzębowska shows that the rhetoric regarding a broad-scale rat extermination programme in Poland in 1945–56 was an extension of both antisemitic discourse and the discursive strategies of Stalinist political purges. Beerendra Pandey's chapter on modernist Partition narratives focuses on the representation of animals in short stories by Saadat Hasan Manto (writing in Urdu), Mohan Rakesh (in Hindi) and Mulk Raj Anand (in English). These animal figures, and all of those in this section, trouble binaries such as citizen–refugee, animal–human and élite–subaltern, pushing back against imperial understandings of the animal. Katharina Alsen, in her exploration of 'Resistant Reindeers' in the contemporary textile art of Britta Marakatt-Labba, reads these nonhuman animal figures as a critical commentary on the representation of Indigenous Sámi culture in the early twentieth century and more recently. Alsen considers how Sámi modern(ist) traditions and Marakatt-Labba's embroidery challenge stereotypical representations and offer strategies of resistance to, and subversion of, cultural subordination and (neo)colonial appropriation. Taken together, the chapters in this section contribute to crucial current debates about the figure of the animal in national and imperial discourse.

Following this, the subsequent cluster of chapters, *Intersections, Encounters*, presents chapters that negotiate, in different ways, moments of human–nonhuman contact, figured as points of metamorphosis, hybridity, affective communion or a violent uncovering of bare life. In the first chapter of this section Lauren Cullen examines turn-of-the-century Canadian wild animal narratives, focusing on the short stories of Charles G. D. Roberts that sit, in terms of genre, on the cusp of modernism. In her chapter, Cullen examines the uniquely Canadian style of Roberts's stories, showing how he draws on contemporary ideas about animal–human continuity and animal psychology to confront and undermine the hierarchy of human superiority and animal victimhood, and to retrieve the agency of the nonhuman animal. Karen Eckersley's 'Encountering Female Human Animal Becomings in Leonora Carrington's Surrealist Hybrid Tales' explores Carrington's biocentric entanglements of human and nonhuman animal that cross the demarcations of subject and species. Considering Carrington's Virginia Fur and the eponymous Jemima from the short story 'Jemima and the Wolf', Eckersley locates, in Carrington's writings, a posthuman resistance to the tyranny of the phallocentric anthropos. Also exploring a short story, Elizabeth Curry's 'Modern Intersections: Reading Anita Scott Coleman's Animals' engages with Coleman's avowal of the animal (and animality) in the story 'Three Dogs and a Rabbit', published in *The Crisis* in 1926, along with the poem 'Idle Wonder'. In these texts, identifications between human characters and animals are made prominent, animal characters exhibit human-ness or human characters appear animalised, and they demonstrate, Curry argues, how Coleman uses animal affinity rather than abjection to explore the dissolution of human boundaries and hierarchies. Animal encounters, then, have many potential resonances.

The final section, *Extinction, War, Proliferation*, contains chapters that range across different visions of apocalyptic destruction, trauma, danger and adversity, at the level of the individual, culture and species, finding protean animal figures who offer an uncertain counter to the ravages of modernity. These chapters invite us to consider literal and figurative animals in our recent past, present and future, as well as the directions in which modernist animal studies may go. Exploring birds and planes in Second World War poetry, Laura Blomvall's '1940s *Avian Noir*' considers the confusion of animal and machine in the recurrent images of avian menace across the work of Elizabeth Bishop, Sylvia Townsend Warner and Muriel Rukeyser work. Articulating the parallels between perceptual distortions in film and in the poetic image, Blomvall argues that the oneiric and threatening aspects of the *noir* aesthetic offer a compelling frame through which to read disjunctive poetic representations of aerial war. In 'Unhoming the Pigeon: Ahmed Ali's *Twilight in Delhi*' Caroline Hovanec focuses on a specific avian species – the pigeon – to consider the violent impacts of colonial modernity, imperial capitalism and environmental catastrophe. Examining the concerns with cultural extinction, loss and unhoming in Ali's novel, Hovanec argues that *Twilight in Delhi* has an important lesson for imagining survival in our own precarious world. Rachel Murray's 'The Modernist Jellyfish' explores how this gelatinous and strange marine life form clogs up the workings of modernity, both as increasing jellyfish blooms that fill the oceans because of anthropogenic climate change, and as symbolic disruptors of thought that produce moments of arrest, but also epiphanic flashes, for Wyndham Lewis, Marianne Moore and H.D. Finally, Kari Weil's Afterword invites us to reflect on the animal within, and on the volume as a whole, grounding the politics of animality in the personal. These chapters encapsulate some of the key themes that this volume explores and raise questions about the present and future state of animals, animal figures and modernist animal studies.

This volume emerged from a site of dialogue and exchange, in a space and time where we seemingly took for granted the opportunities for proximity and scholarly community. Through the intervening time, as this book has come to production, we have been made acutely aware of our own vulnerability as embodied human animals, of the intense fragility of the natural world we share with other life and of the importance of connection and communal responsibility. This awareness colours, however implicitly, the contributions gathered here and has guided us in our curation of this volume. Thus, rather than being an authoritative tome on the modernist animal, we intend the book to be a catalyst for rich conversations, both on and off the page, that continue to uncover and acknowledge a profusion of beastly modernisms.

Works Cited

Adkins, Peter. 2022a. 'Fourwalkers, Taildanglers, Headhangers: Labouring Animals in Ulysses'. *Textual Practice* 36.2: 186–204.
Adkins, Peter. 2022b. *The Modernist Anthropocene: Nonhuman Life and Planetary Change in James Joyce, Virginia Woolf and Djuna Barnes*. Edinburgh: Edinburgh University Press.
Agamben, Giorgio. 1998. *Homo Sacer: Sovereign Power and Bare Life*. Trans. Daniel Heller-Roazen. Stanford: Stanford University Press.
Agamben, Giorgio. 2004. *The Open: Man and Animal*. Trans. Kevin Attell. Stanford: Stanford University Press.
Alaimo, Stacy. 2010. *Bodily Natures: Science, Environment, and the Material Self*. Bloomington: Indiana University Press.
Alt, Christina. 2010. *Virginia Woolf and the Study of Nature*. Cambridge: Cambridge University Press.
Barad, Karen. 2007. *Meeting the Universe Halfway: Quantum Physics and the Entanglement of Matter and Meaning*. Durham, NC: Duke University Press.
Barnes, Djuna. 1922. 'A Portrait of a Man Who Is, At Present, One of the More Significant Figures in Literature'. *Vanity Fair* 18.22 (April): 65, 104.

Benjamin, Lauren. 2020., 'Circe's Feral Beasts: Women and Other Animals in Joyce's Ulysses'. *Journal of Modern Literature* 43.2: 41–59.
Bennett, Jane. 2010. *Vibrant Matter: A Political Ecology of Things*. Durham, NC: Duke University Press.
Boisseron, Bénédicte. 2018. *Afro-Dog: Blackness and the Animal Question*. New York: Columbia University Press.
Borges, Jorges Luis. 1993. 'The Analytical Language of John Wilkins'. Trans. Ruth L. C. Simms, 101–5. In *Other Inquisitions 1937–1952*. Austin: University of Texas Press.
Burton, Antoinette and Renisa Mawani, eds. 2020. *Animalia: An Anti-Imperial Bestiary for Our Times*. Durham, NC, and London: Duke University Press.
Chen, Mel Y. 2012. *Animacies: Biopolitics, Racial Mattering, and Queer Affect*. Durham, NC: Duke University Press.
Deckha, Maneesha. 2008. 'Intersectionality and Posthumanist Vision of Equality'. *Wisconsin Women's Law Journal* 23.2: 249–68.
Deckha, Maneesha. 2012. 'Toward a Postcolonial, Posthumanist Feminist Theory: Centralizing Race and Culture in Feminist Work on Nonhuman Animals'. *Hypatia: A Journal of Feminist Philosophy* 27.3: 527–45.
Deckha, Maneesha. 2013. 'Welfarist *and* Imperial: The Contributions of Anticruelty Laws to Civilizational Discourse'. *American Quarterly* 65.3: 515–48.
Deleuze, Gilles and Félix Guattari. 1986. *Kafka: Toward a Minor Literature*. Trans. Dana Polan. Minneapolis: University of Minnesota Press.
Deleuze, Gilles and Félix Guattari. 1988. *A Thousand Plateaus: Capitalism and Schizophrenia*. Trans. Brian Massumi. London: Athlone Press.
Derrida, Jacques. 2008. *The Animal That Therefore I Am*. Ed. Marie-Louise Mallet, trans. David Wills. New York: Fordham University Press.
Derrida. Jacques. 2009. *The Beast and the Sovereign*. Vol. 1. Ed. Michel Lisse, Marie-Louise Mallet and Ginette Michaud, trans. Geoffrey Bennington. Chicago: University of Chicago Press.
Ebury, Katherine, ed. 2017. 'Joyce, Animals and the Nonhuman'. Special Issue. *Humanities* 6.3.
Eguchi, Maki. 2014. 'The Representation of Sheep in Modern Japanese Literature from Natsume Sōseki to Murakami Haruki'. In *The Semiotics of Animal Representations*. Ed. Kadri Tüür and Morten Tønnessen, 217–38. Leiden: Brill.
Foucault, Michel. 1990. *The History of Sexuality: An Introduction*. New York: Vintage.
Foucault, Michel. 1994. *The Order of Things: An Archaeology of the Human Sciences*. New York: Vintage Books.
Foucault, Michel. 2003. 'Society Must Be Defended'. In *Lectures at the Collège de France, 1975–76*. Trans. David Macey. New York: Picador.
Goldman, Jane. 2007. '"Ce chien est à Moi": Virginia Woolf and the Signifying Dog'. *Woolf Studies Annual* 13: 49–86.
Goldman, Jane. 2016. '*Flush: A Biography*: Speaking, Reading, and Writing with the Companion Species'. In *A Companion to Virginia Woolf*. Ed. Jessica Berman, 163–75. Chichester: Wiley Blackwell.
Haraway, Donna. 1991. 'A Cyborg Manifesto: Science, Technology, and Socialist Feminism in the Late Twentieth Century'. In *Simians, Cyborgs and Women: The Reinvention of Nature*, 149–81. New York: Routledge.

Haraway, Donna. 2003. *The Companion Species Manifesto: Dogs, People, and Significant Others*. Chicago: Prickly Paradigm Press.
Haraway, Donna. 2007. *When Species Meet*. Minneapolis: University of Minnesota Press.
Haraway, Donna. 2016. *Staying with the Trouble: Making Kin in the Chthulucene*. Durham, NC: Duke University Press.
Haynes, Alan. 1983. 'Murderous Millinery: The Struggle for the Plumage Act, 1921'. *History Today* 33 (July): 26–30.
Herman, David. 2016. 'Introduction: Literature beyond the Human'. In *Creatural Fictions: Human–Animal Relationships in Twentieth- and Twenty-First-Century Literature*, 1–18. New York: Palgrave Macmillan.
Hovanec, Caroline. 2018. *Animal Subjects: Literature, Zoology, and British Modernism*. Cambridge: Cambridge University Press.
Jackson, John Wyse and Peter Costello. 1998. *John Stanislaus Joyce: The Voluminous Life and Genius of James Joyce's Father*. London: Fourth Estate.
Jenkins, Stephanie, Kelly Struthers Montford and Chloë Taylor, eds. 2020. *Disability and Animality: Crip Perspectives in Critical Animal Studies*. Abingdon: Routledge.
Joyce, James. 1993. *Dubliners*. New York and London: Garland.
Kleinhans, Belinda. 2016. 'Posthuman Ethics, Violence, Creaturely Suffering and the (Other) Animal: Schnurre's Postwar Animal Stories'. *Humanities Research* 5: 69–88.
McCracken, Saskia. 2021. *(R)evolutionary Animal Tropes in the Works of Charles Darwin and Virginia Woolf*. Doctoral Thesis, University of Glasgow.
Mak, Cliff. 2016. 'Joyce's Indifferent Animals: Boredom and the Subversion of Fables in Finnegan's Wake'., *Modernist Cultures* 11.2: 179–205.
Morrison, Mark S. 2009. '"Their Pineal Glands Aglow": Theosophical Physiology in *Ulysses*'. *James Joyce Quarterly* 46.3/4: 509–27.
Munslow-Ong, Jade. 2019. *Olive Schreiner and African Modernism: Allegory, Empire and Postcolonial Writing*. London: Routledge.
Murray, Rachel. 2020. *The Modernist Exoskeleton: Insects, War, Literary Form*. Edinburgh: Edinburgh University Press.
Nagai, Kaori. 2020. *Imperial Beast Fables: Animals, Cosmopolitanism, and the British Empire*. London: Palgrave Macmillan.
Narayanan, Yamini. 2019. '"Cow Is a Mother, Mothers Can Do Anything for Their Children!" Gaushalas as Landscapes of Anthropatriarchy and Hindu Patriarchy'. *Hypatia: A Journal of Feminist Philosophy* 34: 195–221.
Nicholson, Melanie. 2020. 'Necessary and Unnecessary Monsters: Jorge Luis Borges's Book of Imaginary Beings'. *Journal of Modern Literature* 43.2: 134–51.
Nicholson, Robert. 2001. '"Signatures of All Things I Am Here to Read": The James Joyce Museum at Sandycove'. *James Joyce Quarterly* 38.3/4: 293–8.
Pexa, Christopher. 2016. 'More Than Talking Animals: Charles Alexander Eastman's Animal Peoples and Their Kinship Critiques of United States Colonialism'. *PMLA* 131.3: 652–67.
Rohman, Carrie. 2009. *Stalking the Subject: Modernism and the Animal*. New York: Colombia University Press.
Ryan, Derek. 2013. *Virginia Woolf and the Materiality of Theory: Sex, Animal, Life*. Edinburgh: Edinburgh University Press.

Ryan, Derek. 2019. 'Literature'. In *The Edinburgh Companion to Animal Studies*. Ed. Lynn Turner, Undine Sellbach and Ron Broglio, 321–36. Edinburgh: Edinburgh University Press.

Scott, Bonnie Kime. 1991. '"The Look in the Throat of a Stricken Animal": Joyce as Met by Djuna Barnes'. *Joyce Studies Annual* 2 (Summer): 153–76.

Scott, Bonnie Kime. 1995. *Refiguring Modernism: The Women of 1928*. Bloomington and Indianapolis: Indiana University Press.

Scott, Bonnie Kime. 2012. *In the Hollow of the Wave: Virginia Woolf and Modernist Uses of Nature*. London: Virginia University Press.

Setz, Cathryn. 2019. *Primordial Modernism: Animals, Ideas, Transition 1927–1938*. Edinburgh: Edinburgh University Press.

Spengler, Birgitte and Babette B. Tischleder, eds. 2019. *An Eclectic Bestiary: Encounters in a More-than-Human World*. Bielefeld: Transcript.

Taylor, Nik and Richard Twine. 2014. *The Rise of Critical Animal Studies: From the Margins to the Centre*. London and New York: Routledge.

Weheliye, Alexander G. 2014. 'Introduction' and 'Blackness: The Human'. In *Habeas Viscus: Racializing Assemblages, Biopolitics, and Black Feminist Theories of the Human*, 1–32. Durham, NC: Duke University Press.

Weil, Kari. 2012. *Thinking Animals: Why Animal Studies Now?* New York: Columbia University Press.

Wolfe, Cary. 2003. *Animal Rites: American Culture, the Discourse of Species, and Posthumanist Theory*. Chicago and London: University of Chicago Press.

Wolfe, Cary. 2020. *Ecological Poetics, or Wallace Stevens's Birds*. Chicago: Chicago University Press.

Notes

1. See, for example, the special issue of the *Humanities* journal (2017) on 'Joyce, Animals and the Nonhuman', edited by Katherine Ebury; Cliff Mak, 'Joyce's Indifferent Animals: Boredom and the Subversion of Fables in Finnegan's Wake' (2016); Lauren Benjamin (2020), 'Circe's Feral Beasts: Women and Other Animals in Joyce's Ulysses', *Journal of Modern Literature* (43.2: 41–59); Annalisa Federici, 'From Animal Anthropomorphism to Human Animality in Ulysses: Joyce After Cervantes' (2020–1); and Peter Adkins (2022), 'Fourwalkers, Taildanglers, Headhangers: Labouring Animals in Ulysses', *Textual Practice* (36.2: 186–204).
2. The distinction drawn here is not absolute and there are close intersections between critical animal studies, human–animal studies and animality studies.

PART I

COMPANION SPECIES

I

METAMODERNIST BEASTS, OR FLUSH'S FUTURE: CERIDWEN DOVEY'S *ONLY THE ANIMALS* AND SIGRID NUNEZ'S *MITZ: THE MARMOSET OF BLOOMSBURY*

Derek Ryan

Flush: A Biography (1933) is the only work of fiction written by Virginia Woolf that leaves readers oriented towards an earlier era. Where her other novels end on or around the year of their completion, Woolf's fictional biography of Elizabeth Barrett Browning's cocker spaniel concludes with its protagonist's death in June 1854.[1] The list of 'Authorities' that directly follows the description of Flush's demise reinforces the book's historical gaze by listing the mid-nineteenth-century publications Woolf relied on. Those 'who would like to check the facts or to pursue the subject further' should, we are directed, consult two poems by Barrett Browning, 'To Flush, My Dog' (1844) and 'Flush, or Faunus' (1850), various editions of the Brownings' letters, and Thomas Beames's account of slums in *The Rookeries of London* (1850) (Woolf 1998: 151). As Linden Peach, Jane Goldman and I detail in the Cambridge Edition, Woolf's misleading qualification 'that there are very few authorities for the foregoing biography' (1998: 151) has thrown readers off the scent of the numerous other Victorian sources she drew upon, from Hugh Dalziel's *British Dogs: Their Varieties, History and Characteristics* (1888), key for her discussion of spaniel breeds, to Mrs Sutherland Orr's *Life and Letters of Robert Browning* (1891) and A. G. L'Estrange's *The Life of Mary Russell Mitford* (1870), which provide some of the details of Flush's human companions. The extent of Woolf's research not only puts paid to the idea that *Flush: A Biography* was merely a joke,[2] but demonstrates that she was interested in rescuing him from obscurity and inserting him into his rightful place in (literary) history. As Woolf herself writes in one of her own notes on the text: 'The whole question of dogs' relation to the spirit of the age, whether it is possible to call one dog Elizabethan, another Augustan, another Victorian, together,' she adds with characteristic humour, 'with the influence upon dogs of the poetry and philosophy of their masters, deserves a fuller discussion than can here be given it' (1998, 114).

But *Flush: A Biography* also looks forward and has itself been part of a fuller discussion about human–animal relations sparked by the animal turn in literary criticism. Woolf's decision to write a life of Flush has been understood as a device used to explore links between Victorian and Georgian private and public spheres in terms of gender (Squier 1985; Goldman 2010) and class (Light 2007) oppression, and to explore networks of exploitation connected to slavery (Peach 2000: 71), fascism (Snaith 2002) and eugenics (Peach 2013: 443–7). The book is also now held up as a touchstone of the genre of animal biography. When Woolf only half-seriously wrote in an unpublished note, originally planned to accompany her list of 'Authorities', that she was 'anticipating what will be, in a few years, the rule, perhaps the rage: anyhow the necessity' (1999: 101), she could not have envisaged that Flush would become, several decades later, a celebrated work within a field dedicated to the study of the literature and lives of animals.[3] It is now part of textbooks on the topic alongside other works that are said to 'give voice to animals' (DeMello 2013: 3; see also Weil 2012: 81–97) and is viewed as a complex exploration of canine subjectivity that transgresses generic conventions and transforms the mode of biography itself (Herman 2013; Kendall-Morwick 2014). Some scholars have argued that she engages closely with the behavioural aspects of dogs, whether in relation to comparative psychology (Hovanec 2013: 263–6) or evolutionary theory (Dubino 2014; McCracken 2021: 106–48). Others have focused on how *Flush: A Biography* pushes the boundaries of what we expect a dog's experience to be, by paying attention to smell (Booth 2000; Feuerstein 2013), desire (Smith 2002: 353), gaze (Ryan 2013: 143–150), *logos* and dreams (McCracken 2021: 126–7, 132–5), and reading and numeracy (Goldman 2016: 170–2). A bestseller in its own time and more favourably received by critics than is often assumed, the text's ability to speak to the critical discourse on animality in the early twenty-first century has gained it belated recognition within the modernist canon.

Flush: A Biography's futurity is my main concern in this chapter. But rather than critical fortunes, I focus on the book's literary afterlife. Specifically, I consider two contemporary works of fiction written by an American and a South African–Australian author who follow Woolf in testing how far anthropomorphic language and narrative technique might be used to explore both cross-species companionship and violence. Rooted in what she calls, in her 'Acknowledgments', the 'published fact' of Leonard Woolf's autobiography, Virginia Woolf's letters and diaries, and various other memoirs and biographies (Nunez 2019a: 149), Sigrid Nunez's fictional biography, *Mitz: The Marmoset of Bloomsbury*, first published in 1998, tells the life of the marmoset the Woolfs acquired from Victor Rothschild in 1934.⁴ Ceridwen Dovey's fictional memoir of a tortoise, Plautus, kept by Virginia Woolf (as well as the Tolstoy family and George Orwell, among others), in a section of the 2014 short story collection *Only the Animals*, is more fantastical, playing fast and loose with fact in a manner that perhaps has more in common with *Orlando: A Biography* (1928) (though Woolf is surprisingly omitted in her list of sources – her own kind of 'Authorities' note – published online).⁵ Both texts do, however, make explicit reference to *Flush: A Biography* and as such are examples of what Laura Marcus, in her essay on the legacies of the modernist novel, calls 'direct, rather than diffuse, influences' (2007: 82). In what follows, I suggest that their versions of fictional auto/biography bring modernist strategies for writing about animals into the realm of contemporary literature. While Nunez and Dovey draw on information about the lives of famous writers, animal figures are central to their forging the kind of 'inventive, self-conscious relationship' with modernist literature that David James and Urmila Seshagiri have termed 'metamodernism' (2014: 88), or that is revealed through Michaela Bronstein's definition of 'transhistorical' reading (2018: 7–8).⁶ These books should not be read as merely paying homage to the past, but as making use of the archive of experimental forms and styles from the early twentieth century – in this case, beastly biography – in order to 'reassess', 'reanimate' and sometimes 'repudiate' modernism (James and Seshagiri 2014: 89), to show how the past 'is re-enacted, reused, repurposed, and reimagined by the present' (Bronstein 2018: 1). This is not to downplay the significance of *Flush: A Biography*'s Victorian context, but to show how Woolf transforms Elizabeth Barrett Browning's cocker spaniel into a metamodernist textual beast written into history but ready to pounce on the readers of the future.

Both Nunez and Dovey display a heightened awareness of what Woolf, in the above-mentioned draft 'Authorities' note, described as the 'anthropomorphic delusion' that would view beasts as 'merely extensions of our own identity' (Woolf 1999: 101). While *Mitz: The Marmoset of Bloomsbury* has been recognised as a work of 'biofiction' of primary interest to scholars for its portrayal of Virginia Woolf,⁷ Nunez is clearly concerned with the roles nonhuman animals play in storytelling. When asked in an interview what interested her in writing about animals, she replied:

> Everything. Animals are a great mystery to human beings. We know they have feelings and we have ways of interpreting certain signs and behaviors of theirs, but because they don't have language we really don't know what goes on inside their heads. I have always loved animals and been fascinated by them. (Nunez 2019b)

Lack of knowledge here fuels the desire to write about nonhuman animals rather than hindering it, yet it also ensures a careful approach to, and self-conscious use of, the inevitable anthropomorphism that comes with using human language to explore nonhuman life. In the early reception of *Only the Animals*, meanwhile, Woolf has been something of an understudy to a cast that includes Kafka (the chapter inspired by his 'A Report to an Academy' is one of the collection's highlights), even and most notably in one recent book chapter that opens with a discussion of *Flush: A Biography* and moves on to Dovey and other contemporary texts (see Herman 2018). But the section 'A Terrarium of One's Own' is an example of her wanting, as she put it in an interview, 'to short-circuit the rational retelling' of history centred on human events and experiences. Dovey is cognisant of 'the absurdity of a talking animal soul speaking from beyond the grave' (2014b). Nonetheless, in pushing anthropomorphic voice to a more extreme level than found in *Mitz: The Marmoset of Bloomsbury* or, for that matter, *Flush: A Biography*, Dovey chooses her narrative technique in the spirit of modernism's, and particularly here Woolf's, experiments with an anthropomorphism that contests rather than confirms anthropocentrism.[8]

One strategy Nunez learns from Woolf in order to navigate through the potential pitfalls of anthropomorphism is evident in her use of the interrogative mood to pose questions about animal experience:

> Virginia looked long upon Mitz very often. She wondered about Mitz as she had wondered about the cats and dogs she had known all her life. What was it like to be an animal? How did the world look through a dog's eyes? What did cats think of us? Without such wonder, it is doubtful Virginia ever would have written *Flush*. Now it was Mitz's walnut of a head she wished to crack. Did marmosets dream? Did they remember? Did they regret? What did marmosets want? (2019a, 58)

This passage invokes Woolf's cautious approach to anthropomorphic projection in *Flush: A Biography*, wherein many of her speculations as to his wonderings, observations and motivations are posed as questions. In front of the mirror at the start of Chapter 3, we read: 'Was not the little brown dog opposite himself? But what is "oneself"? Is it the thing people see? Or is it the thing one is?' (1998: 32). Or in the closing pages we read of the biographer imagining Flush dreaming: 'was he dreaming that he hunted rabbits in Spain? Was he coursing up a hot hill-side with dark men shouting "Span! Span!" as the rabbits darted from the brushwood?' (1998: 104). Significantly, human language itself is also up for debate: 'Miss Barrett once exclaimed after a morning's toil, "writing, writing . . ." After all, she may have thought, do words say everything? Can words say anything? Do not words destroy the symbol that lies beyond the reach of words?' (1998: 27). These questions, and the many similar ones posed in Woolf's and Nunez's texts, expose the limits of human knowledge at the same time as they multiply the possibilities of nonhuman worlds. The biographers here place themselves in affinity with Mitz, who herself behaved 'as if the world were a question' (with the speculative 'as if' once again used to imagine cautiously the animal's perspective) (Nunez 2019a: 81). The posing of such questions is not only a marker of modernism's openness to unknowability or unrecognisability but an anticipation of further questions to come. In writing, for instance, that the conundrum 'What was it like to be an animal?' was essential to Woolf's completion of *Flush: A Biography*, Nunez alludes to Thomas Nagel's influential 1974 article, 'What is it Like to be a Bat?' and its sceptical exploration of the limits of anthropomorphism, which would be famously interrogated by J. M. Coetzee's Elizabeth Costello (1999: 31–4) in *The Lives of Animals*. These texts are also part of *Flush: A Biography*'s future.

Dovey's *Only the Animals* plays on Woolf's style in a different way by raising concerns about how animal auto/biographies are often dismissed by readers. An element of self-reflexivity can be detected in Dovey having Plautus the tortoise recall his human keeper reading passages of *Flush: A Biography* aloud:

> She sensed that I didn't like it when the tone veered towards the ironic, tongue-in-cheek style that humans seem to adopt automatically when writing from the perspective of an animal. It was a cheeky book, certainly, provocative even – it fit with her desire at the time to play with the conventions of traditional biography – but that didn't mean it couldn't also be moving. (2014a: 133)

Dovey's response to concerns that writing about nonhuman animals might not be taken seriously is to opt for a more and not less anthropomorphic narrative voice for the tortoise, but she does so very deliberately to undermine anthropocentrism. Plautus points out that the best passages of Woolf's fictional biography are those that focus on smell:

> I was most impressed by the passages in *Flush: A Biography* in which Virginia attempted to understand at a sensory level what it might be like for a dog to experience the world through smell. This was probably due to my own similar hierarchy of senses, with smell right at the top. (2014a: 134)

Dovey then quotes a passage from Woolf's text that imagines what Florence might smell like to Flush, and where these smells are somewhat abstract and only vaguely identifiable to humans: we are told 'how acid shade made the stone smell', and about 'the purple smell' of ripe grapes, the 'raucous smells, crimson smells' of goat and macaroni (Dovey 2014a: 134; Woolf 1998: 87). Earlier in the same passage Woolf's biographer notes:

> there are no more than two words and one-half for what we smell. The human nose is practically non-existent. The greatest poets in the world have smelt nothing but roses on the one hand, and dung on the other. The infinite gradations that lie between are unrecorded. Yet it was in the world of smell that Flush mostly lived. Love was chiefly smell; form and colour were smell; music and architecture, law, politics and science were smell. To him religion itself was smell. (Woolf: 1998, 86)

Dovey has therefore steered her readers to the space opened up in Woolf's text to imagine a canine sensory experience that evades human comprehension.

In their experiments in animal auto/biography, however, neither Nunez nor Dovey goes as far as to present us with what David Herman refers to as 'co-authored acts of narrating' (2018: 194). Grace Moore is right to point out in response to Herman that while attempts to depict cross-species interactions are valuable, such interactions hold 'subtleties' that are beyond human language; the notion of 'joint authorship' is as 'disingenuous' as it is 'enticing' (2020: 212–3). But if both the cautious anthropomorphism of *Mitz: The Marmoset of Bloomsbury* and extravagant anthropomorphism of *Only the Animals* draw attention to the limitations of human language to convey non-human animal narrative, to some extent they do, as the above passages show, 'reflect and help constitute an alternative ontology' that opens up versions of selfhood for animals, as Herman claims of a later section of Dovey's text (Herman 2018: 195). Moreover, in adapting modernist strategies for writing about nonhuman animals, Nunez and Dovey demonstrate how different modes of being and narrative techniques are connected by Woolf, and in their own texts, to material encounters with animals. Like many other works of beastly modernism, *Flush: A Biography* not only is a text that probes ideas of species boundaries but does so by attending to the matter of exploitation – whether of 'half famished, dirty, diseased, uncombed, unbrushed' dogs at the hands of dognappers (1998: 55), the cramped conditions of livestock 'milked and killed and eaten under the bedroom' (1998: 52), or the cruelty of breeding clubs that determine whether certain dogs will be 'encouraged and bred from' or 'cut off' (1998: 7). Nunez and Dovey manipulate anthropomorphic narration to expose not only anthropocentric worldviews but also, we will see, the history of violence that is cause and consequence of them.

Beyond personality portraits and the companionship offered by the Woolfs' marmoset in *Mitz: The Marmoset of Bloomsbury*, asymmetrical power dynamics between human and nonhuman are uncovered. Some exploitative relationships are only hinted at, such as when we read of Leonard eating 'with delight, praising the fish, the meat' or of he and Virginia enjoying their 'passion' of *pâté de foie gras* on a holiday in France (Nunez 2019a: 4, 102). More prominent throughout the book are allusions to networks of colonial captivity. We are told of Leonard's 'mixed feelings' about zoos; an incident in which he and Virginia witnessed an ape who had escaped from the circus; a golden lion marmoset transported to Europe in the mid-eighteenth century to be part of Louis XV's menagerie; and the demand for marmosets among sailors who would purchase them at low prices and 'sell them for a great deal more back home' (Nunez 2019a: 26, 18, 52, 27). The entire novel is framed around Mitz's own story of capture. Echoing the repeated emphasis on chains in Woolf's *Flush: A Biography*, the opening chapter informs readers that 'Mitz had once been chained . . .', with the ellipses then filled in towards the end of the book through a detailed account of the horrid conditions she experienced in South America. We read of 'men with machetes, men with nets', and then of Mitz 'scream[ing] herself hoarse' as 'She bit and scratched at the hands that seized her' and placed her in a box inside which 'she clawed at the bottom, the sides, the top. There was not enough air – yet her lungs seemed full to bursting' (Nunez 2019a: 7–8, 135). Any anthropomorphic language used to imagine the experience of Mitz and her fellow simians captured in this way – for example, when we are told that 'Different stories were passed from tree to tree about the monkeys that disappeared' – only serves to underline the material violence they suffered. We soon discover that an unfed Mitz was squeezed into a cage with other monkeys, 'shrieking, as monkeys in terror and confusion do', and the footsteps of a knife-wielding man who would throw burning ash on paws and bottles against cages (Nunez 2019a: 136–7). Just as Virginia Woolf imagined Flush's plight after being dognapped to an extent not seen in Elizabeth Barrett Browning's letters (see Ryan 2019: 274–5), so here is Mitz's capture depicted with an intensity that surpasses the Woolfs' own remarks about their marmoset.

Plautus may not suffer as Mitz does, but the story she tells reveals how tortoises have also been exploited by humans. In Dovey's text, the tortoise declares herself a lucky exception:

> Many times during my happy years with Virginia, I was grateful for the good fortune of having arrived on her doorstep and nobody else's, for this was London in the 1930s and the pet tortoise craze was in full swing. Virginia followed the travesties of the tortoise trade as they were reported in the papers: millions of us imported each year from North Africa, arriving with broken limbs and shells from being packed into crates one on top of the other; a thousand dead spur-thighed tortoises discovered in baskets on the Barking foreshore. Hardly any that survived the journey made it through their first winter in Britain. Outside schools you could buy a baby tortoise and a goldfish for sixpence, and

> if they both died – as was likely – you could buy another pair the next week. In any local pub, you could find pet tortoises being forced to race across the billiard tables, and given a puddle of beer to drink at the end. (2014a: 136)

Here is a stark example of an anthropomorphised voice being used to shed light on the abuse of nonhuman animals. The passage seemingly alludes to Woolf's 1932 essay 'Oxford Street Tide', which she completed as part of a series of essays on London that she wrote while she was working on *Flush: A Biography* (the first draft of Woolf's fictional biography was, in fact, written in the same notebook as these essays, indicating that the two projects were intertwined). Woolf writes of how 'tortoises repose on litters of grass' waiting for 'a woman [to] stop and add a tortoise to her string of parcels', which 'is perhaps the rarest sight that human eyes can look upon' (2010: 283–4).[9] It should be noted, however, that the Woolfs' complicity in this trade in tortoises – they purchased several over the years – is overlooked by Dovey's description of how sympathetic and caring Virginia was upon Plautus's arrival. To Jacques Raverat, for example, she writes on 30 July 1923 of having 'a tortoise, bought for 2/- yesterday in the High street' (Woolf 1978: 58); while to Lydia Keynes she writes on 5 June 1937 that 'Leonard is engaged in putting his new tortoises to bed in the lily pond. They – we bought 3 – are so active we cant control of them. I am perpetually being sent up the road in pursuit of the father tortoise' (Woolf 1980: 134). Similarly, Plautus's belief that 'in Bloomsbury, during those years before the next war started, I was treated not as a mere pet, but as the worthy subject of great art and poetry' (Dovey 2014a: 136) leaves us wondering if the irony is intended by Dovey, given that Woolf never did write her own testudine story.[10] Meanwhile, the notion that 'Tortoiseshell objects – hair combs, calling card boxes, the rare snuffbox – were banned in my presence, Virginia made sure of it' is contradicted by the fact that Woolf herself owned fashionable tortoiseshell glasses (a pair of which are now in the possession of the National Trust).[11]

If the examples given signal the wider colonial and capitalist networks of animal capture and trade, Nunez's marmoset and Dovey's tortoise are also placed at the heart of encounters involving fascism and war. *Mitz: The Marmoset of Bloomsbury* pieces together details from Leonard's autobiography and Virginia's diaries to reconstruct a trip they took across Europe in 1935 with their marmoset in tow. In *Downhill All the Way* (1967), Leonard records that on 9 May they 'passed in a few yards from civilization to savagery' when they drove across the Dutch border into Nazi Germany, armed only with a letter from Prince Bismarck of the Foreign Office to explain their presence (Woolf 1970: 189). Entering the town of Bonn, they were confronted by German policemen and a large group of 'enthusiastic Nazis' who had gathered to welcome the man the Woolfs suspected must be Hitler (it turned out to be Hermann Göring). If this seemed like a perilous situation for a prominent Jewish intellectual and an eminent novelist, their fears soon subsided, thanks to an unlikely saviour:

> When they saw Mitz, the crowd shrieked with delight. Mile after mile I drove between the two lines of corybantic Germans, and the whole way they shouted 'Heil Hitler! Heil Hitler!' to Mitz and gave her (and secondarily Virginia and me) the Hitler salute with outstretched arm. (Woolf 1970: 191)

As Virginia recorded in her diary that day while the events were unfolding: 'We become obsequious – delighted that is when the officers smile at Mitzi,' with this 'obsequiousness gradually turning to anger' (Woolf 1983: 311).

In Nunez's dramatisation of the event, Mitz takes centre stage as the amusement the officers find in this animal and their embodiment of fascist politics are disturbingly juxtaposed. An officer approaches:

> He threw up his hands, he shook his fists, he lifted one knee and then the other and stamped his feet. He was a swastika himself, all angles, twisted, black and red. He bore down on the car. Leonard felt for the letter in his pocket. Mitz, excited by the noise and the flags and now *this* amusing fellow, leapt onto the steering wheel and screeched. The man stopped in his tracks. Surprise, then puzzlement, then tenderness showed in his face. 'Ah – oh – ah!' he cried. He clapped his hands like a child. '*Das liebe kleine Ding!*'
>
> It was as if the Woolfs had vanished. The storm trooper had eyes only for Mitz. He leaned into the car, and Leonard inhaled a mixture of beer, onion, leather, pomade, and sweat. The man wagged a finger at Mitz, and Virginia closed her eyes and sent up a prayer that Mitz would not bite it. Bite it she did though – but this seemed only to increase his delight. He burbled and cooed, offering wurst fingers to Mitz, one by one. And what was the sweet creature's name? When he heard it he laughed and repeated it several times, slapping his thigh. He loved it – *loved* it! At last he stepped back from the car, clicked his heels together, and raised his arm. '*Heil Hitler!*' (Nunez 2019a: 70–1)

Mitz's anthropomorphic voice can be detected in Nunez's free indirect discourse – 'now *this* amusing fellow' seeming to be her own thoughts – and she appears to be attuned to the man's shifting emotions. Moreover, while Leonard takes a deep breath and Virginia closes her eyes, the marmoset is the only one not rendered passive in front of the transfixed storm trooper. The brief sentence 'It was as if the Woolfs had vanished' is significant from the perspective of the past incident that inspired this part of Nunez's book, as well as the future context in which Nunez is writing. On the one hand, that is, it signals Nunez's foray into more imaginative terrain in focusing on Mitz's experience of the event to a greater extent than the Woolfs did in their written recollections; on the other, it points to the fact that, far from receding from Nazi view, the Woolfs were, as noted a couple of pages later, soon to be added to a Gestapo arrest list (2019a: 73).

Dovey writes of animals less fortunate than Mitz was at the hands of the Nazis. When Plautus remembers 'that Virginia had told Leonard the morning before about the Nazis burning Swastikas into the backs of tortoises' (2014a: 138), she does so while shielding herself from falling bombs. As we are told,

> This lovely literary life with Virginia and the Bloomsbury Set was upended by the London Blitz. I mean this quite literally. One moment I was sunning myself in the Woolfs' drawing room, the next I was buried in the rubble of their home after a bomb hit it while they were out. I felt very calm for the first day I spent hidden away in my shell in the darkness of the ruins. (2014a: 137)

Dovey is not simply using the tortoise to convey the horrors of the war for civilians on the Home Front; she is also alluding to the largely untold history of companion animals caught up in human wars. As historian Hilda Kean powerfully argues, the Second World War is incorrectly labelled the 'People's War' because 'experiencing bombardment was clearly a joint animal–human activity' (2017: 114). While Kean's focus is primarily on dogs and cats, she does touch on tortoises: 'British propaganda asked pet owners to support the war effort partly because of the threat to pets if the Nazis were victorious', the evidence of which included data collected from the occupied Channel Islands, where 'People queued in their hundreds to have their animals killed at the Jersey Animal Shelter. About 2,000 dogs and 3,000 cats were destroyed in five days. Pet tortoises were collected in tomato baskets and released daily' (Kean 2017: 121). Plautus is, in the end, rescued by a mongrel dog named 'Beauty' – Dovey's nod to Anna Sewell signalling a further layer of transhistorical cross-species alliance – and, via an improbably circuitous route that includes time with the unsympathetic Orwell, a wildlife park in Wiltshire and playwright Tom Stoppard (whose 1993 play, *Arcadia*, Dovey took the tortoise's name from), she finds herself in the USSR being presented to the Soviet Space Programme. Here Plautus will become one of those poignantly described as 'one-way passengers' who, at the same time, aided and were victims of the Cold War and its 'Space Race' (Dovey 2014a: 146). Her own death is prefigured when she reflects on the story of 'Laika, the first animal to orbit the earth. She was a stray that Dr Yazdovsky noticed lurking beside the rubbish bins outside the facility and on a whim decided to put in the cabin of *Sputnik II* when it was blasted into orbit around earth in 1957' (2014a: 146). The matter-of-fact way in which we are told that 'The video recorders in the cabin revealed that she was quite happy up there, able to move a bit, bark, and eat food pellets from an automatic dispenser' becomes a darkly ironic kind of anthropomorphic projection when we then read that 'the oxygen in her capsule ran out and she died, but her capsule stayed in orbit for months' (2014a: 146). Plautus suffers the same fate, after being sent up to space in 1968 in 'a Noah's rocket-ark of biological specimens' which included the tortoise in her 'terrarium' (Dovey's play on Woolf's 'a room of one's own' in the section's title now poignantly used to signal the tortoise's lack of freedom) (2014a: 149–50).

Mitz: The Marmoset of Bloomsbury and *Only the Animals* are, I have been suggesting, examples of 'contemporary fictions distinguished by inventive, self-conscious relationships with modernist literature' (James and Seshagiri 2014: 88), and specifically Woolf's experiment in writing animal biography. As metamodernist beasts, Mitz the marmoset and Plautus the tortoise also demand a transhistorical reading as 'an invitation to interaction with multiple historical moments' (Bronstein 2018: 8). If such an approach to contemporary literature necessarily views modernism as a historical phenomenon dependent on particular cultural contexts, it does so precisely in order to mobilise its achievements and gain a greater appreciation of its influence on the later twentieth and early twenty-first century. Crucially, while Nunez and Dovey reanimate and revise Woolf's approach to writing animals in terms of technique and theme, they also speak to their – and our – own moment in which there is increasing recognition of how, as philosopher Christine Overall puts it in introducing the volume *Pets and People*, 'Companion animals are both vulnerable to and dependent upon us' (2017: xvii). Overall asks foundational questions that animal studies scholars and activists have been grappling with in recent years:

> What responsibilities do we owe to them, especially since we have the power and authority to make literal life-and-death decisions about them? What kinds of relationships should we have with our companion animals? What might we learn from them about the nature and limits of our own morality? How should we (re)create our lives with them? (2017: xvii).

Indeed, Woolf herself wrote in an early draft of her fictional biography: 'What does one owe an animal trusted to ones [sic] care?'[12] In responding to *Flush: A Biography*'s future and raising such questions in contemporary fiction, Nunez and Dovey teach us how to care about – and for – modernist beasts.

Works Cited

Booth, Alison. 2000. 'The Scent of a Narrative: Rank Discourse in *Flush* and *Written on the Body*'. *Narrative* 8.1: 3–22.

Bronstein, Michaela. 2018. *Out of Context: The Uses of Modernist Fiction*. Oxford: Oxford University Press.

Coetzee, J. M. 1999. *The Lives of Animals*. Ed. Amy Gutmann. Princeton: Princeton University Press.

DeMello, Margo, ed. 2013. *Speaking for Animals: Animal Autobiographical Writing*. New York: Routledge.

Dovey, Ceridwen. 2014a. *Only the Animals*. London: Atlantic Books.

Dovey, Ceridwen with Potts Point Bookshop. 2014b. Interview. Available at: <https://www.pottspointbookshopblog.com/blog/2014/05/interview-with-ceridwen-dovey-author-of.html> (last accessed 28 June 2022).

Dubino, Jeanne. 2014. 'The Bispecies Environment, Coevolution, and *Flush*'. In *Virginia Woolf: Twenty-First Century Approaches*. Ed. Jeanne Dubino, Gill Lowe, Vara Neverow and Kathryn Simpson, 131–47. Edinburgh: Edinburgh University Press.

Feuerstein, Anna. 2013. 'What Does Power Smell Like? Canine Epistemology and the Politics of the Pet in Virginia Woolf's *Flush*'. Special Issue: 'Woolf and Animals'. Ed. Kristin Czarnecki and Vara Neverow. *Virginia Woolf Miscellany* 84: 32–4.

Godioli, Alberto, Monica Jansen and Carmen Van den Bergh. 2020. 'Thresholds and Tortoises: Modernist Animality in Pirandello's Fiction'. In *Posthumanism in Italian Literature and Film*. Ed. Enrica Maria Ferrara, 51–71. Basingstoke: Palgrave Macmillan.

Goldman, Jane. 2010. 'Who Let the Dogs Out? Samuel Johnson, Thomas Carlyle, Virginia Woolf, and the Little Brown Dog'. In *Virginia Woolf's Bloomsbury: International Influence and Politics*. Ed. Lisa Shahriari and Gina Potts, 46–65. Basingstoke: Palgrave Macmillan.

Goldman, Jane. 2016. '*Flush: A Biography*: Speaking, Reading, and Writing with the Companion Species'. In *A Companion to Virginia Woolf*. Ed. Jessica Berman, 163–76. Oxford: Wiley-Blackwell.

Herman, David. 2013. 'Modernist Life Writing and Nonhuman Lives: Ecologies of Experience in Virginia Woolf's *Flush*'. *Modern Fiction Studies* 59.3: 547–68.

Herman, David. 2018. *Narratology Beyond the Human*. Oxford: Oxford University Press.

Hovanec, Caroline. 2013. 'Philosophical Barnacles and Empiricist Dogs'. *Configurations* 21.3: 245–69.

Ittner, Jutta. 2006. 'Part Spaniel, Part Canine Puzzle: Anthropomorphism in Woolf's *Flush* and Auster's *Timbuktu*'. *Mosaic* 39.4: 181–96.

James, David and Urmila Seshagiri. 2014. 'Metamodernism: Narratives of Continuity and Revolution'. *PMLA* 129.1: 87–100.

Kean, Hilda. 2017. *The Great Cat and Dog Massacre: The Real Story of World War II's Unknown Tragedy*. Chicago: University of Chicago Press.

Kelley, Philip, Scott Lewis, Edward Hagan, Joseph Phelan and Rhian Williams, eds. 2013. *The Brownings' Correspondence*. Vol. 20. Winfield, KA: Wedgestone Press.

Kendall-Morwick, Karalyn. 2014. 'Mongrel Fiction: Canine Bildung and the Feminist Critique of Anthropocentrism in Virginia Woolf's *Flush*'. *Modern Fiction Studies* 60.3: 506–26.

Kersten, Dennis and Usha Wilbers. 2018. 'Introduction: Metamodernism'. *English Studies* 99.7: 719–22.

Latham, Monica. 2012. '"Serv[ing] Under Two Masters": Virginia Woolf's Afterlives in Contemporary Biofictions'. *a/b: Auto/Biography Studies* 27.2: 354–73.

Layne, Bethany. 2014. '"They leave out the person to whom things happened": Re-reading the Biographical Subject in Sigrid Nunez's *Mitz: The Marmoset of Bloomsbury* (1998)'. In *Bloomsbury Influences*. Ed. Elizabeth H. Wright, 30–45. Newcastle upon Tyne: Cambridge Scholars.

Light, Alison. 2007. *Mrs Woolf and the Servants*. London: Penguin.

McCracken, Saskia. 2021. *(R)evolutionary Animal Tropes in the Works of Charles Darwin and Virginia Woolf*. Doctoral Thesis, University of Glasgow.

Marcus, Laura. 2007. 'The Legacies of Modernism'. In *The Cambridge Companion to the Modernist Novel*. Ed. Morag Shiach, 82–97. Cambridge: Cambridge University Press.

Moore, Grace. 2020. '"As Closely Bonded as We are": Animalographies, Kinship, and Conflict in Ceridwen Dovey's *Only the Animals* and Eva Hornung's *Dog Boy*'. *a/b: Auto/Biography Studies* 35.1: 207–29.

Nunez, Sigrid. 2019a. *Mitz: The Marmoset of Bloomsbury*. New York. Soft Skull.

Nunez, Sigrid with Carrie Mullins. 2019b. Interview. *Electric Lit*. Available at: <https://electricliterature.com/sigrid-nunez-mitz-is-a-story-about-virginias-woolf-pet-monkey/> (last accessed 28 June 2022).

Overall, Christine, ed. 2017. *Pets and People: The Ethics of Our Relationships with Companion Animals*. Oxford: Oxford University Press.

Peach, Linden. 2000. *Virginia Woolf (Critical Issues)*. New York: St Martins.

Peach, Linden. 2013. 'Woolf and Eugenics'. In *Virginia Woolf in Context*. Ed. Bryony Randall and Jane Goldman, 439–48. Cambridge: Cambridge University Press.

Pollentier, Caroline. 2014. 'Untimely Metamorphoses: Darwin, Baudelaire, Woolf, and Animal Flânerie'. *Representing the Modern Animal in Culture*. Ed. Jeanne Dubini, Ziba Rashidian and Andrew Smyth, 155–75. New York: Palgrave Macmillan.

Rohman, Carrie. 2018. *Choreographies of the Living: Bioaesthetics in Literature, Art, and Performance*. Oxford: Oxford University Press.

Ryan, Derek. 2013. *Virginia Woolf and the Materiality of Theory: Sex, Animal, Life*. Edinburgh: Edinburgh University Press.

Ryan, Derek. 2015. *Animal Theory: A Critical Introduction*. Edinburgh: Edinburgh University Press.

Ryan, Derek. 2019. '"Was it Flush, or was it Pan?": Virginia Woolf, Ethel Smyth, and Canine Biography'. In *Reading Literary Animals: Medieval to Modern*. Ed. Karen L. Edwards, Derek Ryan and Jane Spencer, 264–81. New York: Routledge.

Smith, Craig. 2002. 'Across the Widest Gulf: Nonhuman Subjectivity in Virginia Woolf's *Flush*'. *Twentieth-Century Literature* 48.3: 348–61.

Snaith, Anna. 2002. 'Of Fanciers, Footnotes, and Fascism: Virginia Woolf's *Flush*'. *Modern Fiction Studies* 48.3: 614–36.

Squier, Susan Merrill. 1985. *Virginia Woolf and London: The Sexual Politics of the City*. Chapel Hill: University of North Caroline Press.

Vermeulen, Timotheus and Robin van den Akker. 2010. 'Notes on Metamodernism'. *Journal of Aesthetics & Culture* 2.1.

Weil, Kari. 2012. *Thinking Animals: Why Animal Studies Now?* New York: Columbia University Press.

Woolf, Leonard. 1970. *Downhill All the Way: An Autobiography of the Years 1919–1939*. London: Hogarth Press.
Woolf, Virginia. 1978. *The Letters of Virginia Woolf, Volume 3: 1923–1928*. Ed. Nigel Nicolson and Joanne Trautmann. New York: Harcourt Brace Jovanovich.
Woolf, Virginia. 1980. *The Letters of Virginia Woolf, Volume 6: 1936–1941*. Ed. Nigel Nicolson and Joanne Trautmann. New York: Harcourt Brace Jovanovich.
Woolf, Virginia. 1983. *The Diary of Virginia Woolf, Volume 4: 1931–1935*. Ed. Anne Olivier Bell, assisted by Andrew McNeillie. New York: Harcourt Brace & Company.
Woolf, Virginia. 1998. *Flush: A Biography*. Ed. Kate Flint. Oxford: Oxford University Press.
Woolf, Virginia. 1999. *Flush: A Biography*. Ed. Elizabeth Steele. Oxford: Shakespeare Head.
Woolf, Virginia. 2010. 'Oxford Street Tide'. In *The Essays of Virginia Woolf, Volume 5: 1929–1932*. Ed. Stuart N. Clarke, 283–9. New York: Houghton Mifflin Harcourt.
Young, Peter. 2003. *Tortoise*. London: Reaktion.

NOTES

1. The date is not given by Woolf, but Flush's death is recorded in a letter Elizabeth Barrett Browning sent to Arabella Moulton-Barrett, 17, 18, 20 June 1854 (see Kelley et al. 2013: 248).
2. Woolf refers variously to *Flush* as a joke in letters to Ethel Smyth, Donald Brace, Ottoline Morrell, Vita Sackville-West and Hugh Walpole. See Woolf, *Letters* 5: 140, 155, 161, 169, 177. At the same time, she repeatedly worries over the book's reception, evident in her diary entries in the days following its publication. See, for example, *Diary*, 4: 184–6.
3. This 'Authorities Note' (in holograph draft, 31 July 1931, Berg Collection, New York Public Library, 197–203) was originally planned to precede the list of sources Woolf includes at the end of Flush. While never published in Woolf's lifetime, the 'corrected' version I cite from here is helpfully reproduced in the source cited.
4. The 2019 reissued edition of *Mitz*, which I refer to in this essay, includes a letter sent by Nigel Nicolson to Nunez upon the book's original publication. In it, Nicolson writes that he thought the marmoset 'horrible' when he saw her, but that the book itself was a 'perfect little gem'. He adds: 'I notice the debt it owes to <u>Flush</u>' (Nicolson qtd in Nunez 2019a: 151).
5. Available at <https://www.ceridwendovey.com/assets/Uploads/Only-the-Animals-sources.pdf> (last accessed 29 June 2022).
6. The term metamodernism has been defined in different ways by critics working in a variety of fields. For a contrasting approach to James and Seshagiri see Vermeulen and van den Akker (2010). For a discussion of 'clashing interpretations' of the term and the work it yields see Kersten and Wilbers (2018).
7. Reading *Mitz* in relation to a range of contemporary texts that present an 'amalgamation of biographical, historical, and scholarly research', critics have emphasised how fictionalising Virginia Woolf allows 'her biographers [to] delve into her imaginary inner life, construct an "as if," and bring the reader into her psyche' (Latham 2012: 356). Bethany Layne similarly urges us to read *Mitz* in relation to Virginia Woolf's life

and writing: 'Nunez's novel thus straddles two different modes of engagement: the adaptive, which engages with Woolf's work, and the biographical, which engages with her life.' She does, however, note similarities and differences between the representations of animal consciousness offered by Nunez and Woolf, arguing that in *Mitz* we find increased 'imaginative empathy' between species (2014: 30, 35).

8. My view of Woolf's anthropomorphism contrasts with that of Ittner (2006). See also Ryan (2013).
9. Focusing on the tortoises in Woolf's essay, Caroline Pollentier argues that the 'human and animal copresence destabilizes the distinction between thinking subject and commodified object' (2014: 166).
10. In this respect Woolf pays less attention to the artistic potential in tortoises than contemporaries such as D. H. Lawrence or Luigi Pirandello (see Rohman 2018: 43–52 and Godiolo et al. 2020).
11. Available at: <https://www.nationaltrustcollections.org.uk/object/768389> (last accessed 28 June 2022). On the history of tortoiseshell trade, see Young (2003: 98–100). Young's book is one of Dovey's listed sources.
12. Holograph draft, 31 July 1931, Berg Collection, New York Public Library, 83. Cited from transcription by Jane Goldman and Saskia McCracken, published as part of the Cambridge Edition of Woolf's *Flush: A Biography*, co-edited by myself, Goldman and Linden Peach. For a discussion of 'pets' and ethics see Ryan (2015: 85–99).

2

CAN FLUSH COUNT?: VIRGINIA WOOLF, ANIMALITY AND NUMBERS

Jane Goldman

'Can Flush Count?' The short answer is 'Yes – But, in more ways than one!' This essay counts some of the ways. The historical, lived dog Flush (c.1840–54), companion of the poet Elizabeth Barrett Browning, given to her by Mary Russell Mitford and the subject of Virginia Woolf's novel *Flush: A Biography* (1933), was apparently taught to count. But this parlour game with a poet is possibly the least interesting aspect of any investigation into numbers and animality in Woolf's bestselling but least critically scrutinised novel. Canine counting and Woolf's own recorded suspicion of measuring – 'Who shall measure the heat and violence of a poet's heart when caught and tangled in a woman's body?' (Woolf 1929: 73) – is here considered in relation to Catullus's famous love lyric against counting and Derrida's dictum 'Counting is a bad procedure', to argue that *Flush: A Biography*, Woolf's much neglected ground-breaking work on animality, really does count.

COUNTING THE FLUSHES

'Can Flush count?' supplements a previous question I asked elsewhere: 'Can Flush read?'. In attempting to respond to the latter I explored Woolf's canine novel in relation to Derrida's animal turn (Goldman 2016). I concluded with the short answer: yes, Flush can read (Goldman 2016: 172)! Flush can read image; he can read humans; he can read human writing. But *which* 'Flush' can read these things? For Flush is legion. Flush, too, is verb, noun and adjective. Flush is text, and more importantly, intertext. How might we collate him?

How do we go about counting the *number* of Flushes that could come running when we call that name? *Flush: A Biography* undermines our faith in a singular, originary Flush.

Nor is Flush simply polysemic; rather, Flush is disseminated. Dissemination, according to Derrida, in 'diverging from polysemy, comprising both more and less than the latter [. . .] interrupts the circulation that transforms into an origin what is actually an after-effect of meaning' (Derrida 1981: 21). 'Counting is a bad procedure', Derrida writes in *Dissemination* (1981), citing Georg Wilhelm Friedrich Hegel's observation in *Lectures on the History of Philosophy* (1892): 'The Spirit is certainly a trinity, but it cannot be added up or counted. Counting is a bad procedure' (Derrida 1981: 24).[1] Derrida takes this up in his account of dissemination itself: 'Another way of working with *numbers*, dissemination, sets up a pharmacy in which it is no longer possible to count by ones, by twos, or by threes; in which everything starts with the dyad' (Derrida 1981: 24). Here he counters the possibility of synthesis or transcendence in Hegel's dialectics: 'The dual opposition (remedy/poison, good/evil, intelligible/sensible, high/low, mind/matter, life/death, inside/outside, speech/writing, etc.) organizes a conflictual, hierarchically structured field which can be neither reduced to unity, nor derived from a primary simplicity, nor dialectically sublated or internalized into a third term' (Derrida 1981: 24–5). Dissemination is the force that exposes counting as a bad procedure: 'Dissemination endlessly opens up a snag in writing that can no longer be mended, a spot where neither meaning, however plural, nor any form of presence can pin/pen down (*agrapher*) the trace. [. . .] This question can no longer be dissociated from a restaging of *arithmos* and of "counting" as a "bad procedure"' (Derrida 1981: 27).

Consider the following kinds of Flush:

- F-1 = Flush.–1: Barrett Browning's Flush was the puppy-son of Flush, Mitford's own dog, also known as Flush senior. The latter also sired another puppy called Flush.
- F0 = Flush.0: the real cocker spaniel, the historical lived dog, the companion of Barrett Browning, given to her by Mitford. As such Flush zero is unknowable.
- F1 = Flush.1: the dog as *represented* by Barrett Browning, in her writings and drawings and in writings and photographs by others who encountered Flush.0 in real life.
- F2 = Flush.2: representations of Flush.1 by various hands, including Woolf's.
- F3 = Flush.3: representations of Flush.2 or representations of representations of Flush.1.

Barrett Browning herself refers to and delights in a multiplicity of Flushes in her letters to Mitford: 'My Flush has no sons nor daughters that I know of. Yours seems to increase & multiply by a very rapid course of arithmetic, indeed. Was Lily my Flush's mother? Not that I am jealous of the new puppies!' (Browning and Browning 1984–2020 [*BC*]: 1319).² She marvels that 'the brother of my Flush is called Flush besides!' (*BC* 1369). 'Oh – do tell me the tale illustrative of the royal race of Flush,' she begs. 'I am prepared for everything from "all the blood of all the Flushes."' (*BC* 441). And on Flush senior: 'as to Master Flush [. . .] he is a very clever Flush [. . .] They are all clever Flushies in fact – & might be, if taken in time as you say, very highly academical Flushies' (*BC* 458). Who *are* 'all' the Flushes?

I have tried in vain to collate and count the different Flushes proliferating from my reading, from F–1 to F3 and mutants beyond. F2 level representations include Woolf's bitch cocker spaniel, Pinka, who was gifted to Woolf by Vita Sackville-West, herself star of *Orlando: A Biography* (1928), Woolf's own textual predecessor for *Flush: A Biography*. Pinka posed as Flush for *Flush: A Biography*, her image gracing the dust-wrapper and the frontispiece, perhaps subversively displacing Flush himself as the real star of the book. The spaniel posed as Flush on the dust-wrapper of the first American edition remains anonymous. Then there is the Flush of Rudolf Besier's play, *The Barretts of Wimpole Street* (1930) (F2), and the dog, actually named Flush, who played Besier's Flush in the Broadway production of the play (F3). This Flush who played Flush was in turn immortalised in Flora Merrill's book, *Flush of Wimpole Street and Broadway* (1933) – is that F4? In May 1933 Merrill's book was previewed by *Variety* magazine as one of three 'Rival Flushes', alongside Woolf's *Flush: A Biography* and Frances Theresa Russell's *Two Poets, a Dog, and a Boy* (1933), which 'also has to deal with Browning's spaniel. Every dog has his day, but Flush seems to be getting three of them' (Anon. 1933: 50). Merrill's *Flush of Wimpole Street and Broadway* is narrated in the first person by Flush, the actor, relating his life and career on stage as the original Flush, and Merrill's dog knows how to pretend to pretend: 'So I was to be an actor! [. . .] I knew that acting was a kind of play. We used to act [in kennels]. I'd pretend I was a big, vicious dog and growl at the other dogs, then I'd pretend I was afraid of them and run away. Acting is playing what you are not. It's a very nice pastime' (Merrill 1933: 22). And in this story the Flushes multiply further. At one point a 'stuffed dog' is considered as an alternative to the live action Flush, but this is foiled when Flush the actor has a son, 'Junior, your namesake, and future understudy' (Merrill 1933: 104).

Then there is the book *Flush*, subtitled *A Biography*, in which Woolf's representations of F1 are found. *Flush* the book is of a different order again to Flush the dog found in its pages, in words and images. The Flush found in the pages of *Flush: A Biography* is multiple. Indeed, he disappears in a *mise-en-abyme* when he encounters, as Barrett Browning reports too (see below), his own mirror image (yet another Flush!) in a series of revelations which unleash his own ontological instability. To begin with, he finds his reflection to confirm his class privilege, according to the eugenic measure of the Spaniel Club:

No sooner had Flush got home than he examined himself carefully in the looking-glass. Heaven be praised, he was a dog of birth and breeding! His head was smooth; his eyes were prominent but not gozzled; his feet were feathered; he was the equal of the best-bred cocker in Wimpole Street. [. . .] When about this time Miss Barrett observed him staring in the glass, she was mistaken. He was a philosopher, she thought, meditating the difference between appearance and reality. On the contrary, he was an aristocrat considering his points. (Woolf 1933: 33)

Woolf's narrative is an intertext with Barrett Browning's letters, where we find Flush before the mirror and dubbed a philosopher: 'My Flush used to bark & howl & whine & moan at the sight of his own reflection – but now he is a philosopher & looks with complacency at his ears' (*BC* 2122; and *BC* 976 quoted below). But it is also an intertext with the breeding points of the Spaniel Club, as mediated by Hugh Dalziel's *British Dogs* (1888), including, for example, the 'Standards of Excellence' (positive and negative) for the various breeds of spaniel (Dalziel 1888 1: 491–3). It is worth dwelling on 'gozzled' here. In fact, there is no such word as 'gozzled' but the context would suggest that it is intended to mean standing out like gooseberries ('gozell' derives from the French *groseille* for gooseberry or currant), which a spaniel's eyes apparently should not do (*OED*). Woolf's source, Dalziel, cites the Spaniel Club's 'description of the eye' of the cocker spaniel and points to the error: 'the word "gozzled" is used but that I presume to be a misprint for "goggled" – prominent, or staring – as there is no English word "gozzled," so far as I know' (Dalziel 1888 1: 430). He then gives the Spaniel Club's description of the 'Eyes': 'Full, not prominent, hazel or brown-coloured, with a general expression of intelligence and gentleness, though decidedly wide-awake, bright, and merry; never gozzled or weak, as in the King Charles and Blenheim kinds' (Dalziel 1888 1: 431). Woolf copies this verbatim in her reading notes (Woolf [n.d.]: 30, 33). In having Flush look admiringly through his ungozzled eyes at his ungozzled eyes, she appears to be deliberately perpetuating (gozzling) the misprint here as a kind of genetic variant, as if pointing up a parallel between textual genetics and dog breeding. Given that the Kennel Club (founded 1873), the Spaniel Club (founded 1885) and Dalziel's book (1888) all postdate Flush's death (1854) by some decades, Woolf is anachronistically imposing standards of which Flush and his contemporary companions could know nothing.

There is a mirror scene to this mirror scene, so to speak, when in Italy the flea-ridden Flush experiences a social levelling as he is shorn of his once magnificent coat:

What am I now? he thought, gazing into the glass. And the glass replied with the brutal sincerity of glasses, 'You are nothing.' He was nobody. Certainly he was no longer a cocker spaniel. But as he gazed, his ears bald now, and uncurled, seemed to twitch. [. . .] To be nothing – is that not, after all, the most satisfactory state in the whole world? (Woolf 1933: 127)

Here all the Spaniel Club breeding points are shorn away, but we would be mistaken if we thought this denuded Flush somehow to be the Ur or pure Flush. Likewise *Flush: A Biography* has its own complicated, textual stemma, recording its genesis (and points) through serialised magazine publication to the first edition, bifurcating into British and American lines (I cite here the first British edition), the Uniform edition and numerous paperback editions. We might also consider how critical writings on Flush and other Flush-related texts in a sense produce further orders of Flush. All of these intertextual Flushes constitute a proliferating interspecies community of 'world-making entanglements' or 'contact zones' (Haraway 2007: 4; Goldman 2016: 172), in which figure-making, and un-making and co-shaping of subjectivities, are in perpetual process. All come running when we call 'Flush'!

Thoroughly tangled in my own taxonomic and semiotic chains, I return to Woolf's slippery, ironic sentence on Flush's literacy: 'Flush could not read what she was writing an inch or two above his head' (Woolf 1933: 52). Woolf, who draws heavily and often verbatim on Barrett Browning, may well be silently nodding over our doggy heads. But did Woolf know from F1 that F0 apparently had basic literacy? Did Woolf, who in 1906 had taught her own dog, Hans (actually a bitch, despite the name), and thereafter 'all her dogs', including Pinka, to 'extinguish the match' 'every time she lit a cigarette' (Adams 2007: 213), *know* that Barrett Browning had taught Flush, in 1843, the alphabet? Yes, indeed! First she gave Flush arithmetic lessons, so that he could play dominos (like a dog she had seen in a newspaper). 'Spurred' by success, she 'next taught Flush how to read by saying the name of a letter and having him kiss the correct one, which for her brothers, she wrote [in 1843], "might be used as straightforward evidence – (against not Flushie but me) of a 'non-compos-mentis' case"' (Adams 2007: 19–20; *BC* 1446). But nearly two centuries on, such evidence graces serious scientific case studies of nonhuman animal minds, consciousness, communicative behaviour, and cultures, and philosophical speculations on modern co-shaping communities, infolding, world-making encounters between species. Yes, as well as knowing the alphabet, the historical lived dog Flush could indeed count, as in 'practise arithmetic' and 'do sums', or at least 'reckon numerically' (*OED*). But Woolf does not mention these feats in her own account of Flush. Cake is frequently mentioned in *Flush: A Biography*, but not as reward for spelling; and nowhere does Flush perform counting.

COUNTING WITH FLUSH AND OTHER ANIMALS

'By the way my Flush learnt to count to *three*, in ten minutes yesterday' (*BC* 1441), his poet companion boasts to Mary Russell Mitford in November 1843, clarifying in another letter that 'Flushie's arithmetic is less complex than you [. . .] imagine':

> I hold up a piece of cake, & say one, two, three; and after 'three', & not sooner, he takes it. It is amusing to see him stir his little head at 'two,' & then correct himself – and still more amusing to observe how, at every unqualified success, he turns round & looks at Arabel for applause. (*BC* 1446)

Barrett Browning's inspiration is a M. Léonard, 'who has a theory upon the rationality & faculty of improvement in animals, & has educated two dogs which he carries about with him' (*BC* 1446). And so she 'begin[s] arithmetic with Flushie, – and am trying to teach him his letters, .. with a .. "Kiss A, Flush – and now kiss B"' (*BC* 1446). Furthermore, Léonard's dog work was verified by *The Athenæum*, which gave

> a notice, & an acknowledgement, that they did, on such & such a day, abase their editorial capacity unto the examination of these educated dogs & were very nearly satisfied of there being no shadow of a 'trick' in them. The Athenæum proposed several hard words, which the dogs spelt, and one or two sums, I believe, which they calculated, – & finished these graver studies with a game at dominos, which was won by the dogs. Whether they talked any dog-latin, I do not know – but if they did, it was'nt [*sic*] a bit more wonderful than the rest. (*BC* 1446)

'No such account is indexed in *The Athenæum* for the period 1841–43,' note the editors of *The Brownings' Correspondence* (*BC* 1446). But *The Athenæum* (17 December 1842), did indeed report that a 'paper on the education of animals', particularly the dog, was presented by M. Léonard (Anon. 1842a: 1092). How splendid to conjecture that Flush may well have delivered this very item himself to his mistress, since she reports in January 1842: 'Papa has just sent up the new Athenæum number by Mr Flush! He ran up stairs, struck his fore paws against my door, sprang dancing with triumph upon the bed, & gave it into my hands with a kiss!' (*BC* 904). A mere seven months after the first advertisement, *The Athenæum* (22 July 1843) reports:

> M. Léonard is here again, having in the interim, tested his theories and the skill of his methods, by applying them to the education (if it may be so styled) of horses; and he is anxious to go, step by step, through his process of training, in the presence of those whom it may interest, with the view to promulgating principles which he believes capable of general application. (Anon. 1843: 675)

My digital searches find no account in *The Athenæum* of Léonard's dogs playing dominos, as Barrett Browning describes, but in 'Cultivation of the Canine Brain', an anonymous correspondent for *The Lancet* (1841) reports on Léonard's private exhibition, witnessed by the writer 'in an adjoining street to Hanover square', of his dogs Philax and Brac, who performed a number of feats involving meat, bread and playing cards, 'evincing the wonderful sagacity and perception of the dogs' (Anon. 1841a: 908), before turning to dominos:

> M. Léonard invited the writer to play a game of dominos with one of them. The younger and slighter animal then seated himself on a chair at the table, and the writer and M Léonard placed themselves opposite. Six dominos were placed on their edges in the usual manner before the dog, and a like number before the writer. The dog having a double number took it up in his mouth, and put it in the middle of the table; the writer placed a corresponding piece on one side; the dog immediately played another correctly, and so on until all the pieces were engaged. Other six dominos were given to each and the writer intentionally placed a *wrong number*. *The dog looked surprised, stared very earnestly at the writer, and at length growled and finally barked angrily.* Finding that no notice was taken of his remonstrances, *he pushed away the wrong domino with his nose, and took up a suitable one from his own pieces and placed it in its stead!* The writer then played correctly; the dog followed and won the game. (Anon 1841a: 908)

The piece concludes by emphasising that the dog's 'play must have been entirely the result of his own observation and judgment. There was no trickery, no mesmerism here.' And Léonard furthermore was entirely unmotivated by money: 'M. Léonard is a gentleman of independent fortune, and the instruction of his dogs has been taken up merely as a curious and amusing investigation' (Anon 1841a: 908). This *Lancet* report on the feats of Philax and Brac was widely disseminated in an accumulating body of accounts of canine and animal intelligence.[3]

Barrett Browning's Flush seems not to have achieved the intellectual prowess of the legendary Philax and Brac, for there is no mention of his counting abilities thereafter. What is going on here, it may be argued, is probably a parlour trick that entirely depends on the numeracy of the human in this shared undertaking between species. In this case, Flush cannot count; but he can read. That is, he can read (without reading) his human companion, and collude with her charade by following her prompts in such a way as to produce between them the pretence of his counting. Do these actions by an applause-seeking dog amount to (add up to) Lacan's 'pretending to pretend', which he reserves only for human animals (Derrida 2008: 128)? On the other hand, science has demonstrated that some dogs *can* actually count and possess 'visual numerosity' (Aulet et al. 2019). The visual stimuli used for one investigation into the latter actually resemble dominos. In canid circles, furthermore, a wolf has better numeracy than a dog (Range et al. 2014). Perhaps, in its domestication, the dog shed some of its ancestral powers of numeracy?

How *Flush* Counts

Flush: A Biography is beginning to count in another sense – as in 'enter into the account or reckoning', to 'count for something' (*OED*). Until quite recently, in the history of proliferating Woolf scholarship *Flush* has counted for very little in critical opinion. Indeed, *Flush* literally was not counted by the editors of the first *Cambridge Companion to Virginia Woolf* (2000), who numbered her novels as nine! (*Flush* is chronologically the eighth of ten.) *Flush*, alas, is nowhere to be found in the List of Abbreviations, although it does get respectful, if passing, mention (twice) by Julia Briggs in her chapter on 'The Novels of the 1930s'. Roe's oversight apparently went unnoticed by reviewers and readers. Ten years later, the Second Edition of *The Cambridge Companion to Virginia Woolf* (2010), restores *Flush* to the List of Abbreviations and reprints Briggs's chapter, but also includes four pages of discussion of *Flush* in a bespoke subsection by Maggie Humm in her chapter on Woolf and visual culture.

Flush: A Biography did not count for most critics, then, but this work did count in other respects that paradoxically explain its not counting for critics. *Flush: A Biography* was a runaway bestseller for the Woolfs' Hogarth Press. On first publication, the novel 'was selected by the Book Society in England for October 1933, and by the American Book-of-the-month Club for September' (Hussey 1996: 89). In the first six months it sold 14,390 copies (Willis 1992: 266), far outstripping the expectations of its author, who had envisaged she would at most 'net £2000 from that six months dogged & dreary grind' (Woolf 1977–84 4: 176).

'*Flush*'s popularity soon proved a liability with some reviewers,' Mark Hussey has observed (Hussey 1996: 89), pointing to a review in *Granta* which Woolf found particularly hurtful. It claims that 'deadly facility [. . .] combined with its popular success' means *Flush: A Biography* represents 'the end of Mrs Woolf as a live force. We must mourn the passing of a potentially great writer who perished for lack of an intelligent audience' (F.C. 1933: 57; Woolf 1977–84 4: 186–7n). However, it is worth noting that *Granta* reviewed *Flush: A Biography* under the heading 'Biography' and alongside *Orlando: A Biography* and *The Waves* (1931), the Uniform Editions of which had just been issued; and the critical stance that it took toward Woolf's work is not attributable only to *Flush: A Biography*:

> Yesterday the Granta said I was now defunct. Orlando Waves Flush represent the death of a potentially great writer. This is only a rain drop; I mean the snub some little pimpled undergraduate likes to administer, just as he would put a frog in ones bed. (Woolf 1977–84 4: 186)

The reviewer, 'F.C.', probably Frank Chapman, finds '*Flush* is related to *Orlando* in more than the word "Biography" [. . .] and both are [. . .] pastiches of Lytton Strachey,' but invokes a minor journalist and fiction writer as the measure of her lapsing talent ('the amused condescending' C. E. Montague):

> It is an obvious comment on the state of literature to-day, when an author capable of writing such fine work as *To the Lighthouse* can sink to the level of *Flush*, and when the latter will obviously be the most popular of her works – it is, inevitably, the choice of the Book Society. (F.C. 1933: 57)

Here *Flush: A Biography* fails against not only the measure of Strachey but that of Woolf's earlier works. Yet, while reviewers were certainly sometimes scathing, the overwhelming majority were very positive. E. J. Scovell, for example, in *Time and Tide* (14 October 1933), counters anyone who thinks Woolf's life of a dog 'strange, and perhaps even a little silly' with a serious account of Woolf's concern in her novels 'with the mind's and body's experience' (Scovell 1933: 1234). If 'psychological insight' is the 'heritage of this generation' of writers, then Woolf 'has the poetic vision that sees its object whole [. . .] the mind gives its colour to whatever comes to it, as well as to whatever it does. Mrs. Woolf is less interested in the variety of experiences than in the personal life that assimilates and colours it all' (Scovell 1933: 1234). Furthermore, Scovell suggests Woolf does not distinguish between human and animal 'personal life':

> So it seems natural that she should be teased by the sight of a dog, going with absorption about his own business, or watching men with intent, melancholy eyes; and in writing about him she should imagine brilliantly his strange existence, between human existence and a wild creature's. (Scovell 1933: 1234)

Vita Sackville-West, writing for *The Week-End Review*, similarly declares Woolf's 'dog is a dog throughout, not one of those deplorable freaks which exist solely, but alas how plentifully, in the whimsical fancy of their creators', and praises, like many other reviewers, Woolf's focalising of the dominant olfactory experience of dogs: 'it is always from the floor-level, in a world of smells and sensations, that we are privileged to observe the two-legged figures towering gigantically and incomprehensively above us' (Sackville-West 1933: [n.p.]).

Flush: A Biography may well stand as the most widely reviewed of all Woolf's works. The archive of Monks House Papers at Sussex holds a folder of nearly 200 press cuttings on this novel[4] so neglected by subsequent academic criticism. The reviews, then, were certainly not as sparse nor as negative as Robin Majumdar and Allen McLaurin imply in *Virginia Woolf: The Critical*

Heritage (1975). They write that 'Virginia Woolf did not take [it] seriously, nor did the reviewers' (Majumdar and McLaurin 1975: 25), pointing in their 'Introduction' to the titles, rather than the content, of two reviews,[5] and reproducing (in part) only one review of *Flush: A Biography* in their volume, by Peter Burra. Burra situates the novel in the context of Woolf's previous works, calling it 'entirely beautiful; but it is a necessary pause, it is not a *tour de force* as its predecessor [*The Waves*] was' (Burra 1934: 113; Majumdar and McLaurin 1975: 321). But in a passage excluded by Majumdar and McLaurin, he makes a serious and moving comparison between the closing scene of 'infinite pathos' in *Jacob's Room* and that in *Flush: A Biography*: 'The light has passed over the surface and has utterly vanished. Flush is brought to an end in the same way. "He had been alive; he was now dead. That was all"' (Burra 1934: 117). Majumdar's and McLaurin's egregious lack of serious attention to the novel itself and to the record of reviews and criticism in such an influential scholarly instrument doubtless contributed to the decades of scholarly neglect. In the decades following Woolf's death, sales of *Flush: A Biography* rapidly declined.[6]

Perhaps Woolf would take some comfort in seeing how much money a first edition of *Flush: A Biography* fetches these days. Because of the big print run, a first edition in dust jacket is not that rare, but in fine condition currently sells for around £500.[7] Compare the value of the dog himself, who cost his owner at least £20 'to the dog-stealers' in ransom money, as Woolf records in her notes to the novel (Woolf 1933: 154). By Barrett Browning's reckoning, it was 20 guineas.[8] Woolf's notes also pointedly document that Barrett Browning's maid, Lily Wilson, was '"an expensive servant" – her wages were £16 a year' (Woolf 1933: 155). In the opening chapter, Woolf has Mitford opine that 'to sell Flush was unthinkable. He was of the rare order of objects that cannot be associated with money. Was he not of the still rarer kind that, because they typify what is spiritual, what is beyond price'; and she concludes chiastically, 'Yes; Flush was worthy of Miss Barrett; Miss Barrett was worthy of Flush' (Woolf 1933: 19).

That opening, affirmatory 'Yes;', which introduces but also unbalances the dyadic chiastic clauses that follow, might be read with Derrida, who declares, in 'A Number of Yes (Nombre de Oui)', 'Already but always a faithful countersignature, a *yes* can never be counted. Promise, mission, emission, it always sends itself off in numbers' (Derrida 1988: 132). Mitford's 'yes' to the dyad of Flush and Barrett Browning reverberates throughout the novel. Derrida rehearses how this performative affirmatory term is both language and not language, and never singular; how a '"second" yes is a priori enveloped in the "first." The "first" would not take place without the project, the bet or the promise, the mission or the emission, the send-off of the second which is already there in it' (Derrida 1988: 131). Woolf's three semi-colons perform a kind of repeated affirmation, like a series of yeses, or indeed kisses, which raise woman and dog above commodification and fiscal evaluation to a status beyond the countable.

47

Not Counting with Catullus

Catullus V
vivamus mea lesbia atque amemus
rumoresque senum severiorum
omnes unius aestimemus assis
soles occidere et redire possunt
nobis cum semel occidit brevis lux
nox est perpetua una dormienda
da mi basia mille deinde centum
dein mille altera dein secunda centum
deinde usque altera mille deinde centum
dein cum milia multa fecerimus
conturbabimus illa ne sciamus
aut ne quis malus inuidere possit
cum tantum sciat esse basiorum

Catullus 5
we must live my lesbia and we must love
and the loose talk of torn-faced old farts
will be worth fuck all to us
suns can set and suns can rise
but once that short light has set for us
the night is one never ending sleep
so give me a thousand kisses then a hundred
then another thousand then a second hundred
then yet another thousand then a hundred
then when we've made many millions
we must mix them all up so we don't know
and no other fucker can be jealous knowing
just how many kisses it is[9]

The speaker of Catullus 5 knows the fatal and ill-starred risks of setting finite limits by counting precisely the number of kisses he shares with his lover Lesbia. Yet he seems to be tempting those very fates in speaking his desire to ward them off in the strict and counted measures of hendecasyllabic quantitative Latin metre. The poem speaks everywhere of exceeding the measure of its own eleven-syllable line by piling up kisses most ill-advisedly in neatly calculable, thrice repeated multiples of eleven: 'da mi basia mille deinde centum' 'give me a thousand kisses then a hundred'. On the other hand, the hendecasyllabic line itself performs structural excess, and Catullus's Phalaecian hendecasyllables are notoriously close to the variable pattern of Sappho's. The reader who manages to count, in the poem's invoice-like repetition of figures, the three lots of 1,100 (MC) kisses (which comes to 3,300 or MMMCCC kisses) is nevertheless soon utterly confounded by lines ten and eleven: 'dein cum milia multa fecerimus/ conturbabimus illa ne sciamus' ('then when we've made many millions / we must mix them all up so we don't know'). Like Derrida's yes, Catullus's kiss is never singular, and we might fuse both by saying: 'Already but always a faithful countersignature, a *kiss* can never be counted. Promise, mission, emission, it always sends itself off in numbers.'

Flush's kissing is likewise excessive and uncountable both in Barrett Browning's correspondence and in Woolf's novel. In the former's letters Flush does more kissing than anyone else bar Robert Browning:

> He is such a companion to me all day long – lying close beside me – & when I move to the sofa, leaping there, beside me still, and always marking his sense of the change of place, by kissing me in a dog-way, most expressively. (*BC* 833)

But Barrett Browning soon drops the distinction of 'dog-way' kissing:

> he can't bear me to look into a glass, because he thinks there is a little brown dog inside every looking glass & he is jealous of its being so close to me. He used to tremble & bark at it, but now he is silently jealous, & contents himself with squeezing close, close to me & kissing me expressively. (*BC* 976)

Drawing on this letter almost verbatim, Woolf introduces this expressive kiss in the later drafts of the novel, augmenting Flush's kisses for the published version:

> Then she would make him stand with her in front of the looking-glass and ask him why he barked and trembled. Was not the little brown dog opposite himself? But what is 'oneself'? Is it the thing people see? Or is it the thing one is? So Flush pondered that question too, and, unable to solve the problem of reality, pressed closer to Miss Barrett and kissed her 'expressively.' That was real at any rate. (Woolf 1933: 45–6)

The poet's letters are teeming with Flush's kisses, reporting, for example, how Flush on instruction 'came, galloping & prancing, kissed me on my lips, & ran out again' (*BC* 1000) and, unbidden, 'never sees me shed tears without running to kiss me & rub his little brown ears against my face' (*BC* 1084).[10] Yet in the constraining form of Barrett Browning's coy sonnet 'Flush, or Faunus', later embedded in Woolf's prose (Woolf 1933: 149), itself saturated in the poet's kiss-filled prose correspondence, the word kiss does not appear (Barrett Browning 1890 3: 78):

> You see this dog. It was but yesterday
> I mused forgetful of his presence here
> Till thought on thought drew downward tear on tear,
> When from the pillow, where wet-cheeked I lay,

> A head as hairy as Faunus, thrust its way
> Right sudden against my face – two golden-clear
> Great eyes astonished mine – a drooping ear
> Did flap me on either cheek to dry the spray!
> I started first, as some Arcadian,
> Amazed by goatly god in twilight grove;
> But, as the bearded vision closelier ran
> My tears off, I knew Flush, and rose above
> Surprise and sadness – thanking the true Pan,
> Who, by low creatures, leads to heights of love.

The proximity of dog's face to human's at lines six and seven may well suggest interspecies kissing, but the poem does not explicitly mark a kiss. Here Flush becomes two ancient pagan deities (the Roman Faunus, half human, half beast, and the equal of the goatly Greek god Pan), intruding on to the pillow of the woman poet with animal force, while disrupting the sonnet's own form of counting. The regular iambic pentameter is disrupted by the hypersyllabic line 5 'A head | as hair | y as | Faunus,| thrust its | way'. Scanned as a catalectic hexameter, the word 'Faunus' thrusts its way centre stage, as the heads of dog and poet now share the horizontal plane of the pillow. It is possible to scan the line with five feet if 'as hairy | as Faunus' is read as two amphibrachs, but this substitution lessens the powerful chiastic internal rhyme of 'us' in 'Faunus' and 'thrust' (reverberating too in Flush), restricting the animal excess of Faunus. Woolf pointedly alludes to this poem in the second and third chapters of her novel. But she waits until the end of the book to cite the poem in full, enclosing, or indeed thrusting, it into the middle of the final death scene between a sentence already anticipating the poem's own 'thrust' – 'Then as he leapt on to the sofa and thrust his face into hers, the words of her own poem came into her mind:' (Woolf 1933: 149) – and one recalling the scene and mood of the poem's composition – 'She had written that poem one day years ago in Wimpole Street when she was very unhappy' (Woolf 1933: 149). The death scene that immediately follows restages or disseminates the poem's primal scene along with the novel's re-echoing scenes and sentences of parallel, chiastic intimacy between dog and woman. Is one final kiss being intimated here?

> She bent down over him for a moment. Her face with its wide mouth and its great eyes and its heavy curls was still oddly like his. Broken asunder, yet made in the same mould, each, perhaps, completed what was dormant in the other. But she was woman; he was dog. Mrs. Browning went on reading. Then she looked at Flush again. But he did not look at her. An extraordinary change had come over him. 'Flush!' she cried. But he was silent. He had been alive; he was now dead. That was all. The drawing-room table, strangely enough, stood perfectly still. (Woolf 1933: 150)

Woolf's closing sentence insists on the finality of Flush's death. He has not returned as a spirit to leave a message 'conveyed by the legs of tables', as Barrett Browning might have hoped, and we are returned to the earlier account of her 'table-spinning' obsession: 'Thus if asked the age of a child, the table "expresses itself intelligently by knocking with its legs, responses according to the alphabet." And if a table could tell you that your own child was four years old, what limit was there to its capacity?' (Woolf 1933: 140). Here the table is credited with the same rudimentary ability to spell and count as Flush himself is alleged to possess. Unlike the dog's, however, the table's numeracy and literacy remain unvindicated by modern science. Woolf shows Flush a cynical materialist when confronted by his mistress's spiritualism:

> There was something in the room, or in the table, or in the petticoats and trousers, that he disliked exceedingly. [. . .] That, to Flush, was a highly unpleasant way of spending a quiet evening. Better far to sit and read one's book. (Woolf 1933: 143, 144)

How does interspecies kissing count, then, for Barrett-Browning and Woolf? Without enumerating them, Woolf makes legible the kisses qua kisses Flush seems to have lavished on the poet, who in her poems and letters withholds or only elliptically hints at the term kiss and all it might suggest of interspecies reciprocity. Earlier, Woolf cites Barrett Browning's self-portrait as Flush in a letter whereby the dog counts for more than her equal by her own estimation:

> She had drawn 'a very neat and characteristic portrait of Flush, humorously made rather like myself,' and she had written under it that it 'only fails of being an excellent substitute for mine through being more worthy than I can be counted'. (Woolf 1933: 38; BC 1393)[11]

This hybrid canine–human self-portrait, then, co-shaped by dog and woman, is a form of affirmatory kissing as their mouths merge into one physiognomy, one flesh. And at this very scene of inscription, to which the final passage returns, Woolf inserts again the sonnet's primal pillow scene where dog kisses woman:

> She was lying, thinking; she had forgotten Flush altogether, and her thoughts were so sad that the tears fell upon the pillow. Then suddenly a hairy head was pressed against her; large bright eyes shone in hers; and she started. Was it Flush, or was it Pan? Was she no longer an invalid in Wimpole Street, but a Greek nymph in some dim grove in Arcady? And did the bearded god himself press his lips to hers? For a moment she was transformed; she was a nymph and Flush was Pan. The sun burnt and love blazed. (Woolf 1933: 38–9)

In referring back to this episode, Woolf explicitly states: 'Once he had roused her with a kiss, and she had thought that he was Pan' (Woolf 1933: 68). It is impossible to count the kisses here. Woolf's question, 'And did the bearded god himself press his lips to hers?' seems to ask whether the pressing lips are Pan's or Flush's, not doubting that a kiss has occurred, as the retrospective comment confirms. Woolf is ribbing the table-turning Victorian poet's recourse to mythology and spiritualism (Flush has been made the medium of Pan). Barrett Browning has kissed a dog and she liked it. Why pretend it was Pan? Why not call it a kiss? The interspecies kiss is here much more explicit than in Barrett Browning's own account of the primal pillow scene in her letter to Mitford (October 1843):

> I, who had had my heart full for hours, took advantage of an early moment of solitude, to cry in it very bitterly. Suddenly a little hairy head thrust itself from behind my pillow into my face, rubbing its ears & nose against me in a responsive agitation, & drying the tears as they came. I had forgotten Flushie, & was startled at the apparition, or rather the sensation, of the hairy head——it was a Faunus or a Pan! In a few moments however, my heart was led away from itself into an assuaging of Flushie, who, if I were determined to cry, was bent upon crying too. Flushie was my Faunus, & powerful for the occasion (.. for 'cutting the knot' as the dramatic critics say, ..) as any sylvan god of them all. (BC 1390)

Yet the rubbing of his ears and nose into her face, the reader infers, comes pretty close to osculation, so too the reciprocal 'assuaging of Flushie'. If Woolf's twentieth-century prose flushes out the term 'kiss' from the elliptically suggestive cover of Barrett Browning's nineteenth-century poems, with the aid of her posthumously published canid-kissing letters, the mutually pressing lips of dog and woman gaining explicit and disseminated representation in *Flush: A Biography*, how much more explicit is Donna Haraway, in the early twenty-first century, on kissing with her own canid companion, Cayenne Pepper, whose '*darter-tongue kisses have been irresistible*':

> *Her red merle Australian Shepherd's quick and lithe tongue has swabbed the tissues of my tonsils, with all their eager immune system receptors* [. . .] *We have had forbidden conversation; we have had oral intercourse* [. . .] *We are training each other in acts of communication we barely understand. We are, constitutively, companion species. We make each other up, in the flesh.* (Haraway 2003: 2–3; emphasis in original)

Better to be kissing than counting! Already but always a faithful countersignature, a yes and a kiss and a Flush can never be counted.

Works Cited

Adams, Maureen. 2007. *Shaggy Muses: The Dogs Who Inspired Virginia Woolf, Emily Dickinson, Elizabeth Barrett Browning, Edith Wharton and Emily Bronte*. New York: Ballantine Books.
Anon. 1841a. 'Cultivation of the Canine Brain'. *The Lancet* 2: 907–8.
Anon. 1841b. 'Cultivation of the Canine Brain'. *The Veterinarian* 13.166 (September): 658–60.
Anon. 1842a. 'Miscellanea: Paris Academy of Sciences'. *The Athenæum* 790 (17 December): 1092.
Anon. 1842b. 'Sagacity of Dogs'. *The St Petersburg English Review* 1: 87–90.
Anon. 1843. 'Our Weekly Gossip'. *The Athenæum* 820 (22 July): 674–5.
Anon. 1933. 'Literati: Rival Flushes'. *Variety* (2 May): 50.
Aulet, Lauren S., Veronica C. Chiu, Ashley Prichard, Mark Spivak, Stella F. Lourenco and Gregory S. Berns. 2019. 'Canine Sense of Quantity: Evidence for Numerical Ratio-Dependent Activation in Parietotemporal Cortex'. *Biology Letters* 15.12 (December). Available at: <https://doi.org/10.1098/rsbl.2019.0666> (last accessed 28 June 2022).
Barret Browning, Elizabeth. 1890. *The Poetical Works of Elizabeth Barrett Browning*. 6 vols. London: Smith, Elder & Co.
Browning, Robert and Elizabeth Barrett Browning. 1984–2020. *The Brownings' Correspondence* [*BC*]. Vols 1–8, ed. Philip Kelley and Ronald Hudson; vols 9–14, ed. Philip Kelley and Scott Lewis; vols 15–19, ed. Philip Kelley, Scott Lewis and Edward Hagan; vols 22–23, ed. Philip Kelley, Scott Lewis, Edward Hagan, Joseph Phelan and Rhian Williams; vols 24–27, ed. Philip Kelley, Edward Hagan and Linda M. Lewis. Kansas: Wedgestone Press. Available at: <https://www.browningscorrespondence.com/> (last accessed 28 June 2022).
Burdett, Osbert. 1933. 'A Storyteller's Holiday'. *The Listener*, 11 October: Supplement xi.
Burra, Peter. 1934. 'Virginia Woolf'. *The Nineteenth Century and After* 115.683: 112–25.
Catullus, Tibullus. 1913. *Catullus. Tibullus. Pervigilium Veneris*. Trans. F. W. Cornish, J. P. Postgate and J. W. Mackail, rev. G. P. Goold. Loeb Classical Library 6. Cambridge, MA: Harvard University Press.
Child, Harold Hannyngton. 1933. 'Brown Beauty'. *Times Literary Supplement* 1653 (5 October): 667.
Dalziel, Hugh. 1888. *British Dogs: Their Varieties, History, Characteristics, Breeding Management, and Exhibition*. Second Edition, 3 vols. London: L. Upcott Gill.
Derrida, Jacques. 1981. *Dissemination*. Trans. Barbara Johnson. Chicago and London: University of Chicago.
Derrida, Jacques. 1988. 'A Number of Yes (Nombre de Oui)'. Trans. Brian Holmes. *Qui Parle*, 2.2, SILENCE AND INTERVENTION (Fall): 118–33.
Derrida, Jacques. 2008. 'And Say the Animal Responded? [to Jacques Lacan]'. In *The Animal That Therefore I Am*. Trans. David Wills, ed. Marie-Louise Mallet, 119–40. New York: Fordham University Press.
F.C. [Frank Chapman?]. 1933. 'Biography'. *Granta* 153.966 (25 October): 57.
Goldman, Jane. 2016. '*Flush: A Biography*: Speaking, Reading and Writing with the Companion Species'. In *A Companion to Virginia Woolf*. Ed. Jessica Berman, 163–75. Oxford: Blackwell.

Haraway, Donna. 2003. *The Companion Species Manifesto: Dogs, People, and Significant Otherness*. Chicago: Prickly Paradigm Press.
Haraway, Donna. 2007. *When Species Meet*. Minneapolis: University of Minnesota Press.
Hegel, Georg Wilhelm Friedrich. 1955. *Lectures on the History of Philosophy*. Trans. E. S. Haldane, 3 vols. London: Routledge & Kegan Paul.
Hussey, Mark. 1996. *Virginia Woolf A to Z : The Essential Reference to Her Life and Writings*. Oxford: Oxford University Press.
Majumdar, Robin and Allen McLaurin, eds. 1975. *Virginia Woolf: The Critical Heritage*. London and Boston: Routledge & Kegan Paul.
Mepham, John. 1991. *Virginia Woolf: A Literary Life*. Basingstoke: Macmillan.
Merrill, Flora. 1933. *Flush of Wimpole Street and Broadway*. New York: Robert M. McBride.
Range, Friederike, Julia Jenikejew, Isabelle Schröder and Zsófia Virányi. 2014. 'Difference in Quantity Discrimination in Dogs and Wolves'. *Frontiers in Psychology* (18 November). Available at: <https://doi.org/10.3389/fpsyg.2014.01299> (last accessed 28 June 2022).
Richardson, H.D. 1847. *Dogs; Their Origins and Varieties*. Dublin: James McGlashan.
Roe, Sue and Susan Sellers, eds. 2000. *The Cambridge Companion to Virginia Woolf*. Cambridge: Cambridge University Press.
Sackville-West, Vita. 1933. 'Lives of the Obscure: *Flush: A Biography*'. *The Week-End Review* (7 October): [n.p.]. SxMs-18/3/B/11, Monks House Papers, The Keep, University of Sussex.
Sample, H. 1869. *The Art of Training Animals*. New York: Jesse Haney.
Scovell, E. J. 1933. [Review of *Flush*], *Time and Tide*, 14 October: 1234.
Sellers, Susan, ed. 2010. *The Cambridge Companion to Virginia Woolf*. Second Edition. Cambridge: Cambridge University Press.
Sherer, John. 1868. *Rural Life*. London: London Printing & Publishing Co.
Willis, Jr, J. H. 1992. *Leonard and Virginia Woolf as Publishers*. Charlottesville: University of Virginia Press.
Woolf, Leonard. 1968. *Downhill All the Way: An Autobigraphy of the Years 1919–1939*. London: Readers Union/Hogarth Press.
Woolf, Virginia. 1928. *Orlando: A Biography*. London: Hogarth.
Woolf, Virginia. 1929. *A Room of One's Own*. London: Hogarth.
Woolf, Virginia. 1933. *Flush: A Biography*. London: Hogarth.
Woolf, Virginia. 1977–84. *The Diary of Virginia Woolf*. Ed. Anne Olivier Bell and Andrew McNeillie. 5 vols. London: Hogarth Press.
Woolf, Virginia. [n.d.]. BERG M12: Flush Holograph and typewritten reading notes 35 pages, numbered 1–35 by the New York Public Library.
Youatt, William. 1845. *The Dog*. London: Longmans.

Notes

1. See Hegel (1955 1: 89): 'In Religion the three make their appearance in a deeper sense as the Trinity, and in Philosophy as the Notion, but enumeration forms a bad method of expression.'

2. For full bibliographical details see Robert Browning and Elizabeth Barrett Browning (1984–2020) in Works Cited. All in-text references [*BC* followed by Letter number] are to the online edition of this work, available at: <https://www.browningscorrespondence.com/> (last accessed 28 June 2022).
3. See Anon. (1841b); Anon (1842b); Youatt (1845: 162–4); Richardson (1847: 106–7); Sherer (1868: 450–2); Sample (1869: 96–7).
4. Monks House Papers, The Keep, University of Sussex: SxMs-18/3/B/11. The contents are listed and discussed in the forthcoming Cambridge University Press edition of *Flush: A Biography*, ed. Linden Peach, Derek Ryan and Jane Goldman.
5. See Child (1933); Burdett (1933).
6. Along with her other two bestselling books in her lifetime, *Orlando: A Biography* and *The Years*, sales of *Flush: A Biography* in the decades following Woolf's death fell far behind the likes of *Mrs Dalloway* and *To the Lighthouse* (L. Woolf 1968: 147–8; Mepham 131).
7. See AbeBooks.co.uk. In 2014–15, the antiquarian bookseller Peter Harrington was advertising a copy at £1,250.00: Available at: <http://www.peterharrington.co.uk/rare-books/catalogue-106-christmas-2014/flush-3/> (last accessed 2014).
8. See *BC* 2585: 'Six guineas, was his ransom – & now I have paid twenty for him to the dogstealers.'
9. My translation of Catullus V. See Catullus (1913: 6, 8).
10. See also Flush kissing and kissed: *BC* 840, 841, 853, 957, 1057, 1099, 1118, 1306, 1436, 1458, 2777, 2803, 2816, 2836.
11. Available at: <https://www.browningscorrespondence.com/amplify/file-store/Browning Correspondence/scans/WPFigures/1558–1.jpg> (last accessed 29 June 2022).

3

CANINE COMPANIONS, RACE AND AFFECTIVE ANTHROPOMORPHISM IN FLORENCE AYSCOUGH'S *THE AUTOBIOGRAPHY OF A CHINESE DOG* (1926) AND MARY GAUNT'S *A BROKEN JOURNEY* (1919)

Juanjuan Wu

In *Flush: A Biography* (1933), an underdog work that recently entered the modernist canon (Ryan 2013: 132), Virginia Woolf configures the ways that border-crossing journeys can lead to agency, conflating Elizabeth Barrett Browning's newly found freedom with that felt by Flush, a cocker spaniel. After being released from a box to which he was confined while travelling from London to Pisa, Flush dashes across the street to explore Italy. With each fresh sensory experience comes a sense of change. 'And just as Mrs Browning was exploring her new freedom and delighting in the discoveries she made, so Flush too was making his discoveries and exploring his freedom,' Woolf writes (Woolf 2016 [1933]: 76). Flush, a 'snob' and an 'aristocrat' back in Victorian upper-class London, becomes 'daily more and more democratic' in this new world (76). The 'moment of liberation' comes with an epiphany as he runs and races, his 'coat flashed', 'eyes blazed' – 'He was the friend of all the world now. All dogs were his brothers' (77). Class and species boundaries disintegrate. Flush's canine subjectivity, along with travel as a trope of agency, serves allegorically and anthropomorphically in Woolf's 'ironic critique of Victorian constructs of class, rank, and gender relationships' (Ittner 2006: 189). Woolf is not alone in this regard. In fact, seven years prior to *Flush: A Biography*, Florence Wheelock Ayscough (1878–1942) employed elements of anthropomorphism to create a canine protagonist who, unlike Flush, who does not speak, has his own voice, to serve a similar and yet different cause.

In Ayscough's *The Autobiography of a Chinese Dog* (1926), Yo Fei, a Chinese dog who crosses the Pacific from Shanghai to New Brunswick, Canada, also enjoys the freedom and excitement foreign travels and new sensory experiences can offer. Amid the 'aromatic scent of spruce trees and balsams', Yo Fei, the narrator, tells us 'I dashed about, my tail uncurled, and rolled in [the snow] with joy' (Ayscough 1926: XIII). However, contrary to Flush, who has fled Victorian society's 'corrupt aristocracy' (Woolf 1933: 77), leaving behind all forms of social constraints, to have 'the fullest, the freest, the happiest years of his life' in Italy (77), Yo Fei's freedom in Canada is not so unequivocally happy. Instead, in the first place, his emotional attachment to his past is enduringly deep, and it sometimes weighs him down, in many ways binding him to his homeland, his culture and his 'countryman' in particular (Ayscough 1926: 65), all that makes him what he is: namely, 'a Chinese dog', a racial identity Ayscough configures for him and underscores by the book title and throughout the entire narrative. Second, Yo Fei's subjectivity is intricately intertwined with a pedagogical project. Ayscough's Yo Fei, well travelled and immersed in Chinese literature, history and folklore, is bestowed with an ethical responsibility to illuminate racial and species relations: 'Does it not seem reasonable that I should share my experiences with those less travelled and less cultivated than myself?' (Foreword i). If race is not an issue Woolf explicitly addresses through Flush, Ayscough gives it serious consideration through Yo Fei, calling Western racism and speciesism into question.

In modernist studies increasing attention has been paid to illuminating how 'the discourses of race, gender, and animality are mutually deployed' in literary works (Rohman 2008: 30). In aligning with this critical trend, this chapter explores the relationship between anthropomorphism, affect and (anti-)imperialism in narratives featuring transcultural encounters in the age of accelerating border-crossing movements that defined modernity in the early decades of the twentieth century. Through a comparative study of the literary representations of two dogs – Yo Fei in Ayscough's *The Autobiography of a Chinese Dog* (1926) and James Buchanan in Mary Gaunt's *A Broken Journey* (1919) – this chapter illuminates the complex roles played by anthropomorphism and animal configurations in Western women's adaptive negotiation of racial, cultural and species alterity and self-representation.

Over the last few decades, traditional anthropomorphism, where the animal is deprived of its own agency and humanised, has been considered to have the potential danger to widen, rather than close, the human/animal divide. In addressing the risks anthropomorphism can pose for reinforcing an anthropocentric complacency, recent scholarship, informed by 'the New Anthropomorphism' in science, as Marjorie Garber describes it in *Dog Love* (1996), starts to address the subversive potential of forms of anthropomorphism connected to empathising imagination. As Dan Wylie argues, anthropomorphic writing can 'embody the proposition that animals – at least certain animals – are in some sense understandable, and have much in common with us to demand an ethically equivalent response and sense of responsibility from others' (2002: 116).

This is echoed by Jane Bennett, whose configuration of 'vital materialism' in *Vibrant Matter* (2010) further inspires new perspectives on anthropomorphism. While commenting on how Charles Darwin's 'inveterate anthropomorphism' backfired, propelling him to see in his worms 'an intelligence and a wilfulness that he recognized as related to his own' (Bennett 2010: 99), Bennett argues for the significance of a degree of anthropomorphism for challenging anthropocentric bias and human privilege. 'In a vital materialism', she maintains, 'an anthropomorphic element in perception can uncover a whole world of resonances and resemblances – sounds and sights that echo and bounce far more than would be possible were the universe to have a hierarchical structure' (2010: 99). Such recent re-evaluations of anthropomorphism inform this chapter and my examinations of animal figurations in relation to race and emotions.

I begin by demonstrating how Ayscough and Gaunt both configure the human–animal bond, one which is forged and consequently deepened during foreign travels, to challenge and transgress discursive assumptions about the human–animal divide, inviting new ways to rethink animal–human relations. I then move on to analysing the ways in which the two different women writers, Gaunt aligned with modernism's imperialism and Ayscough with cosmopolitanism, employ different strategies of anthropomorphism to project their contradictory conceptualisations of race. For Gaunt, I argue, instead of displacing animality on to Chinese people, she strategically filters and constructs an animal identity alien to her Chinese dog. In doing so, she displaces her racial anxiety as a white woman, a proto-feminist incapable of feeling for Chinese people and especially her Chinese sisters. For Ayscough, retaining Yo Fei's Chinese identity is a necessary precondition for her to turn away from imperialist discourses, Western racism and speciesism. The constructed canine subjectivity of Yo Fei, one which is deeply rooted in Chinese ways of life and culture, calls into question modernism's imperialist racial binaries. In exploring the intersection between cross-species relations and interracial dynamics, this chapter sets out to bring a transnational and comparative perspective to 'beastly modernisms', enriching studies of the animal in its relation to race, emotions and transnational modernisms.

'They don't think much of animals'

Before this chapter goes into a detailed examination, some historical and biographical information about the two authors is helpful for situating their animal configurations within the racial discourses on China in the early decades of the twentieth century. Florence Ayscough, daughter to a wealthy Canadian member of the élite amongst Shanghai's earliest and most prominent settlers, spent her entire childhood in Shanghai and later devoted herself to learning local languages and classical literature under the instruction of a Chinese mentor, Mr Nung Chu. With local assistance, she collaborated with her friend, imagist poet Amy Lowell, in translating Chinese classical poetry, which led to the well-received *Fir-Flower Tablets* (1921). She later moved on to translating more Chinese classical poems, introducing Du Fu (712–770), one of the most iconic poets of China's Tang Dynasty, and his poetry to Western readers in *Tu Fu: The Autobiography of a Chinese Poet* (1929) and *Travels of a Chinese Poet: Guest of Rivers and Lakes* (1934). Ayscough's immersion in Chinese language, literature and local ways of living arguably offers her a vantage point, one which inflects her informed, intellectual and sympathetic perception of China, and her openness to and keen interest in its cultural difference on the one hand, and, on the other hand, shapes her self-identity and self-fashioning as 'a citizen of the world' (Ayscough 1932: 11).

Unlike Ayscough, who enjoyed socio-economic privilege, Mary Gaunt embarked on her transnational mobility from economic necessity, one tied to the social inequality and restricted social mobility of middle-class women in the colonial settlement. After her husband's early death, Gaunt exiled herself from colonial Australia, her homeland, to metropolitan London in 1901, the year when the Australian federal movement passed the Immigration Restriction Act as part of the simmering White Australia policy that rigidly excluded people of colour, especially the Chinese. Depressed by the precarity entailed as an immigrant female writer in London's tight and male-dominated market, she embarked on journeys to the empire's periphery, including Africa, primarily to search for materials for new books to secure an income (Hickman 2014: 180). Living a life as an 'unhoused widow', Gaunt often found her state of 'homelessness' looming ever larger in alien lands (1911: 5). Emotional pain became the price she paid to live a life adrift. As a feminist, she was also wary of the universal subjugation of women. Both emotional forces were at work in her travels in China. Gaunt's *A Broken Journey* (1919), an emotional, appealing travel memoir, is constituted in two parts, the first half recounting her lonely, anxiety-ridden wanderings in an unknown part of northern China and the other half depicting the treacherous return journey to England via Europe on the eve of the First World War. James Buchanan, a small local dog, was her only companion, as she claimed.

Ayscough's *The Autobiography of a Chinese Dog* and Gaunt's *A Broken Journey* differ in aspects of genre, subject matter and emotional tone, but the two texts share common ground at least in configuring and foregrounding the animal presence and the sustained emotional relationship of human and non-human animal, though to different degrees. Both Yo Fei and James Buchanan are acquired in China: Yo Fei, a brown dog of the famous Lo-sze breed from Shantung province, was first presented as a gift to a foreign lady by a young Chinese male student who studied Western medicine and was later adopted by Ayscough; James Buchanan was acquired in Peking by Gaunt in 1912. Gaunt does not give us much detail about James Buchanan. In fact, rarely does she pay attention to depicting what he looks like, except for a passing note that he is 'white and black' and approximately ten months old when taken as a travel companion. Nevertheless, she foregrounds the episode in which her dog was badly hurt: James Buchanan was 'badly bitten by a dog, so badly he could no longer walk' and was carried around on a cushion (Gaunt 1919: 36). Gaunt takes care of him, fearing he is going to die. Yet oddly enough, Gaunt lays bare that what really terrifies her is not James Buchanan's death itself, but what loss his death would cause for her. In noting that 'I was terrified lest he should die, and I should be alone in the world' (36), she registers the uses, albeit the emotional ones, to which the dog is put, revealing that her evocation of James Buchanan is, in fact, relentlessly self-serving.

Ayscough likewise evokes a pattern of sentimentality, one which involves the trope of rescuing the suffering animal, as an affective medium to register human–animal intimacy and bonding, but she turns to a different narrative strategy that registers a sense of reciprocity in her relationship with Yo Fei. Taken away from his family and new to his 'foreign home' with his first foreign owner (Ayscough 1926: 3), the rebellious Yo Fei (at the time he was named Buster) attempts to run away before falling seriously ill. Feeling abandoned and not willing to settle into his foreign home, he 'decided to die' (8). Ayscough found him and nursed him back to life, and from hence, he 'made friends' with her – his mistress (8). The bond between them then starts to grow deeper as time passes. Later, when Ayscough is taken down by illness, Yo Fei keeps her company day and night, reversing the mode in which humans relieve the suffering of animals in pain. In doing so, Ayscough seems to place the dog at the centre of this animal–human relationship, inviting readers to perceive him 'as a subject and agent contributing to the encounters (Nyman and Schuurman 2016: 2), as if this relationship is a result of co-production, with the dog taking charge. In reversing the conventional dynamic of how humans 'made friends' with nonhuman animals, Ayscough seems also to imply that there is a higher degree of reciprocity in their mutual care and companionship, from which arises a sense of equality in this human–animal relationship. By this logic, there is less of the one-sidedness that dominates Gaunt's interactions with James Buchanan. In Gaunt's case, the one-sidedness becomes excessive, causing damage to the agency of the nonhuman animal with his disadvantage mired in a relationship resting upon an anthropocentric value system.

Even when they register the animal and human friendship, Ayscough and Gaunt differ from each other in the degrees of self-indulgence that characterise their writing about these canine companions. Ayscough appears largely to refrain from using the nonhuman animal as a site of affect in terms of showing her emotional attachment. On the one hand, there is the inconvenience of making Yo Fei, the focal point of the narration, see into Ayscough's own emotional world, and on the other hand, she is less keen on making the book a projection of herself and, by extension, the world inhabited and dominated by white, Western men and women. As a result, readers access the consciousness and point of view of the dog more than the human. This forms a sharp contrast to Gaunt's text. Gaunt, in her own voice, shows her capacity for self-indulgence, so that her narrative borders on being narcissistic. She frequently draws readers' attention to James Buchanan's affective significance to her as her 'only companion and friend' (1919: 30), and highlights that he 'loved [her] as no one in the world has ever loved [her]' and constantly gives her 'great comfort' (96). It is important to note here that, quite unlike Victorian female travellers who often resort to the conventional tropes of femininity such as self-effacement, Gaunt is open about how she feels and thinks, often overtly foregrounding her emotional sufferings when wandering in a strange land and among people speaking foreign languages (Wu 2021: 732–3). In this vein, she uses the affectionate dog as a site of affect, where her loneliness, insecurity and anxiety among an alien people are projected, displaced and manipulated so that she can fashion herself to fit the persona of a pained Western woman travelling alone in China. This is a persona already well constructed in *A Woman in China* (1914), to which *A Broken Journey* is a sequel.

It is true that, like Ayscough, Gaunt also intentionally avoids the discourses of 'mastery' which, as some feminist ecocritics such as Val Plumwood have highlighted, license ideas of human domination over nonhuman lives (2002: 45). However, throughout *A Broken Journey*, James Buchanan's emotional 'utility' to Gaunt overtakes anything else, as if he is no more than a source of 'affection' and comfort, a form of emotional 'resources' for the human:

> And if anyone thinks I make an absurd fuss about a little dog, I must remind him that I was entirely alone among an alien people, and the little dog's affection meant a tremendous deal to me. He took away all sense of loneliness. Looking back, I know now I could not have gone on, this book would never have been written, if it had not been for James Buchanan. (Gaunt 1919: 96)

Even in this passage that seems to concern James Buchanan most, readers see Gaunt's self, her 'loneliness' and the use of the dog looming ever larger. It reveals an obsession with human rather than animal emotions. The emotional reciprocity between human and nonhuman animals, is frequently disrupted. More importantly, Gaunt fails to explore the dog's complex interior life, unable to imagine canine subjectivity and nonhuman agency.

In the above passage, Gaunt also seems impelled to pre-emptively defend her making 'an absurd fuss about a little dog'. Arguably, she is clear-eyed about how nonhuman animals like dogs are generally treated with indifference by humans. In her own understated words, people 'don't think much of animals' (148). She appears to react against this prevailing denigration of animals, a denigration stemming from the hierarchical dualism enshrined in Western philosophy since

René Descartes that defines human superiority, animal insignificance and the maintenance of this hierarchy. Gaunt's resistance is poignantly articulated in her account of the treacherous journey taking a small dog with her on various transport vehicles crossing Siberia and Europe before reaching England on the eve of the First World War. During this process, the dog's life and his value are constantly slighted, neglected and pitted against human life and value. As a dog, he is not allowed to board the trains and has to be drugged to keep quiet, hidden in a small box and smuggled into the vehicles, a reminder of how nonhuman lives are perceived as lesser than humans', especially in a time of crisis. Echoing Gaunt, Ayscough also demonstrates her awareness and disapproval of this hierarchical dualism. This sentiment is already clear at the outset of *The Autobiography of a Chinese Dog* when Ayscough, citing the Chinese folklore of the weaving lady, poses the question, 'And who shall say that only human beings are of importance in the pattern she weaves?' (Foreword i). Ayscough thus takes a step further as she attempts to challenge the 'alleged human monopoly over reason' (Nyman 2016: 66). Both Gaunt and Ayscough, through recounting their affective relations to dogs, make efforts to confront the thin boundary between the animal and the human, forcing us to attend to the significance of the nonhuman other.

'[H]E HAD ENTIRELY FORGOTTEN HIS ORIGIN'

Race fundamentally marks Ayscough and Gaunt's animal figurations. For Gaunt, her racial identity is that of a white woman who appears to believe in and support the necessity and justice of racial difference with its inherent hierarchy. In fact, in the latter half of *A Woman in China* and across *A Broken Journey*, Gaunt uses her narration to echo the narrow racism she ascribes to Rudyard Kipling (1865–1936), whose poems she quotes frequently. Uppermost is Kipling's 'The Ballad of East and West' (1889). Oddly enough, Gaunt's quotation stops at its first line, 'East is East, and West is West, and never the twain shall meet,' which can be read as an explicit support of the idea that racial and cultural difference between East and West is unbridgeable. She appears to have completely missed the third and fourth lines of the opening stanza: 'But there is neither East nor West, Border, nor Breed, nor Birth/ When two strong men stand face to face, though they come from the ends of the earth!' (Kipling 1989 [1889]: 233). Apparently, Gaunt skirts around Kipling's caution that differences in race, ethnicity, nationality and even birth do not matter and should be supplanted by individual personality, prowess and integrity as criteria for judging one another. In ignoring what Kipling conveys in the remaining part of the poem, Gaunt makes 'East is East, and West is West, and never the twain shall meet' a motto directing how she thinks, feels and reacts to Chinese people as racial others.

Racial perceptions undergirding a mentality of the essentialised hierarchical difference between East and West profoundly problematise Gaunt's representation of her dog, whose Chineseness must be subsumed, assimilated by whiteness.

In fact, she subjects the animal to racial politics. In addition, the animal is constantly instrumentalised to express Gaunt's own racial identity, projecting her mounting racial anxiety as she journeys farther into China's hinterland and away from European presence. This can be seen in various narrative strategies she uses rhetorically to racialise a Chinese dog into non-Chineseness. First and foremost, her naming practice is revealing. Gaunt's first introduction of her dog is already striking, for he bears a name utterly Western and essentially Anglophone. More than that, historically, James Buchanan (1791–1868), the fifteenth president of the United States, was infamous for his ambiguous attitude towards slavery and for his inaction regarding averting the American Civil War (1861–5). Readers can only speculate on what made Gaunt name her Chinese dog after James Buchanan in the first place. However, intentionally or not, this naming practice, with its strong connection to rhetorical colonialism as identified by Mary Stuckey and John Murphy (2001: 82), suggests Gaunt's intention to assimilate a Chinese dog discursively into the Western world, one that decisively sets him apart from the Chinese world, as I discuss later in this chapter.

In addition to establishing racial boundaries through naming, Gaunt in *A Broken Journey* subjects James Buchanan the dog to a progressive erasure of cultural memory. From the outset of their journeys, James Buchanan is said to have 'entirely forgotten his origin' (1919: 16), an origin that means not only where he came from – namely, his physical birthplace – but also his racial and cultural origin. One immediate consequence of entirely losing his race memory is that he no longer has an emotional bond with the Chinese people amongst whom he grew up. This is evident in behaviours such as rejecting any forms of physical proximity to Chinese people, either Gaunt's servants or random people they encounter en route. For instance, readers are frequently told that the small dog, despite being admired by the Chinese, who show their fondness of him, 'utterly declined' to walk with them (96) and 'declined to trust himself with them unless I walked too' (96). Gaunt reminds readers that the reason that James Buchanan does not bite her Chinese servant, Mr Wang, is 'simply because he despised him so' (16) since he is Chinese and, worse still, he is from the lower class. The only occasion on which James Buchanan shows a small dose of willingness to accept the Chinese servant's touch, as Gaunt clarifies, is when he is treated as if he was 'a prince of the blood at least' (96). In both episodes, class-bound pride and vanity are invoked to complicate the racialised reactions towards Chinese people.

On another occasion, Gaunt conflates her abjection of Chinese women with anthropomorphism regarding her depiction of James Buchanan. She recounts her encounters with a native sewing woman when travelling in a boat:

> She [the native woman] had had her feet bound in her youth and was rather crippled in consequence [. . .] She was a foolish soul, like most

> Chinese women, and took great interest in Buchanan, offering him always a share of her own meals, which consisted apparently largely of cucumbers and the tasteless Chinese melon. Now James Buchanan was extremely polite, always accepting what was offered him, but he could not possibly eat cucumber and melon, and when I went to bed at night I often came in contact with something cold and clammy which invariably turned out to be fragments of the sewing-woman's meals. (143)

In this episode, Gaunt reduces the sewing woman, who is 'exceedingly useful to the missionaries' (143), as she points out, to 'a foolish soul' who is 'crippled' from binding her feet in youth. Her comments that this woman is a representative of 'most Chinese women' discloses her general and race-bound contempt for Chinese women as a whole. Indeed, throughout *A Woman in China* and *A Broken Journey*, readers can easily form an impression of Gaunt's perception of Chinese women. Chinese women are homogenised into a hopeless, helpless group centring around their bound feet, a sign of their 'usual agonies' (1914: 170) and 'cruel suffering' (1919: 128). Depicted merely as 'toys and slaves' (1919: 84), Chinese women are pitted against white women, who, exemplified by Gaunt herself, are portrayed as modern citizens, emancipated, mobile and embodying women's rights achieved in a progressive era. A racial boundary is ever present to separate Chinese women from the Western self. Interestingly, Gaunt uses James Buchanan to project her abject feelings towards Chinese women, thus widening, rather than closing, the racial gap. This is clear if we read this episode alongside an earlier one in *A Woman in China* in which Gaunt describes her irritation at being offered food and help by a 'little maimed one-eyed old woman up in the hills of China' (1914: 192). In both cases, local hospitality and good-will from Chinese women, in a morsel of food or other forms, must be politely rejected, so that the boundary between the superior self and the abject other is not collapsed.

In addition to invoking contempt springing from her perceived racial superiority, Gaunt features other economies of emotions closely assigned to racial emotions, to configure James Buchanan's affective reactions towards the Chinese as a means for projecting and solidifying her own racialised feelings. Sociologists such as Eduardo Bonilla-Silva have theorised 'racialized emotions' as emotions constituting the 'fundamental social forces shaping the house of racism' (2019: 2). In echoing Sara Ahmed, who singles out the 'economies of fear' that bear on how 'the language of racism sustains fear through displacement' (2004: 126), Bonilla-Silva uses racialised fear arising from the phenomenon wherein 'Whites fear Blacks in interracial encounters' as an example to illustrate the process of 'race-making' (2019: 3). If we change the 'Blacks' into 'Chinese', it holds true for Gaunt's interracial interactions, in which fear 'works to differentiate between white and [Chinese] bodies' (Ahmed 2004: 126). The difference is that Gaunt displaces her racialised emotions on to the animal other, using James Buchanan to mediate her vexed racial relation to Chinese people. She first emphasises that James Buchanan always casts his 'doubtful' look on Chinese people, who he perceives as 'alien' (Gaunt 1919: 16). As her journey progresses, contempt and doubt are magnified and impinged on by fear. After he is badly hurt by a Chinese dog – a symbolic episode that suggests deep-seated worries over the imminent danger of being left alone among the Chinese – James Buchanan lives in fear of Chinese people. Gaunt renders the sensation of fear on the dog's part most palpable when she, for the first time using direct quotation to invite readers to see into James Buchanan's inner world, records his entreaty: 'Don't leave me, don't leave me to the mercy of the Chinese' (36). As such, the Chinese are imagined, felt and perceived as the very objects of fear, the incarnation of barbarism and capable of nothing but brutality and atrocity.

In fact, Gaunt penned her narratives in the 1910s when, uppermost in her impressions of China was the anti-imperialist Boxer Rebellion, staged between 1899 and 1901, a historical trauma to many Westerners, who perceived from afar the alleged savagery of the Chinese mob as depicted by the Western press. In 1900 the Boxers, determined to expunge foreign influence from China, besieged the foreign legations in Peking, killing a dozen Westerners and many Chinese Christians in the rest of the country. The popular narrative of the Boxer Rebellion strongly reinforced racist stereotypes of the Chinese as a Yellow Peril, a racial ideology feeding on Western 'racist terror of alien cultures, sexual anxieties, and the belief that the West will be overpowered and enveloped by the irresistible, dark, occult forces of the East' (Marchetti 1994: 2). What Gaunt terms 'the Boxer trouble' surfaces and resurfaces in both *A Woman in China* and *A Broken Journey* to an alarming extent: she evokes tales told by missionaries 'who had actually suffered almost to death at the hands of the Boxers' (1919: 133), documents places nearly razed to the ground by frantic Boxers, and recounts conversations with individuals who witnessed the 'troubles and dangers of the Boxer time' (112). In so doing, the history becomes 'alive in the present', shaping the surface of bodies (Ahmed 2004: 126). The passing of a decade does not mean the waning of fear for Gaunt; instead, racist fear circulates and moves across time and space as history becomes 'sticky', to use Ahmed's term (146), and racist fear sticks to the Chinese as a whole. In some sense, the history of 'the Boxer Trouble' that sticks becomes the lens through which Gaunt sees and perceives her Chinese encounters, mediating her interracial interactions and the boundary she uses to set herself apart from the Chinese. If Gaunt, in the former half of her journey, is able to repress her racist fear and anxiety, the moment she is left alone, surrounded by Chinese men and women, racialised emotions erupt, and James Buchanan is passively used as a tool, with attributed emotional value, to articulate her otherwise suppressed feelings towards the Chinese other. The canine companion in Gaunt's text is therefore anthropomorphised into a racialised projection appearing to embody imperialist modernist culture.

'A Chinese Dog'

While in Gaunt's *A Broken Journey*, James Buchanan can be read as a caricature of racialised emotions in the narcissistic and imperialist distortion, Ayscough in *The Autobiography of A Chinese Dog* takes a very different approach insofar as she largely reverses Gaunt's mode. On the one hand, she brings into view the canine subjectivity and agency denied in Gaunt's narrative; on the other hand, she grounds her animal figuration, closely connected to elements of anthropomorphism, and positive to a great extent, in her cosmopolitan vision regarding China's racial and cultural alterity. As a 'citizen in the world', she develops not merely a keen interest in, but also profound respect for, the Chinese difference manifest in Chinese culture in its complex forms. In other words, her immersion in Chinese literature, culture and ways of living provides her with a 'liberal education' (Ayscough 1926: 19), from which she cultivates a responsibility for introducing Chinese cultural difference to the West without subsuming it to increase the sameness of world culture. Ayscough's animal figuration is entangled with this cosmopolitan project.

To portray the canine consciousness and agency upon which Yo Fei's Chineseness is dependent, Ayscough creatively employs a host of narrative strategies in ways that are significantly different from those used by Gaunt. Instead of rendering the animal other voiceless, Ayscough provides Yo Fei with a voice, a history and a capacity for storytelling, thus redrawing the division between the human and the animal. In this way, Yo Fei illustrates what Donna Haraway theorises as 'figures [that] are not representations or didactic illustrations, but rather material-semiotic nodes or knots in which diverse bodies and meanings coshape one another' (2008: 4). As a sign of this strategy, at the outset of the narrative, Yo Fei the dog, in his own voice, traces his own life trajectory originating from Shantung, a province known as the birthplace of Confucianism, the hallmark of Chinese traditional culture. As Yo Fei narrates,

> the great Confucius [551–479 BC] was born in Shantung . . . so was his disciple Mencius [372–289 BC], and in their days, dogs of my breed, the Lo-sze were used in the pursuit of game, so naturally I have a love of the chase in my very blood. (Ayscough 1926: 3)

Blending the origin of Confucianism with that of the Lo-sze dog imparts an important message that the human has been living with the animal since ancient times and that animals are inevitably entangled within human history. In this regard, Ayscough anticipates Erica Fudge, who argues that 'it is impossible to understand human history without also understanding the role that animals played in that history because animals have always held key positions in so-called human society' (2014: 27). Yet as Grace Moore warns, such 'assertions of coexistence sit uncomfortably alongside notions of the "utility" of the animal' (2020: 214). It is true that when Ayscough evokes this cross-species coexistence, the notion of 'utility' is not sidestepped, as we are told that the Lo-sze dogs were 'used' by the humans since Confucius's time. She later returns to the coexistence issue, devoting an entire chapter, through Yo Fei the focaliser, illustrating how dogs, particularly Yo Fei's 'ancestors', his 'lineal and collateral kinsmen' (Ayscough 1926: 51), were domesticated and evolved under the influences of human activities such as religion, imperial preference and selective breeding through China's long history of different dynasties (53).

Ayscough is concerned with how the human and the canine have co-evolved over time upon the premise that the animal is cared for and 'canine feelings' are noted, understood and respected in ways within human power. For instance, she returns to Confucius, Yo Fei's 'great compatriot', to illustrate her point:

> [Confucius] seems to have had a very real comprehension of canine feelings . . . As he understood dogs so well, it was but natural that he should care for them; and it is recorded that he entirely approved the customs of burying a dear 'house-dog' in an old official canopy [as a way of showing respect to the dead]. (52)

Apparently, here the domesticated 'house-dog' is elevated to the status of an honourable man with respectable social status, demonstrating that the frequently emphasised animal subordination in the West may not always apply to the East. This structure of feeling is immediately reinforced by the moving story of a dog in the imperial court in China's Sung Dynasty (960–1279). When an Emperor died, his Lo-sze dog 'whined, moaned, and refused to eat' (52). Sensing its 'pitiful state' (52), the old Emperor's son, now the new Emperor, decreed that the dog be placed on the white mourning cushions and carried in the imperial chair to the royal tomb. The small dog died there, and he was wrapped 'in a royal canopy and buried beside its master' (53). To deny that animals are subordinated might risk romanticising humans' treatment of animals in the East. However, gleaning such affective stories from China's long history does suggest that Ayscough believes in the value of other ways of thinking, feeling and living with nonhuman animals as much as there are other kinds of histories, cultures, civilisations and ways of living outside Euro-America.

In conferring on Yo Fei a profound sense of history, both of Chinese culture and of the canine species, Ayscough makes it possible to enact a cultural and racial identity that is Chinese on the dog's side. This is evident in the narrative strategy Ayscough employs to make Yo Fei a Chinese dog altogether, from his name to his heart. To begin with, like Gaunt, she also turns to the naming practice but approaches it differently. She, through Yo Fei's voice, explains that she changes his name from 'Buster', a name given by the dog's first adopter, to 'Yo Fei' because the latter is 'more in keeping with my personality' (10). The narration then goes on to recount how Ayscough's Chinese mentor tells the story of Yo Fei, a Chinese historical figure esteemed as 'the hero of the twelfth century, who devoted his life to the defence of his country' (11). In the newly established Republican China (1912–49), Yo Fei's story was remembered and conjured back from history, and the spirit of Yo Fei, admired as 'the Prince of Loyalty and Courage', was admitted to the Military Temple in Peking in 1915, as part of the 'Cult of Heroes', to raise public patriotism and nationalism to reinforce China's independence from the West's semi-colonial rule as a new modern state (12). To some extent, Ayscough also attempts to make Yo Fei the dog a defender of his own country in cultural terms.

In this regard, Yo Fei is configured as Chinese not only in origin, in his name, but also in his psychology, which shapes his ability to compare Chinese and Western cultures and reveal the diversity of world cultures free from racial dogmatism. For instance, in a humorous tone, Yo Fei the Chinese dog makes fun of this 'strange Western custom' of naming pets after famous people, noting that it is 'incredibly disrespectful in the eyes of my country-people' (12). On another occasion Yo Fei grounds his comparison and value judgement upon his own lived experiences in both China and Canada. As he tells Western readers, 'In China no hedges divide one man's property from that of his neighbours, only raised paths are used for landmarkers; no white boards such as I have seen here [Canada] state "Trespassers Will be Prosecuted"; I could race and race for miles on end' (38). Such comparisons serve pedagogical purposes. On the one hand, it educates Western readers on Chinese customs relating to matters of private property, which are not necessarily inferior to the Western idea of property rights; on the other hand, his comment that he could race freely in Shanghai illustrates a yearning for a world untainted by a colonial modernity that is propelled by industrialisation and aggressive modernisation.

An affective intimacy between Yo Fei and what he calls 'my country-people', amongst whom he flourishes, significantly marks him as distinct from James Buchanan. Ayscough, throughout *The Autobiography of A Chinese Dog*, uses plural pronouns such as '[w]e the Chinese dog' (8), 'we Chinese' (3; 12; 18) and 'my countrymen' (38: 69; 72; 73) to show Yo Fei's identification with his Chinese origin and racial belongings as much as his emotional closeness to the Chinese. In doing so, Yo Fei is represented very differently from Gaunt's James Buchanan, who grows increasingly distant from, and nurtures contempt and fear for, Chinese people in the wake of the obliteration of his cultural and racial memory. While James Buchanan finds working-class Chinese people repulsive, fearsome and too low to deserve his attention, Yo Fei recognises a natural affective community with them, including Ayscough's servants and other disadvantaged groups. For example, Yo Fei tells of the 'dreadful' life of the 'rickshaw coolie' who lives in a city. The primary source of a rickshaw coolie's dread, as Yo Fei informs us, is 'the people whom he draws in his carriage' because they are 'often thoughtless and cruel; urging him on, swearing at him, prodding him, and sometimes striking him' (14). Here the trope of cruelty links the coolies with animals such as horses as they are configured in Anna Sewell's *Black Beauty* (1877). In this sense, Ayscough appears to reveal, through Yo Fei's voice and his sympathy, the inhuman treatment of the lower-class Chinese workers as much as cruelty against nonhuman animals.

Through comparatively reading animal figurations in Mary Gaunt's self-centred travel narratives and Florence Ayscough's canine autobiography across a span of a decade, this chapter has demonstrated an explicit paradigm shift in forms of anthropomorphism regarding canine subjectivity, agency and animal–human relationships, as well as interracial dynamics in the literary imaginary of the early twentieth-century modernist culture of mobility and intercultural encounters. Gaunt's account of James Buchanan, the voiceless dog wanting cultural, racial memory, falls into the inevitable trap of a form of traditional, old-fashioned and ultimately destructive anthropomorphism inflected by mounting racial anxiety. Her style of anthropomorphising the dog extolls human significance and white exceptionalism at the price of the animal and the non-white. On the contrary, in rejecting such a disservice, Ayscough brings to the view the ways in which the performance of Yo Fei's subjectivity, value system and racial and cultural identity links to an egalitarian, cosmopolitan fashion of perceiving cross-species and interracial relationships. In doing so, she strives to close the human–animal divide as well as the alleged racial, cultural, hierarchical structure between the white and non-white. Her work registers a new fashion of affective, constructive anthropomorphism that acknowledges distinctive animal subjectivity and agency, which enables her to uncover and present a 'world of resonances and resemblances' (Bennett 2010: 99). Moreover, she champions the importance of an empathetic human imagination which respects the coexistence, co-evolution and interaction of the animal and the human, and those of different races and cultures. Ayscough's work provides an anticipatory discourse of 'companion species', to use Haraway's term, that encapsulates the idea that our existence is constantly constitutive with other species. It can be said that Ayscough's positive anthropomorphism encourages what Haraway calls 'an ethics and politics committed to the flourishing of significant otherness' (2003: 3), and in this case, the significant other refers to both nonhuman species and non-white races. In this sense, a degree of empathetic anthropomorphism can be understood as contributing to the mutual understanding of companion species and the course of the flourishing of nonhuman others.

Works Cited

Ahmed, Sara. 2004. 'Affective Economies'. *Social Text* 22.2: 117–39.
Ayscough, Florence. 1926. *A Chinese Mirror: Being Reflections of the Reality Behind Appearance*. Boston and New York: Houghton Mifflin.
Ayscough, Florence. 1926. *The Autobiography of a Chinese Dog*. Boston and New York: Houghton Mifflin.
Ayscough, Florence. 1932. *Firecracker Land: Pictures of the Chinese World for Younger Readers*. New York: Houghton Mifflin.
Bennett, Jane. 2010. *Vibrant Matter: A Political Ecology of Things*. Durham, NC, and London: Duke University Press.
Bonilla-Silva, Eduardo. 2019. 'Feeling Race: Theorizing the Racial Economy of Emotions'. *American Sociological Review* 84.1: 1–25.
Fudge, Erica. 2014. *Pets (The Art of Living)*. London: Routledge.
Garber, Marjorie. 1996. *Dog Love*. New York: Touchstone.
Gaunt, Mary. 1911. *Alone in West Africa*. London: T. W. Laurie.
Gaunt, Mary. 1914. *A Woman in China*. London: T. W. Laurie.
Gaunt, Mary. 1919. *A Broken Journey*. London: T. W. Laurie.
Haraway, Donna J. 2003. *The Companion Species Manifesto: Dogs, People and Significant Otherness*. Vol. 1. Chicago: Prickly Paradigm Press.
Haraway, Donna J. 2008. *When Species Meet*. London: University of Minnesota Press.
Hickman, Bronwen. 2014. *Mary Gaunt: Independent Colonial Woman*. Melbourne: Melbourne Books.
Ittner, Jutia. 2006. 'Part Spaniel, Part Canine Puzzle: Anthropomorphism in Woolf's *Flush* and Auster's *Timbuktu*'. *Mosaic: An Interdisciplinary Critical Journal* 39.4: 181–96.
Kipling, Rudyard. 1989 [1889]. *Complete Verse*. Definitive Edition. New York: Anchor Books.
Marchetti, Gina. 1994. *Romance and the Yellow Peril: Race, Sex, and Discursive Strategies in Hollywood Fiction*. Oakland: University of California Press.
Moore, Grace. 2020. 'Animalographies, Kinship, and Conflict in Ceridwen Dovey's *Only the Animals* and Eva Hornung's *Dog Boy*.' *a/b: Auto/Biography Studies* 35.1: 207–29.
Nyman, Jopi. 2016. 'Re-reading Sentimentalism in Anna Sewell's *Black Beauty*: Affect, Performativity, and Hybrid Spaces'. In *Affect, Space and Animals*. Ed. Jopi Nyman and Nora Schuurman, 65–79. New York: Routledge.
Nyman, Jopi and Nora Schuurman. 2016. 'Introduction'. In *Affect, Space and Animals*. Ed. Jopi Nyman and Nora Schuurman, 1–11. New York: Routledge.
Plumwood, Val. 2002. *Environmental Culture: The Ecological Crisis of Reason*. London: Routledge.
Rohman, Carrie. 2008. *Stalking the Subject: Modernism and the Animal*. New York: Columbia University Press.
Ryan, Derek. 2013. *Virginia Woolf and the Materiality of Theory: Sex, Animal, Life*. Edinburgh: Edinburgh University Press.
Stuckey, Mary and John Murphy. 2001. 'By Any Other Name: Rhetorical Colonialism in North America'. *American Indian Culture and Research Journal* 25.4: 73–98.

Woolf, Virginia. 2016 [1933]. *Flush: A Biography*. London: Penguin Classics.
Wu, Juanjuan. 2021. 'A Broken Journey: Emotions, Race, and Gendered Mobility in Mary Gaunt's Narratives of China'. *Women's Studies* 50.7: 727–46.
Wylie, Dan. 2002. 'The Anthropomorphic Ethic: Fiction and the Animal Mind in Virginia Woolf's *Flush* and Barbara Gowdy's *The White Bone*'. *Interdisciplinary Studies in Literature and Environment* 9.2: 115–31.

PART II

BEASTLY TRACES

4

MAKING AN IMPRESSION DEEPLY: AUTHORISING ANIMALS IN D. H. LAWRENCE

Carrie Rohman

In recent work on animality in modernism and in performance, I have been reframing aesthetic practice as a fundamentally more-than-human undertaking. In that work I assert that human creativity is only the most recent iteration of an artistic impulse that belongs to the living in general. Aesthetics from this perspective must be understood as *bioaesthetics*, wherein a 'bio-impulse' at the root of the aesthetic itself connects human artistic propensities to animality through strategies of excess, display, and intensification.[1] This work of revising our understanding of creatural aesthetic capacities, of re-envisioning the aesthetic domain itself as transhuman in scope, is ethically charged because we must acknowledge the shared status of art-making, one of our most hallowed and formerly 'exceptional' activities. Thinking through the bioaesthetic powers of other animals has led me to consider the ways in which animals might be said to 'authorise' creative projects or practices. This discussion is thus a first step in thinking through what I am calling animal authority in literary and performative practices.

The idea of animals as authors, or as authorising, raises interesting questions about the qualities of authority that are called upon when animals become sources of sanctioning, knowledge or permission, and how those differ from human authorisations. Moreover, suggesting that animals might be authors in some way is more radical than suggesting that they can write or mark because it dares to view animals through a humanised lens of intention or purpose, however much we have problematised those categories as literary scholars. If we were to reframe something like Michel Foucault's outlining of an 'author-function' in discursive practices to accommodate animal authority, the question of the author becomes a much more radically open question than Foucault could have anticipated (Foucault 1969). For instance, how do animal authorities affect the kinship between writing and death that Foucault and Roland Barthes have elaborated? What replaces the apotheosis of *écriture* in an animalised framework? Is it Jacques Derrida's *animot*? Is it a zoopoetics that bears witness to humans' entanglement with life, as a repressed or disavowed given of writing?[2] And is the evocation of an animal authority in creative or artistic work a radical refusal of the proper name, of the individual mark, or does it rather concede that the operations of authentication and verification (tied to self-presence, in at least some sense) ought to be accorded to animals, also? While this discussion will not answer all of these questions, I hope that it might provoke further considerations of what it can mean to think about animals as authors, particularly in the modernist context. Modernism, as I have suggested elsewhere, is itself a bioaesthetic becoming-other, with an emphasis on innovation and becoming-new, so the authorship of modernist animals is of particular interest.

In general, I am proposing that the bioaesthetic critical wager, which locates the fundamental artistic impulse well beyond human capacities, could be understood to signal the ends of human aesthetic authority. In exploring animals as aesthetic authorities, I am keen to take the entire concept of 'authorship' outside of an exclusively human framework, to reconfigure and query it in a more-than-human register. D. H. Lawrence's work is a good foundation for this inquiry because Lawrence wrestles with animal powers, both within and alongside the human, in highly complex ways throughout his writing. His intricate embrace of embodied and intuitive forms of consciousness, and his understandings of human ontology as always embedded in creatural and ecological networks, align with some of his vivid renderings of animal authorship in the modernist era.

Women in Love (1920) uses a multitude of encounters with nonhuman animals that are bioaesthetic in nature, but one set is highly charged around the question of authorship. Chapter 18, 'Rabbit', sits in the exact centre of the novel, at page 235 out of 480 pages in the Cambridge edition. This placement had not occurred to me in the last twenty-five years or so of reading, rereading and teaching the novel, until I started thinking about animal authors in Lawrence. The 'Rabbit' chapter seals the erotic intentions between Gudrun and Gerald, and so it contains a set of critically outworn sexual implications, based on the perception of rabbits as highly propagative, and therefore highly erotic. But as I often remark about Lawrence's work, it is not that the sexual proper is not central: it is rather that the sexual proper must be understood to signal so much more, and so much more richly, in the context of ecological and creatural registers.

The context for the dramatic action of the chapter should be recalled, importantly, as framed by the child Winifred. Winifred, the youngest child in the Crich family, is described as 'detached' and 'ironic', and as one who does 'not notice human beings, unless they were like herself, playful and slightly mocking' (Lawrence 1920: 235). Further, 'the serious people of her life were the animals she had for pets' (235). Winifred's posture toward animals is not necessarily or evenly elevated by Lawrence's treatment of her, but it is crucial to note that the novel's most charged instance of an authorising animal occurs in this chapter, saturated by the child's views. The child's attentions are specifically artistic ones, at that, first to her Pekinese dog, Looloo, and then to the rabbit, named Bismarck.

Both of these creatures have proper, capitalised names, which obviously marks them as domesticated by humans. But this detail has further implications around the role of the proper name in specific relation to authorship. Foucault clarifies that the proper name and the author's name share the oscillation 'between the poles of description and designation' (Foucault 1969: 1480). That is, the author's name signals that *this* writing (or speech) is extraordinary, lasting, something to which others ought to attend. Thus, formally naming Looloo and Bismarck signals this extra quality to the reader, in a way that simply using 'the dog' and 'the rabbit' would not. We might also note that these are attentions to domesticated animality, mediated largely through a child and a woman. Perhaps these details can be seen as a mode of Lawrence's feminism: the extensive focus here on women and children, and domesticated 'pets', would typically be coded as feminine.

The whole chapter is framed by Winifred and Gudrun trying to sketch these two companion animals, in the first drawing and modelling lesson that has been arranged for the child. This is, therefore, a highly self-reflexive chapter, showcasing the making of artwork within an artwork. We might say, then, that the bioaesthetic becomes doubly charged in this portion of the novel. That charge is intensified by the fact that Gudrun is specifically known for her sculptured animal figures. Gerald informs Winifred, his younger sister, that Miss Brangwen 'makes animals and birds in wood and clay, that the people in London write about in the papers, praising them to the skies' (235).

In its initial segments, as the ladies each draw a portrait of Looloo the dog, Lawrence's chapter vacillates to some degree between staid classical portraiture, with a more conventional subject/object dynamic, and a bioaesthetic acknowledgement of animal agency and power. In connection with the latter, Winifred herself suggests that they are aiming to capture or get Looloo's 'Looliness' (235) in their drawings, which at least nods toward an individual subjecthood that is unique to this dog. She also introduces the term 'awful' when she worries aloud that her own sketch of the creature is 'sure to be awful' (236). As I will suggest, this term is significant in multivalent ways for the discussion of animal authority.

Hints of the dog's point of view emerge in Lawrence's descriptions: 'He sat all the time with the resignation and fretfulness of ages on his dark velvety face' (236), and 'He turned his head aside as in chagrin and mortification' (236) when Winifred holds the drawing of him 'under his nose', for Looloo to admire. Looloo the dog also looks at the child 'with reproachful, saturnine eyes, vanquished in his extreme agedness of being' (236). Moreover, the narrator's description, which coincides with Gudrun's initial viewing of Winifred's drawing, turns further toward a reciprocal sense of creatural entanglement: 'It was a grotesque little diagram of a grotesque little animal, so wicked and so comical, a slow smile came over Gudrun's face, unconsciously' (236). Gudrun ultimately agrees that the likeness of the dog is significant.

The repetition of the descriptor 'grotesque' could be misleading here. It is important to recall that Birkin is described in the 'Water-Party' chapter as standing before Ursula with 'a sardonic, flickering laugh on his face. And in another second, he was singing softly to himself, and dancing a *grotesque* step-dance in front of her, his limbs and body shaking loose, his face flickering palely . . . like a shadow' (168–9; emphasis added). Birkin is further described in this scene as malevolent and mocking. In previous work, I have argued that Birkin's grotesque mocking dances are examples of Deleuzean immanence: impersonal antimetaphorical becomings-imperceptible that are highly valued in the novel's framework.[3] The posture or temperament of the dog is perhaps grotesque in the same valued sense. There is a further vacillation, however, that it seems important to mark. When 'a slow smile came over Gudrun's face, unconsciously' (236), at seeing the grotesque little diagram Winifred has made of the dog, there seems an irreverent moment of relishing the wickedness or mischief involved in representation itself. If we are considering whether animals partake in such activities as writing and authoring, the scamp or rascal quality of making a likeness here seems notable.

The early portions of this chapter also contain more overt bioaesthetic linkages between Winifred and her companion animals. For instance, the 'child wore a dress of black-and-white stripes' (237), just as Bismarck is described as 'the great black-and-white rabbit' (239). Thus, the child's garments mirror, to a significant extent, the creature's own embodied designs, or fur markings, which in bioaesthetic terms are often responsible for the lurings, attractions and becomings-artistic that animals perform in order to attract sex partners, and perhaps in order for the rhythmic pleasures alone that these becomings enact. There is clearly some flickering of the child/animal boundary here. That the girl and the rabbit are visually black and white – specifically, the colours of parchment and ink, of the printed page or written word – is especially compelling in reading Bismarck as an authorising force.

The broader significance of bioaesthetic markings is reinforced in Gudrun's characteristic colourful attire. She is described early in the chapter as 'dressed in blue, with woollen yellow stockings, like the Blue coat boys. [Gerald] glanced up in surprise. Her stockings always disconcerted him, the pale-yellow stockings and the rather black shoes' (237). Further into the chapter, when the erotic tensions between the two adults are more activated, Gerald watches the

> soft, full, still body of Gudrun, in its silky cashmere. How silky and rich and soft her body must be. . . . And it did rather annoy him, that Gudrun came dressed in startling colours, like a macaw, when the family was in mourning. Like a macaw she was! He watched the lingering way she took her feet from the ground. And her ankles were pale yellow, and her dress a deep blue. Yet it pleased him. It pleased him very much. He felt the challenge in her very attire – she challenged the whole world. And he smiled as to the note of triumph. (239)

The repetition of 'challenge' signals the territorial aspects of a creatural bioaesthetics. As Gilles Deleuze and Félix Guattari explain, the artist is

> the first person to set out a boundary stone, or to make a mark. Property, collective or individual, is derived from that, even when it is in the service of war and oppression. Property is fundamentally artistic because art is fundamentally *poster, placard*. As [Konrad] Lorenz says, coral fish are posters. The expressive is primary in relation to the possessive. (Deleuze and Guattari 1987: 316)

Elizabeth Grosz helpfully glosses this concept by explaining that the:

> boundary is not self-protective but erotico-proprietorial: it defines a stage of performance, an arena of enchantment, a mise-en-scène for seduction that brings together heterogeneous and otherwise unrelated elements: melody and rhythms, a series of gestures, bows, and dips, a tree or a perch, a nest, a clearing, an audience of rivals, an audience of desired ones. (Grosz 2008: 48)

Again, the piquing element here in relation to authorship is the possessive and forceful enactment of one's 'startling colours': that is, of one's particular aesthetic being. This enchanting, erotico-proprietorial staging of the artistic 'self' seems especially charged in the animal scenes of *Women in Love*, where creatures both human and animal perform and judge others' performances, and where an aesthetic 'outwardness' tests the becomings of individuals, as conventions are surpassed and 'rivals' overcome. When Birkin moves in and out of his 'grotesque step-dance', in which 'his body seemed to hang all loose and quaking in between, like a shadow', he responds to Ursula's assertion that 'we've all gone mad' with '[p]ity we aren't madder' and a sudden kissing of her fingers (168–9). He puts his face near hers here, and would have kissed her again a few moments later, 'had she not started back' (169). The 'outlandish' quality is like that of a 'mad macaw', which Gerald associates with Gudrun, a quality that he both admires and is startled to perceive. Bismarck the rabbit's 'madness' is also a central issue in the chapter, and I will return to that.

The scenes with Bismarck are much more extended, and occupy a larger portion of the chapter, than the portions concerning Looloo. At the outset of this segment, I want to mention that the rabbit's powerful authoritative actions ultimately delay the humans' sketching plans, and so, because the rabbit makes its 'mark' in the chapter, the humans' intentions to make their likenesses of the rabbit are indefinitely deferred. One of Winifred's initial outbursts about drawing Bismarck turns on the framework of the 'awe-ful'. When Gudrun confirms that Winifred wants to take up the rabbit as their next drawing subject, the child responds, 'Oh yes – Oh I do! I want most awfully to do Bismarck. He looks *so* splendid this morning, so *fierce*. He's almost as big as a lion' (237). These remarks correspond with Lawrence's vacillations around animals and animality in his broader work, where his narratorial voices and characters display a 'tension between destroying and acknowledging the radical alterity of the animal other' (Rohman 2009: 100).[4] Moreover, when the child continues to suggest that 'He's a real king, he is' (237), her claim directly echoes the well-known lines in Lawrence's poem 'Snake', in which he describes the serpent as

> like a king,
> Like a king in exile, uncrowned in the underworld,
> Now due to be crowned again. (Lawrence 1923d: 305, ll. 69–70)

Despite the narratorial presentation of the child's views as 'hyperbole' here, the reverence for animal being and subjectivity is marked.

Bismarck is also repeatedly described as a *wonder*, a mystery, which further aligns with Lawrence's tendency to acknowledge a threshold for human pre-eminence, along species lines. That is, 'At times, Lawrence's [work] acknowledges the radical alterity of animal others and deconstructs the typical humanist subject-who-knows by framing the limits of human epistemology' (Rohman 2009: 64). The 'awe-ful' qualities are recapped and recited in Lawrence's hallmark repetitious style, a style that, in part, can be seen as an attempt to produce multivalent meanings, to resist standard concepts and linguistic codes. The section emphasising Bismarck's 'mystery' is partly written in French, as it includes the French governess's comments, and is worth reproducing here at some length, in its translated form:

'Good-day miss,' . . .
'Winifred does so want to do Bismarck's portrait – ! Oh, but all morning it's . . . Bismarck, Bismarck, always Bismarck! It's a rabbit, isn't it miss?
'Yes, it's a big black and white rabbit. Haven't you seen him?' . . .
'No, miss, Winifred has never wanted to show it to me. Many's the time I've asked her, "What is this Bismarck, Winifred?" But she wouldn't tell me. Her Bismarck, it was a mystery.'
'Yes, it's a mystery, really a mystery! . . .'
'Bismarck . . . it's a mystery, Bismarck, he is a marvel,' . . .
'Yes, he is a marvel,' . . .
'Is he really a marvel?' . . .
'Certainly!' . . .
'However, he isn't a king . . . he was only a chancellor.'
'What's a chancellor?' (French and German) (558, explanatory note for 238)

The reprisal of Bismarck's mysterious nature recalls another important moment of vacillation in Lawrence's work, in the poem 'Fish', originally published in 1922 and reprinted in 1923. There, the narrator moves from a posture of envying the fish's vibrancy, to instances of trite anthropomorphism, to an ending posture of awed ignorance. In the poem, the narrator announces toward the ending segments, 'I left off hailing him' (Lawrence 1923e: 292, l. 108). As I have suggested elsewhere, this occasion of humility involves the relinquishing of humanist mastery and autonomy, so that the poem ends by destabilising the conventional ways in which human knowledge and cognition supersede non-human forms of being and knowing.[5]

On the other hand, the rabbit's alignment with the historical Otto von Bismarck, Prince of Bismarck, Duke of Lauenburg, humanises this creature in a highly authoritative way. A conservative Prussian statesman who dominated German and European affairs from the 1860s until 1890, he was the first Chancellor of the German Empire between 1871 and 1890. And so, there is a clear tension between the mysterious alterity of the rabbit and its namesake's role as a highly decorated and powerful political figure. This tension, however, is not unusual in Lawrence. Again, his work often invokes conflicted and ambivalent views of animal power and human relations to that power. The particularity of the designation chancellor is also interesting for the question of animal authority: when Winifred asks Gerald what a chancellor is, he replies a 'sort of judge' (238).

The rabbit's power and authority, his ability to make 'judgements' on some level, are very much at issue throughout the chapter. Winifred, in her 'childish' wisdom, suggests to Gudrun that they ought to leave the rabbit in its hutch and draw him 'listening'; 'he listens with so much of himself,' she notes, a powerful suggestion around this creature's authority (239). But Gudrun wants to bring the rabbit out and asks if they can remove him from his hutch. Winifred warns her, he is 'very strong. He really is *extremely* strong' and the child looks at Gudrun 'in an odd calculating mistrust' (239; emphasis in original). Note here the child's suspicion of human motives and the implied faith in nonhuman powers. Yet Winifred's own desires to control Bismarck also flicker in and out of this chapter. As is usually the case in Lawrence's work, no character is 'clean' in any discourse. With another warning about his fearful kicking, they unlock the door and the 'rabbit exploded in a wild rush round the hutch' (240). And here, in anticipation of the writing to come, Winifred exclaims, 'He scratches most *awfully* sometimes' (240: 5; emphasis added).

The next few lines trace a kind of sadistic insistence inherent in the human characters' desires to control the rabbit for their own ends. By delaying the dangerous encounter with Bismarck for several sentences, and by emphasising the dispositions of the two female characters, the novel makes it clear that the authoritative creature ought really to be left alone:

> Winifred looked up at Gudrun with some misgiving in her wild excitement. Gudrun smiled sardonically with her mouth. Winifred made a strange crooning noise of unaccountable excitement. . . . 'Shall we take him now?' she whispered excitedly, mysteriously, looking up at Gudrun and edging very close. 'Shall we get him now?' –She chuckled wickedly to herself. (240)

There is a distinct linkage between 'mysterious' childhood and animality in the text, but there also seems a linkage here between the wickedness of seizing a resistant animal – an actual nonhuman animal – and the 'unaccountable excitement' of initiating an instance of writing, authoring or representing.

The energetic response of the rabbit to being seized by Gudrun is rendered in great and intensive detail by Lawrence:

> Gudrun thrust in her arm and seized the great, lusty rabbit as it crouched still, she grasped its long ears. It set its four feet flat, and thrust back. There was a long scraping sound as it was hauled forward, and in another instant it was in mid-air, lunging wildly, its body flying like a spring coiled and released, as it lashed out, suspended from the ears. Gudrun held the black-and-white tempest at arms' length, averting her face. But the rabbit was magically strong, it was all she could do to keep her grasp. She almost lost her presence of mind. (240)

I want to suggest that we might read this description as rendering the forces of writing or proto-writing, in a very Derridean sense, wherein an arche-materiality or technicity/prosthetics of language systems precedes speech and writing.[6] We can frame the rabbit's 'madness', its bodily lunging and wild lashing out, as signalling the primordial pan-creatural bid and struggle to write, the creatural attempt to authorise an idea or a text of some kind. This moment can also be read as registering the violence inherent in all acts of writing.

As Gudrun loses her presence of mind while grasping the lunging rabbit, Winifred describes the creature in this way: 'Bismarck, Bismarck, you are behaving *terribly* . . . Oh do put him down, he's *beastly*' (240; second emphasis added). If we stay with the Derridean framework that scholars such as Cary Wolfe privilege, we might say the terrible, beastly experience hints at 'our subjection to and constitution in the materiality and technicity of a language that is always on the scene before we are, as a precondition of our subjectivity' (Wolfe 2010: 89). Note also that the redressing of the rabbit's behaviour is mixed with the implied reprimand of human intervention: 'Oh do put him down.'

Just after this moment, we have the first overt image of what I am calling animal writing or authorship in the novel.

> [Gudrun] stood for a moment astounded by the thunder-storm that had sprung into being in her grip. Then her colour came up, a heavy rage came over her like a cloud. She stood shaken as a house in a storm, and utterly overcome. Her heart was arrested with fury at the mindlessness and the bestial stupidity of this struggle, *her wrists were badly scored by the claws of the beast*, a heavy cruelty welled up in her. (240; emphasis added)

If writing, like other forms of art-making, must also be understood as having its origins in the becoming-aesthetic of all living creatures, and if modernism is particularly 'beastly' in its attentions to human and nonhuman evolutionary and affective linkages, this scene might be read as one of literature's high-voltage descriptions of the dangerous, territorial becoming-other of all creatures in their moments of creative marking.

What might it mean to read this instance of scratching and scoring as an example of writing, authorship or literacy that is animal or creatural in nature? The rabbit scrawls out a text on the arm of a human, writing in claw and blood. This interpretation surely reverberates in profound ways with Lawrence's own investment in his concept of blood-consciousness, the vital instinctual 'knowledge' or bodily unconscious that he theorised in his books *Psychoanalysis and the Unconscious* (1923a) and *Fantasia of the Unconscious* (1923b), as a challenge to Freudian views. In this connection, the work of Bess Van Asselt on cutting as a form of literacy among queer of colour youth provides an insight into how we might further construe the question of animal agency in such instances of authorising. I want to tread as carefully as possible here, while using this analogy, since cutting as a practice is upsetting, controversial, harmful and self-destructive. I am not suggesting a simplified concurrence of practices; nor am I intending to animalise the often marginalised individuals that Van Asselt considers in her discussion. And thus, it may be that this analogy itself is controversial, on some level. The meanings of cutting practices, however, can provide some useful frameworks for thinking about authorship in the present context, as long as we are very clear about the ethical complexities involved in making such a comparison. Van Asselt emphasises the 'tearing and healing' of skin in tattooing and cutting as related to agency, narrative, and storytelling (81). According to Van Asselt, tattoos are considered a validated form of bodily modification in the field of psychology, counting as artefactual literacy. But she argues that no one has framed cutting as literacy, despite its similarity to the act and process of tattooing:

> While the two acts are not completely aligned, it is worthwhile to understand that viewing the manipulation of the flesh as a text pushes us to see and hear a different story told by marginalized queer and trans*+ youth of color. (81)

One important overlapping question around these concerns (human cutting, animal writing) is the question of agency. Van Asselt suggests that when queer of colour youth cut themselves, and one another, 'they can make sense of their world and change their world, if only for a moment' (79). This claim has potential resonances with the question of Bismarck's agency and power in Lawrence's scenes. Certainly, this rabbit *makes his impression* upon the humans who attempt to control him; he changes his world, if only for a moment. Residually, the implied question of physical scarring from an animal swipe in Lawrence's chapter raises the spectre of a permanent reminder of animal 'authorship', written on the body of a human, a permanent reminder of animals' attempts to change their worlds, to turn the angle of a narrative at any given moment. Scarring might also raise the question of legibility in complex ways, in thinking about animal writing and authorship.[7]

The power of this particular animal is something that Lawrence returns to again and again in his own characteristic repetitive and incantatory prose: 'The rabbit made itself into a ball in the air, and lashed out, flinging itself into a bow. It really seemed demoniacal. Gudrun saw Gerald's body tighten, saw a sharp blindness come into his eyes' (241). The image of a bow aligns with many classic images of the pen and sword, the writing implement as powerful, as weapon (and we should continue to acknowledge the fraught complexity of these masculinist images of writing and power). If writing is *carving out* some space of territory, some territory of meaning, then once more, it is difficult to talk about writing without talking about power and force. Gerald's response to the rabbit becoming-bow – 'I know these beggars of old' (241) – is perhaps, among other things, an acknowledgement of the ancient creatural desire to be an agent, to have some capacity to mark, trace, make an impression. This desire is inherently territorial and thus inherently proprietary, and even antagonistic, to some degree. Again, the 'madness' of these desires is distinctly rendered by descriptors like 'demoniacal'.

Lawrence continues to use images of animal power as he writes about Gerald's confrontation with the rabbit:

> The long, demon-like beast lashed out again, spread on the air as if it were flying, looking something like a dragon, then closing up again, inconceivably powerful and explosive. The man's body, strung to its efforts, vibrated strongly. Then a sudden sharp, white-edged wrath came up in him. Swift as lightning he drew back and brought his free hand down like a hawk on the neck of the rabbit. Simultaneously, there came the unearthly, abhorrent scream of a rabbit in the fear of death. It made one immense *writhe*, tore his wrists and his sleeves in a final convulsion, all its belly flashed white in a whirlwind of paws, and then he had slung it round and had it under his arm, fast. It cowered and skulked. His face was gleaming with a smile. (241; emphasis added)

Here we have strike two: Bismarck makes his mark on another human, and the term 'writhe' suggests a kind of embodied cursive or script that the rabbit performatively scrolls into the human's flesh-canvas. Gerald comments to Gudrun, 'You wouldn't think there was all that force in a rabbit' (241). This particular moment plainly has erotic connotations, as the subterranean and 'obscene' (242) connection between the two lovers is sealed or sanctioned by the rabbit's marks. But when Gudrun looks 'unearthly' and when the 'scream of the rabbit, after the violent tussle, seemed to have torn the veil of her consciousness', we can also read the violent tear as that of the work of writing.

There is something about the simultaneity and temporality of the rabbit's scoring that resonates with Roland Barthes's discussion of the modern scriptor, who is

> born simultaneously with the text, is in no way equipped with a being preceding or exceeding the writing, is not the subject of the book as predicate; there is no other time than that of the enunciation and every text is eternally written *here* and *now*' (Barthes 1968: 1324; emphasis in original)

The rabbit's writhing immediacy, the flashing 'white' belly in a whirl of paws that scratch and tear both flesh and cloth: these images evoke the simultaneity of Barthes's scriptor, as opposed to the pre-existing 'author' or 'Author-God' who holds a premeditated meaning in the mind (Barthes 1968: 1324).

I want to continue with a sort of dogged use of Barthes, for a bit longer. Barthes employs the image of *tissue* several times in his classic discussion of authorship, saying the 'text is a tissue of quotations' (Barthes 1968: 1324), the book itself only a 'tissue of signs' (Barthes 1968: 1325). The black and white Bismarck literalises Barthes's tissue of signs as he tears and marks the fleshy tissue of other living beings. Provocatively, perhaps, I propose that the rabbit Bismarck is also shown to undergo what Barthes calls the death of the author, the title of his famous 1968 essay that elevates writing or language itself above the prestige, interiority and 'genius' of the venerated Author. Once Gerald quells the rabbit's power, the chapter continues as such:

> 'He shouldn't be so silly, when he has to be taken out' Winifred was saying, putting out her hand and touching the rabbit tentatively, as it skulked under his arm, motionless as if it were dead. 'He's not dead, is he Gerald?' she asked. 'No, he ought to be,' he said. 'Yes, he ought!' cried the child with a sudden flash of amusement. (241)

Barthes suggests that 'Writing is that neutral, composite, oblique space where our subject slips away, the negative where all identity is lost, starting with the very identity of the body writing' (Barthes 1968: 1322). And, more famously:

> As soon as a fact is narrated no longer with a view to acting directly on reality but intransitively, that is to say, finally outside of any function other than that of the very practice of the symbol itself, this disconnection occurs, the voice loses its origin, the author enters into his own death, writing begins. (Barthes 1968: 1322)

Moreover, Foucault has famously elaborated upon Barthes's ideas, noting that:

> Writing is now linked to sacrifice and to the sacrifice of life itself; it is a voluntary obliteration of the self . . . Where [in the past] a work had the duty of creating immortality, it now attains the right to kill, to become the murderer of its author. (Foucault 1969: 1477)

There is something uncanny about the judge-like Bismarck, a rabbit, being rendered as if dead just after his own moment of potent and profound scoring and marking.

The powers of animal scoring and jabbing are further rehearsed by Lawrence in the poetry of *Birds, Beasts, and Flowers* (1923). In particular, 'Humming-Bird' presents a fantasy of a primordial humming-bird

in some other world
Primeval-dumb, far back
In that most awful stillness
that only gasped and hummed,
Humming-birds raced down the avenues. (Lawrence 1923c: 323, ll. 1–4)[8]

The use of the term 'awful' in this poem resonates with the most awful scratching of Bismarck, and with Winnie's repeated descriptions of that creature as awful. The lines that immediately follow these opening descriptions are of interest because they productively align with current vital materialisms, to some degree.[9] That is, these lines challenge the traditional view of matter as inanimate:

Before anything had a soul,
While life was a heave of Matter, half inanimate,
This little bit chipped off in brilliance
And went whizzing through the slow, vast, succulent
Stems. (324, ll. 5–8)

The first line here (line six of the poem), with its use of 'anything' instead of 'anyone', points to Lawrence's entangled animism, his more-than-human understanding of spirit and soul, which is evident in this often-cited excerpt from his last book, a work of nonfiction called *Apocalypse*:

That I am part of the earth my feet know perfectly, and my blood is part of the sea. My soul knows that I am part of the human race, my soul is an organic part of the great human soul, as my spirit is part of my nation. In my own very self, I am part of my family. There is nothing of me that is alone and absolute except my mind, and we shall find that the mind has no existence by itself, it is only the glitter of the sun on the surface of the waters.

So that my individualism is really an illusion. I am part of the great whole, and I can never escape . . . (Lawrence 1932: 149)

The poem continues to elucidate the hummingbird's tracing/writing:

I believe there were no flowers, then,
In the world where the humming-bird flashed ahead of creation.
I believe he pierced the slow vegetable veins with his long beak.
(324, ll. 9–11)

This description calls to mind the Derridean framework referenced throughout this discussion, in which an arche-materiality or technicity is understood to be that which all living creatures are subjected to, a primary or primordial system of communication that is prosthetic in nature.[10] Reading the beak as a form of non-handed handiness, as an outward exteriorising implement or writing 'tool' that triggers the tracing and iterability at the heart of writing seems productive in this case.[11] Lawrence's stark line 'Probably he was a jabbing, terrifying monster' (324, l. 14) further rehearses, in relation to the hummingbird, the awful carving, tearing violences that he centres in Bismarck's demonic, dragon-like scribing.

Ultimately, I am offering a kind of slant bioaesthetic interpretation of writing and authorship in Lawrence's work, as the blossoming, embodied eroticism of Gerald and Gudrun is scored and underscored by a sanctioning rabbit. The highly self-reflexive framework of artistically rendering Looloo and Bismarck in a sketching tutorial, with a child and a sculptor of animals, provides a potent commentary on aesthetic animals who authorise, mark and write. Moreover, the privileged textual example of the rabbit's scoring and marking showcases his making an impression deeply, in a bloody and demoniacal manner that results in a death of sorts. We can see this scene – akin to the monstrous jabbing of the hummingbird – as Lawrence's perhaps unwitting reflection on the creatural excess, agony, self-obliteration and self-othering at the heart of all writing, all writing by animals and human animals, too.

Works Cited

Barthes, Roland. 2010 [1968]. 'The Death of the Author'. In *The Norton Anthology of Theory and Criticism*. Second Edition. Ed. Vincent B. Leitch, William E. Cain, Laurie A. Finke, Barbara E. Johnson and John McGowan, 1322–6. New York: Norton.

Bennett, Jane. 2010. *Vibrant Matter: A Political Ecology of Things*. Durham, NC: Duke University Press.

Coole, Diana and Samantha Frost, eds. 2010. *New Materialisms: Ontology Agency, and Politics*. Durham, NC: Duke University Press.

Deleuze, Gilles and Félix Guattari. 1987. *A Thousand Plateaus: Capitalism and Schizophrenia*. Trans. Brian Massumi. Minneapolis: University of Minnesota Press.

Driscoll, Kári and Eva Hoffman. 2018. *What is Zoopoetics? Texts, Bodies, Entanglement*. New York: Palgrave MacMillan.

Foucault, Michel. 2010 [1969]. 'What is an Author?' In *The Norton Anthology of Theory and Criticism*. Second Edition. Ed. Vincent B. Leitch, William E. Cain, Laurie A. Finke, Barbara E. Johnson and John McGowan, 1475–90. New York: Norton.

Grosz, Elizabeth. 2008. *Chaos, Territory, Art: Deleuze and the Framing of the Earth*. New York: Columbia University Press.

Lawrence, D. H. 1987 [1920]. *Women in Love*. In *The Works of D. H. Lawrence*. Ed. David Farmer, John Worthen and Lindeth Vasey. Cambridge: Cambridge University Press.

Lawrence, D. H. 2004 [1923a]. *Psychoanalysis and the Unconscious*. In *Psychoanalysis and the Unconscious and Fantasia of the Unconscious*. Ed. Bruce Steele. Cambridge: Cambridge University Press.

Lawrence, D. H. 2004 [1923b]. *Fantasia of the Unconscious*. In *Psychoanalysis and the Unconscious and Fantasia of the Unconscious*. Ed. Bruce Steele. Cambridge: Cambridge University Press.

Lawrence, D. H. 2013 [1923c]. 'Hummingbird'. In *The Poems*. Vol. 1. *The Works of D. H. Lawrence*. Ed. Christopher Pollnitz. Cambridge: Cambridge University Press.

Lawrence, D. H. 2013 [1923d]. 'Snake'. In *The Poems*. Vol. 1. *The Works of D. H. Lawrence*. Ed. Christopher Pollnitz. Cambridge: Cambridge University Press.

Lawrence, D. H. 2013 [1923e]. 'Fish'. In *The Poems*. Vol. 1. *The Works of D. H. Lawrence*. Ed. Christopher Pollnitz. Cambridge: Cambridge University Press.

Lawrence, D. H. 1980 [1932]. *Apocalypse and the Writings on Revelation*. Ed. Mara Kalnins. Cambridge: Cambridge University Press.

Morton, Timothy. (2010). 'Guest Column: Queer Ecology'. *PMLA* 125.2: 273–82.

Rohman, Carrie. 2009. *Stalking the Subject: Modernism and the Animal*. New York: Columbia.

Rohman, Carrie. 2014. 'No Higher Life: Bio-aesthetics in J. M. Coetzee's *Disgrace*'. *Modern Fiction Studies* 60.3: 562–78.

Rohman, Carrie. 2018. *Choreographies of the Living: Bioaesthetics in Literature, Art, and Performance*. New York: Oxford University Press.

Ryan, Derek. 2015. 'Following Snakes and Moths: Modernist Ethics and Posthumanism'. *Twentieth Century Literature* 61.3 (September): 287–304.

Thacker, Eugene. 2010. *After Life*. Chicago: University of Chicago Press.

Van Asselt, Bess Collins. 2022. 'Cutting as a Literacy Practice: Exploring the Fractured Body, Desire, and Rage through Queer and Trans*+ Youth Embodiments'. *Taboo: The Journal of Culture and Education*. 21.1: 74–98.

Wolfe, Cary. 2010. *What is Posthumanism?* Minneapolis: University of Minnesota Press.

Wolfe, Cary. 2013. *Before the Law: Humans and Other Animals in a Biopolitical Frame*. Chicago: University of Chicago Press.

Notes

1. See Rohman, *Choreographies of the Living: Bioaesthetics in Literature, Art, and Performance* (2018). I first used the term *bioaesthetic* in a 2014 publication to signal a cross-species concept of the aesthetic impulse (Rohman 2014: 562–78). My usage of this term counters trends in 'neuroaesthetics' that regard all artistic capacities as exclusively human.
2. For important work on zoopoetic readings of literature, see Driscoll and Hoffmann (2018).
3. See Rohman (2018: 57–62).
4. See Chapters 3 and 4 of Rohman (2009) for an extended discussion of Lawrence's species discourses. See also Derek Ryan (2015).
5. See Rohman (2009: 91–9).
6. See Cary Wolfe, who discusses the trans-species subjection to an 'arche-materiality' that is the basis for living beings to 'engage in communication and social relations at all' (Wolfe 2013: 63), and his discussions of 'the radically ahuman character of what Heidegger called Dasein in relation to technicity and temporality . . . that in no way can be rigorously reserved for the "human"' (74).
7. I want to thank Peter Adkins for suggesting the question of legibility in relation to this work.
8. See also my discussion of the 'dumb' in Lawrence's poem 'Tortoise Shout', as this concept relates to questions of creatural 'intelligence' (Rohman 2018: 44–5).

9. For work in this subfield see, for instance, Jane Bennett, *Vibrant Matter: A Political Ecology of Things* (2010); Eugene Thacker, *After Life* (2010); Timothy Morton, 'Guest Column: Queer Ecology' (2010); and Diana Coole and Samantha Frost, *New Materialisms: Ontology Agency, and Politics* (2010).
10. For a helpful discussion of these prosthetic qualities, see Wolfe (2013: 73–86).
11. I have made related claims about the beak and the signature in Merce Cunningham's animal drawings; see Rohman (2018: Ch. 5).

5

FOLLOWING THE BEAST FAMILIAR: DJUNA BARNES'S FAMILY DRAMAS

Peter Adkins

The unsigned reader report for Djuna Barnes's three-act play, *Biography of Julie van Bartmann*, strikes a note of hesitant praise that would become all too familiar to the author when dealing with publishers and editors in the coming decades:

> This play contains some of the most vigorous and pungent writing that has come to my attention in some time. [. . .] I do not claim to be able to state clearly the theme and the plot of this play. [. . .] The play would be perplexing to an audience, but for the reader it has many stimulating qualities in the midst of a little that is confusing. (Barnes 1924: n.p.)

An 'eloquent and revealing commentary on the more passionate zone of life' (Barnes 1924: n.p.), the play presents the narrative of a world-famous opera singer, Julie van Bartmann, paying a visit to a small American farmstead run by an eccentric and visionary farmer named Basil Born, along with his children Gart, Gustava and Costa. Despite the mixture of admiration and ambivalence in the reader's report, the play was neither published nor performed in Barnes's lifetime. Her first novel, *Ryder* (1928), also set on a farm under the rule of an unconventional patriarch, Wendell Ryder, recycled material from *Biography of Julie van Bartmann* and garnered a similar mixed reception. When her editor at Boni and Liveright, Donald S. Friede, read it, he complained that he 'did not like it half as much as [he had] expected to', voicing his disapproval of its collage of literary 'effects' and fearing that it might be 'the type of book whose sale is purely problematical' (Friede 1927: n.p.). And when, in the 1950s, Barnes once again mined material from her childhood to be reimagined within her drama *The Antiphon*, T. S. Eliot continued the trend. On receiving a typescript of the play in 1954, he explained that he was struggling to comprehend both its language and its plot, and felt it to be extremely obscure.[1] The initial blurb that Eliot wrote for the play ahead of its publication by Faber and Faber in 1958 would reiterate the backhanded compliments of the unsigned reader report for her earlier attempt at a three-act drama, describing it as 'shocking' but 'tedious' and warning potential readers that they 'will not understand it' (quoted in Herring 1996: 276). *The Antiphon*, Eliot suggested, in a sentence that was cut but which has unfortunately stuck, demonstrates the work of a writer for whom 'so much genius [has] been combined with so little talent' (quoted in Herring 1996: 276).[2]

This chapter argues that the responses elicited by these three texts, all of which refashion events from Barnes's unusual upbringing, point to a distinctly beastly literary style. This is beastliness understood as a textual sensibility, in which formal innovation and linguistic experimentation challenge received ideas of animality, human identity and familial relations. As Margot Norris observes in *Beasts of the Modern Imagination*, writers at the turn of the twentieth century, influenced by evolutionary and psychoanalytic discoveries, became interested in developing a form of literature in which they could write 'with their animality speaking' (Norris 1985: 1). And as I have argued elsewhere, Barnes developed a beastly idiom over the course of her writerly life, with her repeated and multiple use of beastly tropes creating a rich textual aesthetic in which beastliness becomes a way of challenging both anthropocentric and androcentric configurations of the human (Adkins 2022: 89–117). Daniela Caselli has also pointed to the way in which Barnes was preoccupied with a literary history of beastly figures, from medieval bestiaries to John Donne and W. B. Yeats (Caselli 2009: 179). Similarly, Bonnie Kime Scott, in a groundbreaking work on Barnes and other female modernist writers, has argued that it is precisely through her use of beastly and animal figures that Barnes challenges binary oppositions between human and animal life (Scott 1995: 71–122). Barnes's interest in the beastly foreshadows the rise of animal studies within literary criticism but also resists a straightforward endorsement of trans-species harmony or a legible animal ethics that sometimes is found in such work. Her beasts often carry a negative charge and, as Carrie Rohman has argued, discard a humanist notion of the human for a mode of 'subjectivity as nonidentity' experienced as 'anonymity, self-obliteration, movement and change' (Rohman 2009: 151; 158).[3] Barnes's beasts more often than not work to undo structures and categories, posing problems and difficulties rather than resolving them. Barnes's beastliness is in this sense akin to what Caselli has described as Barnes's 'improper' mode of modernism, a 'poetics of impropriety, which permeates all aspects of her work and her figure as a modernist author' (Caselli 2009: 2).

This chapter examines the way in which a beastly form of writing is central to Barnes's two family dramas, *Biography of Julie van Bartmann* and *The Antiphon*, arguing that these semi-autobiographical works are premised on exploring the 'beast familiar' (Barnes 2000: 176). This turn of phrase, uttered by Miranda in *The Antiphon*, points to the proximity between the human and the beast as well as the importance of the animal to Barnes's reimagining of familial relations. It also, this chapter argues, speaks to the way in which to read across the breadth of Barnes's oeuvre is to encounter moments of beastly familiarity, where repeated lines, scenes and characters present moments of what Julia Taylor describes as self-referential, 'affectively complex' 'linguistic echoes from earlier works' (Taylor 2012: 66). In the same way that scholars now see the ceaseless processes of revision that characterise Barnes's late poetry as integral to an open-ended poetics (Herring 2015), this chapter suggests that the repeated fictionalised retelling of events from her childhood present a similar aesthetic, in which revision and composition are similarly fundamental to a mode of beastly writing.

'The Beast Salutes You!': *Biography of Julie van Bartmann*

Biography of Julie van Bartmann was written by Barnes in late 1923 and early 1924, begun while she was living in Paris and finished in Cagnes-sur-Mer on the French Riviera. Until recently, those who wanted to read the play had to travel to Barnes's archive at the University of Maryland, which houses the typescript.[4] One of Barnes's earliest attempts to write longform narrative, it establishes a *mise-en-scène* that would recur again and again in her later works.[5] Basil Born, visionary yet myopic smallholder, lives with his three children, Gart, Gustava and Costa, enjoying a leisurely life on his farm in rural north-eastern America, where he can practise his personal philosophy of free love while those around him suffer its consequences. The arrival of opera singer Julie van Bartmann, famous for both her talent and her reputed lasciviousness, and invited by Basil to the farm with the hope that she might perform a private concert for him, is the catalyst for the Born children to see through their father's self-serving ideology. The play ends with Gart shooting his father with a pistol off-stage. Yet, Basil, as his daughter Gustava fears, 'cannot die' and staggers back on to the stage for the final extended speech of the drama, exclaiming to the departing Bartmann that he 'would have honoured you like a man' but now can only acknowledge her as an injured 'beast' (Barnes 2020: 89, 95).

In many respects, the play looks ahead to the publication of Barnes's first novel, *Ryder*, with Wendell Ryder being a clear refashioning of Basil Born, and there are a number of textual parallels between the two narratives. The scene in *Ryder* where the local education authorities arrive to demand that the Ryder children attend school first occurs as a speech in the play (2020: 23–6), while just as the polygamous Ryder sets his wives to work in the pigeon loft, the widowed Basil obliges Gustava to undertake the same duties. Indeed, Basil uses the exact same phrase in relation to Gustava that Barnes will have Wendell make of his daughter, Julie Ryder, describing how she will be like 'her mother' in that she will 'eat, function, die, looking neither backward nor forward' (2020: 31).[6] Basil, like Wendell Ryder, locates his daughter within a personal philosophy in which sexual freedom is equated with fecundity and procreation. A distorted amalgamation of transcendentalism and Darwinian evolution, it places human life within a continuum of animal sexuality, in which, rather than overturning patriarchal power, loosened sexual mores enable the proliferation and deepening of patrilineal genealogies. Importantly, in these shared aspects, *Julie van Bartmann* does not just look ahead to Barnes's later works, but back to her childhood experiences of family life as dictated by the similar philosophies and polygamy of her father, Wald Barnes. Barnes's childhood in rural New York was part-Thoreauvian exercise in self-reliance and part-experiment in a form of socially progressive free living. Barnes's career as a writer was launched under what her biographer Phillip Herring describes as the 'emotional duress' (1996: 41) of having to leave the farm abruptly for New York City when Wald Barnes was threatened with prosecution for bigamy and chose to abandon Barnes's mother.[7] *Julie van Bartmann*, then, stands as an important early example of what Taylor calls a 'non-dichotomous relationship' between 'auto/biography and fiction' in Barnes's writing, where, rather than narrative standing in for autobiography, the text becomes a space for creative retelling and interrogation of personal history (Taylor 2012: 92).

As in many of her subsequent works, *Julie van Bartmann* establishes the linguistic and semantic multivalence of the term beast. Basil Born, like Wendell in *Ryder* and Titus in *The Antiphon*, goes by the name of 'the beast' (2020: 22). A red-haired, short-bodied man, he is associated with an animal vitality and aspires to a masculinity associated with force, strength and butchery. In the opening scene, Basil introduces himself to the newly arrived Julie by describing how he 'kill[s] his own beef' before pickling and smoking it (2020: 29).[8] Scornful of the mannered social conventions of modern life, with 'people in high hats bowing to each other [and] forgetting they have functions' (2020: 86), Basil believes the farmstead presents an environment that he can design according to his principles of animal husbandry, both human and nonhuman, where 'freedom exists in keeping the wood cut, the fire lit [and] the animals productive' (2020: 32). His beastliness, importantly, is not a disavowal of culture, but rather an attempt to marry the natural with the cultural, especially his love of music and the arts. Again, like Wendell, Basil is a figure of vital animality but also artistic sensitivity. The presentation of Basil's two sons, Gart and Costa, his beastly progeny, are figurative of an impossibility to reconcile these two aspects of his identity. Gart, a talented pianist, is presented as a figure of cultural sensitivity who shrinks from the fear that he has 'become abject' under his father's education of 'hid[ing] nothing' (2020: 58). Costa, on the other hand, is presented as barely human, described by Julie as 'a brute, a beast, a beast [who] understands without thought, all the ageless sorrows of simple functions, life, death' (2020: 51) and later as a 'boy with a bull neck and a passion for rape' (2020: 72). These competing aspects of Basil, as symbolised in the schematic presentation of the two sons, represent the irreconcilable contradictions inherent in the concept of beastliness itself. Indeed, this is made explicitly clear in the opening moments of the drama where Gart, playing the piano, engages in a playful *tête-à-tête* with his brother about the art of courtship versus a primitive desire to reproduce, establishing the structural opposition that will motor the play's narrative. As Jacques Derrida observes, the 'beast is not exactly the animal', since it is replete with its own connotations, associations and linguistic history (Derrida 2009: 1). An important part of the semantics of beastliness, Derrida points out, is an internal contradiction around who or what can be properly described as beastly. If *la bête* (the beast) generally designates nonhuman animals, it is notable that the near-sounding and etymologically linked term for stupidity, *bêtise*, cannot apply to them since it implies a transgression and so requires 'regime of propriety' that is, according to a binary understanding of human–animal relations, only found 'in the order of the human'. As such, in French to behave in a beastly (*bête*) way 'no longer refers at all to the essence of the beast' (2009: 138–9). One of the implications of this contradiction is that the more one tries to embrace one's animality, the greater the risk of entrenching one's distance from nonhuman animal life since it will always implicitly uphold the idea of the human from which one is looking to depart. Barnes appears to intuit not only this contradiction in *Julie van Bartmann*, but also the tragic vicissitudes and instabilities it produces, especially in the kind of pseudo-Darwinian transcendentalist philosophies that were circulating in the late nineteenth century of her childhood. It is precisely the hypocrisy of Basil's beastly philosophy that produces the drama's violent denouement, with Gart's rejection of the abject 'devilry' of his father's teaching, in which women are likened to 'beasts in the field', providing the motive for his attempted murder of Basil (2020: 85–6).

Importantly, Basil's animalisation of the women in his life points to a further instability inherent to a notion of beastliness, this time along the fault lines of gender. Gustava is associated with an animalised sexuality throughout the play, described by Basil as 'over fond of the sight of the blood [. . .] simple and great, like a Greek horror' with 'her large pale head' and 'wide-set, uncalculating eyes' (2020: 29). Later, in Act II, Basil will draw upon the analogy of 'prize' livestock 'acquisition' when discussing whether Julie is 'a good woman' with Gart (2020: 60–2). Both moments establish a theme that is returned to in *Ryder* and, most explicitly, in one of the early drafts of *The Antiphon*, where Miranda is described as having been made 'made mutton at sixteen' and offered in 'exchange [. . .] for a goat / With that old farm-hand, Jacobsen' (quoted in Taylor 2012: 43). A further example of what Scott has described as 'a repeated Barnes plot' of 'girls hunted in the field and brought down to earth, to childbed and even death' (1995: 73), the play also offers an insinuation of the most beastly form of sexuality: incest.[9] The opening dialogue on the merits of courtship versus acting on sexual desire, for instance, sees the brothers draw on their sister's virginity for their example of how one should treat female sexuality, while the conversation between Basil and Gart about Julie, in Act II, takes place with father and son having got into bed together at daybreak. Unlike *The Antiphon*, where we find a greater degree of coherence in terms of how power and agency are mapped on to gender and sexuality, *Julie van Bartmann* locates all of its characters within an economy of animalised sexuality that is changeable from one moment to the next. Basil wants to enjoy the fruits of an animal sexuality, while also associating the body and its functions with an abject femininity that he wishes to distance himself from, grasping at distinctions such as while woman is 'monstrous, beautiful, man is active' (2020: 32).

Julie van Bartmann is presented, at least initially, as a figure in the tradition of the *femme fatale*. She is a 'tall handsome woman of thirty-eight dressed in a long trailing gown of saffron, over which is a chinchilla wrap reaching to her feet', at whose 'knee boys have trembled, and girls become hysterical' (2020: 25; 56).[10] Her arrival on the farm is both desired by Basil and a challenge to his authority. A good shot, she goes hunting with him, appropriating both the phallic authority and literal power of the gun. Later, even more explicitly, during a discussion of his shortcomings as a father, Basil will complain that he doesn't like the 'shape of [her] rapier' (2020: 76). Basil is both repulsed by and drawn to this aspect of Julie, confiding to Gart that he finds her all the more 'erotic' and 'beautiful' because she is 'damaged' (2020: 60). Julie as a *femme fatale* occupies a kind of beastly sexuality that Basil lusts for but cannot permit, accusing her of 'com[ing] to destroy' but warning her that 'we shall outlast you' (2020: 31), an assertion not only of Basil as manager of his own farmstead, but of the endurance of his name promised by patrilineal genealogy (the latter of which will become a full-blown obsession in the mind of Wendell Ryder). The play's ending both confirms and complicates Basil's confidence in the family name. Staggering on stage, having been shot, he moves to kiss the hand of Julie but, wounded, 'slips [. . .] and falling on all fours, head lowered, is silent for a long moment' before acquiescing to apparent defeat in his assertion that 'The Beast salutes you!' (2020: 95). A tableau that looks ahead to the endings of *Ryder* and *Nightwood* (1936), which both conclude with protagonists descending to an apparently primitive animality, Basil is reduced to the abject beastliness that he has, until this point, only selectively embraced.

Basil's philosophy of animal vitality, free love and procreation is beastly exactly because it relies on abjecting that which it cannot assimilate within the anthropocentric patrilineal genealogy of which it refuses to let go. The play's tragedy, thus, comes not from Gart's attempted assassination of his father, but from the fact that, despite the intervention of Julie, who is the catalyst for the children to rise up against their father, the family name persists (this will also become a prominent theme in *Ryder*, articulated even in its title). Gustava, speaking 'quietly, almost dully' to Julie after her father's animal descent, tells her: 'Go, go, it is all over. You see what he has managed – accomplished. Go, go, take everything and go. You see yourself – we are reunited – we need nothing – it is all finished – settled –' (2020: 95). As Gustava's sentiment suggests, Basil's descent, ambiguous as it is, holds the potential to signify not defeat but rather a reconciliation of animality with abjection in a fashion that he could not previously achieve. Taking on the name of 'The Beast', Julie's arrival has not displaced Basil's authority but transformed and deepened it.

'A Beastly Brawl in Nature': *The Antiphon*

Barnes's final drama, *The Antiphon*, written three decades after *Biography of Julie van Bartmann*, further develops the beastly idiom we find in her earlier three-act play, while also departing from it in significant respects.[11] The action has moved from rural New York in the early twentieth century to the ruins of Burley Hall in Rutland, England, during 'the war of 1939' (2000: 6), where, on the pretext of a family reunion, the Burley Hobbs family have gathered. Unlike in *Julie van Bartmann* or *Ryder*, however, the patriarch of the family, Titus Hobbs, cut from the same cloth as Basil and Wendell, is present only in his absence.[12] And while the legacy of Titus's actions and ideas continues to propel the events of the narrative, his widow, Augusta, and daughter, Miranda, are afforded more prominent voices in the story being told than the female figures of Barnes's earlier family narratives.[13] *The Antiphon* also differs from Barnes's earlier play in form. A drama written in blank verse, with characters whose names carry clear Shakespearean allusions, and utilising an archaic form of English that also looks back to early modern dramatists, the play eschews the modernist take on melodrama of *Julie van Bartmann* for what Meryl Altman describes as a narrative of 'symbolic intensity' (1991: 272), in which sense is often obscure and requires the active attention and participation of the audience or reader.

One of the central symbols in this family drama is a 'beast-box' (2000: 144), a doll's house first mentioned in Act I and brought on stage at the climax of Act II. Presenting the family history in miniature, Augusta, Titus's widow, discovers the house to contain a doll resembling him, seven of his mistresses and the stick he used to beat her. The only thing missing is the 'stallion yard', or bull's penis, of which he was so proud that 'He asked to be but laid aside it in the grave' (2000: 145), aligning Titus with an animalised phallic symbolism much like his literary predecessors. Pressing her eye against the miniaturised 'cock-loft', however, Augusta 'recoil[s]' in horror at an image of the 'profaned monstrance' of a reconstruction of the rape of Miranda, her daughter, overseen by Titus (2000: 148–50). Miranda's brother Jeremy, wearing the disguise of a coachman and going by the name of Jack Blow, has orchestrated this moment, explaining that the scene in miniature shows her daughter 'not yet seventeen / Thrown to a travelling Cockney thrice her age' (2000: 144). Miranda, he continues, acted 'like the ewe' in not fighting but offering 'up her silly throat for slashing' and making 'that doll's *abattoir* a babe's bordel' (2000: 151). The beast-box, elsewhere referred to as 'Hobb's Ark' (2000: 144), is beastly not only because of what it contains but also because it is, in its stature, a synecdoche for the drama itself. This family drama in miniature, which compels the characters to peer in voyeuristically through the invisible fourth wall, becomes a symbol of the beastly acts of witness and complicity inherent to drama itself and which, as Alex Goody has argued, Barnes is self-reflexively exploring in the play (Goody 2014: 359).

The doll's house is but one of several beastly symbols in the drama that operate at a linguistic, thematic and formal level, which, combined, allow Barnes not only to tell the tragedy of the Burley Hobbs family, but to examine what it means to be a writer with a beastly preoccupation with telling this same family drama over and over. Importantly, these beastly tropes do not combine to make a harmonious or stable system of signification, but, like the set of Burley Hall, remain a 'horrid wrack' of fragments that threaten to topple down upon one another at any given moment (2000: 54). Burley Hall, a location that resembles a 'beastly brawl in nature' (2000: 30), where 'standing before a paneless Gothic window [is] a dressmaker's dummy, in regimentals, surrounded by music stands, horns, fiddles, guncases, bandboxes, masks, toys and broken statues, man and beast' (2000: 7), like the doll's house, is a space that invites reflection on the past and the remnants of it which are carried into the present. It is no longer the actions of the patriarch in themselves that are the focus of the narrative, but rather the trauma he has inflicted, and through which his surviving family members are working. As in *Julie van Bartmann* and *Ryder*, a key aspect of this trauma is a distorted Darwinism that animalises human sexuality. Augusta draws on an image of animalistic engorgement when describing how at Titus's 'rough unbridled head [she] dwined [*sic*] / At his fast leisure', later adding that Titus believed 'he was the stud to breed a kingdom' (2000: 108). The correlative to this is – as Dudley, her son, brutally jokes – that when, in Titus's eyes, she resembled an 'Old barren ox', no longer fit to produce young, and therefore milk, she was cut loose and abandoned (2000: 97). A similar rhetoric of livestock and slaughter is used to frame Miranda's upbringing, in which she was the 'loved' 'lamb' until 'she turned to mutton' (2000: 98), a reference to her rape, which, her mother and brothers imply, soured her unfairly against them.

As I briefly noted in the previous section, Barnes revised the description of Miranda's assault several times, with the earlier, more explicit drafts more clearly framing her attack through the language of animal slaughter. In one version, Titus is described having

> Hauled her in a hay-hook to the barn
> Left her dangling, while in the field below
> He offered to give her, to the farm-hand, for a goat, —
> You know, I've seen heifers dangling from an halter
> Just like that, while he charged the rape blade in. (Quoted in Curry 1991: 291)

This excised speech is spoken by Dudley, who, along with his brother Elisha, taunt and torment their mother and sister over the course of the play. If Costa and Gart in *Julie van Bartmann* are presented schematically, each representing one aspect of their father's split personality, standing for the bestial and the sublimated respectively, Dudley and Elisha are more complex in *The Antiphon*, although no less figurative. Central to their complexity is the degree to which, like Titus, they occupy an uneasy relation between an anthropocentric patriarchal authority and a wish to acknowledge their animal desires. While outwardly they appear more conventional their than father, Dudley is an 'executive, heavily set', who arrives on stage 'chewing a cigar', while Elisha is 'younger and on the smarter side' (2000: 29), like Miranda and Augusta, they carry the trauma of their childhood with them. Dudley, in one of his first lines of dialogue, states: 'if I saw myself, backward, in the mirror, / I am not so sure what sort of beast I'd see' (2000: 32). Here, as in *Julie van Bartmann*, there is an uneasy acknowledgement of a family resemblance to their father and, if not an ambivalent desire to continue his legacy, then, at the least, a sense that they cannot entirely free themselves of it.

As such when, in one of the play's central moments of drama, the brothers emulate their father in a sexualised attack on their mother and sister, it is significant that they don animal masks, with Dudley taking on the appearance of a pig and Elisha an ass. Aligning themselves with animals that have specific cultural connotations of beastliness, insofar as the former is associated with excess and the latter with stupidity, it stands as an act of dissimulation that sanctions their actions and insists on a separation between this beastly act and their true selves.[14] With Elisha forcing Miranda on to her 'four feet' with her 'rump' in the air – declared by Dudley to be her 'best position' – while Dudley 'makes darting motions' at Augusta with a whip (recalling the 'rape blade' used against Miranda in the excised version of her assault) (1998: 176), the masked brothers not only re-enact scenes likely witnessed in childhood but punish the childless Miranda for transgressing their father's philosophy of animal procreation.[15] Immediately prior to the attack, Dudley has decried the 'depopulation in [Miranda's] yaw' (2000: 135), while moments later, Elisha, holding Miranda down, angrily denounces her 'starving puss' (2000: 140), suggesting not only an unhealed, weeping wound but a crude framing of both her perceived promiscuity and her childlessness. Calling her a 'Manless, childless, safeless document', Elisha taunts his sister that despite her 'rank continence to stay / The generations', he intends to 'staff' her (2000: 141).

It is significant that Barnes suggests the failure of the animal masks to provide the brothers with a sense of absolution for their actions or to safely distance their beastly aspects from their human identities. Despite the two men being masked, the stage directions call for it to be clear that Elisha is 'weeping as he mauls [Miranda]' (2000: 141). As Julie Taylor has argued, this stage direction points to the 'complexity of emotions' in the scene, insisting that the roles of victim and perpetrator are not distinct or oppositional since it implies that the brothers are also 'victims of Titus's abuse' (Taylor 2012: 64). Although it is clear where the audience's sympathy should lie in what is the play's most disturbing scene, it is also a moment when we are confronted with the destructive inheritance of their father's beastly philosophy for his sons, as well as his daughter and wife. The beastly currency of these particular animal masks are key here, insofar as they offer a visual metaphor for what was Titus's (and Basil's and Wendell's) desire to be simultaneously at one with an animal identity and to enjoy the autonomy of choosing when to remove this identity in favour of the sovereignty of a male, human authority. Here Barnes's authorial decisions are again ahead of contemporary work on beastliness within the field of animal studies. Derrida singles out Titus Hobbs's namesake, Thomas Hobbes, as one of the architects of modernity's configuration of sovereignty in which the sovereign asserts his power by means of a claim to natural authority, placing himself above the law: a move which insists on his male, human priority but also creates a 'troubling resemblance' between sovereign and beast (Derrida 2009: 17). Both are 'outside the law' by way of a claim to their place within the order of divine creation, which means they 'strangely resemble each other while seeming to be situated at the antipodes' (2009: 17). As Jacques de Ville notes, Derrida here points to the way in which figures such as Hobbes, in their construction of modern philosophy, chased 'after animals to make them flee, to forget them, to repress them, but at the same time also to capture and domesticate them' (de Ville 2012: 359). While Basil, Wendell and Titus all take the diametrically opposite tack, chasing after the beast so as to better shore up their sense of patriarchal sovereignty, Barnes nonetheless foreshadows Derrida's 'attempt to establish the "law" of this contradiction' (de Ville 2012: 359) at the heart of a certain type of beastly masculinity.

This contradiction, or dividedness, is captured tropologically in one of *The Antiphon*'s central visual set pieces: the two halves of a Gryphon carousel car that are positioned at 'either end' of 'a long table' on stage (2000: 7). This fairground representation of a mythical half-eagle, half-lion stands as a split figure that literally frames the drama.[16] One the one hand, it serves as a visual metaphor for the inability of Titus, or his progeny, to reconcile the contradictions inherent in adopting a beastly identity and their impossible desire for an idea of human animality based on sovereignty (Titus is said to have been responsible for its having been 'sawed' in half [2000: 108]). On the other hand, it gestures towards the ever-fragmenting, unstable beastly idioms that Barnes herself was aware had become more and more fractured over the course of her writing. The gryphon also takes on an important dramatic function, becoming imbued with a beastly authority as the play progresses. Augusta, 'inspecting the gryphon', declares it 'a solid beast, an excellent stage, fit for a play' (2000: 158), as if its imposing presence is that which both sanctions and delimits the family drama which is unfolding. Similarly, Jack Blow, the clandestine brother and agent of the play's events, early on in the narrative stands 'before the winged half of the gryphon' and soliloquises on having once

> seen a judge
> Sitting in the credit of his chair,
> So abandon justice that his ears
> Stood in abdication, on his head. (2000: 23)

These moments are two of several instances when Barnes encourages her audience to see the gryphon as standing in judgement over the play's events, foreshadowing the way in which, in the final moments, it will dispense a beastly form of justice. The beast becomes the lens through which the familial drama is resolved, offering a judicial alternative to the legal system (derived from patrilineal conventions of property that Titus and his textual predecessors are so invested in), able to pass judgement in a way that the law cannot and without the pretence of a fair ruling.

The second act concludes with the goodly uncle, Jonathan Burley, Augusta's brother, requesting that Miranda push the two halves of the gryphon together and 'help [him] make of this divided beast / An undivided bed' (2000: 155). This well-intentioned attempt to repair the *unheimlich* 'rip in nature' (2000: 8) within which the play is suspended, as well as the divided family, sets the course for the play's tragic ending. Act III opens with the direction that the stage now shows that the 'gryphon has been brought together', with Miranda sleeping within it (2000: 156). A unified figure at last, when Augusta arrives on stage and climbs into the carousel with her daughter, the play appears to tease divisions reconciled and harmony over fragmentation. It is a peace that does not last, however, with Miranda unwilling to provide the absolution Augusta so desires, while the latter remains in denial of her complicity in Miranda's childhood abuse and subsequent misery. In her 'Cautionary Note' prefacing the drama, Barnes outlines how, for Miranda and Augusta, '[t]heir familiarity is their estrangement' (1998: 79), a sentiment that is declared aloud when Miranda remarks to her mother that 'It has been remarked from advent to the terror / Woman is most beast familiar' (2000: 176). Here familiarity breeds beastliness in the sense of estrangement and horror, adding to the sense of fatalism and inevitability produced in the play's linguistic circularity and refrains, as well as in its apocalyptic setting. In the play's climactic moments, the women struggle with each other on the stairs leading to an upper floor, until Augusta brings a large bell down on Miranda and '[b]oth fall across the gryphon, pulling down the curtains, gilt crown and all' (2000: 201). It is a bleak final image of a unified beastly trope: this 'solid' beastly figure watches with a degree of judicial authority as Dudley and Elisha escape unscathed and then entombs the female members of the family. With the play encouraging its audience to see this final act of violence against women as having been orchestrated by Jack Blow, the figure most frequently aligned with the gryphon in the first act, the beastly tomb provides the visual accompaniment to his departing speech. Returning to the image of the 'beast-box', this time framed as 'a doll's hutch', Blow's final lines declare it to be the 'hour of the uncreate', in which 'villains' are caught, before he exits the stage with what, in the stage directions, is described as an apparent 'indifference' (2000: 202–3).

The play's conclusion, then, is beastly not just in its tropes but also in its form of justice that cannot be mapped on to an idea of just deserts. The doubled, contradictory idiom of the beast insists on both closure and open-endedness, making for a dramatic structure that T. S. Eliot saw as likely to confuse, and which critics have seen as enacting an aesthetics of improperness or ambivalence. Critical appraisals of the play often look to theorise its titular emphasis on antiphony (understood as a musical response made by a voice or choir to another) to provide some form of palatable exegesis. Taylor, for instance, sees antiphony as signalling the way in which trauma requires witness and response (2012: 38–40), while Goody has argued that the play's intended antiphony comes from the audience, who have been 'confronted with the cruelty of their spectatorship [. . .] [as] wolfish pursuers whose insatiable desire for a salacious or shocking entertainment both produces and is produced by an exploitative culture of the spectacle' (2014: 358). While these readings offer convincing theories for antiphonic structures in the play, I want to conclude by suggesting one further antiphony akin to what Barnes, in a poetic fragment from her later years, described as 'a beast / lowing in the isle of [its] dimension' (Barnes n.d.: n.p.). This is the beastly roar that, although unheard, reverberates through the play, the 'gross quiet' (2000: 8) that signifies the absent presence of Titus, the unspoken trauma of his surviving family and the wordless gryphon passing its terrible judgement. It is also a roar that provides an antiphonic response to Barnes's beastly oeuvre, seeming to promise resolution to this on-going retelling of a family drama told through the prism of beastly tropes and narratives, but also keeping everything in suspension, necessarily unresolved and open to further reiteration. Notable as Barnes's final attempt to produce a narrative telling this autobiographical story, it is a beastly antiphon to all that has gone before and will come afterwards. Basil Born, Wendell Ryder and Titus Hobbs stand as figures unable to live up to their aspirations of a transcendent animality, hobbled by the contradiction inherent to such a configuration. Barnes's own writing, instead, embraces the negations, instabilities and paradoxes that come with exploring beastly territories. Her family dramas serve as clear examples of an approach to thinking about animals and animality that resists resolving formal, thematic or tropological components into harmony. She leaves them instead in a state of productive, generative overdetermination and fragmentation, in which an attempt to narrate always seems to call for a further beastly response.

Works Cited

Adams, Carol J. 2010. *The Sexual Politics of Meat: A Feminist-Vegetarian Critical Theory*. New York and London: Continuum.

Adkins, Peter. 2022. *The Modernist Anthropocene: Nonhuman Life and Planetary Change in James Joyce, Virginia Woolf and Djuna Barnes*. Edinburgh: Edinburgh University Press.

Altman, Meryl. 1991. '*The Antiphon*: "No Audience at All?"' In *Silence and Power: A Reevaluation of Djuna Barnes*. Ed. Mary Lynn Broe, 271–85. Carbondale and Edwardsville: Southern Illinois University Press.

Azzarello, Robert. 2012. *Queer Environmentality: Ecology, Evolution and Sexuality in American Literature*. Farnham: Ashgate.

Barnes, Djuna. (n.d.). Untitled poem headed 'Say I am a beast'. Typescript, Djuna Barnes Papers, Special Collections, University of Maryland Libraries (hereafter DBP), Series 3, Box 7, Folder 6.

Barnes, Djuna. 1924. Unsigned reader's report for *Biography of Julie von Bartmann*, DBP, Series 3, Box 5, Folder 8.

Barnes, Djuna. 1957. Letter to T. S. Eliot, 9 January 1957, DBP, Series 2, Box 4, Folder 63.

Barnes, Djuna. 1998. *Selected Works*. London: Faber & Faber.

Barnes, Djuna. 2000. *The Antiphon*. Los Angeles: Green Integer.

Barnes, Djuna. 2020. *Biography of Julie van Bartmann*. Los Angeles: Green Integer.

Caselli, Daniela. 2009. *Improper Modernism: Djuna Barnes's Bewildering Corpus*. London and New York: Routledge.

Caselli, Daniela. 2019. '"If Some Strong Woman": Djuna Barnes's Great Capacity for All Things Uncertain'. In *Shattered Objects: Djuna Barnes's Modernism*. Ed. Elizabeth Pender and Cathryn Setz, 147–62. University Park, PA: Penn State University Press.

Curry, Linda. 1991. '"Tom, Take Mercy": Djuna Barnes's Drafts of *The Antiphon*'. In *Silence and Power: A Reevaluation of Djuna Barnes*. Ed. Mary Lynn Broe, 286–99. Carbondale and Edwardsville: Southern Illinois University Press.

De Ville, Jacques. 2012. 'Deconstructing the Leviathan: Derrida's *The Beast and the Sovereign*'. *Societies* 2: 357–71.

Derrida, Jacques. 2009. *The Beast and the Sovereign: Volume I*. Trans. G. Bennington. Chicago: University of Chicago Press.
Eliot, T. S. 1954. Letter to Djuna Barnes, 24 August 1954, DBP, Series 2, Box 4, Folder 62.
Eliot, T. S. 1957a. Letter to Djuna Barnes, 7 February 1957, DBP, Series 2, Box 4, Folder 63.
Eliot, T. S. 1957b. Letter to Djuna Barnes, 4 June 1957, DBP, Series 2, Box 4, Folder 63.
Friede, Donald S. 1927. Letter to Djuna Barnes, 23 June 1927, DBP, Series 2, Box 2, Folder 10.
Goody, Alex. 2014. '"High and Aloof": Verse, Violence, and the Audience in Djuna Barnes's *The Antiphon*'. *Modern Drama* 57.3: 339–63.
Goody, Alex. 2021. 'Nonhuman Animals and Decorative Modernism in Djuna Barnes and Mina Loy'. *Women: A Cultural Review* 32.1: 8–31.
Herring, Phillip. 1996. *Djuna: The Life and Works of Djuna Barnes*. New York and London: Penguin.
Herring, Scott. 2015. 'Djuna Barnes and the Geriatric Avant-Garde'. *PMLA* 130.1: 69–91.
Kalaidjian, Andrew. 2016. 'The Black Sheep: Djuna Barnes's Dark Pastoral'. In *Creatural Fictions: Human-Animal Relationships in Twentieth- and Twenty-First-Century Literature*. Ed. David Herman, 65–87. Basingstoke: Palgrave Macmillan.
Norris, Margot. 1985. *Beasts of the Modern Imagination: Darwin, Nietzsche, Kafka, Ernst and Lawrence*. Baltimore: Johns Hopkins University Press.
Potter, Rachel. 2019. '*Nightwood*'s Humans'. In *Shattered Objects: Djuna Barnes's Modernism*. Ed. Elizabeth Pender and Cathryn Setz, 61–74. University Park, PA: Penn State University Press.
Rohman, Carrie. 2009. *Stalking the Subject: Modernism and the Animal*. New York: Columbia University Press.
Scott, Bonnie Kime. 1995. *Refiguring Modernism Volume 2: Postmodern Feminist Readings of Woolf, West and Barnes*. Bloomington: Indiana University Press.
Taylor, Julie. 2011. 'Revising *The Antiphon*, Restaging Trauma; or, Where Sexual Politics Meet Textual History'. *Modernism/modernity* 18.1: 125–47.
Taylor, Julie. 2012. *Djuna Barnes and Affective Modernism*. Edinburgh: Edinburgh University Press.

Notes

1. See the letter from Eliot on 24 August 1954, stored in Barnes's archive at the University of Maryland.
2. Barnes's correspondence with Eliot reveals the degree to which the proposed blurb was deeply wounding, with her response describing how she could not 'recall seeing a "blurb" (which I had always thought a means of promoting a book) so tailored to a jacket that so resembles a shroud; and with such fine cruel work of approval and displeasure' (Barnes 1957: n.p.). Eliot's response was defensive, stating that it had been received well by the Faber and Faber board but that he would write something more conventional and shorter in order to please her, sending an abbreviated, austere version of the blurb in the summer of 1957. See correspondence from Eliot to Barnes on 7 February 1957 and 4 June 1957.
3. The rise of modernist animal studies has seen critics re-evaluate Barnes's oeuvre and its implication for our understanding of both modernist studies and literary animal studies. Of particular note is Andrew Kalaidjian's analysis of Barnes's 'dark

pastoral' (Kalaidjian 2016), Robert Azzarello's argument for the inherent queerness of Barnes's interest in human animality (Azzarello 2012), Rachel Potter's account of beastliness within social constructions of human identity in *Nightwood* (Potter 2019) and Alex Goody's discussion of how fashion and clothing mark an uncertain border between the human and the animal in Barnes (Goody 2021).

4. The typescript for the play is in the Djuna Barnes Papers at the University of Maryland. Although the typescript is dated 'November 1923–April 1924' on the final sheet, it is not clear when it was typed and corrected, as Barnes retyped many of her earlier works in the later decades of her life. There are a number of minor corrections to the play in green ink in Barnes's hand, similar to those she made from the 1950s onward, while the last page features extensive corrections to Julie's final speech in black ink that appears to have been written earlier. Green Integer published the play for the first time in 2020.

5. Barnes had previously written a number of one-act plays which, as Goody writes, 'challenged conventional sexuality and morality and refused the Freudian family romance' (Goody 2014: 340). The only longer drama Barnes had written prior to *Julie van Bartmann* was the unpublished and undated *Ann Portuguise*, which Phillip Herring suggests was written around 1920 (Herring 1996: 270).

6. As I have argued elsewhere, this phrase also foreshadows Matthew O'Connor's animalised descriptions of Robin in *Nightwood* (Adkins 2022: 130).

7. As Herring notes, Barnes continued to write to her father and paternal grandmother, Zadel, for many years after leaving, corresponding 'about the farm animals and dogs' but carrying a 'deep sense of grievance' that her career as a writer had begun out of the economic necessity to provide for her mother and siblings (Herring 1996: 41).

8. In this aspect, Basil differs from the lapsed vegetarian Wendell Ryder, who cannot stand the sight of blood and who leaves the messier aspects of livestock raising to his wives and children. For another Barnes narrative which explores what Carol Adams has called the 'association between meat eating and virile maleness' (2010: 25) see her 1917 story, 'The Rabbit'.

9. Claude Lévi-Strauss famously asserted that the 'incest taboo' was one of the universal features of all human cultures, setting the human apart from other animals. Much speculation has been made about sexual abuse and incest in Barnes's own childhood (see Herring 1996: 55–8; Taylor 2012: 7).

10. In this same respect, Julie does not occupy the role of an empowering surrogate mother for Gustava. When, at the end of Act I, Gustava goes to Julie's room and climbs into bed with her, she discovers during their intimate conversation together that Julie is not the great all-consuming figure of female agency that she has long imagined the famous opera singer to be.

11. Barnes started writing *The Antiphon* in earnest in 1950, producing a first draft in 1954 that was subsequently revised multiple times, with editorial input from Eliot and Edwin Muir. For the compositional history of the play see Curry (1991) and Taylor (2011).

12. Like Basil and Wendell, Titus ran 'a farm he never farmed' (2000: 72).

13. Indeed, the character that Miranda most resembles in Barnes's previous work is Robin from *Nightwood*, since she is aligned several times with canine imagery; she is described, for instance, by Augusta as 'the terrier [who] runs back without

the bone' (2000: 187). Miranda's sustained election of silence in Act II also echoes Robin's silence through *Nightwood*.
14. As Goody has shown, earlier drafts of the play find Barnes experimenting with different animal masks, the brothers taking on the appearance of a wolf and a kite, and demonstrating that the degree to which the particular symbolism the masks would elicit was highly considered and influenced by her reading in early modern literature (Goody 2014: 352–3).
15. The dialogue describing Miranda's 'rump' and 'best position' were added to the revised version of the play that Barnes produced for her 1962 *Selected Works*.
16. Bonnie Kime Scott interestingly notes that Barnes had a similar fairground gryphon in her Paris flat in the 1920s. She reads the gryphon differently to me, suggesting it should be understood as a figure of familial unity (Scott 1995: 120–1). Caselli has suggested, on the other hand, that Barnes was drawing on the moment in Dante's *Purgatorio* when the gryphon appears to take Beatrice to heaven (Caselli 2019: 157).

6

THE TAXIDERMIC IMAGINARY IN MODERNIST LITERATURE

Paul Fagan

This chapter foregrounds taxidermy's function in the development of the modernist human–nonhuman imaginary through a new materialist theoretical lens. In it, I map the shifting poetics, politics and problematic ethics of taxidermy in modernist literary expression from the 1860s to the 1950s. This expanded historical scope, beyond the standard limits of the modernist period, allows me to trace the relation between four significant discursive shifts concerning the literary representation of taxidermied bodies: first, the 'enchantment with the authenticity of actual animal bodies' (Bezan and McHugh 2019: 133–4) that the taxidermied animal-as-object introduces to museum dioramas and commodity objects in the nineteenth century; second, the popularity of Victorian anthropomorphic taxidermy, which, in its confusion of taxonomic boundaries and hierarchies, alters the literary representation of both human and nonhuman animals from Charles Dickens to Lewis Carroll; third, an emergent modernist reconsideration of the taxidermied nonhuman animal as a figure of uncanny *in*authenticity, an assemblage of deceitful and ideologically loaded signifiers; and fourth, a late modernist taxidermic literary mode which explores the intersecting topoi of the human becoming-animal, becoming-object and becoming-dead as reflection points for the posthuman themes of living posthumously and the transgressed limit. Within this framework, I historicise the discursive and material interfaces between taxidermic and literary practices in the modernist and late-modernist era through close readings of representative short stories and novels by H. G. Wells, Ernest Hemingway, Virginia Woolf and Myles na Gopaleen (Flann O'Brien). To diverse ends, and with varying degrees of complicity, the texts under analysis interrogate taxidermied objects as commodities through which certain discourses of hygiene, humanism, science, colonialism, race, gender and class gain an unearned legitimacy in the public imagination, with material consequences for both human and nonhuman bodies.

Arrangements of Skin: Historicising Taxidermy

Taxidermy's emergence as a modern technological and commercial practice is marked by Louis Dufresne's 1804 use of the term *taxidermie* from the Greek *taxis* (to arrange) and *derma* (skin), in place of the then common French appellation *empailler* (to stuff with straw) (Aloi 2018: 49). The French naturalist's coinage reflects a change in the art's underlying material practices: while the first documented European natural history collections to include specimens mounted with wires and preservative spices date back to the sixteenth century, it is in the period of industrialisation that methods of preservation were advanced that used stronger chemical poisons, such as arsenical soap, to ward off 'the deterioration of the skin, the odour that came from this deterioration and insect attacks' (Péquignot 2006: 246–7). Yet, Giovanni Aloi identifies this conceptual shift from the craft of stuffing bodies to the art of arranging skins as 'a point at which a new discursive formation begins to emerge' which 'separated the older practices [. . .] related to hunting' from the *modern* 'epistemic focus of scientific taxidermy mounts' (2018: 51). These material and discursive transformations are deeply intertwined in the Victorian imaginary, in which the taxidermied nonhuman animal functions simultaneously as an index of the ideological structures of scientific realism and as an 'effigy of man's subjugation of nature' in industrial and colonial contexts (Aloi 2018: 70).

Pauline Wakeham observes that taxidermy bears a 'doubled status' as 'both a specific technology of representation (the literal stuffing of epidermal shells) and [. . .] a sign system that travels beyond this material practice [. . .] across a range of cultural texts' (2008: 6). In the late eighteenth and early nineteenth centuries, 'modern' scientific conservation techniques were disseminated through handbook publications and treatises, as naturalists began to provide private collectors and museums with specimens of skins and mounted nonhuman animals. The resulting specimens and tableaux served, in turn, as models for the visual illustrations and scientific texts that shaped Victorian understandings of the 'animal', 'nature' and the 'human'. John James Audubon developed his own *ad hoc* method of holding dead birds in life-like poses using wires and threads while he drew them, and many of his influential illustrations in *The Birds of America* (1827–38) were based on joint hunting expeditions and exchanged knowledges and specimens with English taxidermist John Ward and his children. John Gould's celebrated ornithological illustrations in *A Century of Birds from the Himalaya Mountains* (1831–2) drew on a collection of exotic bird skins he accessed through his position as taxidermist to the Zoological Society of London. Robert Havell Jr sold ornithological drawings in his Zoological Gallery on Oxford Street, side by side with 'the birds themselves, stuffed and posed, along with skins and feathers' (Mellby 2012: 486). This circulation of posthumous nonhuman bodies within and between technological, economic, discursive and semiotic systems renders taxidermic practice and modern cultural representations of nonhuman animals inseparable.

The assemblage of organic materials, body parts, chemicals and technologies that was presented to the public as the taxidermied 'animal' offered a new form of indexicality that bolstered the cultural capital of optical and literary realism. Naturalist and museal taxidermy claimed to grant the viewer access to the 'extra-discursive field of "the real"' (Gregory and Purdy 2015: 63) via an auratic object of '"authentic" animality' that presents itself, through the material index of the skin, *as* the animal, not a mere representation (Young 2017: 50). Thus fetishised as an index both of the real material animal body and of science's power to arrest time's flow and conquer the materiality of bodily change, the mounted nonhuman animal corpse functioned as a screen on to which a series of narratives could be projected 'at the complex crossroads of Enlightenment science, colonial trophy hunting and hypermasculine interior design' (Nixon 2011: 316, n3). Even as they come to be recoded as kitsch, even distasteful, in their direct form, these Victorian taxidermic narratives and imaginaries – with their strict anthropocentric taxonomies and ideological coupling of optical realism, scientific knowledge and power over nonhuman bodies – continued to be reproduced in diverse twentieth-century media and commodities 'through malleable semiotic codes' (Wakeham 2008: 6).

As such, historical taxidermy artefacts present the modernist critic with a simulacrum of nonhuman bodies 'that can enable the retrieval of discursive formations, cultural conditions, practices and power/knowledge relationships between humans and animals' (Aloi 2018: 53). Historicising taxidermic practices and their ideological constructions across the modernist period will allow me to connect discrete literary representations of variously exploited, stuffed, mounted, displayed, objectified, and commodified bodies to the specifics of a shifting taxidermic imaginary, in which the material and discursive limits of human and nonhuman skins are constantly redrawn. By paying close attention to the relationship between their writing and these discursive shifts, I will trace the diverse ways in which modernist writers deconstruct scientific, colonial and commodified representations of the mounted animal-as-object. While these forms of representation variously silence and abstract the material reality of violence, modernist depictions work to disclose taxidermy's unspoken discursive and technological linking of power to human and nonhuman bodies.

Animal Objects: Victorian Anthropomorphic Taxidermy

The 1851 Great Exhibition in Hyde Park introduced the Victorian public to the taxidermy of Hermann Ploucquet, a naturalist at the Royal Museum of Stuttgart.

While the majority of the mounts were 'realistic' tableaux, what caught the public imagination were Ploucquet's 'comical groups', including 'frogs having a shave, kittens serving tea, and a marten acting as a schoolmaster' (Morris and Ebenstein 2013: 4–5). A decade later, Walter Potter's *The Death and Burial of Cock Robin* (1861) recreated each stanza of the macabre nursery rhyme in a tableau featuring ninety-eight species of embalmed birds (Morris and Ebenstein 2013: 9), mounted in anthropomorphic poses (in the mourning procession, bearing the coffin, digging the grave), meant to charm and entertain rather than to inform and enlighten their audiences. Potter's subsequent tableaux mounted locally sourced nonhuman animal corpses (squirrels, rats, rabbits, kittens) in increasingly anthropomorphised, class-based and gendered scenes of daily 'British' life (school, tea and croquet parties, cricket games, the gentleman's club, weddings) that endure in the popular cultural imaginary today through toys such as Sylvanian Families.

Indeed, anthropomorphic taxidermy further commodified the art, fuelling the nineteenth-century trend 'to turn animals in to functional objects like lamps, hardened horse-hoof inkwells, bird hats, beetle dresses' (Pyke 2014: n.p.). Magazines such as *Cassell's Household Guide* provided instructions to amateurs for flaying, gutting and stuffing nonhuman animal corpses to produce 'authentic' decorative art objects for the home, and for transforming the leftover body parts into accessories such as 'fish-scale embroidery and pigeon-feather screens' (Young 2017: 50). At the same time, James Rowland Ward's evocatively named Piccadilly shop, The Jungle, commodified and domesticated the bodies of exotic large game in items such as 'a bear as a dumb waiter holding a tray of glasses' and 'umbrella stands made from the feet of elephants' (Jackson 2006: 9). Sourced from throughout, and reflecting the growing reach of, the British Empire, such Wardian furniture 'provided the Victorians with an outlet to act out different dimensions of the colonial experience' (Wirtén 2008: 94), and thus normalised and legitimised the colonial project. By these means, the taxidermied nonhuman animal was transformed from a display in the public spaces and scientific frameworks of the museum exhibit to a tangible commodity in overlapping commercial and domestic spheres. Thus, taxidermy becomes a site of binding economic relations, social codes and cultural practices across public and private spheres that 'records and shapes social identity' (Haraway 1997: 261).

Anthropomorphic taxidermy displays and commodities also transformed the semiotics of human and nonhuman assemblages in the Victorian literary imaginary. Scientific trophy taxidermy is 'boundary-establishing', in so far as it establishes 'clear hierarchies and subdivisions' between the human and the nonhuman, civilisation and the wild, life and death, the subject and object of the gaze (Jackson 2006: 336). As such, it reinforces the logics of optical and literary realism. Shelley Jackson theorises anthropomorphic taxidermy, by contrast, as 'boundary blurring' (2006: 336), confusing the museum's 'vision of a natural world marked by clean boundaries between types and species' (Henning 2007: 673) and drawing 'attention to the links between humans and animals and anxieties related to humans' place in the natural world' (Talairach-Vielmas 2014: 124). As such, anthropomorphic taxidermy creates a cultural imaginary in which the logics of optical and literary realism might be upended in carnivalesque play.

Lin Young observes the boundary-blurring influence of anthropomorphic taxidermy on the 'tangled hierarchy of consciousness' in Carroll's *Alice's Adventures in Wonderland* (1865), expressed through flamingo croquet mallets, hedgehog croquet balls, ravens that may or may not be like writing desks and other forms of sentient Wardian furniture (2017: 47). The taxidermist Mr Venus in Dickens's *Our Mutual Friend* (1864–5) is surrounded by both the trophies of his art and anthropomorphic images such as that of 'two preserved frogs fighting a small-sword duel' (Dickens 1997: 83). Published three years after the *Cock Robin* exhibition, Dickens's novel depicts a comparable scene in which Potter's anthropomorphic tableau is transformed into a defamiliarising zoomorphic scene:

> a pretty little dead bird lying on the counter, with [. . .] a long stiff wire piercing its breast. As if it were Cock Robin, the hero of the ballad, and Mr Venus were the sparrow with his bow and arrow, and Mr Wegg were the fly with his little eye. (Dickens 1997: 84)

In their distinct literary manifestations of the Victorian anthropomorphic taxidermic imaginary, both Carroll and Dickens speak to a confusion of previous semiotic and ontological orders of human and nonhuman bodies. Yet, even as anthropomorphic taxidermy inspires literary representations that play at and with borders of the human and the nonhuman, vibrant and dead matter, in ways that can trouble the assumptions of realism, these representations continue to idealise taxidermy as a narrative- and comedy-generating device. Despite their real differences from these practices, these images from Carroll and Dickens reinforce the fetishism of taxidermy's naturalist, anthropomorphic and commercial modes that veils the material conditions and realities under which nonhuman bodies are transformed into auratic objects and commodities in cycles of production and consumption. They operate at a level of figural abstraction that, even when comic or satirical, fails to test distinctions between the material real and phantasmatic anthropomorphic or zoomorphic performances or inversions of human social codes and discourses. The abject fakeness of the discursive reality created through taxidermy's material assemblages remains to be more rigorously deconstructed and exposed. It is towards this task, I suggest, that modernist literary representations of taxidermy are orientated, with varying degrees of sincerity and irony, complicity and resistance.

Modernist Poetics: The Hoax of Taxidermy

A proto-modernist poetics of the fake drives H. G. Wells's 'The Triumphs of a Taxidermist' (1894). This anonymously published 'interview' between the narrator, Bellows, and a practising taxidermist in the *Pall Mall Gazette* feigns to disclose 'the secrets of taxidermy' as an art of forgery (Wells 1904: 53). Deception, the taxidermist insists, is endemic to the practice, as 'half the great auks in the world are about as genuine as the handkerchief of Saint Veronica, as the Holy Coat of Treves' (Wells 1904: 56). Roland Barthes reminds us that the function of the relic is 'to signify that the event represented has really taken place' (1986: 140). Here, Wells's language foregrounds taxidermy's status as a secularised relic: a hyperreal object whose auratic status is divorced from its material reality and history yet which serves powerful discursive and institutional functions through its constructed indexicality and authenticity, even as it threatens 'to lapse from art into deception, from life to upholstered death' (Haraway 1985: 40). Along with these dubious holy relics, the story is peppered with allusions to actual taxidermy hoaxes. The reference to taxidermied mermaids likely alludes to the Feejee mermaid hoax, in which the torso and head of a monkey was sewn to the back half of a fish and exhibited in P. T. Barnum's American Museum in 1842, and the interviewee's claim to have stuffed a dodo evokes taxidermist Abraham Dee Bartlett's life-size reconstruction of the extinct bird at the 1851 Great Exhibition.

Wells's taxidermist declares that the motivation to forge taxidermied non-human animals is financial in nature; he notes an auk egg has recently fetched £300 and describes sham porcelain eggs as 'brittle capital' (Wells 1904: 56). The economic benefits on both ends of this arrangement mean that the taxidermist has little fear of exposure, as scientists and museum curators 'will hardly care to pull a nice specimen to bits' to discover the fraud (Wells 1904: 56). Yet, the ambitions of Wells's taxidermist are greater than merely to 'imitate nature' for financial gain. He declares himself an artist, whose taxidermied mermaids and hyperreal forgeries of non-existent birds are his 'masterpiece' (Wells 1904: 59). His artistry is shown, in turn, to advance and to legitimise the ambitions of anthropocentric scientific humanism: he has recreated dead matter and, he declares, in the process 'beaten' nature (Wells 1904: 58). He insists that he has 'made' a great auk (declared extinct in 1844), as well as a dodo (extinct since the seventeenth century), and he plans to '*forge* a complete stuffed moa' (extinct c.1500) (Wells 1904: 57). Each of these birds was driven to extinction through human cultural and economic practice: the moa was eradicated by hunting and habitat reduction in its native New Zealand; the dodo's natural habitat was destroyed by human settlement on Mauritius; the auk was hunted for food, fishing bait and down, and its eggs became collector's items. Taxidermy's promised power to arrest time's passage by having 'the animal' live on after death is exposed in Wells's tale as a fake, a fantasy in which nonhuman genocide is reframed, perversely, as a technology of de-extinction.

Thus, Wells identifies taxidermy's 'illusion of reality' as an act of bad faith, 'an appearance of authenticity, which is fabricated through the "narrative art"' by which 'stretched, stitched, and stuffed, taxidermy hides themselves hide, conceal and secret away their stories' (Bezan and McHugh 2019: 132–3). Yet, this revelation is cannily folded back into the author's own art of writing. As Zoé Hardy shows, Wells's text problematises the intertwined representational authenticity of taxidermy and literature across three levels of authorship: first, the taxidermist, who 'attempts to deceive his audience – scientists – into believing in the authenticity of his creations'; second, Bellows, who, 'in his position as a witness narrator, tries to convince his readers of the veracity of his tale'; and third, Wells, who, by presenting his anonymous faux interview alongside advertisements, non-fiction essays and journalism 'printed on the same page' of *The Pall Mall Gazette* 'adds to the story's hybrid status between fact and fiction' (2018: 24).

Wells's turn to hoax poetics marks the emergence of a modernist taxidermic imaginary that is distinguishable from the nineteenth century's dominant realist, anthropomorphic and comic modes. John Attridge identifies modernism's 'preoccupation with masks, hoaxes, role-playing, pseudonymity and other forms of imposture' and details a 'subversive counter-modernism that loves a lie' (2014: 38– 9), as demonstrated by the 'Spectrist' and 'Ern Malley' volumes of faux-modernist 'poetry'; the notorious Bloomsbury Dreadnought Hoax; Samuel Beckett's lecture to Trinity College Dublin on the invented figure of du Chas; Oscar Wilde's and James Joyce's creative interest in the James Macpherson *Ossian* scandal; and diverse modernist parodies, travesties and frauds (see Diepeveen 2014). I have argued elsewhere that 'the power of the false to reorganise and constitute reality is a modernist theme [. . .] that shares a lineage with historical forms of hoax literature' (Fagan 2018: 164). Key to linking Wells's story to this specifically modernist strand of literary hoaxing is the taxidermist's claim to have created '*New* birds. Improvements. Like no birds that was ever seen before' (Wells 1904: 58; emphasis in original). Thus, 'The Triumphs of a Taxidermist' explores not only the modernist project of exposing the bad-faith constructedness and ideological function of realism, but also the modernist theme of the power of the fake performatively to *produce* reality.

By these means, Wells's short story marks the emergence of a proto-modernist self-reflection on the similarities between the arts of the taxidermist and the literary practitioner, for whom 'a real artist in the art' (Wells 1904: 59) conceives their goal not as the bad-faith capturing of 'objective reality' but a poetics of self-aware fragmentation that attends to underlying material realities and processes. Yet, this pre-eminently modernist theme remains thoroughly implicated in taxidermy's position at the nexus of 'both biological tissue and discursive schema overdetermined by colonialism's obsession with racial and species categorisation' (Wakeham 2008: 25). The most shocking aspect of Wells's story is the taxidermist's claim to have stuffed a black man 'and used him as a hat rack' (Wells 1904: 54), an image that grotesquely lampoons yet remains complicit with taxidermy's status 'as a prominent emblem of imperialism' which 'gives form to racism's skin fetish' (McHugh 2019: 241). The appalling image of the black man as Wardian furniture discloses taxidermy as a practice that not only gives cover to but actively fetishises the technological and discursive links between animal commodification and brutal racial dehumanisation.

The taxidermist dismisses Bellows's characterisation of his grotesque creation as 'unpleasant', glossing over its racist overtones to present human taxidermy in positivist utopian terms as 'a promising third course to burial or cremation':

> You could keep all your dear ones by you. Bric-à-brac of that sort stuck about the house would be as good as most company, and much less expensive. You might have them fitted up with clockwork to do things. (Wells 1904: 55)

The image recalls the oft-rehearsed literary anecdote in which Dickens had a single paw of his deceased companion cat, Bob, stuffed and attached to an ivory blade which was engraved 'C.D. In Memory of Bob 1862'. Jenny Pyke distinguishes Dickens's cat-paw letter-opener from the common nineteenth-century practice of memorialising pets by stuffing and displaying them on account of 'its tactile softness and emotional tenderness' as 'an object meant to be held daily' (2014: n.p.). Yet Wells's emphasis on the utilisation of human bodies, and particularly colonised bodies, to work on, zombie-like, after death, challenges, even unwittingly, the speciesism at play in such an implicit emotional distinction between tenderness – when the practice is applied to nonhuman animal bodies – and grotesqueness – when applied, even speculatively, to human bodies.

Wells's human hat-rack is an ambivalent figure that simultaneously lampoons and reinforces the dominant logic of scientific racism, as well as emergent anxieties about a posthuman future. It is an abject figure of humanity's uncertain self-distinction from the nonhuman, and from other humans who are categorised as less-than-human, that must be mastered either through a utopian humanism that doubles down on scientific and colonial violence, or through the realisation of kinship between human and nonhuman animals. At the outset of the modernist era, taxidermy comes to function as an index of the intersecting colonial, racial and patriarchal discursive and material practices in which the exploitation and commodification of real human and nonhuman bodies are inextricably linked.

Modernist Dioramas: The Skin Fetish of Race, Gender, Class

As a response to the conceived unscientific fakeness and cheap gimmickry of anthropomorphic taxidermy and Wardian furniture, an emboldened movement towards taxidermic realism was initiated in the US by Henry Augustus Ward in the 1860s. This American realist tradition culminated in the most renowned disciple of Ward's Natural Science Establishment in Rochester, New York, and the most acclaimed twentieth-century practitioner of the art, Carl Akeley, whose sculptural technique for taxidermy is celebrated by the American Museum of Natural History as having 'elevated the practice from a crude craft to an art form' (2016). The identification of Akeley as the 'father of modern taxidermy' marks the discursive construction of a new point of origin in the practice, which in fact reiterates previous such declarations by Dufresne and others. In each case, more than a century apart, the function of this discursive move remains the same – to indicate that the practice of conserving the nonhuman animal body has been perfected, as its application has been rendered more artful, scientifically more precise, more civilised, more *modern*.

Akeley's 'masterpieces' were the African habitats that he prepared using the 'Akeley method' on nonhuman animals he and his team had killed on expeditions to Africa. These dioramas were mounted in the Field Museum of Natural History in Chicago – where Akeley was chief taxidermist from 1896 to 1909 – and New York's American Museum of Natural History, where he proposed the Hall of African Mammals in 1909 (completed in 1936, a decade after his death). However, this realist project was troubled by contradictions inherent to it. In his practice and its presentation, Akeley 'set himself against faking' and 'wanted no part of the great circus magnate's cultivation of the American popular art form, the hoax' (Haraway 1985: 40), yet he first made his name by mounting Barnum's Jumbo. Despite the dioramas' pretences to scientific objectivity and their connotations of an antimodern return to nature, Akeley's constructed scenes bore all the hallmarks of the narrative trends and cinematic imaginaries of the twentieth century, arranged dramatically to achieve a 'climactic effect' (Brown 2018: 74).

Donna Haraway reads Akeley's project to 'manipulate nature to tell the story of a fierce and savage Africa' as a manifestation of *fin-de-siècle* racial discourses concerning 'genetic hygiene' and 'the politics of eugenics' (1985: 40: 20–1). The African dioramas of the Akeley Hall of African Mammals, set amid the urban jungle of New York, exhibit a romanticised nostalgia for an 'imagined hygienic, pre-Industrial America' and are tasked with the 'regeneration of a miscellaneous, incoherent urban public threatened with genetic and social decadence, threatened with the prolific bodies of the new immigrants, threatened with the failure of manhood' (Haraway 1985: 38, 23). Thus, even as Akeley's work presents itself as a denotational sculptural material practice, 'its connotative specters revise fantasies of white male supremacy in "the sporting crucible" of colonial mastery over nature' (Wakeham 2008: 5).

Ernest Hemingway's writing exhibits the most direct influence of Akeley's 'realist' taxidermy, and the patriarchal naturalist ideology out of which it emerged, on modernist literature. Marcelline Hemingway Sanford's memoirs document family trips to the Field Museum, where she and her brother encountered 'stuffed animals looking lifelike in their original hides' (1999: 38). Kenneth Lynn notes the Hemingway children's fascination with the stuffed elephant that had been killed by Teddy Roosevelt and adds that 'by the time he was ten, [Ernest's] favorite room was the Hall of African Mammals', where Akeley's dioramas were on display (1987: 15). The fascination extended into the author's later life, as 'Akeley's memoir, *In Brightest Africa*, was part of Hemingway's adult library' (Beegel 2000: 77). Specifically, the masculinised 'dangerous game' at the centre of each of Akeley's dioramas, which 'catches the viewer's gaze and holds it in communion' (Haraway 1985: 25), is speculated by Michael S. Reynolds to have 'caught and held [Hemingway's] imagination forever' (1986: 230).

Hemingway's *The Sun Also Rises* (1926) explicitly evokes the theme of taxidermy in Jake and Bill's encounter with a stuffed dog in the window of a taxidermist's shop on their last night in Paris. Over the course of their discussion, Bill draws an overt connection between taxidermy and naturalist writing: 'Going to give all my friends stuffed animals. I'm a nature-writer' (Hemingway 1926: 76). Stephen Gilbert Brown theorises the influence of Akeley's dioramas on the 'aesthetic ideology' of Hemingway's work as a point of intersection between the 'naturalist story-teller' and the modernist writer (2018: 71; 74): the projected realism of Akeley's taxidermy influences Hemingway's sparse, incisive, naturalist writing, as the frozen dramatic scenes of Akeley's dioramas inform Hemingway's 'iceberg theory' of modernist story composition. As in Wells's tale, the connection that Bill draws between these arts is linked to economic pressures that drive the artist–taxidermist to transform the dog's material body into both an aesthetic object and a commodity: 'Simple exchange of values. You give them money. They give you a stuffed dog' (Hemingway 1926: 74).

In the scene, Hemingway applies a literary version of the 'Akeley method' to the taxidermic afterlives of specific nonhuman animals from both private and public spheres. Carlos Baker contends that the image was inspired by Hemingway's Paris landlady's stuffed pet dog (1969: 144), while William Adair identifies it as a reference to 'America's celebrated war dog, Sergeant Stubby, who died 16 March 1926, and was then stuffed and mounted preparatory to being placed in the American Red Cross Museum in Washington, D.C.' (2014: 76). The latter allusion figures the dog in the window as a grotesque parody of fetishistic war propaganda – Stubby 'was awarded medals for heroism, marched in parades, appeared in newsreels, and was photographed with three U.S. presidents' (Adair 2014: 76) – which elucidates the war-wounded Jake's resistance to buying the dog, and to buying into the discourses and narratives projected on to its taxidermied body.

Beyond anchoring the novel to certain taxidermic aesthetic ideologies and their economic and discursive contexts, the taxidermied dog serves as an index of the gendered logic of the gaze that organises both Akeley's dioramas and the recurrent imagery of 'Trophy Hunting as a Trope of Manhood' in Hemingway's writing (Styrchacz 1993: 167). Jake's aversion to the stuffed dog as a figure of the war's butchered bodies, revived and exhibited towards propagandistic ends, extends the motif of the emasculating genital war wound that he has suffered while posted at a 'joke front' (Hemingway 1926: 31). Brown reads Akeley's dioramas as offering Hemingway a masculine ideal towards which his emasculated protagonists can strive:

> At the center of the diorama, constituting its dramatic core, is a dominant male whose prowess is a monument to ideal maleness. [. . .] In this gaze between naturalist hunter and male beast, preserved in the frozen time of each diorama, the self is reborn to the vanishing ideal of frontier masculinity – under radical assault since the turn of the century from the excesses of the Machine Age and the advent of the Suffragette Movement. (2018: 75–6)

In *The Sun Also Rises*, this logic culminates in the scene in which the matador Romero is 'reborn to masculinity in the "gaze of meeting" with the bull' (Brown 2018: 76): 'The bull watched him. [. . .] The bull charged and Romero waited, sighting along the blade' (Hemingway 1926: 222). This masculinised exchange of gazes with the 'wild', nonhuman animal is contrasted with Jake's emasculated deferred gaze from the taxidermied 'pet'. The unmediated encounter with death in the crucible of the bullring enables a rebirth of masculine prowess through a romanticised vitalisation of the exchanged gaze between hunter and beast that is captured in Akeley's taxidermy.

This fantasy, which, in both Akeley's dioramas and Hemingway's texts, is presented formally as naturalist realism, comes under greater scrutiny in a strand of modernist writing in the 1920s which defamiliarises and ironises the domesticated naturalist diorama as an index of colonial nostalgia and modern consumerism. As a representative example, Virginia Woolf's *Orlando: A Biography* (1928) opens with a scene of racial trophy hunting, as the young protagonist is discovered 'in the act of slicing at the head of a Moor which swung from the rafters' (Woolf 2007: 403). The Moor's decapitated head is presented in nonhuman terms, compared in colour and shape to 'an old football' or 'a cocoanut' (Woolf 2007: 403). However, this fantasy is quickly deflated, as it is revealed that while the head had been 'struck [. . .] from the shoulders of a vast Pagan [. . .] in the barbarian fields of Africa' by his forefathers, Orlando can do little more than 'steal away from his mother and the peacocks in the garden and go to his attic room and there lunge and plunge and slice the air with his blade' (Woolf 2007: 403). As this act of colonial savagery is first staged and then collapsed as childish fantasy and play, the scene depicts *both* the real violence against, and grotesque displays of, 'less-than-human' bodies that facilitated Orlando's inherited class position, *and* the ways in which these discursive and material histories continue to be narrativised and simulated in the cultural imaginary.

Orlando's racial, patriarchal and class-based desire for colonial adventure and trophy hunting is sublimated into the acquisition of consumer objects, in the form of Wardian furniture such as 'sofas, resting on lions' paws with swans' necks curving under them' or beds 'of the softest swansdown' (Woolf 2007: 450). The refurnishing of Orlando's ancestral home testifies to the overlapping historical disappearance of wildlife from everyday human life and proliferation of nonhuman animal bodies in the household as nostalgia-laden commodities that serve both as overt markers of class position and as indexes of colonial, patriarchal and racial fantasies. Orlando's metamorphosis, accompanied by 'her Seleuchi hound, which had never left her bed all these days' (Woolf 2007: 467), entails a transgression of both sex/gender boundaries and human/nonhuman limits that further deflates this masculinist fantasy. And yet, even in this scheme, Orlando's encounter with the twentieth-century department store has the same quality as Akeley's dioramas, in its transformation of natural materials into not only displayed objects, but commodities of nostalgia:

> each time the lift stopped and flung its doors open, there was another slice of the world displayed with all the smells of that world clinging to it. She was reminded of the river off Wapping in the time of Elizabeth, where the treasure ships and the merchant ships used to anchor. (Woolf 2007: 544)

Across the many centuries of Orlando's life, Woolf's mock biography reverses and discloses the ideological trajectory displayed in *The Sun Also Rises*, in which an encounter between the emasculated soldier and objectified dog moves towards a revitalising and remasculinising fatal encounter between the matador and the bull. *Orlando: A Biography*, by contrast, opens by deflating trophy hunting as a masculinist fantasy embedded in colonial and racial discourses and practices, and proceeds to queer the binary anthropocentric and gender articulations upon which this fantasy turns. At the same time, a figurative contrapuntal arc traces how the trope of trophy hunting human and nonhuman bodies as a revitalisation of patriarchal colonialism is sublimated, first, into the second-hand experience of colonial adventure offered by Wardian furniture, and then into the commodity fetishism of the department store's modern dioramas.

HUMAN OBJECTS: BECOMING NONHUMAN IN LATE MODERNISM

In late modernist literary encounters with taxidermy, the figure of the taxidermied human animal emerges to interrogate the interfaces between technologies and bodies and to disturb the discursive limits between living and dead matter. In this figure of the human becoming-animal, becoming-object and becoming-dead, literary taxidermy becomes not only a scene of the Othering and subjugation of nonhuman and less-than-human bodies, but also the site of a profound self-Othering and self-mourning for the 'human'. Myles na Gopaleen's short story 'Two in One' is at once representative of this late modernist taxidermic imaginary and a text that engages in a revealing conversation with the proto-modernist forms of Wells's 'Triumphs of a Taxidermist'.

'Two in One' is the murder confessional of a taxidermist who presents himself under the fake name of 'Murphy'. The confession, however, is delayed by the murderer's long progressivist disquisition on the practice's history from the sixteenth century onwards (O'Brien 2013: 84). The material practice of taxidermy itself is as much the text's subject as a set-up for its pot-boiler scenario. While critics have discussed the diverse manifestations of murder that the text puts on display – from Murphy murdering his boss, Kelly, to his final capital punishment for the crime – to date scholarship has not included taxidermy itself within the story's thematics of violence. The entry point to a de-anthropocentrised reading of the macabre late modernist gothic story is not that the murderer is a taxidermist, but that the taxidermist is a murderer.

Murphy's feelings of superiority in his craft – which, he boasts, 'combine[s] the qualities of zoologist, naturalist, chemist, sculptor, artist, and carpenter' – are slighted in the willing denial of his creative expression by his superior, Kelly: 'He knew I had a real interest in the work and a desire to broaden my experience. For that reason, he threw me all the common-place routine jobs that came in' (O'Brien 2013: 84–5). Murphy's resentment turns upon a speciesist hierarchy of animal bodies in terms not of commercial but rather of artistic capital, aligned with the cultural capital attributed to modernist difficulty, that nevertheless maps on to a distinction between the local banal and colonial exoticism:

> If some old lady sent her favourite terrier to be done, that was me; foxes and cats and Shetland ponies and white rabbits – they were all strictly *my* department. I could do a perfect job on such animals in my sleep and got to hate them. But if a crocodile came in, or a Great Borneo spider, or (as once happened) a giraffe – Kelly kept them all for himself. (O'Brien 2013: 85)

As this persecution plays itself out, Kelly figuratively gets under his assistant's skin until Murphy literally gets under Kelly's: killing his boss with a taxidermy instrument and disposing of the traces by disguising himself in, and fusing himself with, his victim's skin, thus 'BECOM[ING] Kelly!' (O'Brien 2013: 86). Contemplating himself in the glass, Murphy evaluates his transformation into the dead spit of Kelly to be 'perfect in every detail' (O'Brien 2013: 86). His grotesque taxidermic masterpiece thus doubles for his macabre 'literary labours' (O'Brien 2013: 84) in a way that is comparable to Wells's taxidermist's self-evaluation as 'a real artist in the art' and his appraisal of his hoax creations as his 'masterpiece' (Wells 1904: 59). Yet the distinctions between the two stories charts the trajectory of the taxidermic imaginary that has been the subject of this chapter: while Well's taxidermist boasts of having defeated nature through hyperreal forgeries of non-existent birds and taxidermied mermaids, na Gopaleen's presents an abject eco-/body horror at the realisation of the continuity between human and nonhuman life.

Yaeli Greenblatt notes that '[f]or Murphy, his victim's remains are both comparable with clothing and practically treated as such, as is apparent in his depiction of 'having "dressed"' in Kelly's skin (2020: 133). The conflation also brings to the fore the unspoken exploitation of nonhuman animal bodies in the technologies of clothing. Elsewhere, the continuity between the human and nonhuman is foregrounded in Murphy's decision to 'treat Kelly the same as any other dead creature that found its way to the workshop' and in his description of his method of skinning Kelly: 'I applied the general technique and flaying pattern appropriate to apes' (O'Brien 2013: 86). From anthropomorphic Victorian mounts through Well's human hat-rack to Hemingway's encounter with the wild animal as the human masculine ideal, there has been an implication that has been redirected at all turns into other anthropocentric discourses (humanism, science, colonialism), but never entirely expunged: namely, that the carefully constructed limits between the human and nonhuman are always liable to be exposed as a construction of underlying economic structures and their discursive linking of knowledges and bodies to power. This implication is foregrounded and complicated in na Gopaleen's image of the human as taxidermied object, as animal.

Na Gopaleen's tale anticipates the late twentieth century's taxidermic imaginary as a site both of kitsch neo-Victorianism and of uncanny eco-horror and abject body horror, especially when applied to the human body, as in *Psycho* (1960) and *The Texas Chainsaw Massacre* (1974). Yet it also reflects backwards on how modernism's proximities to taxidermic material practices reveal a more capacious literary movement than standard accounts, one which develops through diverse points of encounter with naturalism and realism, inhabiting and deconstructing their discursive modes through the hoax poetics of fake interviews, faux biographies, spurious confessions. What distinguishes these modernist writers from purely parodic or satirical approaches to writing taxidermy is their interest in de-fetishising economic processes and material bodies; in reflecting on the resonances between the taxidermist's and the writer's art; in exploring the posthuman intersection between animal, human, technology and object; and in foregrounding taxidermy as a speculative tool for 'questioning our modes of perceiving, constructing, and consuming animals' (Aloi 2018: 34) by harnessing its self-contradictory capacity both to enforce rigidly and to disturb uncannily the coordinates of the living human subject and the inanimate nonhuman object.

Works Cited

Adair, William. 2014. 'Hemingway's *The Sun Also Rises*: The Dog in the Window and Other War Allusions'. *The Hemingway Review* 34.1 (Fall): 76–81.

Aloi, Giovanni, 2018. *Speculative Taxidermy: Natural History, Animal Surfaces, and Art in the Anthropocene*. New York: Columbia University Press.

American Museum of Natural History. 2016. 'The Man Who Made Habitat Dioramas'. Available at: <https://www.amnh.org/explore/news-blogs/news-posts/carl-akeley-dioramas> (last accessed 25 November 2021).

Attridge, John. 2014. 'Mythomaniac Modernism: Lying and Bullshit in Flann O'Brien'. In *Flann O'Brien and Modernism*. Ed. Julian Murphet, Rónán McDonald and Sascha Morrell, 27–40. London: Bloomsbury.

Baker, Carlos. 1969. *Ernest Hemingway: A Life Story*. New York: Scribner.

Barthes, Roland. 1986. *The Rustle of Language*. Trans. Richard Howard. New York: Hill and Wang.

Beegel, Susan F. 2000. 'Eye and Heart: Hemingway's Education as a Naturalist'. In *A Historical Guide to Ernest Hemingway*. Ed. Linda Wagner Martin, 53–92. Oxford: Oxford University Press.

Bezan, Sarah and Susan McHugh. 2019. 'Introduction: Taxidermic Forms and Fictions'. *Configurations* 27.2 (Spring): 131–8.

Brown, Stephen Gilbert. 2018. 'Hemingway and Akeley: Identity Formation and Hemingway's Naturalist Calling'. *The Hemingway Review* 38.1 (Fall): 71–91.

Dickens, Charles. 1997. *Our Mutual Friend*. London: Penguin.

Diepeveen, Leonard, ed. 2014. *Mock Modernism: An Anthology of Parodies, Travesties, Frauds, 1910–35*. Toronto: University of Toronto Press.

Fagan, Paul. 2018. 'Samuel Beckett's "Le Concentrisme" and the Modernist Literary Hoax'. In *Beckett and Modernism*. Ed. Olga Beloborodova, Dirk Van Hulle and Pim Verhulst, 212–28. New York: Palgrave Macmillan.

Greenblatt, Yaeli. 2020. '"the tattered cloak of his perished skin": The Body as Costume in "Two in One", *At Swim-Two-Birds* and *The Third Policeman*'. In *Flann O'Brien: Gallows Humour*. Ed. Ruben Borg and Paul Fagan, 131–45. Cork: Cork University Press.

Gregory, Helen and Anthony Purdy. 2015. 'Present Signs, Dead Things: Indexical Authenticity and Taxidermy's Nonabsent Animal'. *Configurations* 23.1: 61–92.

Haraway, Donna. 1985. 'Teddy Bear Patriarchy: Taxidermy in the Garden of Eden, New York City, 1908–1936'. *Social Text* 11 (Winter): 20–64.

Haraway, Donna. 1997. *Modest-Witness@Second_Millennium.FemaleMan©_Meets_Oncomouse™: Feminism and Technoscience*. New York: Routledge.
Hardy, Zoé. 2018. 'Stuffing the Short Story with Context: Artistic Creation and Gender in H. G. Wells's "The Triumphs of a Taxidermist"'. *Journal of the Short Story in English* 71: 43–56.
Hemingway, Ernest. 1926. *The Sun Also Rises*. New York: Scribner.
Henning, Michelle. 2007. 'Anthropomorphic Taxidermy and the Death of Nature: The Curious Art of Hermann Ploucquet, Walter Potter and Charles Waterton'. *Victorian Literature and Culture* 35.2: 663–78.
Jackson, Shelley. 2006. 'The Original Death and Burial of Cock Robin'. *Conjunctions* 46: 328–46.
Lynn, Kenneth S. 1987. *Hemingway*. New York: Simon and Schuster.
McHugh, Susan. 2019. 'Mourning Humans and Other Animals through Fictional Taxidermy Collections'. *Configurations* 27.2 (Spring): 239–56.
Mellby, Julie. 2012. 'Rare Birds of Paradise'. *The Princeton University Library Chronicle* 73.3 (Spring): 485–7.
Morris, Pat and Joanna Ebenstein. 2013. *Walter Potter's Curious World of Taxidermy*. New York: Penguin.
Nixon, Rob. 2011. *Slow Violence and the Environmentalism of the Poor*. Cambridge, MA: Harvard University Press.
O'Brien, Flann. 2013. *The Short Fiction of Flann O'Brien*. Ed. Neil Murphy and Keith Hopper. Champaign, IL: Dalkey Archive Press.
Péquignot, Amandine. 2006. 'The History of Taxidermy: Clues for Preservation'. *Collections: A Journal for Museum and Archives Professionals* 2.3 (February): 245–55.
Pyke, Jenny. 2014. 'Charles Dickens and the Cat Paw Letter Opener'. *19: Interdisciplinary Studies in the Long Nineteenth Century* 19: n.p. Available at <http://doi.org/10.16995/ntn.701> (last accessed 7 July 2022).
Reynolds, Michael S. 1986. *The Young Hemingway*. New York: Basil Blackwell.
Sanford, Marcelline Hemingway. 1999. *At the Hemingways*. Moscow: University of Idaho Press.
Styrchacz, Thomas. 1993. 'Trophy Hunting as Trope of Manhood in Ernest Hemingway's *Green Hills of Africa*'. *The Hemingway Review* 13.1 (Fall): 36–47.
Talairach-Vielmas, Laurence. 2014. *Fairy Tales, Natural History and Victorian Culture*. London: Palgrave Macmillan.
Wakeham, Pauline. 2008. *Taxidermic Signs: Reconstructing Aboriginality*. Minneapolis: University of Minnesota Press.
Wells, H. G. 1904. *The Stolen Bacillus and Other Incidents*. London: Macmillan and Co.
Wirtén, Eva Hemmungs. 2008. *Terms of Use: Negotiating the Jungle of the Intellectual Commons*. Toronto: University of Toronto Press.
Woolf, Virginia. 2007. *The Selected Works of Virginia Woolf*. Ware: Wordsworth Library.
Young, Lin. 2017. '"To Talk of Many Things": Chaotic Empathy and Anxieties of Victorian Taxidermy in *Alice's Adventures in Wonderland*'. *Victorian Review* 43.1 (Spring): 47–65.

PART III

ANIMAL, NATION, EMPIRE

7

SPECIES CLEANSING: THE RHETORIC OF RAT CONTROL IN THE PEOPLE'S REPUBLIC OF POLAND 1945–1956

Gabriela Jarzębowska

This chapter examines the rhetoric regarding the eradication of rats in Poland between 1945 and 1956, when a broad-scale rat extermination programme was undertaken.[1] There was an intensification of rat control campaigns in Poland at the turn of the 1950s, which can be explained by a sharp increase in the rat population during the period of the war. However, the co-occurrence of the anti-rat propaganda with political purges, as well as strategic and rhetorical resemblances between these two operations, cannot be ignored. Consequently, this Polish case study can be seen as a starting point for analysing how political discourses can shape existing environmental policies and how dominant political narratives influence pest control and sanitary programmes. The exploration of animal figuration in this chapter, therefore, takes a cultural approach to the beastly modernisms that concern the volume as a whole, tracing out the implications of both meanings of that word beastly: cruel and animal-like.

Genocide studies and, most notably, Holocaust studies, have already identified the connections between discursive mechanisms of modernity (including metaphors of purification) and militarised narratives. As I will demonstrate, a similar mechanism may be at play in debates over environmental management and the figuration of nonhuman animals as pests. Rats were traditionally considered vermin and this status was highlighted in the postwar period, when two parallel discourses that shaped the public debate at the time were fused in pest control rhetoric. These discourses were military, promoting the active pursuit of real or imagined adversaries, and the euphemistic discourse of sanitation and epidemiology. I will argue that the rat control discourse which developed during the Stalinist era clearly replicates linguistic and visual tropes of political purges and ethnic cleansing politics. The way that nonhuman animals figure in the rhetoric regarding the management of urban rat populations can thus provide a proper model for investigating how cultural policies of political exclusion work and what kind of persuasive strategies they may follow. My aim is not to discount the real risks associated with the proximity between humans and rats; nor do I compare pest animal species to excluded groups of human individuals. My objective, rather, is to map out strategies of exclusion which draw on beastly figurations that may be common to ethnic and political cleansing and certain strategies of environmental management. I demonstrate how negative ramifications tied to interspecies cohabitation (such as competition over resources and exposure to pathogens) are translated according to narrative schemas that reveal fear, prejudice and biases dominant in their historical moment and embedded in specific political narratives.

My analysis begins by outlining the broader historical context of rat control programmes in early postwar Poland. I provide both an international and a national background for pest control and argue that the latter should be considered as decisive for shaping rat management discourse in this era. I then proceed to rat control discourse analysis, identifying two cultural scripts that shaped social perception of these animals: namely, rat as an enemy and rat as a (disembodied) pathogen. Afterwards, I take a step back to see from which cultural imaginaries of prewar or war origin these scripts come. I argue that they replicate genocidal logic, being the extension of antisemitic discourse on the one hand, and the rhetoric of Stalinist political purges on the other. In the last section I broaden my analysis in order to see how this phenomenon can be situated within the larger cultural landscape of the mid-twentieth century. I argue that anti-rat discourse has deeper underpinnings that exceed strictly genocidal logic and should be considered as an inseparable component of modernity – specifically, modernity's combatant and utilitarian concepts of human relations with a nonhuman world.

Historical Background

The period spanning 1949–56 in Poland witnessed an unprecedented and never since repeated surge in the desire to exterminate rats. Although it was the prewar period that marked the beginning of coordinated rodent control measures in Poland, it was not until the early postwar era that pest control became scientific. What I mean by 'scientific' here is that from being a rather chaotic, reactive and hit-or-miss campaign, pest control was transformed – or at least was meant to be transformed – into a rational, coordinated, proactive effort, based on scientific experiments regarding both the ecology of rats and the effectiveness of particular rodenticides. This was a reflection of a worldwide tendency, as the 1940s marked a widespread interest in rat control science on both sides of the Iron Curtain. In particular, ground-breaking research programmes were undertaken in Baltimore by scientists such as Curt Richter (who invented the toxin alpha-naphthylthiourea, or ANTU) and David E. Davis, John Emlen and John Calhoun with their Rodent Ecology Project (Keiner 2005; Biehler 2013). Due to geopolitical circumstances, Polish scientists were influenced mainly by Soviet colleagues such as Ivan Pavlov and his concept of classical conditioning. No evidence proves that they were familiar with Davis's or Emlen's writings. However, they did make references to Charles Elton (often referred to as the father of modern animal ecology), which demonstrates that the ideas of modern ecology were already present in Polish pest control discourse at that time (Czyżewski 1953; Rybicki 1956).

Although global tendencies should not be under-estimated while looking into postwar rat control discourse in Poland, one needs to stress that the historical context was entirely different. The two critical factors that shaped pest control rhetoric were the Second World War, leaving Poland in a state of total destruction and post-Holocaust trauma, and the Stalinist regime which followed right after. The late 1940s saw huge reconstruction programmes, especially the rebuilding of Warsaw, almost totally destroyed after the Warsaw Uprising in 1944. Those programmes were based on strong social mobilisation, aimed at giving hope to war-traumatised people. However, they were also used as a tool for a symbolic consolidation of a new, Stalinist regime. Propaganda materials portrayed the efforts not only as a reconstruction but as a process of modernisation: building a new, brave, socialist world, emerging from the ashes of the war. And rats were a crucial part of this story.

Polish professional materials from the late 1940s and 1950s emphasised that rat infestations were prevalent during the war and immediately after. This might have been the case, considering the scale of destruction and the number of human and nonhuman bodies buried under the ruins, providing food for scavengers. One needs to remember, however, that, unlike in Baltimore, there were no research programmes in Poland before and right after the war that might have provided specific statistics to prove the population upsurge. Moreover, while rat infestation in the wake of wartime destruction was already clear by 1945, it was not until 1949 that the anti-rat campaign began on such a broad scale. This may support my hypothesis that the nature of this campaign was political and clearly linked to the consolidation of the Stalinist regime that followed in late 1940s, especially as the campaign became distinctly less fervent after the Khrushchev thaw in 1956. What I mean by saying that the rat control campaign was political, is that the Stalinist regime was centred around chasing true or imagined enemies, in order to consolidate the nation around the Party. These foes were mainly human (Germans, Americans, capitalists, 'Kulaks'[2] and so on), but this combatant logic soon began to incorporate nonhuman actors as well. As a troublesome species, destroying the property of humans and spreading disease, rats made a perfect enemy, along with the potato beetle, allegedly dropped by Americans to destroy Polish crops (Steciąg and Wodzińska 2016: n.p.).

As a consequence, propaganda materials from the early postwar period explicitly emphasised the presence of rats in neglected areas as a sign of backwardness and under-development, making rats (or, rather, their absence) a gauge of modernisation processes. As creatures that pose a considerable threat to both public health (as we share pathogens with them) and the national economy (as our competitors for resources), rats can be perceived as embodiments of challenges to be confronted by a state devastated during the war. The vast campaign of didactic propaganda – posters, pamphlets, lectures, commissioned press materials and radio broadcasts – sent a strong message to the public that the extermination of rats was imperative. The key slogan coined in the 1950 was 'Tęp szczury!' (which can be translated as 'Kill rats!' or 'Eradicate rats!'), and it was subsequently included in almost all materials of this type. This extensive campaign, known as 'deratisation',[3] was made possible only by the total centralisation of the profession, scientists' engagement, the introduction of new rodenticides[4] and, last but not least, change in the language used to describe these nonhuman animals. Not a mere nuisance any more, rats were transformed on a linguistic and visual level into a harmful, deceitful foe or a disembodied problem to be solved. This rhetorical shift was possibly due to the symbolic denigration of the rat and the fact that rat population management was combined with a discourse of sanitation.

Two Strategies for the Symbolic Denigration of the Rat

To define species cleansing[5] as a term relevant to the eradication of rats in socialist Poland, we must first examine how the mechanisms of symbolic devaluation work. In the case of methodically executed acts of genocide targeting humans, a common precondition is the dehumanisation of individuals or groups perceived as harmful or threatening to the social order. This concept is typically defined as the denial of a certain person or group's humanity, either uniformly or within a circumscribed context (Oliver 2011: 86). In his writing on the Holocaust, Zygmunt Bauman emphasises the technical and administrative nature of the dehumanisation that precedes genocide, which allows its agents to disregard ethics in their categorisation of human beings (Bauman 1989). Dehumanisation, moreover, carries the linguistic stigma of 'the Other'. One common strategy likens the real or imagined enemy to a nonhuman animal – usually one burdened with negative cultural connotations, such as a cockroach, pig or rat. From this perspective, dehumanisation operates along the border between humans and nonhumans.

However, as Tyler Joshua Kasperbauer aptly demonstrates, similar mechanisms of symbolic denigration can be at play in the way nonhuman animals are portrayed. Being an equivocal example of 'the Other', the animal is deprived of its agency while its death is portrayed using technical terms (Kasperbauer 2018). Of course, nonhuman animals are not homogenous as a group – some of them are denigrated and devalued more than others. Expanding on Giorgio Agamben's figure of *homo sacer*, Robin Mackenzie proposes the term *bestia sacer*, meaning 'subanimals'. For Mackenzie, this category includes species and populations whose welfare is not protected by legislation and whose exploitation has never been legally defined. The category is a dynamic one: within its framework, certain groups or individuals are symbolically excluded from the animal community, depending on their socio-economic or environmental context, often due to the potential harm they cause to the ecosystem or their usefulness to humans (Mackenzie 2011). This concept may help us understand the mechanisms of the symbolic devaluation of rodents in deratisation campaigns. Moreover, in the case of rats, these mechanisms operate beyond the legislative level with deep cultural underpinnings. In the decades discussed here, these precedents were reinforced by extensive propaganda. The tendency to describe the extermination of rodents using language associated with hygiene rather than environmental management reflects the symbolic process by which the rat had been excluded from the vertebrate community and demoted to 'subanimal' status.

Of the two strategies of symbolic devaluation I have identified, the first – 'rat as enemy' – reveals a tendency to anthropomorphise these animals. Anti-rat educational materials from the Stalinist era often used militaristic language portraying rats as invaders:

> For centuries, rats have oppressed us with the plague, attacking mankind with their invisible army of murderous fleas. (Ślusarski 1950: 147)

> The society whose individuals fail to form a unified front to implement wide scale rat eradication will remain at the mercy of any rat left alive. (Brodniewicz 1953: 11)

> Rats wage their own imperialist war, and despite the ceaseless efforts of man, to date, they have not yet been defeated. (Rybicki 1954: 3)

> Each and every citizen of our Nation must join in battle, for only then will victory be achieved. (Ślusarski 1952: 12)

Tellingly, scientific arguments about rats and their necessary eradication were often substantiated by emotional ones that merged descriptive and normative styles:

> A detailed psychological analysis and more scrupulous review of the biological attributes of this rodent, his habits, mode of existence, and

behavior toward other kinds of animals as well as members of his own species suggest that the rat is a crafty and refined aggressor. Threatened by predators or starvation, they become cruel and bloodthirsty murderers. (Kloniecki 1955: 8)

In these linguistic practices, conventional human archetypes ('thief', 'enemy', 'murderer') are applied to nonhuman animals, who thus absorb traits typically associated with *Homo sapiens* ('crafty', 'malicious', 'irreverent'). We might therefore read this anthropomorphic tendency in deratisation propaganda as a form of false ennoblement. It resembles ennoblement on a symbolic level, insofar as rats are ascribed human traits. Yet this 'elevation' is only superficial, for it aims to denigrate the animals morally. The objective is to accentuate their otherness and monstrosity to portray them as valueless and worthy of ruthless extermination. A necessary step in this process is the act of exclusion. In the logic of human genocide, the symbolically dehumanised enemy is less than human and therefore devoid of moral value. The function of zoomorphism is to emphasise symbolically the object's severance from human society. In the case of deratisation, the rat is not fully animal, for it has no sentimental, utilitarian or ecological value to humans. This narrative sets the rat apart as an isolated entity: humanity's mortal nemesis, pest and 'subanimal'. The function of anthropomorphism is to eject the rat from the animal world and imbue it with new meaning: the phantasm of the enemy.

While this paradoxical strategy of 'denigrating anthropomorphism' is mainly specific to militaristic narratives, the second strategy for degrading the rat is tied to narratives of hygiene and epidemiology, according to which these nonhuman animals symbolically disappear. This may be related to a linguistic phenomenon from the late 1940s and early 1950s that conditioned social perceptions of the ethics of rat extermination in Poland as they persist today. I am referring to the acronym DDD (disinfection, disinsection, deratisation), which was often used in former socialist countries to describe discrete campaigns to exclude unwanted nonhuman forms of life (micro- (germs), meso- (insects) and macro-organisms (rodents)) from anthropogenic environments for sanitary and economic reasons. The formation and persistence of this notion were crucial factors shaping the socio-cultural perception of rat extermination in postwar Poland.

This narrative strips the rat of its nuances as animal and symbolically aligns it with the pathogens it carries. The extermination of rats, insects and microbes was consolidated in one term – a gesture that expels the rat from the realm of urban fauna and absorbs it into a hygiene narrative, where it is defined as hazardous filth or waste. In this way, the eradication of rat populations correlates to attempts to purge certain areas of undesirable elements. Killing nonhuman animals has been described euphemistically as a 'set of coordinated activities' represented visually using graphs, tables and infographics (Fig. 7.1).

Figure 7.1 Anon. Map. Courtesy of the Polish National Archive, Szczecin.

This strategy runs counter to anthropomorphism. The analogy to pathogens is very different from false ennoblement, for here, a nonhuman animal with advanced cognitive abilities is metonymically linked to disease. In contrast to cases of anthropomorphism, this correlation is rarely explicit and never adopted as a conscious propaganda tactic. Rather, it is an unconscious psychological mechanism organising discursive practices of deratisation that is catalysed by the advent of the term DDD. The rat's inclusion in hygiene narratives gave rise to a new set of concepts that organised the perception of rats in the collective imaginary by symbolically identifying them with medical conditions. No longer were rats merely a nuisance (as they had been for centuries). Absorbed into a system of bureaucratically organised hygienic and epidemiological practices, they became a problem to be solved. Recalling Bauman's definition, they were 'reduced to a set of quantitative measures' (Bauman 1989: 102), for their death was measured in kilograms, square metres of collected bodies or total tonnage of rat poison consumed.

In sum, the moral denigration that occurs in deratisation rhetoric entails the symbolic exclusion of an entire species from the animal sphere. In militaristic narratives, the rat becomes 'something more' than an animal, for it is symbolically defined as an anthropomorphic adversary of the human species. In the hygiene narrative, however, the rat is 'something less' than mere animal, for it is redefined as a pathogen and classified as a technical issue. In both cases, however, the rat ceases to be an animal on the discursive level.

The Rat as 'the Other': Mechanisms of Ethnic and Political Cleansing in Deratisation Rhetoric

Images of the rat from Stalinist times clearly use the rhetoric of Othering. They reproduce the narrative schemas and projected images of groups that have been morally denigrated and dehumanised by twentieth-century totalitarianisms in the context of genocide or other forms of political exclusion. They are structurally analogical to 'hygienic' metaphors often used to describe ethnic cleansing, as well as the militaristic terminology of political purges. Consequently, they followed two cultural schemas dominant in mid-twentieth-century Poland: the figure of the Jew in prewar and wartime antisemitic propaganda and the figure of the enemy in Stalinist propaganda. In the first instance, deratisation uses iconographic motifs and linguistic templates that invoke the rhetoric of prewar antisemitism. Nazi propaganda frequently portrayed Jewish people as rats, and many scholars have noted the ecological underpinnings of the Holocaust (Bauman 1989; Neumann

Figure 7.2 Bogdan Nowakowski. *Rozwój*. 1925. Courtesy of the Poster Museum, Wilanow. Public Domain.

2012). Here, I will examine two portraits predating 1945 in order to link postwar deratisation rhetoric to prewar antisemitism.

The first portrait is a cover of the magazine *Rozwój* (meaning 'Development') from 1925 (Fig. 7.2), illustrated by Bogdan Nowakowski and depicting a swarm of rats. The rats are fleeing a house, where a man in uniform banishes them by throwing flaming torches. The eagle emblem from the Polish national flag on the man's door suggests that the building symbolises Poland. On closer investigation, we see that the rats have certain traits associated with Jewish stereotypes: payot, caricaturised facial features, and stars of David printed on their hats. This image of rat extermination is rather specific, for the object of extermination is, by implication, the Jewish people, now dehumanised and portrayed as rodents. The image links the rhetoric of pest eradication to a political rhetoric that, like Nazi propaganda, treats Jews as harmful, unsanitary animals that must be eradicated so the modern nation can be built. The extermination of rats-as-Jews is portrayed as an attempt to cleanse Poland-as-home of undesired elements by literally herding them beyond the threshold of the home (*extermino* as exile).

In my second example, a poster advertising 'Delicia' poison (Fig. 7.3), antisemitic and deratisation rhetoric again coincide. The poster is undated but is

Figure 7.3 Anon. *Szczury tępi Delicia*. Undated [c.1940s]. Courtesy of the Polona Archive, Narodowa Library. Public Domain.

likely to be from the time of the Nazi occupation. It portrays two rats in realistic detail – a level of realism conspicuously undermined by the rats' unnaturally red pupils. Even more interesting than the rats themselves are the poster's graphics. Its colour scheme and typography distinctly resemble Nazi aesthetics. While antisemitic allusions may be less evident here than in my previous example, the choice to link rat extermination to Nazi aesthetics would have conjured unambiguous connotations. The relationship between these illustrations lies in their rhetorical contrast: while the earlier image uses the narrative schema of rat eradication to convey an antisemitic message, the 'Delicia' poster references Nazi aesthetics to transpose the logic of extermination (and its attendant emotions) to the animal context. Both posters are therefore visual amalgams of antisemitic and deratisation narratives.

Postwar deratisation propaganda grew out of this historically drawn link between the denigrated figures of the rat and the Jew. I do not suggest that the portrait of the rat in Stalinist propaganda conceals latent antisemitic messaging, but rather that on an iconographic and linguistic level it absorbs motifs and structures that originated in racist rhetoric. I am speaking specifically of motifs such as the image of the rat as thief, epidemiological hazard and threat to the national economy. Today, these analogies may seem less obvious, but we can infer that they were intelligible to the average addressee of deratisation propaganda in the postwar period.

The second linguistic and iconographic tradition that laid the groundwork for postwar deratisation propaganda was Stalinist propaganda about 'the enemy'. This motif offers another context for understanding how the political and the biological intertwine in postwar Polish deratisation rhetoric. While the tendency in totalitarian systems to cast political enemies as vermin has been the subject of extensive scholarship, scholars have not yet acknowledged the practice's bilateral nature.

Rhetoric casting the rat as enemy is rooted in the phantasm of the political enemy circulating in Polish propaganda in the 1950s. This phantasm had a specific function during Stalinism: to mobilise society against real or fabricated threats. Socialist propaganda often used military terminology. For instance, the word *walka* (meaning combat, fight or struggle) was applied to even trivial affairs, such as the fight against alcoholism, minor thefts or poaching. According to this discourse, the enemy can be easily singled out, for they carry repulsive physical traits that reflect their inferior character. To understand the convergence of biological and political narratives in Stalinist deratisation propaganda, we must first consider the notion of 'social vermin' (meaning, roughly, 'social parasite'), common in socialist rhetoric of this period. This term was reserved for individuals who actively harmed the social good (causing economic losses and other kinds of damage) out of negligence, selfishness or loyalty to enemies of the system. These actions would be portrayed as intentional

Figure 7.4 Włodzimierz Zakrzewski. *Demokracja Buduje*. 1945. Poster Museum, Wilanow.

and malice-driven acts of sabotage. The parasite could be a thief, 'Kulak' or poacher, although these details would sometimes be left visually vague, to be filled in later *ad hoc* with the negative archetype most relevant to the moment. On a visual level, the social vermin were often dehumanised and given traits resembling ill-favoured animals.

One instance of the rat motif's presence in Stalinist political propaganda is a poster by Włodzimierz Zakrzewski from 1945 (Fig. 7.4). Zakrzewski depicts a rat gnawing at the foundations of a home. The poster reads: 'Democracy builds, the opposition wants to destroy.' Oppositional forces are portrayed as a rodent destroying the newly erected foundations of the socialist system. While the social vermin concept is not made verbally explicit, the familiarity of the rat-pest archetype makes this connection legible to the poster's addressees. Reading this poster in the context of deratisation rhetoric reveals interesting connections. While deratisation propaganda materials use the stereotype of the enemy to incentivise exterminating rats, the poster inverts this operation: by invoking the negative stereotype of the rat as vermin, it morally condemns 'social vermin'. As was the case with images reproducing antisemitic messaging, the poster relies on a reciprocal relation.

The metaphor functions both ways: the rat is compared to the Jew/social vermin/enemy, while simultaneously, the Jew/social vermin/enemy is likened to the rat. As a result, identifying the source metaphor is no easy task, for it seems to draw from dominant cultural schemas for excluding the Other that devalue individuals or groups within the hierarchy of a given historical and cultural context. The construction of such hierarchies is therefore a dynamic process conditioned by its specific cultural context and the objectives and nuances of the political agenda involved. Degrading a targeted social group by likening its members to rats can simultaneously occur through a counter-rhetoric that devalues nonhuman animals by anthropomorphising them and aligning them with the enemy. In these metaphors the signifier and signified may switch places, yet they both remain discursively bound together by association.

The figure of the Jew in Nazi propaganda and the enemy in Stalinist propaganda have much in common: the dehumanisation of the members of a specific group, the belief that their actions harm the society/nation, and finally, a clear connection to the discourse of hygiene and metaphors of cleansing. Of course, there are also obvious differences between these two figures. For instance, Nazi genocidal discourse had an extensive biological basis (to invoke Bauman again, it was framed as 'a matter of pulling out the weeds') (Bauman 1989: 92), while the rhetoric of Stalinist purges was premised on a political logic that defined the enemy not by their ethnicity but according to their attitude toward the system. In this sense, the rhetoric of the Holocaust coincides with the mechanisms of ethnic cleansing, while Stalinist rhetoric belongs in the category of political purges.

I argue, however, that in the specific case of deratisation propaganda, these two narratives have fused on the rhetorical level. Rat extermination is a biologically oriented operation based on species identity. In this way, it is implicitly pseudo-ethnic, for it does not combat a targeted rat population that has exceeded critical mass and poses a potential threat. On the contrary, it combats rats in general. The rhetoric calling for the eradication of these nonhuman animals suggests that annihilation was the ultimate goal. According to this logic, rats' potential harm is a congenital trait embedded in their species affiliation. At the same time, this perception of rats reproduces the rhetorical schemas used to describe enemies of the system in Stalinist propaganda. This militaristic rhetoric and the consolidation of the rat and social vermin as figures suggest that there is something more to this relation than mere analogy. In Stalinist propaganda, the rat not only resembles the political enemy, but it literally becomes the enemy, absorbing semantic connotations from the image system of political propaganda. In this sense, deratisation rhetoric is doubly derivative: it appropriates the genocidal, 'hygienic' narrative of antisemitism and Stalinist depictions of political enemies.

Species Cleansing as a Militaristic Dimension of Modernisation

For the reasons outlined above, I propose the term 'species cleansing' to describe the methodical extermination of nonhuman animals based on their species identity and the terminology of annihilation coupled with the large-scale social mobilisation accompanying this practice. Stalinist-era propaganda visualises species cleansing according to rhetorical strategies that parallel those of genocide: the symbolic exclusion from society (or, in this case, symbolic exclusion from the community of vertebrates), shifting collective blame for social calamities to one group (scapegoating), and incensing the public actively and enthusiastically to contribute to extermination programmes. The symbolic status of the 'subanimal' was constructed according to cultural conceptions of impurity and purification. This logic, of course, has deep cultural roots tied to a conception of dirt that Mary Douglas has described as the disruption of social order and as 'matter out of place' (1966: 36). Yet species cleansing was made possible only as a consequence of a scientific hygienic superstructure (which, in turn, followed the emergence of germ theory) that informed the cultural schema depicting rats as vectors of disease. This superstructure allowed these nonhuman animals to be fully absorbed into 'hygienic' discursive practices.

The consolidation of discourses of war, sanitation and epidemiology is relevant beyond the specific case of rat extermination. It also impacted antisemitic Nazi rhetoric. Saul Friedlander has argued that it drew its strength from the discursive fusion of older religious and cultural antisemitic tropes (describing Jews as Christ killers, well poisoners, traitors and forces of evil in Western history and society) with 'scientific' or 'biological' narratives exploiting sanitary metaphors. In fact, these two narratives reinforced one another. It was the fusing of the two strands, according to which 'modern' tactics were used to appeal to old prejudices, that made the antisemitic message so powerful (Friedlander 2007).[6]

This fusion, however, has larger cultural underpinnings that exceed strictly genocidal logic. Susan Sontag, for instance, has pointed out that the language surrounding disease also gravitates toward militaristic metaphors. We speak of the 'invasion' of an illness and an organism's 'defence mechanisms'. Sontag notes that the basic metaphors for cancer are directly sourced from militant language. Medicinal terms have a similar inflection: radiotherapy uses metaphors of aerial warfare, according to which patients are 'bombarded' with toxic rays. Chemotherapy, meanwhile, is described as poison-based chemical warfare (Sontag 1978: 65).

Incorporating troublesome nonhuman animals into hygiene rhetoric reproduces this logic. As an embodiment of disease, the alleged pest becomes the object of practices repeating the mechanisms of war. In his comparative analysis of pesticide use and chemical weapons in the twentieth century, Edmund Russell has drawn extensive parallels between his two subjects on the level of propaganda, institutions and actual methods employed. Russell insists that the analogy works both ways: the war with the enemy is portrayed as a war against pests, while the war on pests is conceived according to the schema of the war with the enemy (Russell 2011: 99). As I have demonstrated, this rhetorical reciprocity is also at play in Polish discourse on the elimination of enemies and pests. It reflects a broader mechanism tied to dynamics of modernisation, particularly in the socialist context. Even this brief overview of Polish propaganda materials from 1945 to 1956 reveals how metaphors of cleansing and purification appear frequently in language describing the war on fascism, wartime profiteers, social vermin and other pejorative archetypes. For all these reasons, the language of sanitation and modernisation is deeply tied to military rhetoric.

The rhetorical unification of military and hygiene narratives in Stalinist language is not exclusive to the discourse of rat extermination, although it is particularly evident in this case. This may be because Stalinist propaganda portrayed nature as intensely and intrinsically antimodern – a force that must be tamed and exploited in the name of progress. Such rhetoric conceptualises the natural environment as a dangerous adversary, a residue of the prerevolutionary past that must undergo socialist industrialisation. Consequently, language describing humanity's struggle against nature often draws on military rhetoric to mobilise the public and convince people that they are under siege. Nature became the new enemy for the socialist world (replacing the Third Reich), and the only way to conquer it was to force its unconditional surrender (Gończyński-Jussis 2016: 46; see also Brain 2010).

In this light, we can see how rats (nonhuman animals burdened with negative cultural connotations and disrupting the modernisation regime) are a useful counterpart for the figure of the enemy. By extending the Stalinist portrayal of nature, the territory rats inhabit can be framed as backward and undeveloped, while the reconstruction and modernisation of cities call for the species' annihilation. Socialist modernisation wages war against the rat as a symbol of poverty, disease, wartime destruction and unhygienic backwardness. To paraphrase Bauman's words on genocide again, we might say that killing these nonhuman animals was depicted as an act of creation rather than destruction, for it was linked to the creation of a better, healthier and more modern society (Bauman 1989: 92).

We should bear in mind, however, that the consolidation of military and hygiene rhetoric in environmental discourse of this period is not specific to the Eastern Bloc and belongs in the broader context of modernisation. The mid-twentieth century witnessed a sharp rise in the deployment of combative, violent language to describe relations between humans and their environment. This trend prevailed in countries on the other side of the Iron Curtain, particularly in the United States. In the 1940s and 1950s, there was a sudden rise in unregulated pesticide usage and a new sense of faith that humankind could fully conquer nature (Russell 2011). This process paralleled trends like the emergence of factory farming and the rapid development of laboratory testing on animals. In these same decades, the notion of ecological invasion was used to describe ecological dynamics in military terms. Neel Ahuja has noted that in twentieth-century American politics, the management of species potentially carrying harmful pathogens (understood as the management of biological risk) coincides with the country's territorial and economic expansion (Ahuja 2016). All these trends may stem from a belief system specific to this period that represents humanity's domination over nature (often expressed through military symbols) as an instrument of modernisation and progress. We can read the concerted efforts to exterminate rats in the USA in the 1940s (such as the Baltimore programmes) as a product of these processes. What is more, on both sides of the Iron Curtain, rat extermination propaganda shares this militaristic tone. Lianne McTavish and Jingjing Zheng have demonstrated that extermination campaigns in Alberta in the 1950s (like Stalinist campaigns in Poland) also portrayed the rat as enemy. Their research reveals a clear link between Cold War rhetoric and anti-rat campaigns, while on a visual level, the latter references American propaganda from the Second World War that depicted the Japanese as rats (McTavish and Zheng 2011).

Rat Rhetoric Today

The antagonistic rhetoric used to describe rat extermination in the Stalinist era is therefore the product of several determinants. At the most basic level, it reveals the effects of the escalated language of public debate of this period that castigated the enemy and used military metaphors. More broadly, it is shaped by the Soviet conception of nature in militaristic terms and prewar and wartime visual and linguistic clichés that were often racist in origin. On a broader level, however, it may also be tied to a specific feature of the axiology underlying modernity's antagonistic attitude toward the natural environment and the belief that humans can fully subordinate nature to their needs. This trend thus reflects the overall escalation of public discourse precipitated by the two World Wars followed by the Cold War, and scientific progress, which had seeded the hope that new, chemical methods for exterminating harmful organisms would enable humanity's total emancipation from environmental constraints.

In this light, the escalation of extermination campaigns in postwar Poland and the militaristic and hygiene-oriented rhetoric they employed reflect a specific developmental stage of modernity where military terminology converged with narratives of hygiene and modernisation. In the United States, this narrative was gradually dismissed from the late 1950s. The publication of Rachel Carson's *Silent Spring* (1962) is often cited as a watershed moment in this incremental rhetorical shift in humans' relationship to the environment. In Poland, a similar discursive shift was prompted by the political transformations following the Thaw.

Yet, the figure of the enemy-rat did not disappear from rat control propaganda completely. Indeed, the highly euphemistic, biopolitical narrative of rats as pathogens distinctly shapes public perception of the species today and on-going eradication programmes. Yet, tellingly, this narrative is often replaced (or at least complemented) by a militaristic one when the problem is perceived to have grown severe and more concerted extermination efforts are attempted. When rat control ceases to be taboo (veiled in sterile, sanitary discursive practices) and becomes an issue of public debate, it can transform into a confrontational narrative that uses militaristic metaphors to stoke social fears. Bill de Blasio's $32-million dollar plan announced in 2017 to increase rat control in New York City may be a case in point, for it is clearly framed as 'a war' (Alkousaa 2017).

Therefore, while 'hygiene' discourse has, to a vast extent, taken over contemporary rat-related imaginaries, the military rhetoric still lurks under the surface, to be invoked whenever rat problems appear to get out of control. Further research is needed on the interconnections between contemporary rat control rhetoric and deprecatory rhetoric targeting excluded and under-privileged social groups, such as racist and anti-immigrant discourse. I suspect one could establish clear links between these two narratives, however vastly their dynamics and constitution may differ from Stalinist rhetoric. The latter was the product of a particular historical and geopolitical context – namely, the violent language of a totalitarian regime. But the incorporation of problematic nonhuman animals into political imaginaries and the resulting replication of 'othering' rhetoric can also be observed in contemporary public debate. It could be productive to identify these similarities through cross-species meta-analysis not only to determine how environmental management is discursively organised, but also to explore how the politics of exclusion operate.

Translated by Eliza Rose

The project 'Species Cleansing: The Political Dimension of Rat Extermination after 1945' was funded by the National Centre of Science (Narodowe Centrum Nauki) and its Preludium Competition according to decree 2017/27/N/HS3/00013.

Works Cited

Ahuja, Neel. 2016. *Bioinsecurities: Disease Interventions, Empire, and the Government of Species*. Durham, NC, and London: Duke University Press Books.

Alkousaa, Riham. 2017. 'New York City Declares War on Rats with $32 Million Plan'. *Reuters*. Available at: <https://www.reuters.com/article/us-newyork-rats-idUSKBN19X2YR> (last accessed 7 July 2022).

Bauman, Zygmunt. 1989. *Modernity and the Holocaust*. Ithaca, NY: Cornell University Press.

Biehler, Dawn. 2013. *Pests in the City: Flies, Bedbugs, Cockroaches and Rats*. Seattle: University of Washington Press.

Brain, Stephen. 2010. 'The Great Stalin Plan for the Transformation of Nature'. *Environmental History* 15: 670–700.
Brodniewicz, Aleksander. 1953. *Dlaczego należy tępić szczury?* Biblioteka Popularno-Naukowa Zarządu Dezynfekcji, Dezynsekcji i Deratyzacji w Warszawie, Warsaw.
Czyżewski, Janusz Antoni. 1953. 'Zwalczanie szczurów na dużych obszarach'. *Przeglad epidemiologiczny* 7.4: 277–89.
Douglas, Mary. 1966. *Purity and Danger: An Analysis of Concepts of Pollution and Taboo.* New York: Routledge.
Franklin, Adrian. 2011. 'An Improper Nature? Introduced Animals and "Species Cleansing" in Australia'. In *Human and Other Animals: Critical Perspectives.* Ed. Bob Carter and Charles Nickie, 195–216. Houndmills and New York: Palgrave.
Friedlander, Saul. 2007. *The Years of Extermination: Nazi Germany and the Jews 1939–1945.* New York: HarperCollins.
Gończyński-Jussis, Filip. 2016. '*Przeobraziciele przyrody*: Motyw kształtowania środowiska naturalnego przez *ludzi radzieckich* i ich polskich naśladowców w propagandzie stalinizmu'. *Historyka: Studia metodologiczne* 46: 115–33.
Kasperbauer, Tyler Joshua. 2018. *Subhuman. The Moral Psychology of Human Attitudes to Animals.* New York: Oxford University Press.
Keiner, Christine. 2005. 'Wartime Rat Control, Rodent Ecology, and the Rise and Fall of Chemical Rodenticides'. *Endeavour* 29.3: 119–25.
Kłoniecki, Jan. 1955. *Szczur: Zagadnienie ekonomiczne i zdrowotne.* Stalinogród: Wojewódzki Zarząd Propagandy Rolniczej.
Mackenzie, Robin. 2011. 'How the Politics of Inclusion/Exclusion and the Neuroscience of Dehumanization/Rehumanization Can Contribute to Animal Activists' Strategies: BestiaSacer II'. *Society & Animals* 19: 407–24.
McTavish, Lianne and Jingjing Zheng. 2011. 'Rats in Alberta: Looking at Pest-Control Posters from the 1950s'. *Canadian Historical Review* 92.3: 515–46.
Neumann, Boaz. 2012. 'National Socialism, Holocaust and Ecology'. In *Holocaust and Historical Methodology.* Ed. Dan Stone, 101–23. New York: Berghahn.
Oliver, Sophie. 2011. 'Dehumanization: Perceiving the Body as (In)human'. In *Humiliation, Degradation, Dehumanization: Human Dignity Violated.* Ed. Paulus Kaufmann, Hannes Kuch, Christian Neuhäuser and Elaine Webster, 85–100. Dordrecht: Springer.
Russell, Edmund. 2011. *War and Nature: Fighting Humans and Insects with Chemicals from World War I to Silent Spring.* Cambridge and New York: Cambridge University Press.
Rybicki, Stanisław. 1954. *Organizacja i czynności brygad deratyzacyjnych.* Warsaw: Biblioteka Popularno-Naukowa Zarządu Dezynfekcji, Dezynsekcji i Deratyzacji w Warszawie.
Rybicki, Stanisław. 1956. 'Technika i organizacja prac deratyzacyjnych'. In *Vademecum dezynfektora, dezynsektora i deratyzatora.* Ed. Stanisław Rybicki. Warsaw: Wydawnictwo Lekarskie PZWL.
Ślusarski, Wiesław. 1950. *Szczur gryzoń wojujący.* Spółdzielnia Wydawniczo-Handlowa 'Książka i wiedza', Warsaw.
Ślusarski, Wiesław. 1952. *Szczury!!! Patrz, jaki los chcą nam zgotować te wojownicze i niebezpieczne gryzonie!* Centrala Deratyzacji, Dezynsekcji i Dezynfekcji 'Derodinsekcja', Warsaw.

Sontag, Susan. 1978. *Illness as Metaphor*. New York: Farrar, Straus and Giroux.

Steciąg, Magdalena and Sylwia Wodzińska. 2016. 'The Colorado Beetle's Attack or the Potato Bug in the Cold War Propaganda Service in Poland'. *Language & Ecology*. Available at: <https://www.ecolinguistics-association.org/_files/ugd/ae088a_b985a3d7651d499daf8c109a61c15e25.pdf> (last accessed 18 July 2022).

Notes

1. This chapter is the product of dissertation research conducted in the following archives: Central Archives of Modern Records, National Archive in Łódź, Te National Archive in Szczecin, National Library, Museum of Disinfection, Disinsection and Deratisation, and Poster Museum at Wilanów. In my study, I offer a semiotic and iconographic analysis of propaganda ephemera about rats and deratisation from 1945 to 1956 (posters, pamphlets, proclamations, expert reports, radio commentaries, documents). The actual analyses are omitted from this chapter for the sake of brevity. Here, I attend to the conclusions and conceptual ramifications of my analyses of historical sources and situate these findings within their broader cultural context.
2. A term from Stalinist propaganda referring to land-owning peasants who resisted giving up their land to the state during the postwar land reforms.
3. In Poland's prewar discourse on this problem, the notion of 'deratisation' was not yet in circulation. At the time, the term was already used in several other languages (such as French) and, sporadically, in English, although it was never fully adopted into the English lexicon. It did, however, catch on in Polish, and in the first decade following the war, it became the universal term for the extermination of rodents.
4. Such as ANTU (with the Polish names Anfantina and Antuder) and, in the 1950s, warfarin (with the names Kumader and Kumatox).
5. It was Adrian Franklin who first used the term 'species cleansing' to describe management policies for introduced species in Australia (Franklin 2011).
6. I would like to thank Ethan Kleinberg for suggesting that I use Friedlander's framework to complement this analysis.

8

THE BARKING DOG AND CRYING BIRD IN PARTITION STORIES: BEASTLY MODERNISM AND THE SUBALTERN ANIMISM OF MANTO, RAKESH AND ANAND

Beerendra Pandey

Literary writings on the Partition of India generally portray the horrific violence of the watershed event as beastly instead of tracing it to the beast in the human species. This deflection, with its scapegoating of beasts and Othering of beastliness, masks the grisly deportment of humans towards the Other. In an exception to this trend of blaming the beasts, some modernist writers from India, like Saadat Hasan Manto, Mulk Raj Anand and Mohan Rakesh, appeal to 'subaltern animism' (Narayanan 2017: 488). Narayanan derives this notion of subaltern animism from the concept of subaltern urbanism to recognise the citizenship, agency and resistance of the nonhuman animals in Indian urban spaces in line with the personhood and agency of the marginalised and dispossessed humans in Indian towns and cities.

Subaltern animism does not, however, entail a liberatory promise as much as 'a sensibility toward the nonhuman that has left vestiges among subaltern peoples' (Keller 2005: 129). Although it cannot recover a lost relational living, it does underscore the need for a relational epistemology in the face of what Catherine Keller calls the theology of empire that explains the killing of people and wildlife as manifest destiny and justifies pre-emptive action and demonisation of the Other. The Indian modernist writers I explore in this chapter depict the trauma of Partition violence in deference to a relational epistemology. As they do so, they use disjunctive irony which helps reveal the shared embodiment – animality and humanity – in a paradoxical poise, thereby heightening the effect of both irony and trauma. The intensification of irony and trauma, by their mutual interactions, shocks the reader into a critical engagement with their own animality – a compelling confrontation which recovers subaltern animism from the margins of humanism. The beastly modernism of Manto, Rakesh and Anand acknowledges the shared conditions of human and animal existence, including their marginalisations. My exploration of the language of beastly modernism here first considers two of Manto's stories in Urdu, a vignette titled 'Sharing the Loot' (1948) in *Black Margins* and the 'The Dog of Tetwal' (1951), then Anand's story in English 'The Parrot in the Cage' (1954), and finally Mohan Rakesh's two stories in Hindi – 'The Owner of the Rubble' (1957) and 'God's Dog' (1958).

Manto, considered to be a rebel in his lifetime, reposes no faith in a humanism rooted in religion and philosophy. He shows little deference to God and challenges Him with a Devil-like arrogance: in his own epitaph, he 'wonder[s] if he is a greater short story writer than God' (qtd in Ispahani 1988: 193). Manto's seemingly devilish ego here actually 'expresses the predicament of a creative human spirit that must continue the work of the creation in a world which, it believes, has been permanently abandoned by god' (Chatterjee 2001: 18). Manto does the god's work by using black humour to laugh at the dark sides of humanism modelled on the divine. His configuration of the experiences of subaltern humans and nonhuman animals during the Partition riots swerves away from metropolitan modernism's élitist bludgeons to moral corrections which do not, however, actualise: in Eliot's *The Waste Land* (2001) the much-awaited rain, after all, does not fall.[1] Manto's irony in 'Sharing the Loot' and 'The Dog of Tetwal' diagnoses a humanism diseased by religious restraints and political pieties with a sharpness which, on the one hand, undercuts the closed space between the human and the animal and, on the other hand, dramatises the open space that man and beast co-inhabit.

Manto's black humour communicates the trauma of Partition violence in a way that interrogates the value system of his readers even as he makes them laugh: the mélange of irony's grotesqueness and humour's joyousness produces only a 'dianoetic laugh' (O'Neill 1983: 160), which leaves readers 'laughing so hard they feel as grave as corpses' (Woolf 1979: 299). Manto's irony does not imagine a correction of the grotesque affairs of the world but confronts them with an intensity reminiscent of a Western modernist response 'to a crisis of consciousness that is his bedeviling sense of an irreducible breach between a need for order [. . .] and the disorderliness of reality' (Kadir 1994: 117). The force of the grotesque overwhelms the humorous; so much so that the latter's corrective potency diminishes. What emerges is a disjunctive irony which transmutes the absurdities, brutalities, perversions and traumas into 'an equal poise of opposites: the form of an unresolvable paradox' and without much amelioration (Wilde 1981: 10). The intensity of this irony coalesces with the trauma of Partition violence to produce an affect of shock at the crumbling of humanism. In 'Sharing the Loot', for example, a biting discrepancy ironises the whole concept of the human and the nonhuman animal in critical situations, when the animal in the man arises and the human in the animal is spontaneously expressed. In 'Sharing the Loot', a houseowner helps a group of raiders to loot his own valuables while his dog demonstrates a hostility towards them. There is a telling divergence between the plunderers' display of animalism and the dog's revelation of humanism in his sense of loyalty. The houseowner turns the adverse situation to his favour by complying with the wishes of the looters. This way, he prevents them from harming him and facilitates the intervention of the dog. He loses many of his valuable belongings to the humans but, in contrast, he gets in compensation the love, loyalty and protection of the animal. The polarity, at the centre of which lies the anthropomorphic recognition of the dog's affection and loyalty, relates back to the title, which hints at men sharing both their animality and the booty with other fellows, but not the human attributes of care for and loyalty to the Other that a nonhuman animal – the dog – displays.

If the canine in the vignette is a companion animal, his counterpart in the story 'The Dog of Tetwal' is an anonymous stray which becomes an unfortunate victim of crossfire in the 1948 war between India and Pakistan over territorial rights in Kashmir. Tetwal is the name of a village that lies inside the military line of control in Pakistan. Hostility between the Indian and Pakistani soldiers permeates the story, which narrates the entry of a dog into a camp of frustrated Indian soldiers, who befriend it and attach a label to it bearing an Indian name. When the dog returns, with the label, to the Pakistani side after an absence of a few days, the Pakistani soldiers respond with another label bearing a Pakistani name. As the dog again returns to the Indian side, the poor creature that has been merely looking for companionship becomes an alibi for a bout of crossfiring which terrorises and eventually kills the stray animal. As Hannah Arendt notes, a stray dog has a lesser 'chance to survive' because he is 'just a dog in general' (Arendt 1973: 287), and the general public place upon stray dogs the disgrace of 'worthlessness, ugliness and randomness' (McHugh 2004: 142) and they are tainted as 'trespassers' (Narayanan 2017: 480). Nevertheless, quite a few individuals in South Asia give stray dogs food and do not report them to the municipality for confinement to 'worse conditions than the streets, or more likely extermination' (Fortuny 2014: 276). Stray dogs, thus, oscillate between the zones of disposable and protected life, an ambivalence that makes visible the biopolitics of power and powerlessness vis-à-vis humans and canids.

'The Dog of Tetwal' opens on a strikingly ironic note: the open space of the hills 'in roseate hue' and the 'thin, light clouds [. . .] in the blue sky' come out in sharp contrast to the 'entrenched' space of the soldiers (Manto 2007: 80). The life forms, including animal lives, pulsate with their own particular potentiality: the 'chirping birds', the 'bloom[ing] flowers' and 'honey-bearing bees' are agreeably 'immersed in [. . .] necessary work' (80). Manto's description of the animal environment here produces a state of what Giorgio Agamben terms 'captivation', or predetermined behavioural reflexes to fixed stimuli (Agamben 2004: 52). Captivation is a mode proper to the animals – an absorption which translates as an 'incomparable wealth' for them but which in humans registers as an utter 'poverty' (60). As such, a new difference between the human and the nonhuman animal is that the human is 'simply an animal that has learned to become bored' (70). Manto, like Agamben, compares animals' natural captivation with human boredom:

> For several days now, the soldiers on both sides of the mountain had been restless, as no decisive action was taking place. Lying in their positions, they would get bored and then attempt to recite sh'ers[2] to one another. If no one listened, they would hum to themselves. They remained lying on their stomachs or backs on the rocky ground, and when the order came, let off a round or two. (Manto 2007: 80)

At ironic odds with the animals' disinhibiting environment are the situational enclosures of the soldiers' 'safe positions' (80), which inhibit them in a captivated condition evocative of that of nonhuman animals, whom humans misapprehend as having no interest other than foraging and coupling. The jaded soldiers do nothing except for erratic firing and irregular singing. Despite a separation between the animals and the soldiers, a striking proximity between them is disclosed in boredom, where humans find themselves 'delivered over to things that refuse themselves' (Agamben 2004: 65). Boredom has bound the soldiers to things that nonetheless offer them nothing; they are taken up by things that refuse their revelation. Thus, the point of Manto's irony, which emerges from the zone of indistinction – the humAnimal – turns on the soldiers' animal-like betraying of a behavioural reflex to the fixed stimulus – firing at the perceived enemy. They are unable to kill their boredom, which foregrounds itself as 'the autoimmune disease of the anthropological machine – the surplus of animality that is disavowed', which results in biopolitical counterreactions (Lewis 2012: 294). When the machine takes over, its ironic character comes to the fore: while safeguarding the human, it forces out and externalises the underlying animal. Manto, like Agamben, makes his readers realise that the human merely resides in a suspension of that animality which would render inoperative the anthropological machine of humanism.

In a biopolitical counterresponse to boredom, Indian soldier Banta Singh catches a stray dog by his tail and says: 'The poor thing is a refugee!' (Manto 2007: 82). He names him Chapad Jhunjhun and cuddles him. The affectionate attitude of the Indian soldiers is not, however, simply an act of compassionate humanitarianism; instead, it is bound up in the nation-state's obsession with affixing identities. Fellow Indian soldier Jamadar Harnam Singh, who tentatively takes the dog to be Indian, correlates his sniffing face with language and an articulation of his desire for leftover food, but he consistently ignores the gesture embodied in the canine's wagging of his tail. Giving importance to the signification of the dog's face, Harnam Singh gives him a biscuit to eat but he immediately doubts the canine's Hindustani identity. Overcome with misgivings, he summarily dismisses the gesture of wagging, which, in Agambenian logic, is 'pure praxis' (2000: 79): an unfolding of an ontological realm of ethics, the ironic absence of which, in the nationalistic naming of the canine refugee, exposes the statist, teleological and identarian philanthropy of the warring soldiers. Nationalism is the palpable butt of Manto's irony: he scorns the fastening of nationalist labels on the dog by both the Indian and Pakistani soldiers. The Pakistani soldiers even ludicrously replace the dog's Indian name with a nonsensical name of their own – Sapar Sunsun. Besides the implied ridicule, the naming also amounts to rendering the dog as a pet, which connotes the owner's biopolitical dominance over the animal as a piece of movable property.

In ironic contrast to the identarian blindness of the soldiers on both sides, the dog sees them as humans, and not as Indians or Pakistanis. He expects them to mete out to him the usual human treatment as per the age-old trust between canids and hominids. This canine–human trust is based on mutual give and take; the dog reciprocates for the crumbs and the cuddles with a 'cheerful' companionship vis-à-vis the bored soldiers (Manto 2007: 83). Such a symbiosis seems to substantiate companionable thinking, but Manto indicates that the soldiers do not qualify for universal shareability, because the logic of Partition has so amplified alterity that even the common heritage of 'Heer'[3] song looks ironically incongruous (81). The absurdity of alterity and Partition logic also leads to the ridiculous division of even the dog as 'Hindustani or Pakistani' (83). Such assertions of absolute difference make the soldiers suffer from 'soul blindness' 'with respect to non-human animals' (Cavell 2008: 93). Manto uses the imagery of darkness as an objective correlative to the soldiers' internal negativity, and pits it against the imagery of light in order to dramatise its cutting contrast: 'In the blink of an eye, just as when one presses a button and the electricity generates light, the sun's rays flooded the mountainous region of Tetwal' (Manto 2007: 83). Whereas light suggests the positive vibrations in the natural nonhuman world, its counterpart reveals the negative dynamics of the human world.

Manto's irony challenges this disavowed underside of humanism that reinforces prejudice and the ideological logic of Otherness, a belief system which legitimates the atrocities enacted on both underdogs and nonhumans. It is highly ironic that when the winter and summer work out 'peace with one another' (80), the Indian and Pakistani soldiers, through their soul-blindness, maximise difference despite their sameness. They shut their eyes to the moral beauty of the canine wisdom; the stray dog recognises no alterity and provides companionship to whichever of the two groups he is with. The chilling irony is that he is killed for this very reason – his scrambling to both sides makes the militarised line of the divide look patently preposterous. The soul-blind soldiers see the politics of universal shareability inherent in the companionable deportment of the dog, but they fail to recognise the dog as a subject. Their uncanny way of seeing everything and yet seeing nothing keeps Manto's irony in a disjunctive equilibrium – an unresolved incongruity verging on the pessimistic. His ironic prose makes the readers bear witness to the monstrousness of Partition. The story ends with an irony-intensified shock at human insensitivity: 'Jamadar Harnam Singh took the warm barrel of the gun in his hand and said, "He died a dog's death"' (87). The ironic intensity here – that foregrounds the soldier's brutal behaviour and the victim's abject position of voicelessness – challenges the complacency of humanism with the agency of subaltern animism.

Like Saadat Hasan Manto, Mulk Raj Anand's beastly modernism in 'The Parrot of the Cage' is evident in his ability to blend incisive irony with traumatic shock, a key feature of his subaltern animism. Similar to Manto, Anand uses an ironic register to shock an evasive humanity into an engagement with the Other – a homeless old woman and a caged parrot. Evasiveness and engagement are closely connected through the creatural vulnerability the old woman shares with her companion bird.

The parrot acts as a surrogate – a substitute child – to Rukmani, a wrinkled and toothless woman who waits for the Deputy Collector of the City of Amritsar in the hope of compensation. Finding himself in alien surroundings, the parrot keeps bursting into two cries, '*Rukmaniai ni Rukmaniai!*' and '*Ni tun kithe hain?*'[4] (Anand 1995: 53, 54). After ignoring the parrot's repeated cries for a long time, she finally answers back – an answer in which she reveals herself as a refugee, who had escaped from the Partition riots in Lahore only the previous night on a train. The nearby gram-seller mocks her for waiting there and, instead, advises her to go to the Durbar Sahib temple for food. Rukmani, however, continues to wait and when finally the Deputy Collector comes out of his office to go elsewhere in his official car, she runs towards the vehicle where the *lathi*[5] is being wielded on the crowd of refugees who are clamouring for help. The state apparatus is portrayed as callous and brutal. While the cries of the refugees that are ringing in the air – '*Hujoor, Mai-Baap*, hear us! *Sarkar! Dipty Sahib!*'[6] – do not reach the ears of the Deputy Collector, the police action triggers a melee in which Rukmani is trampled. Meanwhile, the parrot flaps feverishly as his frequent cries – '*Rukmaniai! Ni Rukmaniai!*' and '*Ni tun kithe hain!* . . . *Ni tun kithe hain!*' – take on a shrill tone (57). The gram-seller thinks that the old woman has been killed in the stampede.

The possible death of the woman in the eyes of the gram-seller spontaneously elicits his sympathetic response. In a moment he changes from a well-meaning mocker trying to make the gullible woman see her harsh reality into an empathetic rescuer. He pushes forward to take charge of her, but then, to his pleasant surprise, she shows signs of life. He drags her away to a safe spot and simultaneously offers gram to the parrot. The gram-seller's gesture, compelled by his surrender to the immediate danger for the endangered and the distraught, foregrounds his empathy – a natural perception of the Other's pain – against the most dehumanising tendency of modern bureaucracy, which is, at the same time, its most rationalising quality. The intensity of the irony in the valorisation of the gram-seller's momentary but timely intervention, in contradistinction to the Deputy Collector's callousness, galvanises responsibility towards the Other – both humans and non-humans. The story, however, concludes on an uncertain note for the refugee – to the parrot's incessant cries, Rukmani finally answers: '. . . I do not know where I am! I do not know . . .' (57). As the story ends with these words, Rukmani remains without shelter, the implication being that the parrot will keep on crying.

Anand configures the eponymous parrot as a crying companion, a disruptive doppelgänger, an allegory of entrapment in general and, in the case of Rukmani, an externalisation of her confinement within a desperation exacerbated by a false hope of receiving monetary help from the Deputy Collector. The official's unfeeling attitude stands in sharp and ironic contrast to the genuine, immediate surrendering of the subaltern gram-seller to the situation of creatural life in crisis. The political edge of the irony, however, lies not so much in the contrast obtaining as in the rupture of the given discourse of humanism by a moment of pure praxis.

Another partition story which valorises subaltern animism is Mohan Rakesh's 'The Owner of the Rubble'. My reading of the story focuses on the shock stemming from an ironic (dis)similarity between animal and human behaviour – an (in)congruity which coalesces with the traumatic situation. The cumulative effect generated by this irony gathers such momentum that it exposes the language of xenophobia mystifying the Indian historiography of Partition. The intensity of the demystification dizzies the Indian reader's consciousness, lulled to moral smugness vis-à-vis the Pakistanis.

The story starts on a note of shock for Gani Miyan and other fellow Pakistanis, who have come back to Amritsar after seven and a half years. The city, once their home and hearth, lies transformed into a city of only Indians, to a few of whom they are 'guests' (Rakesh 2007: 93), but to most of whom they are strangers, 'watched' with 'eagerness and curiosity' and feared as the Demon Other from whose proximity the city-dwellers 'turn away' (91). Post-Partition Amritsar, which had been so severely hit by vicious riots against Muslims, is on the cusp of remaking its own notion of the community: as Gyanendra Pandey writes, 'Frequently "our people" and "theirs" are being reconstituted, different senses of "us" and "them" are in contention' (1999: 44–5). The community forges itself as the subject of history – a rut into which the official historiography of Partition has fallen – by demonising the outsiders (externally the Pakistanis and internally the antisocial elements who had contributed to the ferocity of the riots). The community engages in this realignment in order to recreate, after the big rupture, a coherent and stable identity of its own. Demonisation of the Other, particularly the external Other, by their animalisation as a snake or a dog goes a long way towards reshaping both the community and its history. An implied demonisation of the visitors from Pakistan at the outset of the story works as a ploy to transfer the city-dwellers' own barbarous actions of murders and usurpations to the humans-reduced-to-animals – the Muslim Other – so that the perpetrators may feel absolved of their own bestiality. Rakesh intimates this through the trope of xenophobia on the one hand and references to the perpetration of violence against the Muslims during the Partition riots on the other hand.

The irony underpinning the attitude of the 'still so suspicious' city-dwellers in 'The Owner of the Rubble' is that they fail to see not only the surprise and sadness of the visiting Muslims at the land grab, arson and usurpation, but also the tell-tale signs of mayhem still visible in 'the still piles of rubble everywhere', in the 'midst' of which 'the new buildings present a strange sight' (93). That ethnocentric Othering that lies at the centre of the Amritsarians' fear of the Muslims becomes ostensible in a young sister's rebuke of her crying child brother, who has bumped into Gani in Bansan Bazar Lane: 'Stop crying, you little devil! If you don't, that Muslim will catch you and take you away!' (93). This perception of Gani as a source of evil is ironically antithetical to the old man's own fear of and trauma at the Indians' raptor-like preying on the Muslim body and scavenging of their property: 'His throat was dry, and his legs were shaking [. . .] Two well-fed kites were sitting absolutely still on the electric wires running past the house' (93). Here, Rakesh displaces human-to-human violence to a voracious nonhuman animal world – the kites function as agents of torment and torture. Gani shakes with trepidation at the possibility of the Indian community's aggression transposed on to the rapacity and violence of a bird of prey that would pluck out human flesh in a frenzy. Despite his fear, he moves on but halts when he comes across his erstwhile neighbour, Manori (a child then but now a young man), near what used to be his house. The trope of xenophobia strategically returns as they reach the spot: a rumour about an attempted abduction of a crying child is aimed at investing Gani (and his ilk) with malevolent monstrousness so that the Indians' own involvement in or complicity with the annihilation of the Muslim Other remains nullified in their own eyes. Rakesh subtly ironises the ideology of scapegoating as a way of normalising the Indians' own moral turpitude.

Having thus subtly challenged the politics of the construction of the Other, Rakesh steers readers towards the climax when Manori points out to Gani a heap of rubble which the young man identifies as the old man's erstwhile house.

Its dilapidated condition shocks Gani even more than the homicide of his son, daughter-in-law and grandchildren. Shock, the cognition of trauma, manifests somatically in his dry mouth and infirm knees. The house, now mere debris, ironically disinters the trauma buried deep inside him: he starts sobbing as he rests his head against the still standing but charred doorframe. Gani stands at a crossroad: whether to move towards a normalisation of the trauma, or towards finding out the perpetrator as is expected by his former neighbours, peering from their windows. Rakesh indicates Gani's choice of the first route through the symbolism of 'a long worm' issuing from the doorframe and squirming towards an open drain (95). The choice allows Gani to plumb the depths of his traumatic past and to wriggle through it so that he may eventually exorcise his ghosts.

It is, however, difficult for Gani to reconcile himself to the trauma, for there are no willing mourners with whom to grieve over the monumental tragedy. The community remains bolted inside, waiting for some histrionics to unfold. At this juncture, the narrator apprises readers of the gruesome dinner-time murder of the entire family by Rakkha, and of the callous conduct of the community members who had witnessed the incident through their windows but with closed doors and locked hearts. The narrator also relates the ransacking and torching of the house by members of the community and Rakkha's sole ownership of its remains – the heap of the rubble. Since the arson, Rakkha, however, has been displaying dog-like aggressive protection of his territory against any intruders. But with Rakkha still uninformed of the goings-on at his claimed property, Gani has an opportunity for unhindered mourning. However, with the house now in ruins and no one to join him in his bereavement, the theatre of mourning becomes, ironically, the debris itself and the co-mourner turns out to be the lone doorframe: 'Then he put his arms around the doorframe and wailed, "Speak to me, Chirag! Say something! Tell me where you are. O Kishwar! O Sultana! My children! O God, why is Gani still alive?"' (96). Irony here intensifies and adds to the shock of the trauma; what should have been a collective sharing of Gani's grief is reduced to an unattended and unheard cry of pain. Rakesh here foregrounds the reality of the disassociation of the experiential with the intra-personal[7] in the process of mourning in the immediate aftermath of post-Partition Amritsar.

Ironically enough, the very killer – the much-maligned wrestler, Rakkha – substitutes for the community in Gani's grieving process. This man, to whom the community has attributed the rampaging animality of 'the wild bull', comes to the site with a 'grunt' (97). By so banishing Rakkha to the Otherness of the nonhuman animal world, the community not only 'distances' itself from the troublemaking of the Partition riots but also 'consign[s] the violence to a domain "elsewhere"' (Pandey 1999: 27): 'the handiwork of "outsiders"' (26). The arrival of the troublemaker, residing outside the mainstream of the *mohalla* (community), raises the possibility of a showdown, but the community is disappointed to see Gani extend his arms towards Rakkha and evacuate his trauma:

> 'Tell me Rakkha, how did it happen?' Gani asked as he wiped his eyes. 'You loved each other like brothers. Couldn't he have hidden in your house? . . . Rakkha, he depended on you. He used to say that, as long as Rakkha was around, nobody would dare to hurt him. But when death finally came, even Rakkha couldn't help.' (Rakesh 2007: 97–8)

The irony of the very predator innocently being perceived as the protector jolts the murderer, such that he whispers to God for mercy. The more the unsuspecting father grieves before him with an intercession for forgiveness for the killer, the more shocked the wrestler becomes. This shock produces sparks in Rakkha's dormant humanity: 'Gani noticed that Rakkha's lips had become dry and that deep, dark circles hung under his eyes' (98). This stands in strikingly ironic contrast to the inhumanity of the community, which has been Othering the wrestler as a marauding bull. Alterations become noticeable in Rakkha's face and he undergoes a transition from the condition of his animalistic predaciousness to an upwelling of shame and sorrow that shows up in the affective changes to his lips and eyes. Gani's mournful face catches Rakkha 'naked', 'initiating in him a process of reversal' (Derrida 2004: 114). The day Gani leaves for Pakistan, somewhat unburdened of the trauma, Rakkha too remembers his 'pilgrimage [. . .] to Vaishno Devi' (Rakesh 2007: 99). The divesting mourning, to which Rakkha has contributed, definitely calms the devil in him; his memory of the difficult pilgrimage to the shrine located in the Trikuta hills for a blessing for an elimination of a demonic streak points to a softening of the hardened heart of the bully.

Though softened, Rakkha's dog-like propensity to react to any intrusions into his territory continues. He 'instinctively' lashes out at a buffalo near his rubble with a stick and produces a bark-like sound, 'Tat, tat, . . . tat, tat!', in what looks like a protective display of belligerence (Rakesh 2007: 99). That his body language no longer smacks of predatory aggression, though, is reinforced with a masterstroke of irony at the finale. A dog resting in a corner of the debris, flustered by Rakkha's presence there, barks at him and chases him away, in order to announce his own unequivocal ownership of the rubble – a supremacy he seals with a continued 'growl' (99). The mongrel goes on a barking spree, which attests to the ruffian's culpability. As a result, Rakkha experiences further remorse. The dog's barks become an incitement to a new ethic as the canine testimony helps complete the process of reversal in Rakkha, who, therefore, concedes his ownership of the rubble to the barking beast. The dog's role in Rakkha's turnaround, unlike the community's failure to enable a change of heart in either the wrestler or themselves, stands out. Rakesh here accords ethical pulchritude to the mongrel and the scoundrel – both of them now inhabiting an indeterminate zone of the humAnimal, which registers as a trenchantly ironic absence in the community.

The climactic irony of the story, disjunctive in nature and typical of modernism, does not, however, resolve the paradox between hospitality and hostility towards the stranger that it posits, even as it ruptures the language of Otherness embedded in Indian post-Partition discourse. The irony functions pointedly to seek a shift of register from animalisation of the Other towards humanisation but, at the same time, it recognises that the traumatised Indian self remains trapped in a circle of knowledge and ignorance. Rakesh's modernism demystifies the discourse of Otherness shoring up the Indian historiography of the trauma of Partition while paradoxically suggesting a continuity of ignorance, since the text shows no inkling of a reversal in the xenophobic attitude of the *mohalla*. The disjunctive irony merely heightens awareness of destabilising the rigidity of a self-arrogated moral subjectivity.

A similar disjunctive-ironic dramatisation of the rigidity of the community and, conversely, the Other's (Rakkha's) propinquity to canine becoming features in Rakesh's story 'God's Dog'. The disjunctive irony in this tale threatens to rise to the level of satire. The butt of the joke is the corrupt Indian bureaucracy to which the task of allocating land to the evacuees from the other side of the border has devolved. Rakesh makes the apathetic, corrupt officials reveal themselves so that their outrageous deviation from Gandhian ethics as the cornerstone of India's independence is transparently exposed. Thus, the protagonist, while feigning animality with the performativity of a dog – as we shall see – wonders 'if Mahatma Gandhi struggled for freedom so that these people could misuse the freedom he won for us? Corrupt it? Give it a bad name? Tie it up in their petty files and let it rot?' (Rakesh 1994: 124). Sluggish, bribery-ridden bureaucracy has been adding to the trauma of the hapless refugees from Pakistan. What this analysis spotlights is Rakesh's reprehension of bureaucracy and community while, at the same time, his irony fails to effect a regeneration.

The locus of irony in 'God's Dog' turns out to be 'naturism' – a cosmology, according to which 'this enigmatic, earthly cosmos' strips itself in a way that tantalises us with becoming animal, becoming 'a part of the inanimate world whose life swells within and unfolds all around us' (Abram 2010: 77, 3). Amidst the civilised activities going on in the office compound, which forms the setting of the story, what stands out is the contrasting natural world:

> It was September and the entire compound was bathed in sunlight. A few baby sparrows, who were learning how to fly, had hopped down from the branch of a tree and were trying to reach it again. A few large crows were strolling up and down the porch. (Rakesh 1994: 119)

This invitation to become animal, however, goes unnoticed by the community that has collected there for office work. It does not dawn upon the people that this nonhuman animal world, 'lively, creative and filled with unexpected possibilities', can bring sudden illumination about new 'forms of agency' (Calarco 2021: 28). Their adaptation to the established system of office trappings makes them bribe the officials in order to get them to accomplish their official tasks – and that after a lot of kowtowing to them.

The protagonist, a middle-aged man, stands as an exception to the grovelling community. Fed up with the office system which has reduced him and his family to a dog's life, he arrives in the compound with his entire family – an elderly widow, her young daughter, and his sick son. He has decided to turn literally into a dog with the purpose of really becoming agentive with regard to his application for replacing an allotted piece of land, which is nothing but a pit-like hollow, with a smaller chunk of arable land. For two years, the application has made no headway because, without bribery, it cannot 'travel from one room to the next' and 'move from one desk to the next' (Rakesh 1994: 121). Feigning a canine self, he says that he is God's dog and that he will go barking on His behalf until the officers' eardrums split, no matter how severe a punishment he attracts for this action. He also takes off his shirt and tries to unknot his *tehmat*[8] to go completely naked. His performance of animality here shows him in a state of what Søren Kierkegaard terms 'negative freedom', since 'there is nothing that holds him' (Kierkegaard 1989: 166, 262) – not even his clothes, which he has decided to discard to be naked like a dog. He remains in the interstices between actuality when he presses for prompt action on his application and performativity as he threatens to go naked while producing dog-like barks. The end result of these two selves of the protagonist – the empirical self as man and the performing self as dog – brings about a double demystification: first, the actuality of the bribery-ridden trappings of a government office, and second, the poignant exposé of the underdog's half-starved status. The demystification, catalysed by the 'moment of ironic performativity that makes possible ethics as a form of radical self-formation, as opposed to the mere adherence to preexisting codes, norms, and other constructions', 'stings us to wakefulness' (Miller 2009: 68–9). This stinging arousal from slumber makes us see our nakedness even when we are clothed.

The performance of irony by the protagonist of 'God's Dog' works to undress officialdom and the community whose possible repugnance towards him has no meaning. As he tells the *chaprasi* (clerk), neither coercion nor disgust matters for him any longer because he has become 'shameless and fearless' (Rakesh 1994: 121). After having dehumanised himself, he has become empowered enough to maintain his composure, which ironically registers as a woeful lack in both officialdom and members of the community that quickly gather at the spot to project their disapproval of his behaviour:

'You are not the only son of a bitch here. All of you here are dogs', the man continued. 'All of you are dogs, and I am also a dog! The only difference is that you are the dogs of the government – you tear people to bits and bark at the orders of the government! I am a God's dog. I live by his grace and bark at his command . . . Pet dogs of man, go and chew on the bones thrown away by him; go wag your tails and beg . . .' (122)

In this passage, degradation takes canine form and the dog marks a shrinking from the human to the animal. Here, the protagonist, in a process of ironic *dédoublement*, laughs at the jest of his own debasement. The intra-subjective compass of irony at work here renders the self-humiliation both subject and object of the comedy. He, like the government personnel and the common people, has already fallen to the stature of a dog. The whole point of the irony here is the dichotomy of a self that oscillates between being God's watchdog and being a pet dog, between moral beauty and moral ugliness.

The protagonist's canine comedy, buttressed with the threat to go naked, embarrasses the officials. Their embarrassment, which stems from their apprehension that the performativity contravenes the prohibition of bribery, especially awakens the Deputy Collector from his stupor. Subsequently, the 'files move' and 'within half an hour' the middle-aged petitioner is allotted a piece of arable land for which he has been applying for two years (125). The promptness evinced by the nodal officer is, however, not due to his *lajjA* (shame), which 'becomes the internal governor that guides one not only in not doing what is inappropriate, but also . . . for not doing what is appropriate' (Bhawuk 2017: 117), but an unexpected occasion of climactic embarrassment that the dog-man's stripping induces in this so-called 'textile' man. After this awkward moment of interruption, the usual situation of bribery will continue; neither the Deputy Collector's nor the crowd's clothes cover their inescapable nakedness. The protagonist's animalistic behaviour does not spark in them the shame that is an internalised reaction to the consciousness of exposure. This is what Jacques Derrida means by his famous statement: 'An animal looks at us and we are naked before it. Thinking perhaps begins there' (2004: 122). Thinking, which arises from the interstitial space between the animal and the human, is where the ethical regime begins. But Rakesh dramatises its denial in both officialdom and the community. For the regime of thinking to take over, the prerequisite, as Bhawuk implies, is '*lajjA* . . . wisdom [which] guides us to choose desires that are appropriate and those that are not' (2017: 123). The crowd in 'God's Dog' – the second target of the protagonist's performativity – abjectly lacks the *lajjA* and is deaf to the performer's repeated calls for barking. The irony generated by his animalistic performance, despite being so incisive and affective, does not jolt the community towards the wisdom of no longer pandering to bribery. The overall effect of the dissimulative irony on the readers, however, is not 'the gloom' once again enveloping the office compound but the potential ethical radiance (Rakesh 1994: 125).

The modernist irony of Mohan Rakesh, Mulk Raj Anand and Saadat Hasan Manto cannot dispel the despair brought about by the ego of humanism. But, by unravelling the limits of humanism and dramatising its affinity with animalism, this irony makes the hitherto disavowed beastliness a most striking site for a rethinking of humanist subjectivity at the time of Partition, when the inhuman within the human had manifested in the outbreak of violence. Unlike metropolitan modernism's irony, which displaces animality to the margins of society and merely prescribes a correction from an élitist position, the irony of these writers derives its potency from their subscription to subaltern animism. Though disjunctive in nature, their irony confronts the chaotic world head on from the lowly position of the beast and, from inside it, clinches an ethically aesthetic closure which acts as a shock to the thought of a post-Partition public fed a diet of the high politics of Partition marred by communal, national and élite relapsing into blame, countergame and demonisation. The shock jolts them into cognition of the subaltern animism which recognises both the animality that is intrinsic to the human and the humanity that is immanent to the animal. The meta-ironic shockwaves produced by Manto and Rakesh gesture towards the alternative politics manifested in the moral agency of the commonplace dog. Their historiography of subaltern animism explodes the high politics of historical debate that elides the commoners – the subalterns – who have been the parties directly affected by the watershed event that many people understand as South Asia's Holocaust. Manto and Rakesh's representation of the trauma of Partition arises from their deep embeddedness in the composite culture of undivided India. And this is why Anand also succeeds in his own way in trenchantly representing the sense of confusion and uprooting that many in North India faced at the time of Partition. As Anand uses the caged parrot as an allegory to reveal that the core of the refugees' identity exists in their ancestral place, he plays out the crisis in humanism which, as I have shown, also turns out to be humanism not in crisis. Humanism, for Anand, emerges as a dialectical concept, evoking both approval and disapproval. Anand's Partition stories expose humanism's underside of suffering and oppression, towards which the State apparatus shows apathy. But the story also uncovers a subaltern animal-humanism wherein a common person absorbed into humanism reinfuses it, through a spontaneous intervention, with practical meaning.

Works Cited

Abram, David. 2010. *Becoming Animal: An Earthly Cosmology*. New York: Pantheon.

Agamben, Giorgio. 2000. *Means without End: Notes on Politics*. Trans. Vincenzo Binetti and Cesare Casarino. Minneapolis: University of Minnesota Press.

Agamben, Giorgio. 2004. *The Open: Man and Animal*. Trans. Kevin Attell. Stanford: Stanford University Press.

Anand, Mulk Raj. 1995 [1954]. 'The Parrot in the Cage'. In *Orphans of the Storm: Stories on the Partition of India*. Ed. Saros Cowasjee and K. S. Duggal, 53–8. New Delhi: UBSPD.

Arendt, Hannah. 1973 [1951]. *The Origins of Totalitarianism*. San Diego: Harvest/HBJ.

Bhawuk, Dharm P. S. 2017. '*lajjA* in Indian Psychology: Spiritual, Social, and Literary Perspectives'. In *The Value of Shame: Exploring a Health Resource in Cultural Contexts*. Ed. Elisabeth Vanderheiden and Claude-Hélène Mayer, 109–34. Cham: Springer.

Calarco, Matthew. 2021. *Animal Studies: The Key Concepts*. London: Routledge.

Cavell, Stanley. 2008. 'Companionable Thinking'. In *Philosophy and Animal Life*. Ed Stanley Cavell, Cora Diamond, John McDowell, Ian Hacking and Cary Wolfe, 92–126. New York: Columbia University Press.

Chatterjee, Partha. 2001. 'Democracy and the Violence of the State: A Political Negotiation of Death'. *Inter-Asia Cultural Studies* 2.1: 7–21.

Derrida, Jacques. 2004 [2002]. 'The Animal That Therefore I Am'. In *Animal Philosophy: Essential Readings in Continental Though*. Ed. Matthew Calarco and Peter Atterton, trans. David Wills, 113–28. London: Continuum.

Eliot, T. S. 2001 [1922]. *The Waste Land: Authoritative Text, Contexts, Criticism*. Ed. Michael North. New York: Norton.

Fortuny, Kim. 2014. 'Islam, Westernization, and the Posthumanist Place: The Case of the Istanbul Street Dog'. *Interdisciplinary Studies in Literature and Environment* 21.2: 271–97.

Ispahani, Mahnaz. 1988. 'Saadat Hasan Manto'. *Grand Street* 7.4: 183–93.

Kadir, Djelal. 1994. 'On the *ars combinatoria* of Plato's *Cratylus* and Its Latest Peripeties'. In *Plato and Postmodernism*. Ed. Steven Shankman, 115–21. Glenside, PA: Aldine Press.

Keller, Catherine. 2005. *God and Power: Counter-Apocalyptic Journeys*. Minneapolis: Fortress Press.

Kierkegaard, Søren. 1989. *Kierkegaard's Writings, II : The Concept of Irony, with Continual Reference to Socrates Together with Notes of Schelling's Berlin Lectures*. Ed. and trans. Howard V. Hong and Edna H. Hong. Princeton, NJ: Princeton University Press.

Kumar, Sukrita Paul. 1990. *The New Story: A Scrutiny of Modernity in Hindi and Urdu Short Fiction*. New Delhi: Allied Publishers.

Lewis, Tyson. 2012. 'King of the Wild Things: Children and the Passionate Attachments of the Anthropological Machine'. In *Philosophy in Children's Literature*. Ed. Peter Costello, 285–98. London: Lexington.

McHugh, Susan. 2004. *Dog*. London: Reaktion.

Manto, Saadat Hasan. 1995 [1948]. 'Sharing the Loot'. In *Black Margins. India Partitioned: The Other Face of Freedom, Vol. I*. Ed. and trans. Mushirul Hasa, n 88–99. New Delhi: Roli.

Manto, Saadat Hasan. 2007 [1951]. 'The Dog of Tetwal'. Trans. Ravikant and Tarun K. Saint. *Manoa* 19.1: 80–7.

Miller, Paul Allen. 2009. 'Ethics and Irony'. *SubStance* 38.3: 51–71.

Narayanan, Yamini. 2017. 'Street Dogs at the Intersection of Colonialism and Informality: "Subaltern Animism" as a Posthuman Critique of Indian Cities'. *Environment and Planning D: Society and Space* 35.3: 475–94.

O'Neill, Patrick. 1983. 'The Comedy of Entropy: The Contexts of Black Humour'. *Canadian Review of Comparative Literature* 10.2: 145–66.

Pandey, Gyanendra. 1999. *Memory, History, and the Question of Violence: Reflections on the Reconstruction of Partition*. Calcutta: K. P. Bagchi.

Rakesh, Mohan. 1994 [1958]. 'God's Dog'. In *Stories About the Partition of India, Vol. II*, 119–25. New Delhi: Indus.

Rakesh, Mohan. 2007 [1957]. 'The Owner of the Rubble'. Trans. Alok Bhalla. *Manoa* 19.1: 91, 93–9.

Wilde, Alan. 1981. *Horizons of Assent: Modernism, Postmodernism, and the Ironic Imagination*. Philadelphia: University of Pennsylvania Press.

Woolf, Virginia. 1979 [1907]. 'Friendship's Gallery'. Ed. and intro. Ellen Hawkes. *Twentieth Century Literature* 25.3-4: 270–303.

Notes

1. Noted Hindi critic Namwar Singh finds that Manto's vernacular modernity of class consciousness and well-established positions on community rights – those of the Hindus and the Muslims in the 1920s–1940s – veers 'towards the real' (Singh qtd in Kumar1990: 5). The tendency to be realistic is a far cry from the West's modernism which struggles with papering over an ugly reality even as it enters the literary consciousness.
2. An Urdu word, meaning poems.
3. A poetic narration, written in 1766 by Waris Shah, of the popular tragic Punjabi romance between Heer Sial and Dheedo Ranjha.
4. A Punjabi expression, meaning 'Where are you?'
5. A *lathi* is a heavy stick, often made of bamboo bound with iron, used in India as a weapon, especially by the police (as in dispersing a crowd).
6. These three italicised expressions are used in rural part of India to refer to a person who helps the poor or the needy.
7. Mourning, in South Asia, is basically a community affair: the neighbourhood gathers together at the residence of the deceased for a period of mourning, consisting of prayers and other cultural customs.
8. This is the Punjabi version of the *lungi*; it has folds at the front and is traditional dress for Punjabi men.

9

RESISTANT REINDEERS: HUMAN–ANIMAL RELATIONS AND CULTURAL SELF-APPROPRIATION IN SÁMI ART AND LITERATURE

Katharina Alsen

At the centre of the small-scale embroidered scene is a solid brownish entity, depicted in abstract and minimalist form. It is shaped like a bottleneck with a sketchy crown at the top, which almost doubles its total size. As if the figure was wrapped in barbed wire, it is surrounded by amorphous black lines which create a physical distance from the other pictorial actors: to the left and the right, there are three identifiably human figures, two adults and one infant. These three are shown in more detail than the first figure, with distinct facial and sartorial attributes.[1] Although there is no further indication of body structure, the context makes it clear that the abstract brownish entity is supposed to (re)present a reindeer torso and head, and the surrounding black lines show a number of reindeer antlers.

The composition defies easy interpretation. Is the nonhuman animal meant to be alive or dead? Do we look at them from the side or below, indicating either a same-level or an inferior positioning (and perspective) of the spectator? Although the stylised reindeer seems to be bound in chains, immobilised and exposed to human-driven violence, they are displayed in a powerful topological arrangement and posture. The crowned torso is placed in an elevated position, the human figures kneel down facing them as if they were some sort of ritual sculpture or higher being. The composition recalls the symbolic imagery of sacrifice or martyrdom. The attitude towards the nonhuman animal figure can be read as both humiliating and submissive.

In addition, the vast number of antlers render the reindeer visible not only as an individual animal, but also as a representative of their species. A plurality of reindeers is suggested by pictorial means: while the antlers are depicted, the animate bodies they once grew out of and were connected to are absent and gesture towards an absent presence. The antlers – which both male and female reindeers grow and shed annually – convey ambiguous meaning, oscillating between life and death, agency and objectification, resistance and surrender.

The narrative embroideries by textile artist and painter Britta Marakatt-Labba (b. 1951), whose works were among others exhibited at Documenta 14 (2017) as part of Sámi Artist Group, show motifs of traditional Sámi lifestyle in cyclical and linear arrangements. Above all, they depict the close relationship between human and nonhuman animal life in barren landscapes, epitomised by reindeers who coexist and interact with human figures in various ways. Modern transformation of living conditions and society, however, which accompanied the industrialisation and urbanisation of the European mainland, does not play a pictorial role. The absence of dominant features of Western modern life and the very medium of embroidery, which has become relatively rare today, may at first glance seem to establish a rather antimodern(ist) attitude and suggest a romanticised, somewhat ahistorical reading of 'natural' environments.[2]

Figure 9.1 Marakatt-Labba, Britta. 2003–2007. *Historjá* (*History*) (Detail). Embroidery, print, applications and wool on linen. 39 cm × 23.5 m. Oslo: KORO Public Art Norway. © Britta Marakatt-Labba / BONO, Oslo 2022. Photo: Cathrine Wang.

Figure 9.2 Marakatt-Labba, Britta. 2003–2007. *Historjá* (Overview at The Arctic University of Norway, Tromsø). © Britta Marakatt-Labba / BONO, Oslo 2022. Photo: Larissa Acharya.

On closer inspection though, many of Marakatt-Labba's motifs are anything but pastoral and tranquil. Instead, they portray a highly constructed notion of 'nature', unfolding scenes of violence, pain and collective mourning for both animals and humans, and equally addressing issues of environmental pollution and climate change.[3]

In the 23.5-metre-long, multipart frieze *History* (2003–7), there are both scenes of reindeers fighting against acts of domestication and scenes of apparently balanced interspecies life and work routines. Power relations and the sense of community are never simple matters in Marakatt-Labba's critical visual storytelling. *History* gives an insight into complex networks, entanglements and dependencies as heterogenous forms of human–animal encounter (Böhm and Ullrich 2019: 2) and combines literal with metaphorical dimensions. The scene outlined above, depicting an enchained reindeer surrounded by antlers and three human figures, allows for diverse interpretations and indicates different stages of conflict escalation compressed in just one embroidered detail.

Approaching Reindeers: Key Arguments

The Sámi are an Indigenous people who inhabit the transnational area of Sápmi (previously also referred to by the exonym 'Lapland') in northern Norway, Sweden, Finland and the Russian Kola peninsula.[4] The history of the Sámi across national borders has been a long one of territorial and cultural colonialism, forced assimilation and construction 'as the racialized others' (Heith 2012: 159). Mobility, hunting and reindeer herding have, among other things, always been central features of the Sámi lifestyle.

The textiles by Marakatt-Labba can help address a set of critical research questions. For this chapter, I will read the works as reverberations of Nordic modern art and literature, more precisely as critically affirmative commentaries on the dominant representation and reception of Indigenous Sámi culture from the first decades of the twentieth century. Not only negative forms of critique, but also (hyper-)affirmation, including methods of imitative exaggeration, overserious realism or over-identification, can act as strategies of subversion and resistance, especially in the context of repressive political systems (Arns and Sasse 2006: 444–5). Recurring representational features of Sámi culture, which have often been stereotyped and romanticised by non-Indigenous modern artists and publics, involve a semi-nomadic, transhuman lifestyle, the abovementioned absence of modern urban influence and a mythologically charged, intimate relation to what is perceived as 'nature'. The latter also includes the regional fauna of Sápmi. Since reindeers are the most common megafaunal species, they have become significant symbols for northern Scandinavia and been framed as charismatic 'animal landmarks' of the whole region,[5] most notably in the (originally non-Sámi) tradition of national romanticist landscape painting since the early nineteenth century.

As I have argued, human–reindeer encounters are significant, yet ambivalent, motifs in Marakatt-Labba's visual worlds. In so doing, I understand her artistic approach as showing (so-called) antimodern 'natural' environments and cultural practices in a (so-called) premodernist medium as a strategy of subversive affirmation and cultural self-appropriation which challenges dominant conventions of representing and imagining Sámi lifestyle now and then. Cultural self-appropriation has been described as a critical epistemic practice by dominated and hermeneutically marginalised social groups which aims at revealing and overcoming hermeneutical gaps and (re)gaining interpretational sovereignty (Serrano Zamora 2017; Fricker 2007). In this case, the strategy is also connected to the wider theoretical and historical context of appropriation art (Puranen 2009).

However, theories of cultural self-appropriation and subversive affirmation do not answer only to contemporary Sámi art in which the entanglements of history and present, of 'nature' and politics, become particularly tangible – as seen in Marakatt-Labba's embroideries. In fact, this theoretical perspective can also shed new light on the modern(ist) precursors. The three first, and so far most studied, Sámi modern artists – at least in the narrow sense of Western modern art – are Johan Turi (1854–1936), Nils Nilsson Skum (1872–1951) and John Savio (1902–38). Their works will be included in my analysis as examples of the variety and multidimensionality of Sámi depictions of human–reindeer relations, and specifically the animal agency in these portrayals. It is important to recognise that there is no such thing as modernism in the singular, but rather a diversity of international modernist aesthetic practices that makes it necessary to speak of modernisms in the plural (Harney and Phillips 2018: 3). In addition to a critical art historical approach informed by postcolonial theory and Indigenous studies, this chapter focuses on issues from the cross-disciplinary field of human–animal studies and addresses three key arguments.

First, the very subject matter of reindeers in modern(ist) works by Turi, Skum and Savio can be read as motifs of resistance, reclaiming the power of interpretation of cultural symbols which have been assimilated into the Western canon, and opting for interpretive pluralism. In this light, dominant non-Sámi pictorial conventions have been transferred into testimonies of painterly self-(re)presentation with emancipatory effect. Animals used to serve as identity-creating elements in the iconography of national romanticism and helped coin the typical 'brand image(ry)' of Nordic nations and their respective cultural majorities. Typical landmarks in flora and fauna, among them reindeers, which are intimately linked to the life of the Sámi, were taken over by non-Sámi artists. At the turn of the century, the landscape was considered '*the* genre of Nordic painting', conveying 'the impression of a symbiotic relationship between man and nature in the north of Europe' (Alsen and Landmann 2016: 136), most often without regard to cultural differences and underlying political hierarchies.

The Sámi settlement areas, however, are not and have never been equivalent to a nation-state, and thus pursue(d) different aesthetics and political targets. Depending on the definition from either a geographical, linguistic or political viewpoint, Scandinavia is a subregion in northern Europe with varying dimensions. Norway, Sweden and Denmark are traditionally regarded as the core Scandinavian countries. Together with Finland and Iceland, they form the Nordic countries. The Nordics also include Greenland (with the Indigenous Inuit) and the Faroes as autonomous territories of Denmark and Åland as a Swedish-speaking autonomous region of Finland. Sápmi has for centuries been divided between different nation-states, with the Sámi on the receiving end of oppressive colonising policies.

Second, many works by modern Sámi artists do not show the semi-domesticated species of reindeers in situations free from conflict but in vivid scenes of rebellion against and in opposition to the dominating group of humans. This too contradicts the popular animal brand imagery of national romanticist iconography with its atmospheric landscapes and idyllising, homogenising tendencies. Sámi depictions of conflictual human–reindeer interaction, especially in the oeuvre of John Savio, exhibit a resistant subtext which seems to mirror the socio-political positioning of human Sámi life in the context of restrictive assimilation policies within the Nordic national states. In that light, the motif of reindeers rearing back and fighting against attempts at domestication can be read as images of both nonhuman animal *and* human self-empowerment in the wider sense. The images demonstrate that cohabitation has many faces and that power relations are always more complex than they may seem from the perspective of the (societal) majority.

In terms of the ideologies and practices of colonialism, the Nordics have for a long time claimed the status of a so-called 'Nordic exceptionalism' within European colonising countries. The (neo-)colonial entanglements within and of the North and the (ongoing) history of marginalisation of the Sámi and other minorities or Indigenous peoples, however, have attracted increased scholarly and public attention during the last decade (Loftsdóttir and Jensen 2012; Körber and Volquardsen 2014).

My third aim is to examine the agency of the depicted reindeers beyond their mere illustrative and conventional metaphorical level. In doing so, I will harness the concept of 'material metaphor', which goes beyond simple logics of substitution and asks about expectations and effects of relational agency instead (Steinbrecher and Borgards 2016). The perspective of nonhuman animals as material metaphors in art and literature concerns forms of tacit agency following the ideas of new materialism. In the Sámi artworks considered here, both explicit and implicit narratives of resistance are linked to the (re)presentation of reindeers, thereby countervoicing dominant narratives of cultural subordination as well as modernist aesthetics.

Self-Reflective Note: Decentring Perspectives

Writing about Indigenous art as a non-Indigenous scholar requires 'critical care' (Garneau 2020) in several respects. Academic cultural analysis 'has a long history of analysing the "other"' (Svalastog et al. 2021) and is prone to perform practices of (explicit or tacit) exclusion (Crowther 2003: 121). Practices of 'othering' most often ignore the socially constructed privileges they are based on; they can provoke reiterations of hegemonic power and a patronising attitude. Exclusion also involves 'soft' factors such as governance of terminology or methodology, and the predominance of selected mainstream scientific communities. Since the Western academic world has for a long time claimed 'theory as thoroughly Western, [and] has constructed all the rules by which the indigenous world has been theorized, indigenous voices have been overwhelmingly silenced' (Smith 1999: 29). In the process, Indigenous cultures and knowledges have been instrumentalised and appropriated by members of the majority society, which has been described as the phenomenon of an 'ongoing epistemicide of Indigenous thought' (Svalastog et al. 2021). In the last few decades, however, cross-disciplinary scholarship in Indigenous studies, critical race and critical whiteness studies, and postcolonial and decolonial theory have disclosed and reframed the asymmetries of knowledge production in many regards. Bearing this in mind, notions such as 'resistance', which I deploy as a key term in this chapter, take on a multidimensional meaning which non-Indigenous writers cannot fully grasp (Garneau 2020). The critical concept of a 'double perspective', for instance, frames the multiplicity of Indigenous knowledges and stories, which reach beyond a Western perspective on time, space and place, as 'not two perceptions of the same world, but the parallel existence of two (possibly overlapping) worlds at the same time' (Svalastog et al. 2021). This concept supports the idea of Indigenous resistance in (ongoing) colonial experiences in the sense that

> [n]on-Indigenous people do not need to fully understand Indigenous peoples' unique double perspectives, for if they did, the knowledge contained therein would be open to dominant system colonization. Indeed, our goal is not to ask individuals to increase their own understanding of the exotic 'other'. Rather, we ask for recognition that the double perception exists and is a valuable cultural tool. (Svalastog et al. 2021)

As a non-Indigenous scholar, I have no first-hand knowledge of Sámi cultures. I have been able to educate myself only through mediated forms of expertise (academic courses, books, museum tours, verbal exchange). Within the field of Indigenous studies, it has become common practice to outline the biographical background of the respective author as a sign of cultural responsibility. This can help establish a relational positioning for the researching subject and avoid the illusion of academic neutrality or objectivity (Smith 1999: 137–8). The reading of Sámi visual art and literature I undertake in this chapter is hence to be understood as an interpretative approach among many other possible readings. In brief summary, this means: '[A]s a non-Indigenous scholar you have to *decentre yourself*' (Skille 2021: 10). The move towards a decentralisation of 'familiar' epistemological frameworks can be tackled with the so-called 'four Rs': reciprocity, relevance, responsibility and reverence (Pidgeon 2018). As a complement to this, most recent scholarship has added a critical understanding of heterogeneity to the list (Skille 2021: 2), acknowledging the complexity of heterogeneity in Indigenous communities, involving different subgroups and individuals – as well as unique artistic productions.

Working towards a decentralisation of established knowledge is, in a different context, also a key concern of the cross-disciplinary field of human–animal studies. The objective is to establish a framework for more-than-anthropocentric research which balances out the relationalities and entanglements of human and nonhuman animal life and agency. As literary scholar Roland Borgards (2017: 53) has pointed out, a distinction has to be drawn between different concepts of anthropocentrism. While the perspectives of an ontological anthropocentrism advocate the status of human exceptionalism in a rather naive way, epistemological anthropocentrism helps reflect on the conditions and limits of (more-than-)human knowledge production. As long as it is human actors who conduct research, epistemological anthropocentrism will be ineluctable to some extent. This makes it all the more important to avoid imperial strategies of thought, to develop a sensitivity for the powers and asymmetries of knowledge production in research, and to work towards a constant decentralisation of one's own perspectives by methodological means.

Modern(ist) Sámi Art and the Ethnographic Eye

The subject matter and mode of (re)presentation in Marakatt-Labba's embroideries take up different features from Sámi art and literature of the early twentieth century, in which reindeers and human–animal relations had already been key elements. In 1910, it was self-taught writer Johan Turi (1854–1936) who published the first ever secular book in a Sámi language, *Muittalus samid birra* (*An Account of the Sámi*), with the assistance of non-Sámi ethnographer and artist Emilie Demant Hatt (1873–1958).[6] The aim of the project was to introduce the richness of Sámi knowledges to a wider, non-Indigenous public. In correlation with the written part of the book, Turi produced a set of ink drawings which stylistically resemble ancient northern rock and parietal art. For the most part, the illustrations show large groups of reindeers, humans and some accompanying dogs from a great distance. In terms of style, Turi's visual narratives of human–animal interaction in *An Account of the Sámi* seem to exhibit a rather countermodernist approach and clearly differ from the pictorial principles of the contemporary European avant-garde movements. His drawings abjure techniques of central perspective or deep-view effects, and make use of fine lines and two-dimensional silhouettes.[7] The illustration for the instructive chapter 'Reindeer Corral in Autumn', however, experiments with a bird's-eye view. It shows the traditional practice of separating groups of reindeers who migrate from north to south in winter, in order to allocate them to the different Sámi *siida*, the local communities. The spectator looks down at a circular corral which is divided into three parts and filled with reindeers and human figures who are, quite surprisingly, not seen from above but modelled from a lateral line of sight. While most of the human figures, both male and female, hold sticks in their hands and seem to be moving around, the reindeers' positions are rather static; they seem to stand still next to each other. In the bottom and one top corner, there are a few reindeers and dogs located outside of the corral, which has no visible entrance. Turi's small-scale, detailed image composition, comprising a large number of similar-looking, nearly stereotyped figures in interaction, stylistically resembles the embroideries by Marakatt-Labba. The scenes of both artists transport tranquil, somewhat mute atmospheres, which seem to be charged with extra meaning: the circularity of Turi's corral, for instance, bears similarities to the pictorial principles of ritual objects in Sámi cosmology. Traditional depictions of ceremonial Sámi drums featured a similar oval shape filled with human and non-human animals and functioned as objects of embedded knowledge (Joy 2018: 173–85). Besides Marakatt-Labba, contemporary artists such as Keviselie / Hans Ragnar Mathisen (b. 1945), who was also a founding member of the Sámi Artist Group and exhibited at Documenta 14, have taken up the cosmologically charged circular structures and cyclical storytelling for their work.

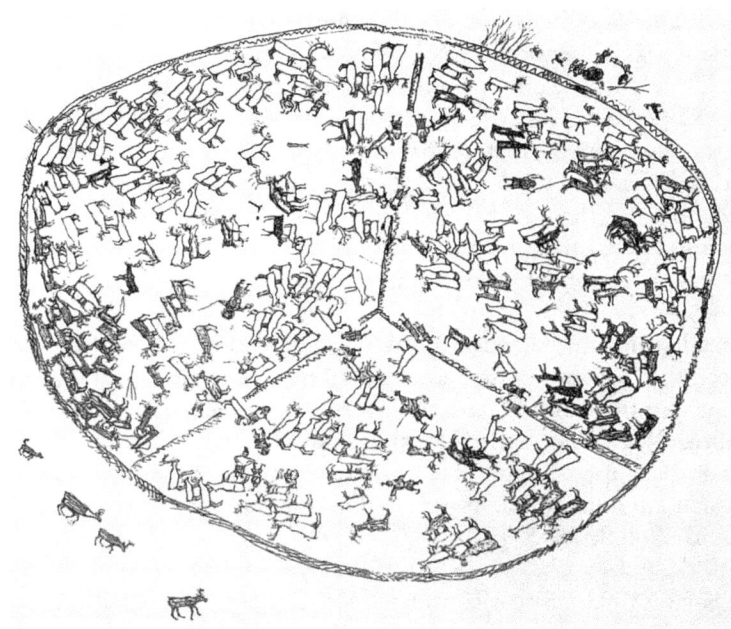

Figure 9.3 Johan Turi. 1910. *Reindeer Corral in Autumn*. Ink drawing. Illustration from *Muittalus samid birra (An Account of the Sámi)*.

Turi's début in 1910 was a success at the time and has subsequently been translated into numerous languages. For a long time, however, the book was investigated only from an ethnographic perspective,[8] and, in consequence, has often been rashly misread as 'mere' functional writing and handicraft, disregarding the literary and art historical relevance in its own right. Such hierarchical value judgements, seeking to perpetuate a clear distinction between art and craft – or, more precisely, between supposedly 'high' fine art of aesthetic value and 'low' applied art serving only a practical function – are nothing new and have a long discursive tradition, especially in art criticism and mainstream academic discourses about cultural minorities and Indigenous cultures. The established categories and canons of Western art, however, do not represent the actual diversity of cultural practices in diverse societies. The Sámi term for fine art in the Western sense, *dáidda*, is a Finnish-based neologism that was added to Sámi languages only in the 1970s, in addition to *duodji*, the original word for craft.[9] Such rigid conceptual boundaries, however, do not correspond to the multidimensional logics and aesthetics of Turi's artistic production. Due to conceptual misunderstandings, modern and traditional art from Sápmi, and also from the Inuit in Greenland, has 'has long been reduced to the constructed pair of aesthetics and ethnology' (Alsen and Landmann 2016: 282). The same applied to the artistic works by autodidact Nils Nilsson Skum (1872–1951), who is today considered one of the central agents of modern Sámi art. In 1938, he published the book *Same sita* (*Sámi Village*), exhibiting verbal and visual narratives of Sámi lifestyle, which was by then persistently under threat due to the restrictive assimilation policies of the national states. Skum's central motifs are large reindeer herds roaming through barren, hilly and snow-white landscapes, seen from a far distance. With their works, Turi and Skum created countervoices to the external representation and foreign interpretation of their cultures. Still, a

> problem in the reception of art of indigenous provenance has always been the (generally unreflected) attribution of a representative character to it – in this reading, an artwork stands as representative for the entire culture [. . .]. The artistic quality and meaning of the works is shelved and the superordinate factor of presumed authenticity emphasized, which amounts to an abbreviated and inadequate reception. (Alsen and Landmann 2016: 57)

John Savio (1902–38)[10] is considered the first Sámi artist with a formal arts education and is known for his expressionist woodcuts, similar in style and technique to works by influential representatives of (Nordic) modernism such as Edvard Munch (1863–1944). The motifs of Savio's graphics range from reindeer wildlife to cohabitation of reindeers, dogs and humans, including scenes of dynamic and conflictual human–reindeer interaction. Such scenes of tumult most often show domestication attempts by human figures with the aid of ropes or other tools which are physically resisted by the reindeers. Physical confrontation and violence, however, are not in general shown as something extraordinary or only belonging to the interaction between human and nonhuman animals. In Savio's works, violence asserts itself as an integral part of reindeer wildlife, too, in particular in the form of ritualised antler fights as a common behavioural pattern. Until today, antler fights haven often been misinterpreted as 'unnatural', deficient behaviour by human spectators, as, for example, the audience's reactions to the installation *Soma* (2010) by German artist Carsten Höller (b. 1961) have shown. In this installation, Höller let living reindeers dwell in an artificial paddock at the Hamburger Bahnhof museum in Berlin for three months. Audience members were even allowed to stay overnight to watch the 'aesthetic actors', the reindeers, around the clock.[11] A striking formal feature of Savio's woodcuts, however, in particular in comparison to his early contemporaries Turi and Skum, is the pictorial focus on individual nonhuman animal and human figures instead of larger groups or communities. Still, the figures depicted do not resemble individual portrayals and are, rather, stylised as typical representatives of their species, gender and cultures. Moreover, Savio's works do not pursue instructive goals.

HUMAN–ANIMAL RELATIONS IN SÁMI ART AND LITERATURE

Figure 9.4 John Savio. Between 1925 and 1938. *Mann med reinokse* (*Almei hergin / Man with Bull Reindeer*). Hand-coloured woodcut on paper. 26.5 cm × 22.5 cm. Oslo: National Museum of Art, Architecture and Design.

The tension-fraught woodcut *Man with Bull Reindeer* shows a scene which has many variations in Savio's oeuvre: a reindeer defending themselves against a rope in their antlers, which has been thrown by a male human figure dressed in traditional Sámi clothes. The two antagonists form a diagonal axis which can indicate their pictorial roles as both opponents in harsh polarity and as an ambiguous conflicting unity, tangibly connected by the rope between them. It is not possible to identify which of them is dominating the fight. They are surrounded by lively linear structures which help underline the overall expressivity and create a restless pictorial space. In Savio's woodcuts, human and nonhuman animal actors never merge visually with the 'natural' environments around them, but stand out by means of sharp dark–light contrasts. This explicit focus on scenes of interaction and conflict which do not blur into the surrounding landscape differs from that of other modernist representations of similar themes, such as in the oil painting *Sámi Working with Reindeer* (1943) by Danish artist Emilie Demant Hatt, who initially assisted Johan Turi in writing the book *An Account of the Sámi* and was keen on experiencing the semi-nomadic lifestyle herself.

Figure 9.5 John Savio. Undated. *Pulkkjøring* (*Hærgevuodje* or *Heargevuoddji* / *Sleighride*). Woodcut on paper. 25.2 cm × 19.5 cm. Kirkenes: The Savio Museum.

The woodcut *Sleighride* transports an increased level of dynamic movement and ambiguous physical violence into human–animal interaction. The reindeer and the human figure are depicted from behind; the sleigh as such is barely recognisable at first sight. Two jumping dogs accompany the duo, one of them constituting the foreground of the image. The reindeer has large antlers which reach high into the sky and shows spread legs in a peculiar position that would make it anatomically impossible to run. The most interesting detail, however, is the ambiguous visual reference between human and reindeer corporeality. A pair of reindeer antlers is depicted on the back of the sleigh, and by means of perspective, they even seem to be a part of the human clothing. As a result, the human figure remains as an active aggressor, holding up a whip and exploiting the physical strength of the nonhuman animal for his own purposes. On the other hand, though, the 'reindeer-ish' physiognomy becomes part of the human visual appearance through the antlers on the back. The overall image composition renders the reindeer visible as a superordinate actor in two ways. Although being violently harnessed for the purpose of human mobility, the reindeer's physiognomy takes over the human visual appearance, and the reindeer figure itself is located at the top of the image with large crown-like antlers.

Cultural Self-Appropriation and Subversive Affirmation

The tradition of national romanticist landscape painting is considered a typically Nordic genre, if not *the* typical genre, embracing the peripheral status of the North in contrast to Central European urban milieus. These landscape works convey the impression of a close, emotionally charged relationship between 'nature' and human and nonhuman animals as a visual strategy of what is referred to as 'place-making' practices today (Cassel 2019). In terms of the Sápmi region in the very North, the motifs used to be barren, yet sublime, landscapes with reindeers as their dominant animal actors. Since Sápmi is, and has always been, a cross-national region which is inhabited by both the Indigenous Sámi and members of the majority society, the question of authorship and the privilege and power of interpretation become all the more relevant. In the ideology of national romanticism which formed the mainstream canon of the nineteenth and early twentieth centuries, Sápmi has long been romanticised, stereotyped and appropriated by non-Indigenous painters and writers, while Indigenous positions were silenced.

Figure 9.6 John Savio. Between 1928 and 1934. *Alene (Okto / Alone)*. Woodcut on paper. 28 cm x 32,5 cm. Oslo: National Museum of Art, Architecture and Design.

The woodcut *Alene*, by John Savio, showing a solitary, proudly posing reindeer on hill with a view across a spacious landscape, takes up (or, better, imitates) central pictorial principles of the national romanticist paradigm, and turns them into a Sámi perspective in its own right.[12] I read this as a critical strategy of cultural self-appropriation (Fricker 2007; Serrano Zamora 2017) and subversive affirmation (Arns and Sasse 2006). Acts of subversive affirmation operate with modes of structural invisibility (through imitation, simulation, mimicry and camouflage) or over-identification, and make 'use of the tactics of resistance through apparent affirmation' (Arns and Sasse 2006: 444). This is especially useful in the context of repressive political situations. Such strategies allow (presumably) subordinated social actors to take part in official discourses while simultaneously gaining the agency to undermine them. Therein lies their critical and emancipatory function. In all, 'there is always a surplus which destabilises affirmation and turns it into its opposite' – or at least has the potential to do so. This function is similar to the idea of cultural self-appropriation as a critical epistemic practice by dominated and hermeneutically marginalised groups who aim to overcome the status of hermeneutical marginalisation and epistemic injustice (Serrano Zamora 2017: 300). The reappropriation of interpretative power over Indigenous cultural techniques and knowledges takes its starting point here, in the reappropriation of stereotyped motifs which were harnessed by non-Indigenous artists. In particular, the multifaceted Sámi portrayals of reindeers who always seem to be situated in ambiguous interaction with human figures, oscillating between resistance and surrender, gesture towards such an ideal of (structural) transformation.

The works by Sámi artists examined in this chapter, Marakatt-Labba and her modern(ist) predecessors, Turi, Skum and Savio, do not show explicit or brutal criticism of repressive societal circumstances in their painterly modulations of reindeer life. Instead they actively integrate established stereotypes into their works, either by means of motif, medium and technique, or by the adaptation of certain genre specifics of mainstream culture. While giving an insight into significant traditions of Sámi lifestyle, the artworks can simultaneously be read as examples of silent and subtle resistance.[13]

Animal Agency: Reindeers and/as Material Metaphors

The theoretical concept of 'material metaphor', which has been introduced to the field of human–animal studies by literary scholars Aline Steinbrecher and Roland Borgards (2016), is based on the assumption that nonhuman animals have more than one active role in terms of human–animal relations and (inter-species) cultural production. Nonhuman animals are living creatures *and* serve as cultural signifiers who are charged with meaning. They are integrated into processes of meaning production with specific, yet variable, forms of agency. Cultural historian Mieke Roscher has discussed central perspectives on and of more-than-human agency in recent scholarship with the overall aim of avoiding banal conclusions and repetitive, static projections. The mere idea that 'agency is the ability to have an effect' will not do, since 'everything affects everything else in some way or another' (Carter and Charles 2013: 328). Another common trap of banal labelling can be mistaking the attribution of 'nonhuman charisma' (Lorimer 2007) and the resulting increased (human) attention as a form of agency of selected animal species of interest. Thus, Roscher points out that not 'all agency is of the same quality', which is a helpful conceptual reminder, and calls for diversification of the semantically challenging 'master trope' agency (2019: 167). A general differentiation between a 'weak' notion of agency (*Wirkungsmacht*), following the ideas of Bruno Latour's actor–network theory (2005), and a 'strong' notion (*Handlungsmacht*) can be further supplemented with critical understandings of relational, entangled and embodied agency, as well as an increased awareness of the historicity of such concepts (Roscher 2016: 57–61). Interestingly enough, it is especially acts of resistance, performed by nonhuman animals against life forms that have been imposed upon them by humans, and transgressions of human role expectations, which Roscher names as examples of influential acts of relational animal agency (Roscher 2016: 49).

Bearing these critical considerations about (the limits of) the concept of agency in mind, the perspective of nonhuman animals as material metaphors offers a useful theoretical compromise for analysing nonhuman animals in human-made cultural artefacts without losing track of the other role of nonhuman animals in human–animal relations, which is the role as a living creature with an impact on various levels. Material metaphors deny simple logics of substitution in which nonhuman animals are considered only as representatives of meaning implemented by humans. If that was the case, the nonhuman animals depicted or written about could easily be substituted by 'literal meanings', which would follow a naive understanding of anthropocentric world-making. Instead, Steinbrecher and Borgards opt for a change of perspective and emphasise the interactive and material aspects of nonhuman animals in art in three aspects. First, material metaphors originate from the encounter and cohabitation of human and nonhuman animals. Second, material metaphors can be read as traces of the respective underlying human–animal relationships. Third, these traces will affect future animal relations and, thus, they also have an impact on the on-going relationships they emerge from (Steinbrecher and Borgards 2016: 165). The last aspect, which has the strong potential of changing existing 'realities', demonstrates the importance of relational interspecies meaning-making. Of course, the impact of an epistemological anthropocentrism and anthropogenic influence can never be totally denied, since it is still human actors who interpret the cultural productions involving nonhuman animals. However, in the perspective of material metaphors, nonhuman animal actors take on a formative, world-changing and world-making role. Steinbrecher and Borgards (2016: 157) suggest we think of the living animal and the represented animal not as two separate entities, but *together* – without indicating a hierarchy between human and nonhuman animal impact.

If one considers the reindeers in the works by Marakatt-Labba and the modern(ist) Sámi artists as material metaphors which reference both the living nonhuman animals *and* their pictorial representation, the complexity of negotiating resistance in terms of both human and nonhuman animal actors becomes even more obvious. On the one hand, the reindeers reference the complexity of (semi-)domesticated living animals, bear witness to lived relationships in which human attempts at control do not succeed without complications, and show a variety of acts of resistance which function in the logics of more-than-human agency in a strong, formative sense. On the other hand, the symbolic level of the nonhuman animal depictions becomes permeable for human experiences and a commentary of Sámi resistance against attempted territorial and cultural subordination by societal majorities. In doing so, the representation of resistance is

Figure 9.7 John Savio. Between 1928 and 1938. *Gutter med lasso (Gánddat suohpaniin / Boys with Lasso)*. Woodcut on paper. 20.5 x 29 cm. Oslo: National Museum of Art, Architecture and Design.

ambiguous and can be found in depictions of vivid fights as well as in supposedly tranquil, close-to-'nature' scenes which follow, as I have argued, the strategies of cultural self-appropriation and subversive affirmation. None of the analytical approaches I have presented in this chapter would work on its own; they only work *together*, in interrelation.

The general ambiguity and the broad range of interpretation of reindeer depictions in Sámi art finds its epitome in a woodcut by John Savio, which may have a disturbing effect at first sight. The work *Boys with Lasso* shows three male human figures who walk in a row, bending slightly forward while holding reindeer antlers on to their foreheads. A fourth person stands in the front of the scene, turning his back to the spectator and holding a rolled-up lasso in his hands. His body position indicates that he is ready to throw it right away. This image of the attempt at 'becoming' a reindeer offers a variety of interpretations. Obviously, the human figures perform an imitation of reindeer corporeality and behaviour. This could be read either as a simple leisure activity of children about the species they have most contact with in daily life, or alternatively as an act of holding reindeers up to ridicule by mocking processes of domestication, or as a sign of deep respect and admiration for reindeer life as a result of a close human–animal relationship.

The reindeer depictions in modern(ist) and contemporary Sámi art which I have examined in this chapter can be read as images of both nonhuman animal *and* human empowerment in challenging hierarchical environments. Informed by Indigenous studies, post- and decolonial theory and human–animal studies, the (re)presentations of nonhuman animals and humans in cohabitation, and the related issues of (a)symmetries of power, have proven to be more complex than they may seem from privileged (societal, academic or species) positions. They countervoice dominant narratives of both cultural subordination and a naive nature–culture divide, and illustrate how the perspective of Indigenous and animal epistemologies are enriching contributions to mainstream readings of modernist aesthetics.

WORKS CITED

Alsen, Katharina and Annika Landmann. 2016. *Nordic Painting: The Rise of Modernity*. London and New York: Random House.
Arns, Inke and Sylvia Sasse. 2006. 'Subversive Affirmation: On Mimesis as a Strategy of Resistance'. In *East Art Map: Contemporary Art and Eastern Europe*. Ed. IRWIN, 444–55. Cambridge, MA: MIT Press.
Böhm, Alexandra and Jessica Ullrich. 2019. 'Introduction – Animal Encounters: Contact, Interaction and Relationality'. In *Animal Encounters: Kontakt, Interaktion und Relationalität*. Ed. Alexandra Böhm and Jessica Ullrich, 1–21. Berlin: J. B. Metzler.
Borgards, Roland. 2017. 'Märchentiere'. In *Macht und Ohnmacht: Erfahrungen im Märchen und im Leben*. Ed. Harlinda Lox and Sabine Lutkat, 49–71. Krummwisch: Königsfurt-Urania.

Carter, Bob and Nickie Charles. 2013. 'Animals, Agency and Resistance'. *Journal for the Theory of Social Behaviour* 43.3: 322–40.
Cassel, Susanna Heldt. 2019. 'Branding Sámi Tourism: Practices of Indigenous Participation and Place-Making'. In *The Nordic Wave in Place Branding: Poetics, Practices, Politics*. Ed. Cecilia Cassinger, Andrea Lucarelli and Szilvia Gyimóthy, 139–52. Cheltenham, UK, and Northampton, MA: Edward Elgar.
Crowther, Paul. 2003. 'Cultural Exclusion, Normativity, and the Definition of Art'. *The Journal of Aesthetics and Art Criticism* 61.2: 121–31.
Fricker, Miranda. 2007. *Epistemic Injustice: Power and the Ethics of Knowing*. Oxford: Oxford University Press.
Garneau, David. 2020. 'Writing about Indigenous Art with Critical Care'. *C-Magazine*, 145. Available at: <https://cmagazine.com/issues/145/writing-about-indigenous-art-with-critical-care> (last accessed 28 February 2022).
Guttorm, Gunvor. 2018. 'Stories Created in Stitches'. *Afterall: A Journal of Art, Context and Enquiry* 45: 18–23.
Harney, Elizabeth and Ruth B. Phillips. 2018. 'Inside Modernity. Indigeneity, Coloniality, Modernisms'. In *Mapping Modernisms: Art, Indigeneity, Colonialism*. Ed. Elizabeth Harney and Ruth B. Phillips, 1–29. Durham: Durham University Press.
Hautala-Hirvioja, Tuija. 2014. 'Early Sámi Visual Artists – Western Fine Arts Meets Sámi Culture'. *Barents Studies* 1.1: 11–40.
Heith, Anne. 2012. 'Aesthetics and Ethnicity : The Role of Boundaries in Sámi and Tornedalian Art'. In *Whiteness and Postcolonialism in the Nordic Region : Exceptionalism, Migrant Others and National Identities*. Ed. Kristín Loftsdóttir and Lars Jensen, 159–73. Farnham: Taylor & Francis.
Joy, Francis. 2018. *Sámi Shamanism, Cosmology and Art as Systems of Embedded Knowledge*. Rovaniemi: University of Lapland.
Körber, Lill-Ann and Ebbe Volquardsen. 2014. 'The Postcolonial North Atlantic: An Introduction'. In *The Postcolonial North Atlantic: Iceland, Greenland and the Faroe Islands*. Ed. Lill-Ann Körber and Ebbe Volquardsen, 7–25. Berlin: Nordeuropa-Institut.
Kreuger, Anders. 2018. 'Britta Marakatt-Labba: "Images Are Always Stories"'. *Afterall: A Journal of Art, Context and Enquiry* 45: 4–17.
Loftsdóttir, Kristín and Lars Jensen. 2012. 'Nordic Exceptionalism and the Nordic "Others"'. In *Whiteness and Postcolonialism in the Nordic Region: Exceptionalism, Migrant Others and National Identities*. Ed. Kristín Loftsdóttir and Lars Jensen, 1–11. Farnham: Taylor & Francis.
Lorimer, Jamie. 2007. 'Nonhuman Charisma'. *Environment and Planning D: Society and Space* 25: 911–32.
Morton, Timothy. 2007. *Ecology Without Nature: Rethinking Environmental Aesthetics*. Cambridge, MA: Harvard University Press.
Pidgeon, Michelle. 2018. 'Moving between Theory and Practice within an Indigenous Research Paradigm'. *Qualitative Research* 31.4: 418–36.
Puranen, Jorma 2009. 'Imaginary Homecoming'. In *Appropriation*. Ed. David Evans, 135–6. Whitechapel Gallery/Cambridge, MA: MIT Press
Roscher, Mieke. 2016. 'Zwischen Wirkungsmacht und Handlungsmacht: Sozialgeschichtliche Perspektiven auf tierliche Agency'. In *Das Handeln der Tiere: Tierliche Agency im*

Fokus der Human–Animal Studies. Ed. Sven Wirth, Anett Laue, Markus Kurth, Katharina Dornenzweig, Leonie Bossert and Karsten Balgar, 43–66. Bielefeld: Transcript.

Roscher, Mieke. 2019. 'Actors or Agents? Defining the Concept of Relational Agency in (Historical) Wildlife Encounters'. *Animal Encounters: Kontakt, Interaktion und Relationalität*. Ed. Alexandra Böhm and Jessica Ullrich, 149–70. Berlin: J. B. Metzler.

Roters, Annalena. 2022. *Mit Tieren denken: Zur Ästhetik von lebenden Tieren in zeitgenössischer Kunst*. Berlin: Neofelis.

Serrano Zamora, Justo. 2017. 'Overcoming Hermeneutical Injustice: Self-Appropriation and the Epistemic Practices of the Oppressed'. *The Journal of Speculative Philosophy* 31.2: 299–310.

Skille, Eivind Åsrum. 2021. 'Doing Research into Indigenous Issues Being Non-Indigenous'. *Qualitative Research*. Available at: <https://doi.org/10.1177/14687941211005947> (last accessed 28 February 2022).

Skum, Nils Nilsson. 1938. *Same sita – lappbyn: Bilder og lapsk text*. Ed. Ernst Lauritz Manker. Stockholm: Thule.

Smith, Linda Tuhiwai. 1999. *Decolonizing Methodologies: Research and Indigenous People*. London and New York: Zed Books/Dunedin: University of Otago Press.

Steinbrecher, Aline, and Roland Borgards. 2016. 'Doggen, Bologneser, Bullenbeisser: Hunde in historischen Quellen um 1800 und in *Danton's Tod* von Georg Büchner'. In *Tierisch! Das Tier und die Wissenschaft*. Ed. Meret Fehlmann, Margot Michel and Rebecca Niederhauser, 151–71. Zurich: VDF Hochschulverlag.

Svalastog, Anna Lydia, Shawn Wilson, Harald Gaski, Kate Senior and Richard Chenchall. 2021. 'Double Perspective in the Colonial Present'. *Social Theory and Health*. Available at: <https://doi.org/10.1057/s41285-020-00156-8> (last accessed 28 February 2022).

Svonni, Mikael. 2009. 'Johan Turi: First Author of the Sámi'. *Scandinavian Studies* 8.4: 483–90.

Turi, Johan. 1910. *Muittalus samid birra: En bog om lappernes liv*. Ed. Emilie Demant Hatt. Stockholm: Nordiska Bokhandeln.

Ullrich, Jessica. 2016. 'Tiere und Bildende Kunst'. In *Tiere: Kulturwissenschaftliches Handbuch*. Ed. Roland Borgards, 195–215. Stuttgart: J. B. Metzler.

Notes

1. The clothing indicates traditional Sámi *gákti* costumes in blue and red colours, with *goikkehat* shoes – usually made of reindeer skin – and the horn-shaped *ládjogahpir* headgear which used to be worn by Sámi women in everyday life until the early twentieth century (Guttorm 2018: 19, 22).
2. I place the term 'nature' in quotation marks due to the social constructedness of the nature–culture divide. Among others, Timothy Morton provides an in-depth critical reading of dualist concepts of 'nature' and 'the ecological imaginary' (2007: 1).
3. The recent documentary film *Historjá – Stygn for Sápmi* (*Stitches for Sápmi*, 2022), written and directed by Thomas Jackson, grapples with environmental issues in Marakatt-Labba's oeuvre in more detail.
4. Following new archaeological research, some have suggested we speak of all inhabitants of the Sápmi region as 'immigrants', which would include speakers both of

Sámi or Baltic Finnic and of North Germanic languages, instead of considering the Sámi 'Indigenous' (Kreuger 2018: 10).
5. 'Charismatic megafauna' of the Sápmi region, both extinct and extant, was also the topic of the exhibition of the same name at the Arktikum museum and science centre in Rovaniemi, Finland (16 March 2021–25 May 2022).
6. The collaborative process behind the bilingual publication (North Sámi and Danish) is further described in Svonni (2009).
7. Some of Turi's late works, however, indicate changes of style and show experiments with 'Western' pictorial conventions (Alsen and Landmann 2016: 51–7).
8. The primary ethnographic interest can also be explained by Turi's biographical background: before becoming an artist in advanced age, he worked as a hunter and fisherman and was, like all of his family, active in reindeer herding.
9. In this text, I generally refer to the North Sámi spelling, which has the largest amount of speakers (about 20,000). However, varying spellings can be found in the different Sámi languages: for example, in Lule and Southern Sámi.
10. A comprehensive biography-oriented approach to the practices of John Savio, Johan Turi and Nils Nilsson Skum can be found in Hautala-Hirvioja (2014).
11. The interaction between living reindeers and human spectators in *Soma* is further discussed in Roters (2022: 89–119). The term 'aesthetic actor' in animal aesthetics has been introduced by Ullrich (2016: 203).
12. Moreover, the motif of the solitary reindeer plays with another dominant attribution of modernist Nordic art, which is melancholic Nordic individuum (and artist).
13. A radically different mode of criticism with the aid of reindeers as both motif and material pursue the sculptures and installations by contemporary Sámi artist Máret Ánne Sara (b. 1983), who works with the shock effect of accumulated reindeer skulls. Her works were, amongst others, part of the renamed Sámi Pavilion (instead of Nordic Pavilion) at the 59th Venice Biennale (23 April–22 November 2022).

PART IV

INTERSECTIONS, ENCOUNTERS

10

ANIMAL–HUMAN ENTANGLEMENTS IN THE CANADIAN WILD ANIMAL STORIES OF CHARLES G. D. ROBERTS

Lauren Cullen

> *I saw, deep in the eyes of the animals, the human soul look out upon me.*
> – Edward Carpenter, *Towards Democracy* (1905)

In a letter addressed to H. Gerald Wade in 1933 following a review of his realistic wild animal stories, Canadian author Charles G. D. Roberts lamented that Rudyard Kipling's Mowgli stories

> are not by any means nature yarns in the same *genre* as mine, but rather the order of the old fabliaux. My stories are *a new departure* in animal stories, dealing with the *psychology* of animals, as I have pointed out in several of my prefaces, and has been fully and ably expounded in the (English) *National Review* for July 1931. (Roberts 1989: 455; emphasis in original)

Roberts's fascination with nonhuman animal (hereafter animal) psychology was bound up with his aspiration to present truthful depictions of animals in fiction and came on the heels of theories of evolution and comparative psychology. The wild animal short story genre first emerged in the late nineteenth century, which Adrian Hunter describes as a period in which a 'three-way alignment between realism, the short story, and various forms of cultural radicalism and avant-gardism came into being', signalling the advent of a new modernist moment (Hunter 2016: 206). A genre co-developed by two Canadian writers,

Ernest Thompson Seton and Charles G. D. Roberts, the wild animal story has long been touted as 'distinctly Canadian' for its style, focus on wild rather than domestic animals, and form (Atwood 2012: 73). In the first instance, Roberts's use of animal–human encounters in the wild works as a formal strategy to encode suspense and unpredictability within the fabric of the short story. 'The originality of the new form', remarks W. J. Keith, 'consisted in its shifting of the main focus from the human to the animal world,' and Roberts's use of heterodiegetic narration, as opposed to the autodiegetic narration employed by Anna Sewell, Margaret Marshall Saunders and Virginia Woolf, marks an experimental innovation that stands in contrast to the animal fable and (auto) biography (Keith 1969: 88). In this chapter, I analyse how attention to the lived experiences of animals in the wilderness raises important questions not only about animal agency and the limits of humanism, but also about the entangled nature of animal–human relations in settler society. As Caroline Hovanec puts it, 'in the Anthropocene, no "wilderness" entirely untouched by human activities exists. It's entanglements all the way down' (Hovanec 2019: 93). This chapter argues that Roberts's wild animal stories work to deconstruct anthropocentric hierarchies, with survival functioning as a means of blurring the animal–human boundary in the Canadian wilderness. To that end, I provide close readings of wild animal stories to reveal how Roberts challenges ideas about animal victimhood and human supremacy to present them instead as cognitively complex, agential characters.

As a writer whose reputation developed during the final decades of the nineteenth century and the beginnings of the twentieth, it would seem that Roberts found his career split between two periods at odds with one another: the Victorian era and modernism. While attention has been given to Roberts's modernist (and antimodernist) sensibilities, these analyses have mainly focused on his poetry and not on his successful yet controversial wild animal short stories.[1] By terming his stories 'psychological romances constructed on the framework of natural science', Roberts's attempt to know, understand and depict animal life speaks to the modernist preoccupation which 'drove Woolf and her contemporaries to the very limits of literary and scientific representation' (Hovanec 2018: 3). The wild animal short story genre illuminates the 'interplay between anthropocentric and biocentric storytelling traditions' by acknowledging and refuting anthropocentric distinctions made between civilisation and wilderness, instinct and rationality, and (agential) character and (passive) object (Herman 2018: 4). Animals, and animal characters, operate with more than just instinct, as shown, for example, in Roberts's 'The King of the Mamozekel' (1902), in which the titular moose shirks death through knowledge-building and experience. After a close encounter where he witnesses the death of a fellow moose, the king concludes 'he now knew [men] to be dangerous, and also knew that their chief power lay in the long dark tubes which spit fire and made fierce sounds' (Roberts 1902: 332).

Indeed, the critique of 'the animal' as a discursive category was a thread that ran through Roberts's works formally, thematically and characterologically. As my analysis shows, the wild animal story functions as a transitional fiction by embracing realist, naturalist and experimental formal elements in the short story form to represent animal life. In his treatment of animal characters, Roberts draws on both theories of evolution and the burgeoning comparative psychology tradition, speaking to modernist concerns about animal subjectivity and the confluences of animal–human kinship. Importantly, Roberts also reveals an awareness of the consequences of human hubris, colonialism and settler expansion on animals. This chapter argues that, through its treatment of the wild animal character in the short story form, the wild animal story genre posits a bridge between forms and movements, time periods and cultural preoccupations to reconsider, in turn, the parameters of modernism.

The Modern Canadian Animal

Reading for a Victorian-to-modernist shift, Roberts's stories provide important case studies that trouble the borderlands between these seemingly disparate periods. Carrie Rohman asserts that 'for those in modernist studies, the animal problem takes on a particularly charged valence since modernism comes on the heels of Darwin's catastrophic blow to human privilege vis-à-vis the species question' (Rohman 2008: 1). My discussion engages with and builds on Rohman's contention by illustrating how late nineteenth- into twentieth-century writers responded to Darwin's theories and questioned the complexity and hierarchical nature of animal–human relationships. Roberts's birth in 1860 coincided with developing theories of evolution that were being widely discussed and engaged with by novelists, artists, poets and playwrights internationally, and were at the heart of the Nature Fakers debate.[2] In 1903, American naturalist John Burroughs penned an article in the *Atlantic Monthly* criticising writers on animals, including Canadians Roberts and Thompson Seton, for fabricating a 'sham natural history' through their literary representations of animals who could communicate, learn and reason. This article ignited a fierce literary debate over animal intelligence, sentience and behaviour that spanned 'four years of magazine and newspaper articles, book prefaces, and a full editorial in the *New York Times*' (Lutts 2006: n.p.).[3] What set Roberts and the other 'Nature Fakers' apart from other writers on animals was their unflinching collective claim that their works represented truthful, realistic depictions of animal behaviour, consciousness and emotion exemplified through dynamic, central animal characters in North America. Thus, rather than extol the virtues of humans against those of his nonhuman animal characters, Roberts connects them with narratives built on survival.

These species entanglements were specific to Roberts's experiences as a white settler growing up on the edge of the wilderness in Canada. Roberts lived a rather solitary existence as a child, educated by his Reverend father, and actively sought the companionship of animals, tame and wild, by the marshlands of the Tantramar in rural New Brunswick, in eastern Canada. Moreover, as '[t]he childhood of Charles G.D. Roberts coincided with the birth of the Canadian nation', the cultural and political ramifications of this reality colour his works (Adams 1986: 9). Canada was a nascent nation with a powerful girding of British culture before and after its Confederation in 1867, and Canadians belonged legitimately within the fold of nineteenth-century writers and were part of the broader Anglophone dialogue. Roberts's wild animal stories were included in school readers in Canadian classrooms and published by American, Canadian and English publishers. Likewise, Roberts's animal stories were admired by German Nobel laureate Thomas Mann, and Roberts further corresponded with English and Irish writers Rudyard Kipling and Oscar Wilde, as well as President Theodore Roosevelt and E. Pauline Johnson (Roberts 1989: 33, 496). Moreover, as Don Conway notes, T. S. Eliot 'was a notable presence for at least seven of the thirteen years of Roberts's London sojourn' (Conway 1984: 77). Roberts found immense international success with book publications, with a review in *Country Life* in 1907 touting the view that Roberts's *Kindred of the Wild* (1902), *Watchers of the Trails* (1904) and *Red Fox* (1905) were 'the most successful books' of the modern animal story form (*Country Life* 1907: clxvii).

Critics such as Thomas Dunlap, Terry Whalen and Margaret Atwood have acknowledged Roberts's contributions to Canadian literature, and literature about animals more generally. In her ground-breaking book about the roots and substance of Canadian literature past and present, *Survival* (2012), Atwood dedicates an entire chapter to the presence of 'animal victims' as unique to Canadian literature, a view likewise held by Marian Scholtmeijer, whose chapter on 'Animal Victims in the Wild' contains an analysis of Roberts's work (Scholtmeijer 1993). Examining animals for their symbolic currency, Atwood circumvents reading animals as subjects in and of themselves, choosing instead to explore their role as vehicles for understanding the 'national psyche', since her thesis considers the main preoccupations of Canadian prose and poetry as survival and victimhood. She views Canada's identification with nature and fauna as a potential representation of national guilt, stating pointedly that 'Canada after all was founded on the fur trade, and an animal cannot painlessly be separated from its skin' (Atwood 2012: 81). Yet Nicole Shukin's *Animal Capital* (2009), which provides a critique of the central role of animal exploitation under capitalism, notes that in emphasising the symbolic nature of animal life, cultural analyses neglect the corporality and lived experiences of animal beings. In this way, the beaver exemplifies 'Canada's fetish insofar as it configures the nation as a life form that is born rather than made' (Shukin 2009: 3). For Shukin, the 'rendering' of animal life takes on a double meaning as representational, 'making a copy', and material/literal, 'the industrial boiling down and recycling of animal remains' (Shukin 2009: 20). To this end, Roberts's 'renderings' of animal characters can draw attention to these political–economic sensibilities, albeit in a more subtle way.

The development and prominence of animals as both symbols and characters in the Canadian literary imagination is therefore tied to Canada's cultural, political, economic and environmental legacies. However, John Sandlos, in his survey of Canadian literature about animals, points out that while much attention has been drawn to the realistic wild animal story's contribution to both the development of the Canadian short story and animals in the Canadian literary canon, critics have failed to acknowledge the extent to which these animal stories engage with 'the philosophical implications of late-nineteenth and early-twentieth-century natural science . . . to promote a sympathetic identification between the reader and animal characters' (Sandlos 2000: 81). This chapter posits that central to these scientific conversations was an increasing awareness of the entangled lives of humans and animals in Canada, with the backdrop of the back-to-nature movement, and a transatlantic interest in environmental issues, conservation and the treatment of animals both captive and wild, mediated by the authority that Roberts presented.

Ideas surrounding animal–human continuity and animal psychology undergird the realistic animal story, and these frameworks are explicitly referenced in the prefaces to Roberts's collections, including *Watchers of the Trails* (1904), in which Roberts clarifies:

> the stories of which this volume is made up are avowedly fiction. They are, at the same time, true, in that the material of which they are moulded consists of facts, – facts as precise as painstaking observation and anxious regard for truth can make them. (Roberts 1904: vii)

These wild animal stories are sketches whose subject matter and commentary on animal–human relationships is distinctly modern. Roberts's keen interest in animal psychology complicates our usual sense of the form of short fiction, and the anthropocentrism inherent in realist fiction. He poses a challenge to form and genre by which animals feature as protagonists who are emotional and rational, and whose stories represent the world through nonhuman perspectives. Stories hinge on fitness and ability, as well as the implacability of luck and chance in the wilderness. And although Terry Whalen contends 'Roberts never loses sight, as many critics have asserted, of the spiritual ascendency of the human being', although Roberts's narratives often leave space for a more antianthropocentric interpretation that evaluates the (unfairly advantaged) violent methods of destruction at the disposal of humans, and the slow violence committed by acts of settlement (Whalen 1984: 139). In 'The Tiger of the Sea' from

Neighbours Unknown (1911), for instance, Gardner, a yachtsman, is 'seized with a fool idea' to hunt an orca for his trophy (Roberts 1911: 223). After missing his shot, he takes aim at and kills the orca's calf, leaving his own life hanging in the balance as the mother orca seeks retribution. While Roberts states Gardner 'was not wantonly cruel, only thoughtless', he delivers a narrative that underlines the cost of human hubris and selfishness, when the mother orca must be killed by another man to guarantee Gardner's survival (Roberts 1911: 26).

Consequently, while animals play the leading characters in these stories, the realistic wild animal story genre does not obscure the role of the human; rather, these multispecies narratives draw attention to the increasing number of ways humans and animals interact with each other and their environments. Martina Seifert writes that the wild animal story 'follows the short-story convention of isolating and dramatizing a single incident that contains within it a multitude of implications' (Seifert 2007: 49), and among these implications are those of entanglement. The result is a form of multispecies narrative in which readers are encouraged to look beyond distinctions between species. For posthumanist Donna Haraway, 'multispecies storytelling' generates 'stories in which multispecies players, who are enmeshed in partial and flawed translations across difference, redo ways of living and dying attuned to still possible finite flourishing, still possible recuperation' (Haraway 2016: 10). The locating of his stories in the North American wilderness, where species encounters were often violent struggles for territory, resources and life, means that animals crawl, fly, gallop, swim and hop from the margins to occupy central roles in their stories. Roberts was attentive to the 'partial and flawed translations across difference' that frustrated understandings of animal, and especially non-domesticated animal, life. In his stories, animals are not presumed to be human, and they do not 'speak' in human language like other animal characters of the period, such as Saunders's *Beautiful Joe*.[4] Roberts's narratives explore the tension between likeness and alterity by illustrating the rationality and motivations, in addition to instinct, of his animal characters as they interact with their environments and other 'kindred of the wild'.

Although it is important to acknowledge that Roberts's narratives often reproduce and amplify anthropocentric conceptions of animal–human relationships, I nevertheless contend that Roberts's detached position as narrator and observer gives space for reader interpretation of this anthropocentrism. That is not to say that the short stories carry no ethical or moral weight. Rather, the realism of the wild animal story was meant to serve a higher moral and sympathetic purpose. As Seton puts it: '[W]e and the beasts are kin. Man has nothing that the animals have not at least a vestige of, and the animals have nothing that man does not in some degree share' (Seton 1898: 1). This contention of animal–human continuity based on both science and religion demonstrates an awareness of an emerging modernist dialogue on mental and biological evolution in animals and also a growing animal rights rhetoric. Roberts repeatedly invokes or relies on animal consciousness and writes animal characters that are self-reflective and emotional, and make inferences about their circumstances and predicaments. While a species-crossing spoken language continues to be a barrier between seamless animal–human communication, animals, and their textual representations in the animal story, communicate in a variety of ways, including through signs, body language and verbal cues that engage both textual characters and readers. With narratives informed by science and attentive to developments in psychology, Roberts's animal characters provide an important lens to examine and re-examine these wider cultural and literary ontologies surrounding animal psychology and selfhood.

Roberts's Animals

Roberts's stories can be grouped into broad categories dependent on plot and characterisation: the animal biography, the animal adventure story, the 'anecdote of observation' animal encounter stories and what I term 'split-sympathy' stories, such as the path-forging 'Do Seek Their Meat from God' (1892). Since many of Roberts's stories follow a familiar narrative structure, I draw most of my close reading examples from *Kindred of the Wild* (1902). The animal biography reflects an extended narrative, tracing the life of an animal from birth until death, and, at times, functioning as a condensed *Bildungsroman* in its attention to the psychological and emotional development of the animal protagonist. These stories all employ heterodiegetic narration with variable internal and external focalisation. More simply put, there is no first-person point of view, no narrating 'I', but rather narration that focuses on character action and behaviour. Stories such as 'Strayed' (1889) and 'The Homesickness of Kehonka' (1902) feature animal characters who attempt to forge lives away from human intervention, 'stories told by persons to make sense of and provide a rationale or justification for their action' (Herman 2020: 53). But for Roberts's characters, animal–human relationships are precarious, entangled and often violent.

One of Roberts's first successful wild animal stories, 'Do Seek Their Meat from God' appeared in print in 1892. A short story focusing on the survival of two families, panther and human, it was considered 'too innovative' when Roberts first sought to publish it and was finally accepted by *Harper's Weekly* 'after considerable hesitation and for less than the usual writer's fee' (Seifert 2007: 44). The innovation that baffled and stalled the success of Roberts's publication was his detached and unsentimental depiction of wild animal life, mediated through heterodiegetic narration, as opposed to the traditional autodiegetic narration in animal (auto)biographies, and the intertwining of animal and human worlds. He sets up the premise of 'Do Seek Their Meat from God' in a straightforward manner: Encroachment of settlers on the land had driven away 'deer and smaller game. Hence the sharp hunger of the panther parents, and hence it came that on this night they hunted together' (Roberts 1895: 4). Their eventual target is a human child, a situation which instigates the human and nonhuman animal conflict in the story and the death of the panther parents. The consequence of this killing is described in 'unflinchingly graphic' terms (Adams 1986: 19):

> Not many weeks afterwards the settler was following the fresh trail of a bear which had killed his sheep. The trail led him at last along the slope of a deep ravine, from whose bottom came the brawl of a swollen and obstructed stream. In the ravine he found a shallow cave, behind a great white rock. The cave was plainly a wild beast's lair, and he entered circumspectly. There were bones scattered about, and on some dry herbage in the deepest corner of the den, he found the dead bodies, now rapidly decaying, of two small panther cubs. (Roberts 1895: 16–17)

What is so jarring about the story is not only the importance (and violence) of species relations in the wild, but also the blurring of animal–human lives in language and representation. The death of the panther cubs is clearly likened to the tragedy of two dead human children, given that they are described in the first instance as 'dead bodies' and only later identified as 'small panther cubs'. The story's resolution, in other words, is not one of human heroism over animal conquest; instead, the pathos lies in understanding that human encroachment and intervention often mean an unnecessarily violent end to animal life.

Another explicit example of human intrusion comes with 'The Homesickness of Kehonka'. In this story, the capture and attempted domestication of a wild animal is conveyed through the life-narrative of a young goose, who is stolen from his family's nest and raised by a backwoods farmer. Kehonka's freedom is circumscribed when his wings are clipped; however, he never loses his desire to return to the wild, and this 'homesickness' is reflected in his frequent ruminations about migrating south and attempts to forge relationships with the flock of geese near the goose pond. When spring arrives, Kehonka's desire to join this 'alien flock' becomes urgent, and he tries to fly, despite his clipped wings (Roberts 1902: 129):

> His first desperate effort carried him half a mile. Then he dropped to earth, in a bed of withered salt-grass all awash with the full tide of Tantramar. Resting amid the salt-grass, he tasted such exaltation of freedom that his heart forgot its soreness over the flock which had vanished. (Roberts 1902: 131)

Overcome by a newly formed fellowship with the wild goose group, Kehonka forgets 'his captivity and clipped wing' (Roberts 1902: 132). Unable to keep up with the flock, he begins a fragmented journey to find them, during which his wings give out and he falls frequently along the Tantramar river. As with most of Roberts's narratives, animal death is immediate and violent. Earthbound, Kehonka is ambushed by a fox: '[T]he struggle lasted scarcely more than two heart-beats' and his limp body is carried swiftly back into the woods (Roberts 1902: 140). As this story shows, Roberts's representation of Kehonka holds formal and political weight. As a psychologically complex protagonist, Kehonka demands the same readerly attention and empathy that a human protagonist would garner, while his demise, due to human intervention, forces a refashioning of the ethical optics surrounding hunting, environmental destruction and domestication.

Roberts's animal characters are consequently fleshed out, fully formed and central, often even more so than his human characters. Moreover, with the short story form, animals come sharply into focus. Characters are not marginal, nor is their precarity reliant on being written out in favour of human character action. Instead, this precarity is due to the inherent violence and danger of the wilderness. Indeed, as Roberts writes, 'death stalks joy forever among the kindred of the wild' (Roberts 1902: 36). Moreover, Roberts's wordplay in calling animals 'wild folk', 'kindred' and 'persons' also forges a linguistic kinship, and specifically disrupts the uncertain boundary between animals and humans. In not actively employing rights rhetoric throughout his prose, Roberts sidesteps a Victorian didacticism in favour of a more modernist representation of animal–human kinship based on confluences in behaviours and concerns specific to psychology and the environment. This sets himself apart from other writers of his time, such as Seton, London and even Woolf, who often lean more towards overtly anthropomorphic depictions of talking animals or animal narrators.

While Kehonka meets a tragic end, the titular eagle in the adventure story 'The Lord of the Air' (1902) manages a triumphant escape and return to freedom from both Indigenous and settler hands. Significantly, Roberts illuminates different cultural relationships with animals. For the Indigenous character, the eagle is initially 'inoffensive' and rather a source of inspiration: 'He had often watched, with feelings as near akin to jealousy as his arrogant heart could entertain, the spearing of suckers and whitefish. And now the sight determined him to go fishing on his own account' (Roberts 1902: 69). Though the Indigenous character engages in trade because he 'had freed himself from the conservatism of his race', the relinquishing of this reciprocal and appreciative relationship with animals amounts to nothing.[5] Consequently, eliding racial, class and cultural differences, Roberts positions both the Indigenous trapper and the American animal-trophy collector as threats to animal existence. Once trapped, the eagle sits in his cage, where the stifling nature of the enclosure is palpable with his immobility:

> Now when any one of his jailers approached and sought to win his confidence, he would shrink within himself and harden his feathers with wild inward aversion, but his eye of piercing gold would neither dim nor waver, and a clear perception of the limits of his chain would prevent any futile and ignoble struggle to escape. (Roberts 1902: 86–7)

Here, the eagle plays into a juxtaposing object–subject dynamic, as a live specimen whose importance exists for the American as symbolic domination of the wilderness and for the Indigenous character as economic transaction, while also markedly resisting this status by not giving in to their affections. He visibly resists domestication, too, reflected by Roberts's repetitive imagery of the eagle drawing his energy inwards, collapsing his wings, shrinking but maintaining a visual awareness of both his surroundings and his situation. When the American arrives, excited to claim a live specimen of a species that 'year after year had baffled his woodcraft and eluded his rifle', he brings with him a leather anklet to be fitted so that the eagle may leave his cage (Roberts 1902: 87). While the Indigenous 'jailer' had long accepted that 'them's the kind that don't tame', it is the American's 'confidence in his knowledge of the wild folk' that secures the eagle's freedom (Roberts 1902: 88). Seizing the opportunity to escape, 'the king bounded upward' when the cage was opened (Roberts 1902: 90).

Roberts often repeats plot formulations in his adventure stories, such as animal-to-animal combat, seen in 'When Twilight Falls on the Stump Lots', and egocentric human hunting, as in 'The Treason of Nature', which raises two central concerns: the conflicting roles of instinct and reason, and the role that settlers play in the fabric of the wilderness that was being articulated at the beginning of the twentieth century. For many of those living in the settlements, survival forms the basis of their encounters with animals while others seek out animal kin out of curiosity. This curiosity often manifests itself in perilous encounters between children and animals. Many of Roberts's stories feature a character called 'the Boy', a potentially autobiographical figure: his father is a pastor who teaches his son and gives him access to natural history books, and he spends most of his time alone since he is not enrolled in the local school. As Keith stresses, 'in denying him a proper name, Roberts deliberately places [the Boy] on the same footing as animals' (Keith 1969: 97). The archetype, bordering on allegory, of the unnamed Boy thus works to distance the reader from the human individual in salutary ways, in redressing the implicit imbalance of narratives that depict animal–human relationships.

For the Boy, the multiple ways in which humans interact with animals and the resulting conflicted feelings about responsibility towards those animals is played out in short stories, the most explicit being the first story of *Kindred of the Wild*, 'The Moonlight Trails'. In this story, the Boy is first described as concerned with the welfare of animals, going so far as to state his love for them and to be 'fiercely intolerant' of cruelty towards them (Roberts 1902: 40). Then, with a hired man named Andy, the Boy experiences 'the wild spirit of adventure, the hunting zest of elemental man', as they set traps for rabbits (Roberts 1902: 42). The Boy's youth and excitement are juxtaposed with the playful nature of the rabbits. While they are not seen by the Boy, their 'fine triplicate tracks' in a 'pattern of mirth' reflect the 'play of care-free children, almost a kind of confused dance, a spontaneous expression of the joy of life' (Roberts 1902: 34). But the rabbits are *not* care-free children, as Roberts clarifies, for they are nonhuman animals with their own form of communication through signs: 'No onlooker not of the clef-nose, long-ear clan could have told in what the signal consisted, or what was its full significance' (Roberts 1902: 36). There is no attempt to decipher or translate these signs as a recognition of alterity that resists translation. His compassion blinkered by the thrill of the hunt, the Boy's revelatory return to his previous sympathies occurs only when he sees 'the cruel marks of the noose under [the rabbit's] jaws and behind its ears' (Roberts 1902: 51). Horrified by the reality of hunting and trapping, the Boy throws his animal 'trophy' into the snow and declares that neither he nor Andy will snare any more rabbits.

We encounter the Boy once more in 'The Boy and Hushwing', where he is determined to test his woodcraft against an owl's, in order to trap and observe him. The Boy's fascination with Hushwing as a skilful hunter leads him to track the owl to 'give him a taste of what it feels like to be hunted' (Roberts 1902: 160). However, in his desire to trap, but not kill, Hushwing, the Boy reveals two key insights that complicate dominant structures of animal–human relationships that place human as superior to animal. First, that 'the Boy' 'felt impelled to try his skill against' Hushwing's suggests that he is an intelligent and worthy adversary and mentor. Second, the Boy understands his knowledge of 'woodcraft' is linked to his understanding of animal behaviour, and he, in turn, 'becomes animal' in order to observe them: he creeps 'soundless as a snake', spies 'as a fish-hawk' and '[lies] still as a watching lynx' (Roberts 1902: 160–1).[6] He sets his trap, which involves a string that, when pulled, forced 'broken twigs [to] scratch seductively on the stump, like the claws of a small animal', and waits patiently (Roberts 1902: 169). Slipping (albeit briefly) into Hushwing's thoughts, the narrator suggests that 'Hushwing knew his fate was wholly in the hands of this master being, whom no wild thing dared to hunt' (Roberts 1902: 170). Here, Roberts's variable focalisation, shifting from the Boy's to Hushwing's thoughts, presents Hushwing with his own subjectivity and interiority. In other words, the use of variable instead of fixed focalisation opens up the narratological perspective to more-than-human characters.

The Boy's feeling of 'mastery' is short-lived, however, and reversed by Roberts by the conclusion of the story. Much like the eagle, as a wild creature Hushwing resists the confines of captivity through his persistent defiance of human authority. Even when he is released in the loft, Hushwing is visibly marked out by his potential for violence: the Boy must be careful to avoid 'the keen talons' and the 'hissing and snapping [from] his formidable beak' when he approaches the owl (Roberts 1902: 173–4). Moreover, in a spectacular moment of encounter, the Boy stares at Hushwing and Hushwing stares back, destabilising the expected hierarchical power dynamic inherent in this master–captive relationship: 'The daunting mastery of the human gaze, which could prevail over the gaze of the panther or the wolf, was lost upon the tameless spirit of Hushwing' (Roberts 1902: 175). This challenge meets the Boy's approval, made possible by youthful inquisitiveness and curiosity rather than desire to bend the owl to his will. Realising that he cannot make a pet out of Hushwing, the Boy instead resolves to study his hunting in the loft for a fortnight, again employing his knowledge of animal behaviour by sitting motionless in hiding. Hushwing's freedom is regained when a thief attempts to invade the loft to steal grain, and Hushwing, with his cunning hearing, disturbs and attacks him with his claws and wings. Here, Hushwing simultaneously assumes dominion of his space and secures it through his depiction as a consistent threat to both human and animal. In a stunning reversal of power, the thief mistakes Hushwing for a 'hobgoblin' – 'Nothing was further from his imagination than that his assailant should be a mere owl' – and Hushwing flees (Roberts 1902: 175). In his absence, Hushwing experiences a linguistic and hierarchical promotion as well, rechristened 'Master Hushwing' by the Boy's father (Roberts 1902: 177). This scene marks a potential transgression of Cary Wolfe's 'discourse of species', 'a constellation of signifiers to structure how we address others of whatever sort (not just nonhuman animals) – and the living and breathing creatures who fall outside the taxonomy of Homo sapiens' (Wolfe 2003: xx). With this phrase, Wolfe draws attention to sites in which human and animal similarity and difference, often a means of upholding human superiority, may be challenged. In this conclusion, Hushwing is celebrated at once for his specifically 'animal' abilities, and he is rewarded with a human designation. His elevation can be read as unsettling, and even inverting, the privileged status of the human. I concede that Roberts's use of the term 'Master', a semantic signifier reserved exclusively for humans, exemplifies an allegiance to humanist epistemology; however, I also see its use here, suggestive of a form of dominion over other beings, including humans, as upending the animal–human relations at play in the narrative.

This upending gesture is significant, as it redresses the accepted hierarchies that maintain human supremacy, and is continued in Roberts's attention to animal gaze. In 'The Haunter of the Pine Gloom', it is the Boy who feels 'afraid in his own woods' because he realises he is being watched by a lynx (Roberts 1902: 199). As the hunter, the lynx reverses the position of human and animal. However, this radical shift in agency does not necessarily affect the expected outcome of the plot. The Boy, again, is eager to test his abilities against a wild animal: 'He had a pet theory that the human animal was more competent, as a mere animal, than it gets the credit of being; and it was his particular pride to outdo the wild creatures at their own games' (Roberts 1902: 202). But these skills take the form of the Boy mimicking their behaviours, and he prides himself above all on his keen eyesight. The Boy does, however, recognise his limitations in this narrative. He reads a big black bear as the 'undisputed Master of the Woods', and begins to carry a rifle when he realises that he is being watched by the lynx (Roberts 1902: 105). Unable to accept this reversal of animal–human hierarchy, the Boy takes it upon himself to become the steward of the forest and stalks the lynx to death. Michel Poirier contends that in these scenes where humans are in 'great peril', 'the sympathies of the writer naturally go out to him', meaning that 'the man almost invariably escapes unhurt' (Poirier 1927: 403). However, while such an outcome proves true in many of Roberts's narratives, we should not assume that Roberts's sympathies always lie with the human. In 'The Watchers of the Campfire', Roberts articulates an ecocritical attention to humanity's destruction of the natural world through sprinklings of the effects of human settlement on the area: 'the ancient forest [has] fallen under the axes of the lumbermen' and the panther had been 'declared' by 'some hunters' as 'extinct' (Roberts 1902: 255, 264).

The impartiality that Roberts displays towards the outcome of animal–human or even animal–animal encounters signals his desire to tread the middle ground. As many critics have pointed out, Roberts attempts to produce a realistic, objective depiction of the nonhuman realm to 'avoid . . . the melodramatic, the visionary, and the sentimental' (Roberts 1904: ix). Often, these scenes of violence come at the price of animal life that ends brutally but does not trivialise lived animal experience. Instead, animals prove worthy adversaries of human characters in their intelligence and strength. Animal–human kinship is strengthened by these similarities, and Roberts makes this apparent not only through characters like the 'semi-human' bear of 'Black Swamp' (1911), but also through form, the most striking examples of which are 'Savoury Meats', 'Wild Motherhood' and 'Do Seek Their Meat from God'. In all three stories human and animal interests are pitted against each other, with survival as the common link between human and animal. Formally, Roberts employs what I term 'split-sympathy' narratives in which reader identification shifts among multiple, rich, intertwined plots. What gives depth to these stories and, indeed, complicates a solely anthropocentric reading of the plot is that Roberts provides significant backstories for both human and nonhuman characters, and positions all creatures within a family network.

In 'Wild Motherhood', for instance, we see a triangulation between moose, wolf and human families. The reader is first introduced to a family of moose travelling through deep snow, in which they 'can neither flee nor fight', to take the risk at finding food and shelter during the hard winter (Roberts 1902: 98). A moose calf falls down a rock crevice, where he is stuck without any chance of escape. His mother stays with him while the rest of the herd moves on. The narrative then shifts, with a formal break indicating part two of the story, to a family of wolves that inhabit a cave. Here, too, is struggle, as 'there was famine' and, more troubling, the she-wolf has been wounded by a human steel trap: '[s]he had gnawed off her own paw as the price of freedom. She could not hunt' and '[t]he wapiti deer had migrated to safer ranges' (Roberts 1902: 101). Since the wolf and his mate's survival are dependent on the hunt, the he-wolf, though aware of the threat of the human, nevertheless must venture outside of the cave.

Another formal break welcomes the third and initially disparate narrative about a family of settlers. The man, much like the male wolf, is depended upon by his wife and child, both in ill-health. The solution to their plight is fresh meat, casting the man as predator, akin to the wolf. This family does not appear to live within the confines of the settlement or in proximity to other families. Left in isolation 'in a cabin of unutterable loneliness', they appear as reliant upon nature as the nonhuman animals (Roberts 1902: 107). Yet, the reader is also privy to Roberts's commentary on the 'curious improvidence of the backwoodsman [in cutting] down every tree in the neighbourhood of the cabin', which distinguishes his motives and actions from those of the wild animals. Ironically, chopping down the forest deprives the man and his family of warmth and shelter and exacerbates their illness. The man not only invades nature but also upsets its balance and disturbs the forest. Furthermore, Roberts does not paper over, or absolve the man of, this fact. From his hiding place, the backwoodsman audibly disrupts the scene by 'slapping the silences in the face' (Roberts 1902: 112). He shoots first the wolf and then the moose, who collapses with her muzzle touched to her calf. Once outside of the dynamic of survival with the conflict resolved, the man's place in the fabric of the wilderness becomes distorted. With a bizarre change of heart, the man saves the calf and concludes the tale by sparing him for 'the boy to play with and bring up' (Roberts 1902: 113). Does this act offer further possibilities for interspecies entanglements? Or does it simply re-enact the human–companion animal relationship made possible through domestication? While the man's actions bring about the story's end, the narrative's ambiguity complicates a conclusion celebrating human dominion, and instead demands a more thoughtful reflection on animal–human encounter.

The critical dynamics at work in Roberts's short stories contest accepted hierarchies of intelligence, strength and emotion, and provide an alternative politics of animal–human relationships made possible by the creation of this new genre. In its embrace of American naturalism, Victorian realism and the modernist short story form, the wild animal story fashions a forceful discourse of animal–human kinship within a North American geography. The result is a transitional fiction that complicates, redresses and even, sometimes, subverts the 'human' as separate and apart from the 'wilderness' folk. Roberts's tight plotlines and captivating animal characters contribute to a larger narrative undercurrent that speaks to some of our most pressing predicaments regarding environmental destruction, species displacement, extinction and climate change. As my analysis has shown, scenes of violence are not brief encounter but entanglement, causing a domino effect through communities, both human and nonhuman. In its effect, survival is a captivating and unsettling narrative premise in the Canadian wild animal short story that not only disrupts the animal–human boundary, but also makes legible the crucial and continuous confluences of environments, species and subjectivities in modernist literature and culture.

Works Cited

Adams, John Coldwell. 1986. *Sir Charles God Damn: The Life of Sir Charles G. D. Roberts*. Toronto: University of Toronto Press.

Atwood, Margaret. 2012. *Survival: A Thematic Guide to Canadian Literature*. Toronto: House of Anansi Press.

Conway, Don. 1984. 'Roberts and Modernism: The Achievement of "The Squatter"'. In *The Sir Charles G. D. Roberts Symposium*. Ed. Glenn Clever, 77–88. Halifax: Nimbus.

Country Life. 1907. 'Realism & Romance, Nature & Humour'. *Country Life* 22.570 (7 Dec.): clxvii.

Haraway, Donna. 2016. *Staying with the Trouble: Making Kin in the Chtulucene*. Durham, NC: Duke University Press.

Herman, David. 2018. *Narratology Beyond the Human: Storytelling and Animal Life*. Oxford: Oxford University Press.

Herman, David. 2020. 'Narratology Beyond the Human: Self-Narratives and Inter-Species Identities'. In *The Palgrave Handbook of Animals and Literature*. Ed. Susan McHugh, Robert McKay and John Miller, 51–64. Basingstoke: Palgrave.

Hovanec, Caroline. 2018. *Animal Subjects: Literature, Zoology, and British Modernism*. Cambridge: Cambridge University Press.

Hovanec, Caroline. 2019. 'Darwin's Earthworms in the Anthropocene'. *Victorian Review* 45.1 (Spring): 81–96.

Hunter, Adrian. 2016. 'The Rise of Short Fiction'. In *Late Victorian into Modern*. Ed. Laura Marcus, Michèle Mendelssohn and Kirsten E. Shepherd-Barr, 204–17. Oxford: Oxford University Press.

Irvine, Dean. 2010. 'Modernisms in English Canada'. In *The Oxford Handbook of Modernisms*. Ed. Peter Brooker, Andrzej Gąsiorek, Deborah Longworth and Andrew Thacker. Oxford: Oxford University Press.

Keith, W. J. 1969. *Charles G. D. Roberts*. Toronto: Copp Clark.
Lutts, Ralph. 1990. *The Nature Fakers: Wildlife, Science, and Sentiment*. Charlottesville: University of Virginia Press.
Lutts, Ralph. 2006. 'Nature Fakers Controversy'. In *The Encyclopedia of Religion and Nature*. Ed. Bron Taylor. London: Continuum.
Morton, Peter. 1984. *The Vital Science: Biology and the Literary Imagination, 1860–1900*. London: Allen & Unwin.
Poirier, Michel. 1927. 'The Animal Story in Canadian Literature'. *Queen's Quarterly* 34 (April): 398–419.
Roberts, Charles G. D. 1895. *Earth's Enigmas: A Volume of Stories*. Boston: Lamson, Wolffe.
Roberts, Charles G. D. 1989. *The Collected Letters of Charles G. D. Roberts*. Ed. Laurel Boone. Fredericton, New Brunswick: Goose Lane.
Roberts, Charles G. D. 1902. *The Kindred of the Wild*. London: Duckworth.
Roberts, Charles G. D. 1904. *The Watchers of the Trails*. Toronto: Copp, Clark.
Roberts, Charles G. D. 1911. *Neighbours Unknown*. New York: MacMillan.
Roberts, Charles G. D. 1974. 'A Note on Modernism'. In *Selected Poetry and Critical Prose Charles G. D. Roberts*. Ed. W. J. Keith, 296–301. Toronto: University of Toronto Press.
Rohman, Carrie. 2008. *Stalking the Subject: Modernism and the Animal*. New York: Columbia University Press.
Sandlos, John. 2000. 'From Within Fur and Feathers: Animals in Canadian Literature'. *TOPIA: Canadian Journal of Cultural Studies* 4: 73–91.
Scholtmeijer, Marian Louise. 1993. *Animal Victims in Modern Fiction: From Sanctity to Sacrifice*. Toronto: University of Toronto Press.
Seifert, Martina. 2007. 'Canadian Animal Stories: Charles G. D. Roberts, "Do Seek Their Meat from God" (1892)'. In *The Canadian Short Story: Interpretations*. Ed. Reingard Nischik, 41–52. Rochester, NY: Camden House.
Seton, Ernest Thompson. 1898. *Wild Animals I Have Known*. New York: Scribner.
Shepherd-Barr, Kirsten. 2015. *Theatre and Evolution from Ibsen to Beckett*. New York: Columbia University Press.
Shukin, Nicole. 2009. *Animal Capital: Rendering Life in Biopolitical Times*. Minneapolis: University of Minnesota Press.
Whalen, Terry. 1984. 'Roberts and the Tradition of American Naturalism'. In *The Sir Charles G. D. Roberts Symposium*. Ed. Glenn Clever, 127–42. Halifax: Nimbus.
Ware, Tracy. 2016. 'Cosmopolitan Nationalism: Canadian Literature of the Confederation Period, 1867–1914.' In *The Oxford Handbook of Canadian Literature*. Ed. Cynthia Sugars. Oxford:Oxford University Press.
Wolfe, Cary. 2003. *Zoontologies: The Question of the Animal*. Minneapolis: University of Minnesota Press.

Notes

1. For Roberts on modernism, see Roberts, 'A Note on Modernism' (1974: 296–301). For criticism on modernism and Roberts's poetry, see Don Conway, 'Roberts and Modernism: The Achievement of "The Squatter"' (1984); and Dean Irvine, 'Modernisms in English Canada' (2010).

2. For more on the overlapping discourses of evolution and the arts, see Kirsten Shepherd-Barr, *Theatre and Evolution from Ibsen to Beckett* (2015); and Peter Morton, *The Vital Science: Biology and the Literary Imagination, 1860–1900* (1984).
3. For more about this subject see Ralph H. Lutts, *The Nature Fakers: Wildlife, Science, and Sentiment* (1990).
4. Terry Whalen's 'Roberts and the Tradition of American Naturalism' (1984) provides a compelling comparison of Roberts's and American Jack London's corpus. For Whalen, Roberts writes in 'the wider tradition of mimetic' while 'London writes in closer kinship with the anthropomorphic mode of Kipling' (130–1).
5. In considering Roberts's role in the 'cosmopolitan nationalism' of early Canadian literature Tracy Ware highlights that his 'several poems on Aboriginal mythology, whatever their shortcomings, demonstrate that he was not exclusively Eurocentric, and the Senecas and the Sarcees made him an honorary chief' (Ware 2016: 297).
6. Also noted by Keith (1969: 99).

11

ENCOUNTERING FEMALE HUMAN ANIMAL BECOMINGS IN LEONORA CARRINGTON'S SURREALIST HYBRID TALES

Karen Eckersley

Surrealist Leonora Carrington's proclamation that she was born a 'female human animal' (Carrington 1998a: 372) situates her as an artist and author who identified as a hybrid, bringing her into conversation with a posthuman and feminist politics. In her essay 'What is a Woman?' (1970), Carrington intimates that her human–animal positioning is not mere aesthetic choice but rather an ontological state, a political manoeuvre that disrupts humanism's normative models of the Vitruvian white man. It signposts a call to action aimed at women in order to forge an alliance with the natural world against what she perceives as patriarchal 'Masters' (Carrington 1998a: 375).

Carrington's remedy for an imminent apocalypse induced by a tyrannical male anthropos demands adopting a multiplicity of perspectives and ontologies for her proposed hybrid and 'humanoid female' (Carrington 1998a: 373):

> The idea that 'Our Masters' are Right and must be loved, honoured and obeyed is, I think, one of the most destructive lies that have been instilled into the female psyche. It has become most horribly obvious what these Masters have done to our planet and her organic life. If women remain passive I think there is very little hope for the survival of life on this Earth. (Carrington 1998a: 375)

Carrington's call to action provokes both a politics of transgression and a rebellion in her attack upon the 'destructive lies' of 'Our Masters'. Moreover, she catalyses a dynamic that requires alliance and *sympoiesis*, where she suggests that women and 'organic life' are kin that must come together to ensure 'the survival of life'. As I argue in this chapter, the politics exhibited in 'What is a Woman?' aptly introduce the hybrid human–animal themes of Carrington's short stories – laying the ground for characters who embody such transgressions and alliances in a manner that anticipates a posthuman approach. Crucially, I posit that Carrington employs the human–animal hybrid figure as a feminist catalyst for change: one which transgresses and subverts the 'passive' position that she critiques in a manner that demonstrates a strategy in confronting ecological crisis, whilst at the same time forging a feminist politics that contributes to contemporary environmental debates. In this way, Carrington also challenges the male surrealists' penchant for visions of female passivity, by harnessing the figure of the hybrid in order to redesign and articulate an active female position. To this end, I investigate how Carrington's modernist hybrids anticipate feminist Rosi Braidotti's posthuman subjects, exhibiting modes of 'becoming-animal' and multiple ecologies of belonging and navigating a path beyond an androcentric humanism. Carrington's short stories 'As They Rode Along the Edge' (1937–40) and 'Jemima and the Wolf' (2017)[1] are thus precise anticipations of the 'geostories' (Haraway 2016: 49) that Donna Haraway proposes as a route out of the narratives repeatedly dictated by 'Species Man'. Carrington's tales stage a revolt via their cast of disparate, hybrid bodies and etch an interspecies cartography that gives voice to contemporary feminist and ecological thinking.

In their account from *A Thousand Plateaus: Capitalism and Schizophrenia* (1980), Gilles Deleuze and Félix Guattari explain their concept of 'becoming animal' as a process of intensive and affective encounters between humans and nonhumans. This process involves casting off majoritarian modes of thought (including humanist principles) and instead moving towards what they describe as 'minoritarian' positions in order to embrace a potential unfettered by humanist dichotomies. Crucially, it marks a process or movement *towards*, rather than arriving at a fixed destination point: a praxis emphatically evident in Carrington's nomadic human-animal speakers. The 'becoming animal' is always in flux in a manner that mirrors the surrealist hybrid's ontological ambiguity, thus forging a creative space for the feminist identity, as Deleuze and Guattari explain further in *Kafka: Toward a Minor Literature* (1975):

> To become animal is to participate in movement, to stake out the path of escape in all its positivity, to cross a threshold, to reach a continuum of intensities that are valuable only in themselves, to find a world of pure intensities where all forms come undone, as do all the significations, signifiers, and signifieds, to the benefit of an unformed matter of deterritorialized flux, of nonsignifying signs. (Deleuze and Guattari 1986, 13).

Posthuman thinker Rosi Braidotti adopts a feminist reading of Deleuze and Guattari's theory of 'becoming animal' in a bid to offer alternatives to humanism. Braidotti insists that the 'becoming animal' has the potential to 'scramble the master-code of phallocentrism', thereby 'loosening its power over the body' (Braidotti 2002: 124). Her development of Deleuze and Guattari's frameworks opens up original feminist readings of the hybrid figure in Carrington's surrealist work. Braidotti seizes the concept of a *becoming* politics, viewing it as an opportunity for so-called 'minoritarian' others in its potential slippage in between ontologies. Notions of human and animal are ruptured and replaced with a sliding continuum of movement which dislodges Cartesian essentialist principles where 'all forms come undone', as Deleuze and Guattari explain. In this way, the fixed, stable subjectivity envisaged and consolidated by humanism is unsettled in a manner that also accurately describes Carrington's hybrid figure, who is similarly in flux, fully adhering to neither humanity nor animality, and instead depicted as crossing 'a threshold'. As Braidotti adds, these becoming modes show how we 'live in permanent processes of transition, hybridization and nomadization and these in-between states and stages defy the established modes of theoretical representation' (Braidotti 2002: 2). In this chapter I investigate how Braidotti's reading of this malleable, 'becoming animal' mode illuminates Carrington's hybrid figures who occupy, and operate within, indeterminate territories which circumnavigate humanist cartographies.

The 'becoming animal' female hybrid figures in Carrington's tales also mark their estrangement from the male white body as the measure of all things: a practice that Braidotti identifies as a tool in Enlightenment humanism's habit of subordinating all those who fall outside of its parameters. In *The Posthuman* (2013), Braidotti suggests that it is Leonardo da Vinci's Vitruvian Man who has become the ultimate and most pervasive symbol of androcentric humanism. In this 'ideal of bodily perfection', Braidotti posits that humanism has found its 'universal model': a European white man, 'self-regulating' and imbued with the 'intrinsically moral powers of human reason' (Braidotti 2013: 13). I suggest that this figure has shaken off its animal heritage in order to assume its superiority over all other species. Carrington's hybrids embrace their inherent wildness by eschewing man's codes of controlled civility and restraint, and so reclaim an animal ancestry whilst gesturing towards a posthuman future. In this way, her work chimes with Braidotti's postulation that 'feminism is *not* a humanism' (Braidotti 2017: 21) where female figures turn to their animality in order to disrupt the male symbolic order but also to conjure a more balanced and posthuman landscape to replace it. Braidotti suggests that the antidote to Man falsely claiming to be the measure of all things is to enact a 'colossal hybridization of the species' where 'What comes to the fore instead is a human–nonhuman continuum' (Braidotti 2017: 26). I investigate the extent to which Carrington's female, hybrid figures recurrently embody and conspicuously enact this continuum.

Carrington's own biocentric perspective in 'What is a Woman?' provides an appropriate cue to begin a posthuman analysis of her short stories. She is dismissive of René Descartes, casting his 'I think, therefore I am' as '[s]ome kind of pretension', and replaces it instead with a metamorphic ontology in the form of a female body that is 'changing every second' (Carrington 1998a: 373). Carrington's perception of an imminent manmade disaster and her call to women to facilitate change and recovery anticipates Donna Haraway's feminist politics, which argues for the eschewal of 'Species Man's' dominance over all life. Like Carrington, Haraway suggests that we 'refuse' 'Species Man's' reign, which she describes in similarly condemnatory terms in her book *Staying with the Trouble: Making Kin in the Chthulucene* (2016):

> The story of Species Man as the agent of the Anthropocene is an almost laughable rerun of the great phallic humanizing and modernizing Adventure, where man, made in the image of a vanished god, takes on superpowers in his secular-sacred ascent, only to end in tragic detumescence, once again. Autopoietic, self-making man came down once again, this time in a tragic system failure, turning biodiverse ecosystems into flipped-out deserts. (Haraway 2016: 47)

Haraway correlates the annihilation of the natural world with the singular ego of Cartesian man (and his representative humanism), who subordinates and denigrates all who fall outside of his epistemological category in a manner that mirrors Carrington's concerns in 'What is a Woman?' Not only are there parallels between both writers' calls to refuse such a tyrannical system, but they are similarly aligned in the creative, posthumanist approach they propose in order to circumnavigate it. Rather than slipping into a reductive trap that rants against the humanist framework, thus reinforcing its binaries, Haraway proposes new frameworks which resonate with the method and subject matter Carrington had given voice to several decades earlier. Haraway abandons Anthropocene-bound, utilitarian individualism in favour of forging a more inclusive landscape that knits species together, a praxis that could also accurately describe Carrington's interconnected creaturely approach in her writing and visual art: 'That History must give way to geostories, to Gaia stories, to symchthonic stories; terrans do webbed, braided, and tentacular living and dying in sympoietic multispecies string figures; they do not do History' (Haraway 2016: 49). Haraway's call for tales of 'sympoietic multispecies' uncannily resembles the principles that underpin Carrington's writing and art where her audience is brought into close proximity and alliance with not only other animal species, but crucially their own animal genealogy. Such a radical reconfiguration of traditional tales that forge anticipatory 'geostories' often manifests in Carrington's writing as a recourse to fairy-tale domains, where she invokes imaginary realms that hark back to childhood. It is these frameworks that, I suggest, enable original readings of Carrington's work in this chapter. Her hybrid configurations, conjuring transformative landscapes that reimagine a humanity entangled within the natural world, serve to re-index and rewire humanist principles. In this way, I investigate how Carrington's band of beastly modernist hybrids fosters a feminist move towards ecological recovery in order to reconfigure a phallocentric Anthropocene.

Born in Lancashire to an upper middle-class family, Carrington rebelled early on, scribbling on the walls of the Crookhey Hall mansion where she grew up, and getting expelled from several schools where one cast her 'ineducable' (Aberth 2010: 15). She sought solace with animals, frequently etching non-human realms in her early visual oeuvre and story writing. Her *Self-Portrait (Inn of the Dawn Horse)* (1937–8), for example, was painted around the same time that she wrote many of her short stories and features both a hyena alter ego, whose pose mirrors her own, and a horse glimpsed galloping away through an open window. After a brief spell at the Ozenfant Academy of Fine Arts in London, Carrington went to Paris, where she was welcomed into André Breton's surrealist circle, achieving critical acclaim with exhibits of her own. Her relationship with fellow surrealist Max Ernst, who was twenty-six years her senior, helped to catapult her into the minds and imaginations of the surrealist movement. At the same time, it threatened to compromise her own artistic integrity because her youth and beauty positioned her as a potential muse to the male artist's gaze. As Anna Watz notes in *Surrealist Women's Writing: A Critical Exploration* (2020), whilst the surrealists were interested in the collective project of unsettling subjectivity, the 'troubling of identity sought by Breton and Ernst [. . .] was often conceived as simulating a "feminine" subject position': one that they correlated with a passivity and hysteria that Carrington's work and politics sought to contradict. Watz adds that whereas 'Breton and Ernst envision psychic, and by extension social, revolution resulting from their troubling of identity, several of Carrington's stories contain a critical reflection on the gendered and political blind spots of such a project' (Watz 2020: 46, 43). I posit that Carrington challenged the male surrealists' 'blind spots' and their predilection for visions of female passivity, symbolised in the *femme-enfant*, by forging an active and agentive human–animal hybrid.

Carrington's short story 'As They Rode Along the Edge' is one of a series of tales she wrote between 1937 and 1939. It has been published most recently as one of a collection in *The Complete Stories of Leonora Carrington* (2017) by Dorothy Project. This surreal tale opens with the provocatively named protagonist Virginia Fur riding a so-called wheel through her forest homeland with a menagerie of cats, immediately establishing her as one among a human–animal assemblage. The liminality of her existence is established in the opening pages when we discover that, despite exhibiting traces of a human ontology, she lives 'in a village long abandoned by human beings' (Carrington 2017: 40). Significantly, Virginia's house has holes all over that she has deliberately 'pierced for the fig tree that grew in the kitchen' (Carrington 2017: 40). In this way, Virginia thrives within a setting which is appropriately metamorphic and porous: a realm that is palpably in flux in a manner that aptly introduces the protagonist's own shape-shifting physicality and character. Carrington presents Virginia as an emphatic hybrid force who slides across the human–animal continuum, one that Braidotti posits as key to adopting posthuman positioning. as this extract from the opening page of the story demonstrates:

> This was something to see: fifty black cats, and as many yellow ones, and then her, and one couldn't really be altogether sure that she was a human being. Her smell alone threw doubt on it – a mixture of spices and game, the stables, fur and grasses [. . .] Her name was Virginia Fur, she had a mane of hair yards long and enormous hands with dirty nails; yet the citizens of the mountain respected her and she too always showed a deference for their customs. (Carrington 2017: 39).

Virginia's 'dirty nails' situate her as an earthly being: a character who is at one with the soil and embraces the uncleanliness that Carrington suggests all religion ascribes to women in 'The Cabbage is a Rose' (1975). In this later essay, she critiques the religious thinking that 'declare[s] women to be feeble-minded, unclean, generally inferior creatures to males' (Carrington 1998b: 377). Aside from her nails and her bestial name, Virginia's 'mane of hair' also aligns her with equine characteristics, whilst her 'enormous hands' suggest that she transgresses anthropocentric proportion and scale.

As Janet Lyon explains in her chapter 'Carrington's Sensorium', *'there is no right or wrong body in Carrington'* (Lyon 2017: 169: emphasis in original), and her rupturing of anthropocentric scale and perspective constructs new modes that question the hierarchical supremacy that the human species anoints itself with:

> In the Carringtonian milieu, this dissolution of scale is part of a larger fundamental condition: in this milieu, no life is slotted for sanctity or degradation in advance. No living thing deserves, *a priori*, to live or die more than any other living thing. [. . .] No body or manifestation of life has more value than another. (Lyon 2017: 169)

Lyon here highlights how Carrington's narrative landscape is one that corresponds with Haraway's 'geostories': tales which operate outside of the humanist orbit, exploding the rational boundaries of Cartesian thinking to etch instead an open-ended, human–animal continuum that functions on an often vast and incomprehensible scale. The fact that Virginia's initial appearance is blurred in among 'fifty cats' speaks to the non-hierarchical and posthuman ontology that Lyon underlines in her analysis, where those who do presume to 'live or die more than any other' are held to account in an often violent and transgressive manner. Carrington draws attention to a conspicuous animality in this extract in the description of Virginia's potent smell, which is a key signifier of her ambiguous ontology. Despite her apparently anomalous and hybridised presence, she is, however, presented as a reciprocal agent in this landscape, one who is respected and, at the same time, exhibits a 'deference' to others, speaking to this space as a balanced and therefore posthuman milieu.

In many ways, 'As They Rode Along the Edge' is enacted as a quest, where Virginia, accompanied by an extraordinary menagerie of animals, eventually seeks revenge for the murder of her boar lover at the hands of Saint Alexander – a figure who, in presuming that his religiosity accords him superiority, is destined for an unpleasant end. Situated in the wilds of the woods within the mountains, it is the setting of a multitude of animal species and hybrid life who exist in a rich ecosystem that exhibits sympoietic balance, as the dynamic between Virginia and the landscape's residents suggests. This vibrant assemblage of life that anticipates Haraway's calls for 'tentacular' tales is threatened by the appearance of Saint Alexander. Saint Alexander's ambitions for Virginia Fur to 'enter the Church', so that he can 'win her soul' (Carrington 2017: 41), play out Carrington's critique of the way in which religious male masters seek to 'enfeeble' and control women. He wishes to sacrifice her, promising that she will be rewarded with a 'beautiful spot' in his graveyard, 'right next to the statue of the Holy Virgin' (Carrington 2017: 41). With no intention of conforming to Saint Alexander's religious regime, Virginia instead becomes a thief, filling her bag 'with holy plates' in a comic interlude (Carrington 2017: 44), and eventually escaping with one hundred cats behind her in a transgressive manoeuvre. Her journey across the forest is one that takes place in the company of its beasts: creatures who appear to be drawn to Virginia's own animality. Further galvanised by their co-mingling, this assemblage of animal and hybrid life replaces the singular symbolism of Saint Alexander and his cold church with a more collective, animal politics:

> The wheel crossed the woods at a hissing speed. Bats and moths were imprisoned in Virginia's hair; she gestured to the beasts with her strange hands that the hunt was over; she opened her mouth and a blind nightingale flew in: she swallowed it and sang in the nightingale's voice: 'Little Jesus is dead, and we've had a fine dinner.' (Carrington 2017: 44)

Saint Alexander's piety is dismissed as Virginia and her assemblage of beasts triumph, enjoying the fact that his attempts to sacrifice her to religion are thwarted. Rather, her own animality and her kinship with other creatures are cast as an active and emancipating force that speaks to the strategy of becoming-animal.

Here, Virginia is empowered by her nomadic and hybrid force, emblematised by the cyclical vision of a wheel that eschews humanism's hierarchical frameworks, and emphasising her tentacular entanglements with the creatures of the woods. Her immersion within this twilight, liminal sphere that criss-crosses between human and nonhuman space is emphasised by the way in which bats and moths become caught in her hair. Moths are particularly significant. As conspicuously metamorphic creatures, they aptly complement Virginia's own on-going, shape-shifting ontology. Swallowing a nightingale appears to symbolise how Virginia is given voice by connecting with animals. This contrasts with the eternal silence that Saint Alexander has planned for her in death in his graveyard. The fact that it is Virginia who sings as a result of swallowing the nightingale suggests Carrington's own feminist politics, as this is a bird species where only the male gives song. Transferring his voice to Virginia gives further agency to her female-animal hybrid figure, thereby speaking to the active gender politics that Carrington calls for women to adopt.

It is significant that the episode where Saint Alexander espouses his religious rhetoric and attempts to convert Virginia is juxtaposed with a scene of seduction. Following her escape from the church, Carrington introduces Virginia's ostentatious lover, Igname. Igname is a boar, whose name suggests an audacious embrace with disgrace and dishonour in its etymological relations with ignominy. Importantly, his attraction to Virginia is apparently stirred by her hybrid animality. Rather than lie sacrificed and dead in Saint Alexander's graveyard next to the 'Holy Virgin', the ironically named Virginia would rather lie in bed with Igname, a feeling that he shares: 'He admired most her fruity smell and her long hair, always full of nocturnal animals. He decided she was very beautiful and probably a virgin. Igname rolled in the mud luxuriously, thinking of Virginia's charms' (Carrington 2017: 45).

The significance of smell is highlighted again in this short story and is a key defining characteristic of Carrington's protagonists, who engage all of their animal senses rather than relying solely upon sight. Virginia's 'fruity smell' acts as an aphrodisiac to Igname, whilst Saint Alexander's human odour, by contrast, is described as 'sickening' (Carrington 2017: 40). Similarly, Virginia's attraction to Igname is underpinned by his position as one among a creaturely multiverse, where the young nightjar attached to his head and his wig of squirrel's tails only adds to his beauty. Carrington subverts the famed surrealist male gaze into a female one here, playfully detailing how Igname teasingly hides 'his russet buttocks, as he did not want to show all his beauty at one go' (Carrington 2017: 46). In this way, human figures – particularly religiously inclined ones – are relegated to the periphery in the tale, while those who display their animality are central to its concerns. Saint Alexander wants to 'win' Virginia and take her like a trophy. Igname is instead generous in his affection for her, explaining that his 'body is exploding with love' (Carrington 2017: 47). Carrington presents their bestial sexuality as an affirmative life force, thereby transgressing religious humanist codes that insist upon denial, ritual sacrifice and empty symbolism. Saint Alexander's cold and inert churchyard, stone statues and 'Flowers of Mortification' (Carrington 2017: 42) are contrasted with the excesses and vivacity of creatural life stirred by the spectacle of Virginia and Igname's courtship. The stillness of Saint Alexander's church is replaced with the intense colour and sexual dynamic pulsing between the lovers in a scene which highlights Virginia's wild animality, as well as the transgressive politics of her hybridity:

> She spat into the stewpot and put her lips into the boiling liquid and swallowed a big mouthful. With a savage cry she brought her head back out of the pot; she jumped round Igname, tearing her hair out by the roots; Igname stood up, and together they danced a dance of ecstasy. The cats caterwauled and stuck their claws into one another's necks, and then threw themselves in a mass onto Igname and Virginia, who disappeared under a mountain of cats. Where they made love. (Carrington 2017: 47)

This scene is a swirling vortex that complements the nomadic mode of becoming animal where the creatures, and the landscape itself, appear to be in flux. The courtship episode is imbued with movement, energised by the animal dynamics at play between Virginia and Igname but also the caterwauling cats who play a part in the ceremony of the couple's love-making. Virginia's hybridity is cast in this scene as a subversive force. Her spitting into the stewpot and tearing out her hair speak to a primal and animal instinct that resonates with Carrington's own rebellion against the so-called civilising forces of Man and religion that she takes to task in her essays. Virginia's grotesque and violent animal manifestation – further emphasised in its jarring juxtaposition with the implied purity of her name – also counters the male surrealists' penchant for the *femme-enfant*: a role that Carrington herself refused to be subsumed into, thus rupturing the male scopophilic gaze. Carrington's hybrid protagonist experiences a further wild metamorphosis after she ingests the 'boiling liquid' (Carrington 2017: 47) from her stewpot, suggestive of a culinary alchemy that triggers further uninhibited behaviour. Now firmly distanced from the inert space of Saint Alexander's church, Virginia is both an energised and, importantly, an energising force whose wild vivacity spills over immanently, casting a spell upon those around her. This transformation is not coerced in the manner that Alexander's church rhetoric would effect. Rather, this wilder metamorphosis is enabled through Virginia's own free will and desire to act in a way that Carrington calls for in 'What is a Woman?'

The tale's denouement is catalysed by Igname's death: he is slain and sacrificed for his meat by human hunters at Saint Alexander's behest. For this act, Virginia and an animal assemblage of extraordinary scale seek revenge and set about interrupting the religious party's convent meal, where they intend to feast on Igname's flesh. Carrington's prescient posthumanist ethics are demonstrated in Virginia's assertion that what humans call hunting is, in fact, murder. She descends upon the religious meal, accompanied by a copious, wild menagerie of co-species, allies who are motivated by the same sense of injustice and the need for redress against male masters:

> The door crashed open and all the beasts of the forest entered crying, 'Kill him, kill him.' In the turmoil that followed one could barely make out a human form sitting on a wheel that turned with incredible speed, who shouted with the others: 'Kill him!' (Carrington 2017: 56)

The collective revenge that the animals and Virginia seek is symbolic of the creatures' confrontation with the domineering speciesism of humanist practice exhibited in Saint Alexander's religious moralising and in his carnophallogocentric meal.[2] In the tale Carrington challenges the centrality of human characters and replaces them with a non-speciesist framework: the sympoietic landscape celebrated by Haraway which recognises animals as our kin. The fact that Virginia can hardly be made out as a 'human form' suggests that not only has she fully embraced her animal ontology, but also that she is, most importantly, very much one among an assemblage of life, not poised over others upon an anthropocentric throne. She is the embodiment of the becoming-animal and posthuman identity as Braidotti imagines it, a 'transversal entity, fully immersed in and immanent to a network of relations' (Braidotti 2013: 193). In this manner, Carrington etches an animal milieu overriding humanist perspectives and forging malleable scales that rupture the human's presumed centrality. Virginia's dismissal of Saint Alexander demonstrates this refusal of hierarchy. Instead, Carrington conjures unstable, shifting and metamorphic realms that do not prioritise one body or species over another, as Lyon notes. This manoeuvre is suggestive of a feminist politics in that it eschews what Braidotti dismisses as the habit of casting 'Man' as the gold standard by which we define ourselves. As she explains in *Anthropocene Feminism* (2017): 'Neither "Man" as the universal humanistic measure of all things nor Anthropos as the emblem of an exceptional species can claim the central position . . . this shift marks a sort of "anthropological exodus" from the dominant configurations of the human' (Braidotti 2017: 26).

An 'anthropological exodus' is precisely what Carrington facilitates in the final pages of 'As They Rode Along the Edge' in the characters' quest for revenge and move towards an animal kinship, synonymous with Braidotti's call for a 'hybridization of species'. In the example of the hybrid figure of Virginia Fur we witness how a posthuman, vitalist feminism is enabled in the vision of her position upon a 'human–nonhuman continuum' which refuses to valorise humanism as the exception. What emerges in the continuum and hybrid visions and practices of Carrington's story is the movement of always becoming and fostering entanglements across subject and species lines. As Braidotti further explains in a praxis that could describe Carrington's characters, '"Becoming" [. . .] is about affinities and the capacity both to sustain and generate inter-connectedness' (Braidotti 2002: 8). In Carrington's vision of the surrealist hybrid figure, such open-ended praxis is fully harnessed and enabled, fostering feminist politics that escape humanism's reductive, fixed parameters in both their transgressive powers and in their evocation of an alliance and sympoietic balance. In this way, her hybrid ontology is one that conjures a portal out of what Haraway critiques as the repeated tales of 'Species Man'.

Such active becomings are further manifest in the case of Carrington's 'Jemima and the Wolf': a story only recently published for the first time, situated as the final tale in the complete collection with 'As They Rode Along the Edge'. Whilst Virginia is introduced at the beginning of that narrative as an already hybrid figure in the wild amalgam of the forest, Jemima appears at first as a singular and human girl, as yet uninitiated into the becoming-animal mode and held hostage in a family home she despises. Carrington does, however, hint at the metamorphoses to come, establishing the teenage girl as a transgressive misfit, reminiscent of Carrington's own rebellious childhood when she was expelled from several educational institutions. Jemima's governess is called upon to make 'a normal girl' of her. This involves taming her wildness and bringing her into line with the civilised behaviour expected of a young lady born into an upper-class life. Jemima's mother, a woman who conforms to such codes, is disappointed with her daughter and upset to hear that the doll she gave her has not become a treasured toy but has instead had her head broken 'against a rock' (Carrington 2017: 193). Her mother's ambitions for Jemima consist of making her 'become a very beautiful woman' but she sees her 'ridiculous' behaviour as a serious foil to her plans, casting her thirteen-year-old daughter as 'that she-devil' (Carrington 2017: 195). Demonstrating parallels with Virginia spitting into the stewpot, Jemima similarly 'spat on the beautiful carpet' (Carrington 2017: 195) when the governess confronts her about her behaviour, exhibiting a transgressive wildness that foreshadows the mode of becoming-animal she eventually adopts.

In the same way as Virginia Fur's sexuality is portrayed as an animal force, so too is Jemima's animated by her attraction to a mysterious figure who exhibits a hybridity that eludes epistemological categories. Following the altercation with her mother and governess, Jemima seeks refuge outdoors, hiding herself 'in the branches of a great tree' as she laughs at her family's futile attempts to tame her. Whilst lurking in her tree, she catches sight of her father with a man whose appearance both captivates and confounds her:

It seemed to her that this man had the head of a wolf. Intrigued, she bent forward to see better. 'It's the changing shadows that produce the impression,' she said to herself. 'But I'm sure he's got the head of a wolf. He's devilishly beautiful, damn it, more beautiful than other men.' [. . .] With his untidy grey hair and thin face, he really did look more like an animal than a man; close up, his yellow eyes had a hunted look. His clothes were very correct. (Carrington 2017: 196)

This mysterious figure is later identified as Ambrose Barbary – a contradictory conundrum of a name that suits his apparent hybridity. Ambrose attracts Jemima via his palpable animality, which immediately intoxicates her in the way that Virginia is similarly drawn to the boar Igname. This key feature is one that makes him 'more beautiful than other men'. His claim to 'know a lot about the habits of animals' only serves to heighten the teenager's sexual curiosity. Indeed, Jemima ponders how the 'human language is strange on his lips' (Carrington 2017: 197), as if his nonhuman otherness is what arouses her the most. Jemima's transgressive character, highlighted by her mother, who casts her as a 'she-devil', is also foreshadowed in Ambrose, whose own devilish beauty speaks to an immediate resonance between these two figures. As the two men return to the house, Jemima climbs down from her tree and goes towards the shed that only she and her animal companions use. The building, like Virginia's house with its fig tree growing through the middle, contains a hole through which Jemima enters. Like the feast where Virginia and her animal community convene around a stewpot, Jemima's own animal menagerie appear together to eat, albeit on a smaller scale. Cats jump in at the window and a large female bat appears with her seven suckling babies. As Jemima mingles with this animal community, her own inherent wildness becomes increasingly apparent, moving beyond the more obviously rebellious spitting towards exhibiting a seemingly creaturely ontology herself as she proclaims that the 'flies taste good today' (Carrington 2017: 198). Whilst Carrington appears to relish the alterity of this creatural scene, she also invokes an intimacy and familiarity between Jemima and her animal companions. The baby bats suckling their mother underline how, as posthuman thinker and physicist Karen Barad explains, '"Human" bodies are not inherently different from animal ones' (Barad 2007: 152). Later, hearing her governess calling, Jemima emerges from the shed and, like Virginia, finds creatures become caught in her hair, eating 'lots of little insects' and 'spitting out their scaly feet' (Carrington 2017: 199). This source of sustenance is cast as preferable to the more conventional drink and snacks which await her in her room, where she 'poured the milk into a flowerpot, and ignored the biscuits' (Carrington 2017: 200). In this way, Carrington intimates Jemima's sense of kinship with this animal community, where she exhibits a tangible entanglement with this nonhuman realm in a manner further highlighted by her refusal of the human custom of 'milk' and 'biscuits'.

When Jemima finally meets Ambrose Barbary formally in the family home, Carrington introduces him as both the object of her teenage desires but also a conduit into the animal world, to which she already feels a sense of kinship. In her chapter 'The Gender of Sound' (1992), Anne Carson suggests that women and wolves share an affinity in their more proximate ties to the wild and the earth in a manner that resonates with Carrington's portrayal of the uncanny connection between Jemima and Ambrose:

> The wolf is a conventional symbol of marginality in Greek poetry. The wolf is an outlaw. He lives beyond the boundary of usefully cultivated and inhabited space marked off as the polis, in that blank no man's land called to apeiron ('the unbounded'). Women, in the ancient view, share this territory spiritually and metaphorically in virtue of a 'natural' female affinity for all that is lawless, formless and in need of the civilizing hand of man. (Carson 1992: 119–42)

Both Jemima and Ambrose occupy a liminal and unmappable space on the margins of the human and beyond 'usefully cultivated and inhabited space'; they are equally 'unbounded' and lupine in the way that Carson identifies. Similarly, Carla Freccero discusses the connection between humans and wolves, explaining that the wolf–human hybrid in particular demonstrates a 'history of interdependence' (Freccero 2017: M102). Jemima's and Ambrose's entanglement speaks to the fact that, whilst they project a human appearance, there are visible traces of an inherent animality within them which appears to surge more palpably when they are in one another's company. This animal kinship in their united becoming-animal is indicative of an emancipatory passage out of the civilised and thus inhibited human world within which Jemima feels imprisoned. Their union appears to catalyse their animality and predisposition for metamorphosis, as the following climactic episodes suggest.

Ambrose presents Jemima with a gift and proposes that they meet early in the gardens before breakfast. Jemima eagerly unwraps the present and is delighted to find inside the head of a rooster 'five times larger than any other'; she appraises it as 'beautiful' (Carrington 2017: 202). She kisses it three times, thereby revising conventional definitions of beauty beyond those conceived by her mother. Pressing the rooster's head to her heart, she falls asleep but is seized by a series of nightmares. Jemima dreams of the wolf as a metamorphic form, possessing 'sometimes the body of all animals mixed with his own' (Carrington 2017: 202), speaking to the shapeshifting and hybrid themes of the narrative. At 4am, she is drawn to the window and sees a shadow in the garden, recognising it, 'though it changed into a plant, bird, animal, man' (Carrington 2017: 202). Jemima enters the garden with a sense of uneasy anticipation whilst following this shadow, knowing that she is pursuing the wolf and yet unable to 'distinguish the precise form of his body'. Ambrose is in flux, anticipating the becoming-animal posited by Braidotti as a route out of humanist frameworks, occupying an in-between state that triggers Jemima's own metamorphosis in their immanent relations. Such an in-between is emphasised in the recurrent liminal motifs that are invoked in Carrington's short story: Jemima's status as a teenager, neither child nor adult; Ambrose's shifting appearance as a human–animal that cannot be definitively categorised; the twilight hour when the moon hangs still, yet the daylight will soon be upon them; and the garden realm itself, which is both an outside space and one that is curated and manipulated by man – not fully wild and yet not entirely containable either. The two characters come together, with Jemima touching his face with her fingertips. With her touch she 'had the feeling his face was changing colour' (Carrington 2017: 203) and the sun casts a yellow light before he disappears with such suddenness that she describes their last scene together as experiencing 'whiplash' (Carrington 2017: 204). In this intimate scene it is as if Jemima has become an agentive force herself, where it is her touch that triggers a visible shift in the wolf's appearance. Indeed, Carrington forges the couple as exhibiting a sympoietic connection where Ambrose's slippage towards the status of a plant similarly seems to trigger a significant and reciprocal metamorphosis in Jemima:

> But her feet had changed. She bent down to see better and to satisfy herself that a metamorphosis had really occurred. Fine, soft fur had grown between her toes, a fur that stopped on the instep where she found little hairs barely visible to the naked eye. With a gaping mouth she looked at her two feet and murmured. 'I'm of the same blood. Will I be as beautiful as he? [. . .] What wonderful changes will I see in just a few days?' (Carrington 2017: 204)

Jemima's 'acute loneliness' and sense of despair are transformed by the becoming-animal metamorphosis she witnesses in herself, thrilled not only by the shapeshift she observes so far, but also by the changes to come. Such a transformation brings Jemima into closer proximity with the wolf as she notes that their entanglement is complete, they are now 'of the same blood' (Carrington 2017: 204). Through this connection, Jemima is further positioned as a posthuman figure: one immanent to a network of others, in flux and becoming rather than the stable, individualist ego of humanism. Here she presents an 'affective, interactive entity endowed with intelligent flesh and an embodied mind' (Braidotti 2017: 39). Her increasingly hybrid form speaks to what Braidotti labels the posthuman nomadic body which is 'open-ended, inter-relational and trans-species', exploding the 'boundaries of humanism at skin level' (Braidotti 2002: 124). Jemima's transgressions thus far in the short story, which defy the tales of 'Species Man', also move towards a symbol of alliance and entanglement, where Jemima's and the wolf's co-mingling ontologies resonate in affirmative posthuman becomings. It is a mode that is positively estranged from the fortress of human civilisation that her family home represents.

I suggest that Jemima has now experienced an awakening to the world beyond 'Species Man', as Haraway critiques it, embracing a metamorphic ontology in order to begin to craft her own narrative destiny that seeks a reunion with her animal heritage. Feeling at one with the wolf, Jemima expresses an increasing sense of alienation from her family home and seeks to reunite with Ambrose, beginning a solo quest to find him. She abandons the patriarchal rule of home and its humanist conventions, climbing a tree to look into the distance, spying a landscape that shares parallels with the world in which Virginia Fur resides. It is one of 'miles of forest and a gigantic castle', bringing the narrative into a fairy-tale sphere, albeit an increasingly dark and at times gothic one. In this way, there is a sense that Carrington is intimating her story's connections with Red Riding Hood in Jemima's journey into the woods. However, in this version, it is the young female figure who seeks out the wolf rather than the animal predating upon her, as we witness in the traditional tale. Entering this wild and earthly milieu brings Carrington's Jemima character into conversation with Virginia Fur as a fellow creature who registers upon a spectrum of human–nonhuman hybridity. Jemima is not the vulnerable *femme-enfant* but rather a wild and creaturely force herself who controls her own destiny. This fairy-tale multiverse recalls Lyon's discussion of Carrington's capacity to invoke landscapes which are out of humanist scale and perspective. Jemima stumbles upon a figure whom she presumes is a young child and whose gender is unclear. However, he is quick to point out that he is twenty years old and so older than her. This strange boy, described as 'pale, fragile' (Carrington 2017: 207) as if a ghost, is Ambrose's son, called Mimoo. He details his father in the terms that Jemima is familiar with as a multitude of creatures: 'A fox, a wolf, a cat, an eagle, a stag, a horse, a rooster' (Carrington 2017: 209). Jemima demands that he take her to his father's castle so as to continue her metamorphosis on her trajectory of becoming-animal.

Jemima's surprise discovery that Ambrose Barbary and his family are, in fact, all ghosts, who walk the line between the living and the dead, closes the tale in an emphatically hybrid and posthuman zone. Worn out with fatigue from her journey through an increasingly frozen landscape, Jemima finally lies down on an enormous stone, reading the words written into it with 'deep gothic letters, *Here lies Ambrose Barbary and his wife Lucind. Wolf, dear Master, do not walk too often in the footsteps of the living*' (Carrington 2017: 212; emphasis in original). On this final page, Carrington's tale enacts a full exit from the stories of 'Species Man', forging a geostory that melds temporality, space and ontologies in recurrently hybridised manoeuvres. Ambrose figuring as a human–wolf, dead but still walking '*in the footsteps of the living*', places him upon an on-going, becoming trajectory: a figure who criss-crosses between thresholds, even in death. Jemima's increasing connection with this figure galvanises her own becoming-animal figuration, staged as a protest that answers Carrington's call to action in her 'What is a Woman?' essay whilst also committing to a mode of connection and entanglement that forges a human–animal continuum in the manner we also witness in 'As they Rode Along the Edge'. In this way, both Jemima and Virginia are characters who anticipate the tentacular figures Haraway proposes, forging a portal away from the frameworks of 'Species Man' and his pervasive 'History', where the male masters that Carrington critiques pose a threat to the planet and her organic life. In the hybrid figures from Carrington's stories here, we witness both a rebellion and a transgression against a humanist symbolic order that imposes patriarchal rule, and a creative posthuman cartography that navigates a path away from such rule. As such, Carrington's brand of beastly modernism leads us into a posthuman landscape that gives voice to a feminist politics and a more balanced ecological approach. It reminds us, most importantly, that animals are ourselves and our kin. In Carrington's animal hybrid figures we learn how *becoming* is about our capacity both to 'sustain and generate interconnectedness' (Braidotti 2002: 8). As Carrington so presciently warns, this is a vital strategy in countering a neglectful, androcentric anthropos that threatens the existence of all species.

WORKS CITED

Aberth, Susan L. 2010. *Leonora Carrington Surrealism, Alchemy and Art*. Farnham: Lund Humphries.
Barad, Karen. 2007. *Meeting the Universe Halfway*. Durham, NC: Duke University Press.
Braidotti, Rosi. 2002. *Metamorphoses Towards a Materialist Theory of Becoming*. Cambridge: Polity Press.
Braidotti, Rosi. 2013. *The Posthuman*. Cambridge: Polity Press.
Braidotti, Rosi. 2017. 'Four Theses on Posthuman Feminism'. In *Anthropocene Feminism*. Ed. Richard Grusin, 21–48. London: University of Minnesota Press.
Carrington, Leonora. 1998a. 'What is a Woman?' In *Surrealist Women: An International Anthology*. Ed. Penelope Rosemont, 372–5. Austin: University of Texas Press.
Carrington, Leonora. 1998b. 'The Cabbage is a Rose'. In *Surrealist Women: An International Anthology*. Ed. Penelope Rosemont, 375–7. Austin: University of Texas Press.
Carrington, Leonora. 2017. *The Complete Stories of Leonora Carrington*. St Louis: Dorothy Project.
Carson, Anne. 1992. 'The Gender of Sound'. In *Glass, Irony and God*. New York: New Directions, 119–42.
Deleuze, Gilles and Félix Guattari. 1986. *Kafka: Toward a Minor Literature*. Trans. Dana Polan. London: University of Minnesota Press.
Deleuze, Gilles and Félix Guattari. 2004. *A Thousand Plateaus: Capitalism and Schizophrenia*. Trans. Brian Massumi. London: Continuum.

Derrida, Jacques. 1991. '"Eating Well", or the Calculation of the Subject'. In *Who Comes After the Subject*. Ed. Eduardo Cadava, Peter Connor and Jean-Luc Nancy (eds), 96–119. New York: Routledge.

Freccero, Carla. 2017. 'Wolf, or Homo Homini Lupus'. In *Arts of Living on a Damaged Planet*. Ed. Anna Tsing, Heather Swanson, Elaine Gan and Nils Bubandt, M91–M103. London: University of Minnesota Press.

Haraway, Donna J. 2016. *Staying with the Trouble: Making Kin in the Chthulucene*. Durham, NC, and London: Duke University Press.

Lyon, Janet. 2017. 'Carrington's Sensorium'. In *Leonora Carrington and the International Avant-garde*. Ed. Jonathan P. Eburne and Catriona McAra, 163–76. Manchester: Manchester University Press.

Watz, Anna. 2020. *Surrealist Women's Writing: A Critical Exploration*. Manchester: Manchester University Press.

Wolfe, Cary. 2003. *Animal Rites: American Culture, the Discourse of Species, and Posthumanist Theory*. Chicago and London: University of Chicago Press.

Notes

1. 'Jemima and the Wolf' was published for the first time, together with 'The Sand Camel' and 'Mr. Gregory's Fly', in Leonora Carrington, *The Complete Stories of Leonora Carrington* (2017).
2. See Jacques Derrida, '"Eating Well", or the Calculation of the Subject' (1991). Derrida explains the term 'carnophallogocentrism' as one which highlights the way in which subjectivity is most specifically the privilege of meat-eating men, implying 'carnivorous virility' and species supremacy (1991: 113). In *Animal Rites*, Cary Wolfe explains that eating animals facilitates a 'transcendence of the human . . . by killing off and disavowal of the animal' (2003: 66).

12

MODERN INTERSECTIONS: READING ANITA SCOTT COLEMAN'S ANIMALS

Elizabeth Curry

In May 1926, when *Opportunity* magazine announced the winners of its second annual writing contest, the Casper Holstein Awards, it was no small affair. Celebrating a range of authorial forms, from poetry to investigative journalism, the contest culminated in a dinner party at New York's Fifth Avenue Restaurant attended by 400 writers, political actors and socialites – many of them well-known figures of the Harlem Renaissance, including Jean Toomer, Alain Locke, Paul Robeson and Carl Van Vechten ('The Awards Dinner' 1926: 186). These awards not only bestowed recognition and cash prizes upon the celebrated, but most essentially made available a sizeable public platform for promising Black writers from around the country. From this dais, the name of one such writer then beginning to emerge as a literary voice from beyond the New York locus was announced: Anita Scott Coleman. Awarded second place for her personal experience sketch 'The Dark Horse', Coleman's introduction was broadcast prominently through this prize.

A poet who also wrote fiction and essays, Coleman's work appeared frequently in African American periodicals between 1925 and 1938, but her central occupation concerned family life on the ranch (Davis and Mitchell 2008: 24). In a short biography published in tandem with the Holstein awards, self-described 'ex-schoolteacher' Coleman sums up her position as that of a married woman 'engaged in raising children and chickens' on a ranch in New Mexico (Coleman 1926: 188). This brief self-portrait not only distinguishes Coleman through geography and occupation, but it also emphasises an important theme that crops up often in her writing: a keen awareness of the side-by-side lives of humans and nonhuman animals. The unpretentious and humorous discursive parallel Coleman draws between children and chickens, who both require raising, corresponds to similar associations and linguistic dyads that appear throughout her work, which take for granted notions of interspecies linkages. For Coleman, who did indeed raise five children and untold chickens before moving to Los Angeles in mid-life, her positionality as a Black woman at home on a ranch in New Mexico would seem to foreground a perspective that surfaces often in her poetry and prose. Her work disarticulates antiblack racism and dehumanisation while it simultaneously resists the instrumentalisation of nonhuman figures as necessarily reproachable in the process.

In this chapter, I observe how Coleman's work within the Harlem Renaissance modernist milieu explores nonhuman animality not outside the prism of America's racial imaginary, but in a way that reconceptualises many of its animalising compulsions. Given how race, and Blackness specifically, directly figure in the animalising ontologies that many modernist texts explore, a critical focus on how racialisation and animalisation intersect with modernist themes and aesthetics reveals much about both constructions, as Coleman's poetry and prose demonstrate. Engaging critical work in Black studies and postcolonial studies that consider animal representation, I read Coleman's work as but one example of (heretofore overlooked) modernist experimentation concerned with the parallel rupture of race and animality as co-constituting colonial categories of devaluation. Within modernism's bestiary, where often the human becomes strange and the nonhuman becomes familiar, Coleman imagines something different: scenes of interspecies mingling where lines of division blur and merge to redraw formations that disrupt the work of whiteness as a force of dehumanisation. Instead, dyadic pairings align interspecies linkages through both affective and positional bonds that highlight how such alliances resist white hegemonic subordination. Binary *oppositions* are reinscribed through Coleman's work to be *parallelisms* between humans and animals that reveal race and animality to be co-constructs of what Aimé Césaire calls the 'howling savagery' of the 'Western humanist' (Césaire 1950: 37). Approaching a writer long overlooked, this chapter surveys Coleman as an important figure to consider as we rework the beastly modern with the aim of challenging systems of racialisation and animalisation.

Though unfortunately 'The Dark Horse' is now lost – either to history or to an as-yet-uncatalogued archive – its mention survives alongside a number of Coleman's published essays, short stories and poems presented in the recently assembled collection *Western Echoes of the Harlem Renaissance* (2008).[1] Within this collection, themes and discursive parallelisms arise between humans and nonhuman animals that challenge notions of their figurations as somehow removed from the American racial imaginary. Coleman's poetry and prose borrow from animalising stereotypes around Black bestiality and then soften or reverse those tropes so that animality comes to figure as something at odds with the beastly. The most prominent example of this reversal appears in her story 'Three Dogs and a Rabbit', which, a year prior to the Holstein awards, had earned Coleman a writing prize from *The Crisis* in 1925. A frame narrative, the story formally mirrors the disorienting layers of 'civility' that ostensibly separate human and nonhuman as recognisable relations. Additionally, her poem 'Idle Wonder', published in *Opportunity* in 1938, creates not so much a reversal as a thinking through animality when its speaker speculates about feline consciousness, then to meditate further on Black labour and conditions of servile captivity. Both pieces offer possibilities to read closely the work of an artist who, though celebrated at the time, was also marginalised by social forces that limited a wider circulation of Black voices within modernism. These works also suggest new possibilities for reading race alongside questions of the animal (and reading animals while always considering racial constructions) as a way to think around white normativity and discourses of dehumanisation. Interestingly, these works also point to an early twentieth-century concern among Black writers with representations of animals that differ markedly from white modernist depictions. For instance, while works by white writers noted for their radical takes on animality (such as Djuna Barnes's *Nightwood* or Franz Kafka's *The Metamorphosis*) explore and acknowledge the beastly animalism inherent in being human, writers like Coleman (and, notably, Zora Neale Hurston and Jean Toomer as well) portray animals not as atavistic or primitive, but redemptive in their dignity and fullness. In opposition to modernist texts that render the animal (and the human animal) as monstrously other, Coleman's prose and poetry demonstrate how racialisation and compulsive animalisation fundamentally distort their subjects. Instead, her work puts forward a notion of the human animal that is not so distinctly above or different from the rest of the living world. This chapter represents an effort to expand understandings of how Coleman – among other writers of the Harlem Renaissance – were long since asserting animal figurations that refigure what it means to be human.

Prose Work

Through figurations of bodily entanglements, 'Three Dogs and a Rabbit' illustrates how race and animality are always ensnared in a Eurocentric American culture that seeks to devour nonwhite bodies. One of her best-known works, the short story was an entry Coleman submitted to an annual fiction contest held by *The Crisis*, for which she won third prize.[2] In the tale, past and present – memory and reality – merge across the species barrier to conjure a challenge to what Claire Jean Kim identifies as 'the centuries-old racial trope [of] Black bestiality' (Kim 2015: 6). Instead, it offers a way of reading that Sharon Holland proposes as one that avoids 'defining the human against the animal other', whereby both discursively exist in binary tension; rather, the story achieves 'a potentiality for togetherness' that does not seek the lack in one to establish the greatness of the other (Holland 2016: 168). 'Three Dogs' tells the tale of a woman standing trial, offering testimonial defence for her part in harbouring a Black man as he fled three policemen. She confesses to this act and justifies it through a narrative that relies on the animal as a figure of sentimentality. She explains to the attendant jury that in the fleeing man, 'only a little terror-mad rabbit' was visible, the very same rabbit, in fact, that she had rescued at great personal peril decades earlier from three hound dogs and her white enslaver (93). In this story, the connection between human and animal manifests as one of parallel vulnerability subject to forces of white brutality bent on domination. The narrative engages animal figures as a means of enacting resistance through empathy (rather than fear or malice) in its audience, and thereby inverts the dominating ends that animalisation often pursues. As a scholar of Coleman's work, Laura Barrett notes that the story explores 'the intersection of personal and national, individual and race, oral and written traditions' (Barrett 2013: 59). A piece that stands decidedly within the modernist context and also outside the narrowness of the modernism canon, 'Three Dogs' is but one example of a text that explores how race and animality collide to interrupt the deployment of violence as usual through commingling figurations.

The story operates through a frame narrative with an unidentified narrator quoting at length a lively man named Timothy Phipps, who advised the narrator to 'write, write, write' the oral tale that Phipps recounts (85). This piece of short fiction that 'consciously examines layers of storytelling' engages a series of narrative voices that unintentionally illustrate how added layers of discourse ultimately distort their subjects (Barrett 2013: 61). Chronicling three narrative voices (the narrator, Phipps and Mrs Ritton as she stands trial), the story successively draws the reader closer to a central figure incapable of speaking: a frightened rabbit. Each voice presents a set of perspectives that differ in interpretive capacity, and which remain readily identifiable by the shorthand of their punctuation. Near the beginning of the story, Phipps explains that 'the only plot in this rigamarole [. . .] is running, hard to catch' before he goes on to elaborate emphatically his gendered theories around beauty and its rarity among women (85). Fortunately for Phipps, who 'clings like a leech to the belief that beautiful temples are invariably beautiful within', the small, attractive Mrs Ritton (the central human figure around which the story revolves) provides a tidy sense of validity to his subjective claim. He interprets the story he tells to be one that affirms 'the power of her beauty' (92). Phipps would seem to engage what Achille Mbembe refers to as a 'racist conscience', whereby 'appearance is taken as the true reality of things' (Mbembe 2017: 112). But Mrs Ritton's story as the central kernel disrupts Phipps's interpretive voice, since she speaks as well. Her voice (as related by Phipps and documented by the narrator) is the third perspective the story follows as she testifies from a courtroom witness stand, presenting her own defence against four charges, which include hampering police in their duty and harbouring 'a criminal' (87). Mrs Ritton's verbal testimony ultimately tells a very different story, one that is not about gendered beauty, but about the verve of 'nonhuman vitality' in confrontation with brutal human violence (Bennett 2010: 14).

From the witness stand, Mrs Ritton tells two stories that take the reader to the core of liveliness that the story ultimately pursues in its alignment with nonhuman animality. She relates a pair of nearly identical actions, performed decades apart, as central to both stories; both stemmed from the 'only two impulses' Mrs Ritton ever answered, having not 'been born so unfettered' as the white courtroom she addresses (89). In the first story, she explains, in a line that breaks off, 'I was ten years old, when my master –' thereby testifying to having survived as a child under American chattel slavery (90). In her testimony, she describes how, during that time, she journeyed overland with the Ritton family from their holding in the South to a new homestead out west. Long days on the trail, she explains, left them eventually exhausted and starving. Then, one night, they stop to camp in what the girl observes to be a 'lovely spot . . . a luxurious resting place for weary bodies' (90). To assuage the party's hunger, 'three hounds – faithful brutes that had trailed beside [them] all the weary miles', are sent to chase down dinner (91). The dogs quickly succeed in scaring up a rabbit, who runs, bounds, turns, swirls and finally plunges, 'terror-mad', into the girl's lap – a frantic 'flight-blind' attempt to escape that she observes with almost unmediated identification (91). This concentrated observation of the rabbit's plight compels her to cover 'the tiny trembling creature' in her hands as she fends off the springing dogs; she then manages 'to conceal [her] captive in the large old-fashioned pocket' of her skirt where it rests, presumably motionless (91). Arriving a moment later, 'Master', hungry and ireful, asks which way the rabbit went (91). Mrs Ritton explains to the court:

> When I replied 'Don't know,' he became quite angry and beat me. Gentlemen, the scars of that long ago flogging I shall carry to my grave. Our food was nearly gone and it was I, the slave-girl, who knew the lack most sorely. But I did not give the rabbit over to my master. (91)

The power of this scene – both for the reader and for the story's courtroom audience to whom the testimony is addressed – is in the bareness of the modes of defence it describes. Using her body alone, the girl withstands the violence of a brutal assault, terror and hunger to enact resistance to animal suffering and death. In shielding the rabbit, the girl does more than protect the small creature from death and devouring; she rejects and endures in her own bare and unarmed flesh the basest justifications for which men kill animals: hunger (which is here extreme), fear, violent will, rapacious entitlement and assumed dominance over nature and all that exists in it. She asserts her body between these ideological and physical forces on an impulse, a connection with the creaturely, in recognition of the small animal's determination to live in the face of a howling chase. In a body deemed available to violence – as violable – by both her white captors and the law, the girl enacts an improbable inverse: she creates a space of inviolability for the smaller creature, preserving the unspeaking animal at the centre of the story.

As Mrs Ritton continues her testimony, she explains that the horrific scene of violence she endured was witnessed by the white man's son – the future Colonel Ritton – who then 'changed from that day' toward the girl he had always teased (92). She tells the assembled 'Gentlemen' in the courtroom that he – her husband – taught her 'to forget the scars of serfdom' and to find 'the joys of freedom' from the social positionality assured by her status as Mrs Ritton (92). Her account pauses here when Phipps interrupts her narrative and testimony to praise the 'little old white-haired woman standing alone' in 'her loveliness', captivating the room with 'the power of her beauty' (92). With this interjection, Phipps and the narrator tie together the construction of Mrs Ritton's personhood in the eyes of the courtroom by entangling her beauty, her passing whiteness, and her demonstration of courage and compassion for the hunted rabbit. Her protection of the animal and her display of courage and moral commitment had transformed her access to respected personhood, which was further 'guaranteed' through her marriage to the military officer, Colonel Ritton. As this particular notion of what it means to be a respectable person is so enmeshed in the American military state, the narrator does not further identify her beyond her married surname. As Alexander Weheliye explains, 'full access to legal personhood has been a systematic absence' for people of colour (Weheliye 2014: 11). In 'Three Dogs', race, gender and animality are tied together to construct certain versions of what it means to be human in the eyes of the law and white heteropatriarchal culture that abides by 'the colonial model of comparing humans to animals' within a society where subjugation and domination structure mainstream discourses of animality (Mbembe 2017: 21).

But Coleman is not through with the construction of personhood as separate, above or outside of the nonhuman sphere. Though human–nonhuman boundary lines remain distinct in Mrs Ritton's first remembrance, in the story's final scene these boundaries blur into something momentous. Concluding her testimony to address the charges at hand, Mrs Ritton recalls the day she glanced out the window to witness a man running down the street. Fleeing three white policemen on foot, the man compelled Mrs Ritton to 'look closer' to observe 'that he was black' (93). From the witness stand she relates: '[t]hen a queer thing happened' as the memory of that 'hilly slope' from years ago surrounded her, and suddenly the man 'who was running so wildly' appeared to be 'only a little terror-mad rabbit' (93). The sequence of this memory spills from her recognition of the man's Blackness – a mode of identification Mrs Ritton had thrust aside – to a visceral terror that guides her association back to the rabbit. This association becomes more than memory or resemblance, however, as Mrs Ritton explains that the forms of man and rabbit exceeded distinction, and as she looked on, 'they merged and both were one' (93). Both man and rabbit running for their lives take on the form of a transgressive creature, at once distinct and combined, simultaneously appearing as vital beings legible to white American society as exploitable and killable. Species separation breaks down to make material the connection that both experience as living beings, who are also bounded by a logic outside of themselves, one that renders them subject to violent debasement by Euroamerican brutality. On an impulse, as he darts into her house, Mrs Ritton shelters Phipps – who is here revealed to be the 'hard to catch' man – and like the rabbit, she never gives him over (85). In both scenarios, concealment is critical; hiding their forms is an act that Mrs Ritton impulsively recognises as the only mode of defence against the violence of white hysteria, a practice she had adopted for her own being by passing in order to live freely.

The work of Mrs Ritton's narrative is in its production of symmetry between man and rabbit that discursively merges their figures to draw a phenomenological connection between the two. This connection is important in the context of the story's courtroom because it critically illustrates how white sympathy seeks sentimentalised animals as it also creates bestialised humans. As Bénédicte Boisseron observes, within the US court system, so-called justice is contingent on 'a racially invested denial of personhood' (Boisseron 2018: 9). 'Three Dogs' demonstrates very clearly how the conceptual gymnastics required to receive legal justice while Black in America hinges on pushing the proper buttons of sentimentality to activate white sympathy so that it recognises persons and their rights. Paradoxically, those buttons light up for charismatic, docile, small and frightened animals, even while such creatures are also subject to various exploitative and inhumane actions by that same culture. Animality here does not function as a means of 'othering' in the service of subjugating; rather, its intention is to humanise both the small animal and Phipps, and to link them through experiences of vulnerability to harm and unjust entrapment. In the context of Euroamerican histories of bestialising Black men, animalisation in this story partially inverts that logic, not only by ascribing rabbit-like qualities to the man (he is fleeing, frightened and outnumbered by beings ferocious and merciless), but by blurring the lines of distinction between the two. That 'both were one' gestures toward the body as the site of connection, not only through shared vulnerability but through the commonality of embodied being – of being as always within bodily form. Outside of deliberative logic or even the pursuit of justice, it is an affective impulse that overtakes Mrs Ritton in each of her lifesaving encounters. The story's power derives from its core associations between affective connections; it draws the reader's attention to what Jane Bennett calls 'the common materiality of all that is' (Bennett 2010: 122). A connection through affect – a sense of what it means to share the very thing of being – spurs Mrs Ritton's impulses and consequent protective actions to shield the hunted, who otherwise lack any chance of escape, and thus to stand physically in the way of predation that hunts with hungry entitlement. What is more, the story re-authors what it means to be human as well. It illustrates what Dana Luciano and Mel Y. Chen point to in the humaneness of the human, which is 'to feel for others [. . .] and to respond to [their] suffering' (2015: 190). Mrs Ritton reacts not only through identification, but as an immediate response to the desperate plight of another being.

Despite the story's title and the connection it draws between the three policemen and the three dogs who first chased down the rabbit, it is worth noting that Mrs Ritton's testimony does not explicitly align these figures. Rather, she declares that the policemen, though three in number and chasing down 'the rabbit', instead share 'the visage of [her] master' (93). Importantly, with this refusal to impugn the dogs as agents of white violence (a colonialist tactic that Boisseron extensively explores), the narrative affirms another connection, this time to animal actors who are assigned roles by dominating forces of white control. Coleman's story prefigures Joshua Bennett's twenty-first-century call 'ultimately to abolish the forms of antiblack thought that have maintained the fissure between human and animal', as it refuses to affirm this fissure with an easy analogy (Bennett 2020: 4). Instead, the story 'animalises' the police such that they take on the inhuman form of the white enslaver. Aimé Césaire, in *Discourse on Colonialism* (1950), writes that the coloniser 'gets into the habit of seeing the other man as *an animal*, accustoms himself to treating him like an animal, and tends objectively to transform *himself* into an animal' (Césaire 1950: 41). In Coleman's short story this psychological process is rendered literally and inversely: Mrs Ritton's so-called 'Master' treats her as 'an animal' and seemingly becomes one by doing so. In the final scene, it is the 'master's' face, not the hounds', that subsumes those of the police. That is, the men pursuing violent domination resemble only themselves, and thus call into question the very construction of the term 'animal' and its perverse usages. Coleman's story asserts that nonhuman animals themselves have no part in this framework around which a power structure has been assembled but are collateral damage in the carnage of colonial human self-destruction.

Ultimately, 'Three Dogs and a Rabbit' inverts animality as a concept – as a designator of abuseability – and through a merging of forms and figures, it emphasises the shared circumstances of bodily vulnerability and necessary flight. Inversions here proliferate to offer productive vantage points from which to apprehend better the previously concealed. In this story, Black bestiality is inverted such that white domination and 'law enforcement' appear beastly; the logic of violence is inverted such that it is combatted not through revenge but through nonviolence and safeguarding. The figure of the rabbit, nested inside layers of narrative scaffolding, emits a pulsing vibrancy – a harmless and fearful relatability not only across species boundaries, but across juridical barriers that buttress the white courtroom as well. Coleman's story exemplifies how exclusion from full acceptance within the American legal rubric of personhood enables Phipps and Mrs Ritton to escape ways of seeing that are conditioned by Eurocentric fantasies of domination and supremacy, though both must still navigate this terrain as a means of survival by traversing territories of animal sentimentality first. In her verbal testimony before a white courtroom, Mrs Ritton does not appeal for recognition of her humanity vis-à-vis an ontologic equation with the white master or the policemen, but rather turns away from 'the human' and toward the rabbit as a redemptive counterfigure to the unhinged ferocity of 'Man' (Wynter 2003: 260). 'Three Dogs and a Rabbit' illustrates how a steely protection of life in the face of white brutality depends on an impulse in which care eclipses fear. It illustrates the connection between vulnerable lives – both of them treated as prey by predatory creatures – and the propulsion to safeguard life because it lives.

POETIC FIGURES

Figurative representations that push beyond affective connection between human and animal continue in Coleman's poetry, exploring as it does the figure of the nonhuman as capable of the same psychic longings and frustrations that haunt human subjects confined to the domestic realm. Offering a catalogue of queries into the nature of being, of consciousness and of social subjugation, many of Coleman's poetic works demonstrate a preoccupation with nonhuman subjects, presaging the more recent 'nonhuman turn' embraced by a growing list of scholars (Luciano and Chen 2015: 189). Such critical investigations into the global historical construction of race as dependent on conceptions of animality importantly look primarily to the animal and the nonhuman as sites not of rejection, but of interest, enquiry and possibility. In *Being Property Once Myself: Blackness and the End of Man* (2020), Joshua Bennett surveys the 'ongoing entanglement of blackness and animality' to watch how 'black authors cultivated a poetics of persistence and interspecies empathy' (5). This turn toward the animal, and, by extension, a turn away from interest or inclusion in white American notions of the human, appears irrepressibly over time in the poetic works of Anita Scott Coleman, surfacing in poems such as 'She Was Not Wise', 'The Dust of the Streets' (1929) and 'Respective Flight' (1948).

Most notably, the route from nonhuman to human is explicitly encountered in Coleman's poem 'Idle Wonder', published in *Opportunity* in 1938.[3]

The short verse poem draws a comparison between human and house cat as it muses on animal consciousness and the assumptions of those who rationalise oppression and possession. Through this parallel encounter, the poem foregrounds empathetic curiosity about companion species as a means of understanding human social relationships. The poem's speaker begins by pondering her cat, assuming it leads a life of satisfaction, but then questions that assumption by drawing a comparison between the cat and the subjugated position of a Black acquaintance. The poem appeared originally in *Opportunity* in 1938 as follows:

> Idle Wonder
> My cat is so sleek and contented;
>   She is a real house-cat
> She has not seen any other cat
> since she came to live with me.
>
> I wonder does she think,
> I wonder does she dream
> I wonder does she ever imagine
> Herself out, among cats
> I wonder is she like poor Agnes
>
> Agnes lives with the white folks
> And they think she is contented
> And actually delighted with being
>   their house-maid. (Coleman 1948: 202)

Beginning from a space of idle observation, as its title asserts, the speaker's domestic assurance informs the musings around her cat's smooth figure and presumed satisfaction. An impression of repose is suggested by the cat's 'contented' air. As the sentence runs on, it even suggests that her contentment correlates with a lack of contact with other cats, such that she can repose unbothered by their company. Despite or because of the cat's isolation from other felines, she is decreed authentic in her domesticated position; observed to be relaxed and fit, she seemingly wants for little in the way of comforts or companionship, and so lives as 'a real house-cat' is meant to live.

It is remarkable how little scholarly theory around race and animals, or within animal studies itself, looks specifically at cats. This is despite the fact that Jacques Derrida's (2008) musings about his own cat's consciousness opened the scholarly floodgates for a serious consideration of animal being among Western humanists. As books like Kim's and Boisseron's reveal, dogs and often farm animals are creatures in whom animal studies remains heavily invested. This is exemplified by Donna Haraway's *When Species Meet* (2007), which gives scant attention to cats and only then to a small family of feral cats as 'interpellated into the modern biopolitical state', whom she hopes to safeguard for both their 'subject status' and as agents of rodent control (2007: 277). Indeed, America has a vexed relationship with cats, especially among their devoted advocates who have yet to reach collective consensus around how 'feral' they should be encouraged to be. Thus, Coleman's use of the signifier 'house-cat' is itself a radical position in some ways that marks the speaker herself as a proponent of the domestic. She naturalises this subject position and asserts it to be the position in which real personhood resides, for both human and feline.

But the speaker goes on in the next stanza to question further whether these assumptions of fulfilment and definition are misconstrued, pondering her cat's interiority and likening her to 'poor Agnes'. Through the imagined subjectivity of the cat and her potential personhood – she might, after all, think, dream and imagine – she brings to the speaker's attention Agnes, a Black acquaintance who works as a live-in maid for white people. Her employers, in their position of assumed powerful benevolence, believe her to be happy. Though they hold her in socio-economic captivity, they assume she is 'delighted' to inhabit that realm. The hyphenated connection the speaker draws between 'house-maid' and 'house-cat' not only links the two subjects by their house-boundedness, but it also emphasises the domesticating work that the enclosures of home do in ostensibly offering comfortable lives to those within, despite *how* they occupy that space. Revealing how subjugation operates through the exercise of privilege on the part of the subjugator, the poem illustrates how the privilege to draw assumptions about the happiness of others (whether human or animal) who must reside inside a home they did not choose belongs to people who believe they possess the power to confer favours through the superiority of their position. Those who benefit, from labour or from companionship, infer their own paternalistic benevolence and enact a bourgeois complicity in the structures of domination that gird such an arrangement. The poem suggests that the workings of white supremacy and white innocence may creep into human–animal relationships unnoticed when assumptions about others' experiences glorify those who presume control.

'Idle Wonder' goes even further than drawing attention to the privileged assumptions of those in domestic control, in that it also depicts a troubled connection between the isolation of the cat and that of Agnes. If the speaker views the cat as authentic and pleased in its isolation from other cats, it implies that Agnes's employers attribute part of her delight to living away from Black people, exclusively in a space of whiteness. But the poem provides immediate evidence to the contrary; Agnes has spoken of her thoughts, dreams and imaginings of escape from the confines of domestic labour and economic internment.

The dissonance between her white employers' false beliefs and the truth of Agnes's desires are what compel the speaker to question her own assumptions. The speaker's wondering about animal interiority and speculating about the falsity of her own conjectures takes its route through the animal to the person, just as Coleman's story 'Three Dogs and a Rabbit' does, and thus enacts Joshua Bennett's poetic means of 'getting out of animality *by going through it*' (2020: 2, emphasis in original). Through the cat, an appreciation for its interiority emerges in concert with lamentation for Agnes's position. Still, it is worth noting that although the poem projects a form of interspecies empathy in which the cat's experience is taken seriously and is imaginatively encountered, it does not directly reflect human empathy here. Instead, the speaker's empathy for Agnes takes a more indirect and sardonic tone, going through the white folks to comment on how erroneous their assumptions are. The poem performs a talking around what Agnes truly thinks to indicate more precisely how discontented and trapped she is. The speaker's musing about Agnes's interior state would be inadequate, the poem suggests, because she already knows the answers to these questions, and the unhappiness of her position exceeds the parallelism by which the verse is constructed. To go beyond this dyadic formation would be to weigh down both halves of the poem with a more complete articulation of what Zakiyyah Jackson calls the 'abjectly animalized', or the 'burden of "the animal"' wherein the appropriation of lives by Euroamericans structures the spaces – interior and exterior – in which both figures dwell (Jackson 2020: 12).

In recognising modernism as distinctively inquisitive about nonhuman animals and the human connection to other beings, attending to works that lay bare the work of racialising constructions is critical if we are to understand better how 'the animal' came to be, and can be recovered and ultimately set free. Coleman's poetry and prose present formulations of human–nonhuman pairs (house-cat : house-maid, rabbit : man, children : chickens) that reject the hierarchical assumptions inherent in the modern construction of the Euroamerican human, or '*homo modernus*' as Denise da Silva terms the invention of such a being, and opposes this construction with adamant interspecies likenesses (Da Silva 2007: 4). Through her literary contributions, Coleman proposes a realm of parallel existences in which each pair occupies a space of being that, while subject to the forces of white judgement and control, nonetheless refuse to submit to the ideo-logic of those demands. By pushing against the indexed gradations of value that white hegemonic ideology assigns, Coleman's discursive parallels reject the bases of Euroamerican presumptions around racialisation and animalisation, namely that some lives are inherently more valuable than others, that some humans are more animal that others, that some humans are not animals and that animalising comparisons need be derogatory. Instead, her work foregrounds a poetics of the posthuman figure, one that embraces discursive correlations between humanity and animality to create pairings of similarity rather than opposition. In this way, she reinscribes *the* other as *an* other.

WORKS CITED

Barrett, Laura. 2013. '"Mark my words": Speech, Writing, and Identity in Three Harlem Renaissance Stories'. *Journal of Modern Literature* 37.1: 58–76.
Bennett, Jane. 2010. *Vibrant Matter: A Political Ecology of Things*. Durham, NC: Duke University Press.
Bennett, Joshua. 2020. *Being Property Once Myself: Blackness and the End of Man*. Cambridge, MA: Harvard University Press.
Boisseron, Bénédicte. 2018. *Afro-Dog: Blackness and the Animal Question*. New York: Columbia University Press.
Césaire, Aimé. 2000 [1950]. *Discourse on Colonialism*. New York: Monthly Review.
Coleman, Anita Scott. 1926. 'Our Prize Winners and What They Say of Themselves'. *Opportunity* 189: 188–9.
Coleman, Anita Scott. 1948. 'Idle Wonder'. In *Reason for Singing*. Prairie City, IL: Decker Press.
Coleman, Anita Scott. 2008a. *Western Echoes of the Harlem Renaissance: The Life and Writings of Anita Scott Coleman*. Ed. Cynthia J. Davis and Verner D. Mitchell. Norman: University of Oklahoma Press.
Coleman, Anita Scott. 2008b. *Unfinished Masterpiece: The Harlem Renaissance Fiction of Anita Scott Coleman*. Ed. Laurie Champion and Bruce A. Glasrud. Lubbock: Texas Tech University Press.
Da Silva, Denise. 2007. *Toward a Global Idea of Race*. Minneapolis: University of Minnesota Press.
Davis, Cynthia J. and Verner D. Mitchell, eds. 2008. *Western Echoes of the Harlem Renaissance: The Life and Writings of Anita Scott Coleman*. Norman: University of Oklahoma Press.
Derrida, Jacques. 2008 [1997]. *The Animal That Therefore I Am*. New York: Fordham University Press.
Haraway, Donna. 2007. *When Species Meet*. Minneapolis: University of Minnesota Press.
Holland, Sharon. 2016. 'Hum/Animal All Together'. *PMLA* 131.1: 167–9.
Jackson, Zakiyyah Iman. 2020. *Becoming Human: Matter and Meaning in an Antiblack World*. New York: NYU Press.
Kim, Claire Jean. 2015. *Dangerous Crossings: Race, Species, and Nature in a Multicultural Age*. Cambridge: Cambridge University Press.
Luciano, Dana and Mel Y. Chen. 2015. 'Has the Queer Ever Been Human? Introduction'. *GLQ: A Journal of Lesbian and Gay Studies* 21.2-3: 183–207.
Mbembe, Achille. 2017. *Critique of Black Reason*. Trans. Laurent Dubois. Durham, NC: Duke University Press.
'The Awards Dinner'. 1926. *Opportunity* 126: 186.
Weheliye, Alexander G. 2014. 'Introduction' and 'Blackness: The Human'. In *Habeas Viscus: Racializing Assemblages, Biopolitics, and Black Feminist Theories of the Human*, 1–32. Durham, NC: Duke University Press.

Wynter, Sylvia. 2003. 'Unsettling the Coloniality of Being/Power/Truth/Freedom: Towards the Human, After Man, Its Overrepresentation – An Argument'. *CR: The New Centennial Review* 3.3: 257–337.

Notes

1. Another Coleman volume was also published that same year: *Unfinished Masterpiece: The Harlem Renaissance Fiction of Anita Scott Coleman*.
2. It was judged in second place by H. G. Wells, who served on the contest judging panel along with Sinclair Lewis, Charles Chesnutt and Mary White Ovington (Davis and Mitchell 2008: 23).
3. The only full collection of Coleman's work published during her lifetime was a compilation of poetry titled *Reason for Singing* (1948); 'Idle Wonder' appears in that collection.

PART V

EXTINCTION, WAR, PROLIFERATION

13

1940s *AVIAN NOIR*

Laura Blomvall

THE MENACE OF BIRDS

In a long tradition of Western war literature stretching back to Ancient Greece, birds have appeared in military imagery, from the war cries of Trojan soldiers in *The Iliad* pouring out 'like the clamour of cranes' (Homer 2014: 129), to Aristophanes' allusions to the Peloponnesian War in his comic fantasy play, *The Birds*. Embodying the fears and fantasies of twentieth-century aerial warfare, in literary representations of the Second World War this surreal imagery resurfaces in a figurative conflation of birds and aircraft. This chapter examines what I term '*avian noir*' in the 1940s: war poetry that goes beyond the trope of flight and the aeroplane's engineered resemblance to a bird with outstretched wings, by exploring the destructive dominance of the aerially positioned beast – bird or machine. From Elizabeth Bishop to Sylvia Townsend-Warner, poets represented the threat of bomber planes by employing rapid and unexpected juxtapositions inherited from modernism, surrealism and the visual language of cinema, but materially underpinned in the 1940s by the lived experience of total war. Especially in female and queer lyric poetry, imagery confusing birds and planes represented distant violence capable of infiltrating women's intimate spaces. *Avian noir*, as explored in this chapter, thus touches on wider questions over the relationship between the material otherness of birds and the other, othered voices of *noir* in wartime modernism.

This 1940s *avian noir* formed part of a global mid-century moment exploring aerial warfare through the visual language of birds, in a performative reflection on the role of the poetic image within the modern war lyric. The speaker in Anna Akhmatova's 'The Wind of War' ('Veter Voiny', 1941), poetically documenting aerial warfare during the siege of Leningrad, depicts bomber planes as 'birds of death' (Haughton 2004: 7). Bertolt Brecht's poem 'This Summer's Sky' ('Der Himmel dieses Sommers', 1953) describes bomber planes that appear in the horizon 'like young starlings, their beaks wide open for food' (Haughton 2004: 36). In London, H.D. writes in 'R.A.F.' (1941) of 'the flying shadow / of high wings // moving / over the grass' (Keery 2020: 34). The speaker in Stephen Spender's poem 'To Poets and Airmen' calls a bomber plane an 'all-night screeching metal bird' (Spender 1942: 101) and, in Edith Sitwell's 'Lullaby' (1940), the plane takes the form of a 'steel bird' with 'steel wings' (Sitwell 1940: 13). Whether a flying shadow, a bringer of death, a creature of metal or steel, or young birds hungry to be fed, from Leningrad to London avian species provide a visual language in poetry for evoking the fantasies and fears of bombers capable of inflicting mass civilian casualties. Terrifying and dream-like characteristics oversaturate the most central resemblance between birds and planes – the act of occupying space in the sky – as the speakers of these poems use images of avian menace to gesture towards atrocities that are fundamentally human. If, in Homer, war cries carry through the air like birds, in twentieth-century warfare the presence of military technology in the sky means birds can figuratively represent the aerial distance of violence. However, in the twentieth century the sounds of war extend to an embodied conflation of birds and instruments of warfare within the technological language of modernity that blurs boundaries between nonhuman nature and machines.

A number of cultural shifts underpinned the use of avian imagery in 1940s modernism. From one perspective, these images could be seen as constituting a distinct subgenre of the frequently cited pastoral turn of the Second World War. Reflecting on his translation of Virgil's *Georgics*, published to critical and commercial success in 1940, Cecil Day-Lewis wondered how 'it takes a seismic event such as a war' to reveal a rural patriotism in 'most of us rootless moderns' ('On Translating Poetry' [1970], qtd in Stanford 2004: 177). In her analysis of Virginia Woolf's *Between the Acts* (1941), Marina MacKay observes how the 'context of war exacerbates the conservative function of the imagined countryside', and how, during the war, 'idealised rural England once again became the literary mainstay of nostalgic longings for community and continuity' (MacKay 2010: 24–5). Leo Mellor's study of literary representations of metropolitan bombsites, focused on urban rather than rural representations of war, analyses the importance of '[t]he creation of implausibly lush zones in the midst of London', 'one of the most unexpected transformations that resulted from incendiary and high-explosive bomb attacks' (Mellor 2011: 166). The presence of nonhuman nature was therefore not just essential to pastoral and georgic poetry and countryside fiction; it now also formed a part of the urban settings in the wartime imagination.

However, this pastoral turn also frequently implied a critically underexplored animal turn during the war. In her notes to *Between the Acts*, Woolf recounts this return of nature in the wartime city specifically in reference to nonhuman animals: 'They have gone back to the 18th century. Nature prevails. I suppose badgers & foxes wd. come back if this went on, & owls & nightingales . . . Odd if this should be the end of town life' (Lee 1997: 718). To Woolf, wartime London has ecologically returned to a past century, as she wonders whether 'the end of town life' will come after nonhuman animals return to the city. Aerial warfare transformed the organised anonymous crowds of the modernist city, revealing the coexistence of nature and buildings, human and nonhuman animals, bricks and foliage, surreal in their dream-like and unexpected connections. In an apocalyptic narrative of regression, the presence of nonhuman animals is symptomatic of an urban dystopia that spells the end of modernism and modernity.

These nonhuman animals include birds, such as the 'owls & nightingales' Woolf imagines taking over London. Elizabeth Berridge's poem 'Bombed Church' (1946) reveals some of the distinguishing characteristics of birds within this animal turn of wartime modernism. In the poem's urban church, it is creatures with wings that overtake the fragmented ecclesiastical space: 'a black owl chant[s] the lesson' and '[b]ats descend and flap' in the place of the verger (Reilly 1984: 20). The bird especially captures the vertical vulnerabilities of rapidly transformed architectural structures, as it descends from the sky through opened roofs and walls to occupy buildings. Meanwhile, in the countryside of *Between the Acts* (1941), aeroplanes assume the appearance of birds as they interrupt the rhythms of rural life with their noisy engines in the sky, when twelve planes appear overhead 'in perfect formation like a flight of wild duck', interrupting Miss La Trobe's pageant (Woolf 2000: 119). The surreal city is matched by the surreal sky with its confusing juxtapositions of engines and birdsong, technology and nature, metal and feathers. This wartime avian turn thus represents a crucial context for utilising the aesthetics of modernism to interrogate the possibilities of its end.

Critics have frequently cited the significance of surrealism in wartime culture. Mellor, for one, notes both 'the organicist turn in the use of surrealist methods in British poetry and art' (Mellor 2011: 91–2), and 'how surrealism provided the conditions of possibility for various aesthetic strategies to engage with wartime London' (Mellor 2011: 93). However, the figure of the bird opens a particular interest in the kinetic and figurative logic of dreams in surrealism. Hitchcock's *Spellbound* (1945) – a psychological thriller about the growing intimacy between a psychotherapist (Ingrid Bergman) and a man suffering from dissociative amnesia (Gregory Peck) – includes a dream sequence designed by Salvador Dalí. The sequence climaxes with the shadow of a bird chasing Peck's character:

> [DR. ANTHONY EDWARDES / JOHN BALLANTYNE]: Suddenly I was running. Then I heard something beating over my head. It was a great pair of wings. The wings chased me, and they almost caught up with me, as I came down the hill. (Hitchcock 1945: 1:29:17 to 1:29:26)

From the top left corner of the screen, the shadow of the wings expands until it overtakes the running character and the frame dissolves back to Gregory Peck's face, recounting the dream to Ingrid Bergman. The dark avian shape thus captures the moment of dissolve between recalled dream and the waking present, where the dream and the dreamer momentarily overlap. The speed of the avian shadow evokes both the speed of the dream (its metamorphosing images, the suspense of the final avian chase) and the speed of cinematic transitions. In surrealist art, birds make frequent appearances, from Max Ernst's human–bird hybrids to René Magritte's avian windows in the sky. Indeed, in a 1927 essay, Dalí, while comparing the possibilities of photography to poetry, used an avian image to draw these parallels between the two media:

> The [camera's] mechanism, perfect and exact, proves, by its economical structure, the joy of its poetical functioning [. . .] out of the pure crystalline objectivity of the glass there emerges a spiritual bird of thirty-six greys and forty new manners of inspiration. (Finkelstein 1998: 45–6)

The image of a bird captures the poetic possibilities of the camera implicit in its 'economical structure' and the 'crystalline objectivity' of its lens. Eighteen years later, at the end of yet another world war, the winged shadow chasing the dreamer in *Spellbound* captures the possibility of birds to convey the speed of the visual metamorphoses of surrealist cinema, while evoking wartime anxieties over flying shapes in the sky.

Indeed, these *avian noir* poems converse with the visual speed of cinema with increasing directness. These poems' visual language of birds engages in a technical and aesthetic dialogue with the film's ability to cut from one image to another in order to activate the imagination of the audience. In the new 'cinematographic poems' of the early twentieth century, the film-maker Jean Epstein, for example, identified similarities between modern poetry and cinema, noting how '[t]he film like contemporary literature accelerates unstable metamorphoses' (quoted in Marcus 2007: 2). In 'Tapestry of Great Fear' ('Tapisserie de la grande peur'), written in August 1940 in response to scenes at Dunkirk, the French surrealist poet Louis Aragon puts this cinematographic lyricism into practice. To capture the 'modern terror' of war in a pastoral landscape, the poem 'accelerates unstable metamorphoses' from 'flying fish' to a growing list of hybrid, bird-like creatures:

> And hydra-headed birds like Lerna's hydra
> What are they writing, white on blue, in the sky?
> Skimmers of earth, steel birds that stitch the air
> To the stone houses, strident comet-birds . . . (Haughton 2004: 14)
>
> [Qu'écrit-il blanc sur bleu dans le ciel celui-ci
> Hydre-oiseau qui fait songer à l'hydre de Lerne
> Écumeur de la terre oiseau-pierre qui coud
> L'air aux maisons oiseau strident oiseau-comète . . .]

In Aragon's poem, the 'steel birds' of modern warfare undergo various figurative transformations, from 'hydra-headed birds' to 'comet-birds'. In the original French, the repetition of the word 'oiseau' in three compounds – 'hydre-oiseau', 'oiseau-pierre' and 'oiseau-comète' – further foregrounds the accelerating transformations of the birds' hybrid forms. In the context of the Second World War, the rapidity of his avian metamorphoses also conveys the amorphous, movable and momentary threat of aerial warfare. Within his poem on Dunkirk's 'modern terror', the birds evoke the speed of planes and the changeable dangers in the sky.

The speed of metaphor and cinematic visual editing is therefore particularly apt to describe these dangerous aerial movements. As Susan Stewart writes, 'the work of metaphor is to draw on the material qualities of the phenomenon to reshape and reform it, to hypothesize about what had formerly been fixed' (Stewart 2011: 74). In 1940s poetry, the rapid metamorphoses of the formerly fixed birds to evoke fear over the true nature of winged shapes in the sky are both plane-like and cinematic in the speed of their visual alternations. The aesthetics of speed and 'unstable metamorphoses' underpin the operation of metaphor. These aesthetics were therefore central to the visual mechanisms of war poetry, which developed the twentieth-century dialogue with film in the 1940s. Birds, with their dynamic movement across the sky, open possibilities for exploiting the visual instability of figurative language and cinematic cuts in the war lyric.

In 1940s war poems, the rapid transformations of avian imagery are thus indebted both to the speed of planes and the accelerating visual metamorphoses familiar from the page and the screen. In his wartime poem 'The Edge of Day' (1951), Laurie Lee employs images of incendiary and high explosive bombs to describe birds at dawn as '[t]he starlike birds catch fire' and '[t]he birdlike stars droop down and die' (Keery 2020: 193). The poem's speaker also uses astral imagery reminiscent of Aragon's 'comet-birds': in Lee's poem, 'blackbirds scream with comet tails' and 'starlings, aimed like meteors, / Bounce from the garden wall' (Keery 2020: 193). However, the main part of the poem's accelerating avian transformations draws on images of electricity and fire:

> The thrush's tinder throat strikes up,
> The sparrow chips hot sparks
> From flinty tongue, and all the sky
> Showers with electric larks. (Keery 2020: 193)

The Blitz and the cinema share, with different intentions and ends, dramatic lighting effects in their artificial and intense illumination of dark spaces. Indeed, the cinematic visual language of the Blitz is evident in films like Humphrey Jennings's 1943 *Fires Were Started*, depicting firemen working in nocturnal burning London. Lee, like Jennings, had first-hand experience of both film production and the Blitz. Lee lived with Day-Lewis and the novelist Rosamond Lehmann in London during the air raids and worked in the Ministry of Information making wartime documentaries for the GPO Film Unit and the Crown Film Unit. Lee's experience of 1940s film-making and of living through the Blitz are the two salient contemporaneous contexts that underpin the light and fire effects of his rapidly changing avian imagery, from the 'electric larks' to the 'thrush's tinder throat'.

The sexually suggestive *chiaroscuro* effects of the 'great O of the sun' forming in the horizon 'with smoky, smut-red lips' to break the 'mouldering atoms of the dark' (Keery 2020: 193) in the poem are evocative of the new style of American *film noir* with its *femmes fatales* and dramatic light effects overtaking cinemas on both sides of the Atlantic in the 1940s.[1] Known for its theatrical play with dark and shadow both as an aesthetic and as a wider theme, the term *film noir* was first coined by French critic Nino Frank when this new style of cinema reached Paris in 1946: a term which, as William Luhr notes, 'translates as "black film" and refers to the darkness of the themes as well as the visuals of the film' (Luhr 2012: 20). The poetry of the 1940s shared the social and cultural contexts of the emerging *film noir*. In fact, critics often diagnose the essence of *noir* outside of film. James Naremore, for example, argues that *noir* sensibility 'was expressed through many things besides cinema', and a more representative artist of *noir*'s origins would not be a film-maker, but 'the somewhat Rimbaud-like personality Boris Vian', a surrealist author and jazz musician (Naremore 2008: 11).

While the term *film noir* is notoriously enigmatic,[2] it is a productive cultural and critical category for untangling the aesthetic implications of 1940s dominant cinematic style on the visual language of the poetry in the same period – poetry which arose from the same wartime mood of ethical and existential questioning. Frank first introduced the term *film noir* to explain how crime films had left the traditional formula of detective films behind in order to explore the reality of the 1940s, where 'atrocities, which there has never been a good reason to conceal, do exist' ('à certaines atrocités qui existent effectivement et qu'il n'a jamais servi à rien d'occulter') (Frank 1946; my translation). From the first use of the term, considering the darkness of human violence was more essential to distinguishing *film noir* than its detectives and investigative storylines. By exploring *avian noir* in lyric poetry, I want to sharpen and expand the idea of *noir* not only by examining its presence in lyric poetry, but also by investigating how *avian noir* includes rural environments, female speakers and queer voices in an aesthetic that critics have almost entirely delineated as urban and male. In 1940s rural writing, the avian, with the speed of its flight and elevated position in the sky, enables the evocation of rapid visual transformations and vertical dynamics of domination and vulnerability. Moreover, the image of the bird becomes a key poetic vehicle for accessing other elements of otherness – female, queer, rural – through its entanglement with *noir* themes of secret sexualities, mutability of dreams and nihilistic violence.

Distant and Intimate Violence

In the first critical account of *film noir*, Raymond Borde and Étienne Chaumeton identified in 1955 this new cinematic style by its 'oneiric, strange, erotic, ambivalent, and cruel' elements (Borde and Chaumeton 2002: 2). In her poem 'Death of Miss Green's Cottage' (1944), Sylvia Townsend Warner activates some of these *noir* elements by juxtaposing a rural scene of female intimacy with the distant violence of war. In the poem, a bomb has landed on a cottage where the speaker had been 'in love' (Warner 2008: 295). Its bird-like roof, '[s]loped like the tailfeathers of a sitting dove', takes flight after the explosion: '[w]ith a fluster it spread its wings of grey stone, / And went its piecemeal way into the dark' (Warner 2008: 294). The dove with 'wings of grey stone' visualises the architectural damage of a rural cottage from aerial bombardment. The speaker thus reaches for an avian image to convey how the violence of modern war destroys the affective history of an intimately shared domestic space. Indeed, the coexistence of the 'erotic' and the 'cruel' in the continuities between intimate spaces and distant violence were part of the lived experience on the British Home Front, including the entanglement of the wartime homes of Townsend Warner and her partner, Valentine Ackland, in the conflict. In 1940, an incendiary bomb fell through the roof of their home in Frome Vauchurch. In 1942, their house was selected as a machine-gun post in the event of a German landing on the Dorset coast. This intersection of the intimate domestic space with wartime organised violence underpins the 'oneiric' and 'strange' image of the stones of their home taking flight like a dove in the aftermath of bombing. The poem's *avian noir* thus enables a lyric discourse exploring how the violence of war compromises intimate spaces that protect romantic relationships between women. Like the fade-out of a cinematic scene, the avian home disappears 'piecemeal into the dark'.

Townsend Warner had, in fact, used the image of a plane to mourn the loss of female intimacy before the Second World War. In 1930 (the same year Ackland and Townsend Warner moved to live in Miss Green's Cottage), Townsend Warner's close female friend, the author Bea Howe, was getting married. Visiting Howe to say goodbye to 'her nymph', Townsend Warner saw Howe's wedding-dress 'spread in her bedroom – an enormous rectangular ghost – like an aeroplane, shrouded in tissue-paper and dust-sheets' (Harman 2015: 93). Writing about the replacement of intimate female friendship with heterosexual marriage, Townsend Warner conflates the spectral absence of a living, breathing body inside the dress with an 'aeroplane'. In 1930, planes evoked memories of the Zeppelin planes of the First World War. In 1944, in 'Death of Miss Green's Cottage', the loss of past female intimacy still reverberated within her portrayal of a bomber plane. The poem's speaker reaches for surreal aesthetics in her metaphorical juxtapositions, this time of grey stones and dove's tail-feathers, just like Townsend Warner had earlier – strangely but strikingly – connected the shape of a dress on a bed with the shape of a plane in the sky.

On the other side of the Atlantic, Elizabeth Bishop's poem 'Roosters' (1946) represents another avian evocation of aerial warfare that infiltrates women's intimate space, its *noir* even more dream-like because of its dark bedroom setting. Written after the Japanese attack on Pearl Harbor in December 1941, the speaker of the poem is at home in the early hours of the morning, using the pronoun 'we' in an intimate register that fits with the intimacy of its dusk setting. Sounds of roosters invade this interior space, as the poem turns into a layered avian allegory of aerial warfare:

> At four o'clock
> in the gun-metal blue dark
> we hear the first crow of the first cock
>
> just below
> the gun-metal blue window
> and immediately there is an echo
>
> off in the distance,
> then one from the backyard fence,
> then one, with horrible insistence,
>
> grates like a wet match from the broccoli patch,
> flares, and all over town begins to catch. (Bishop 2011: 36)

In setting the scene, the violence of war colours both the transparent openings of the home and the early morning sky associated with the privacy of sleep, as the speaker describes the morning darkness, as well as the window, as 'gun-metal blue'. As the avian description expands, the speaker in Bishop's poem uses metaphors of the metallic materials of bomber planes and their incendiary impact to evoke the birds' plumage, describing the birds' 'flame-feather' and 'metallic feathers' that 'oxidize' 'on the grey ash-heap'. The dream-like imagery maps on to the night-time of the poem as Bishop metaphorically obscures the distinctions between planes and birds. In the *avian noir* of its intimate setting and violent, invasive imagery of birds, 'Roosters' also bears similarities to Frances Cornford's poem 'Daybreak' (1954), where the speaker describes the cock crow as a 'long metallic cry of dung and dew' interrupting the speaker, who lies 'warm in bed' in the 'graying light' (Keery 2020: 38). Both Bishop and Cornford use the word 'metallic' to confuse the sound and appearance of roosters with the materials familiar from planes, interfering with the intimate boundaries of the bedroom.

For Borde and Chaumenton, as Naremore summarises in his introduction, the 'erotic treatment of violence' is essential to the new style of *film noir* (Borde and Chaumenton 2002: xix). Wartime poems by Townsend Warner, Bishop and Cornford, with their suggestive bedroom settings of the aubade and elegies for sexual and emotional histories of women, are deeply concerned with sexuality and violence in their *avian noir*. However, instead of representing female seducers or female victims familiar from *film noir*, the female voices of these poems are invested in using avian imagery in unique ways to explore the porousness of the bedroom's boundaries in the context of new and violent technologies of warfare. In 'Roosters', where the 'virile' birds 'terrorize' their hens and 'by twos . . . fight each other' in 'mid-air', lyricism itself is complicit and corrupted by its ability to perform and evoke the erotic and violent as the subconscious forces of war (Bishop 2011: 36, 38). The poem's irregular rhymes, sometimes appearing in twos with a third half-rhyme, at other times producing three perfect rhymes, breaking the satisfaction of an even pairing with a third, clamorous element, seem lyrically to parallel the 'horrible insistence' of the sounds of the cock crows and their 'echo . . . off in the distance' (Bishop 2011: 36). Mutlu Konuk Blasing reads these rhyming triplets as 'gaudy', like the roosters, insist[ing] on being heard' (Blasing 1995: 90). The wider implications of Bishop's use of avian imagery and soundscapes relate to how birds in particular become complicit in the aggression and sexual undertones of the scene, as the poem lyrically performs the invasion of the intimacy of the bedroom, implicit in the poem's aubade setting, with the 'fighting blood' of the birds heard outside (Bishop 2011: 38).

Indeed, in 1940s *avian noir* poetry, the poetic image of the bird is intertextually entangled with its associations with music and the soundscapes of lyric poetry. Comparing Keats's 'Ode to a Nightingale' (1819) to Bishop's 'Roosters' shows how wartime lyric poetry both mobilises and distorts these allusions. In Keats's 'Ode to a Nightingale', as in the opening of 'Roosters', the focus is on hearing the bird, instead of seeing it; as Susan Stewart notes, 'Keats skillfully emphasizes that he *cannot see* [. . .] The night wandering of the sleepless melancholic is carefully worked through the meandering *sound* through the darkness' (Stewart 2002: 282–3; emphasis in original). Bishop's nocturnal avian soundscapes meanwhile 'terrorize': the Romantic song of Keats's nightingale, with its 'full-throated ease', turns into the 'uncontrolled, traditional cries' floating 'deep from the raw throats' of the morning roosters:

> Deep from the protruding chests
> in green-gold medals dressed,
> planned to command and terrorize the rest,
>
> the many wives
> who lead hens' lives
> of being courted and despised;
>
> deep from the raw throats
> a senseless order floats
> all over town. A rooster gloats
>
> over our beds . . . .. (Bishop 2011: 36–7)

Instead of the Keatsian temptation of 'easeful death', the birdsong in Bishop's poem erupts as military orders leading to the mass casualties of modern warfare: leaving no home untouched, the sound of the roosters spreads through the air 'all over town', 'over our churches' and 'over our beds'. Continuing the violence of *avian noir* in the shape of another winged symbol of poetic inspiration, Pegasus, Lynette Roberts's poem 'Crossed and Uncrossed' (1944) also fuses its avian imagery with memories of the Blitz. In the poem, written after a visit to the bombed East End of London in June 1942, the firemen cling 'to buildings like swallows / flat and exhausted under the storm', while 'Pegasus melted and fell / Meteor of shining light on to a stone court / and only wing grave' (Roberts 2005: 20). Flat and exhausted, melting and falling, the winged creatures in the poem infuse the avian imagery of the bombs' impact with a fragility and vulnerability distinct from the open aggression of Bishop's birds. However, ending with the 'wing grave', Roberts's poem ties its winged symbol of poetic inspiration to similarly deadly outcomes. Across different poets' wartime writing, the avian becomes a vehicle for exploring the violent impact of aerial violence.

In 1940s *avian noir*, this complicity of lyric language is evident in the defamiliarisation of the bird as a symbol for the expressive powers of poetry. In the early 1940s verse of W. H. Auden, as in that of Bishop, poetic imagery transforms birds into mechanically engineered harbingers of death from air, mobilising the symbolic associations of the bird to draw uncomfortably close connections between lyric poetry and violence. Written between 1940 and 1942, Auden's lyrics to Benjamin Britten's choral piece 'Hymn to St Cecilia' (1942) evoke the symbol of the bird to represent the patron saint of music: the lyrics compare her to 'a black swan', who, 'as death came forth', '[p]oured forth her song in perfect calm' (Auden 2007: 278). However, the Second World War is another audible subtext in Auden's lyrics, visualising the death-bringing swan as a mechanical plane in the air. St Cecilia's swan-like music 'thundered out on the Roman air': it is 'her great engine' in death (Auden 2007: 278). 'Hymn to St Cecilia' was the final collaboration between Britten and Auden; unlike Auden, Britten felt compelled to return to England during the war and finished his composition on the voyage home across the Atlantic in April 1942, as the aerial bombing of civilians in Britain was escalating. Auden's lyrics for the composition reflect on the place of music during wartime and, by extension, the place of lyric poetry, which has its roots in music.

From Bishop to Roberts and Auden, 1940s verse thus employs *avian noir* as a figurative language to evoke aerial warfare and to suggest the complicity of lyric poetry with the darker forces that motivate war, as well as some of its more terrifying effects. In this sense, the aesthetic foregrounding of dark themes in *avian noir* is comparable to the way the word '"*noir*" in *film noir* referred as much to its visual textures as to its themes', as Luhr argues:

> [*Film noir*'s] use of *chiaroscuro* lighting and ominous darkness gave viewers the sense that they were watching more than a 'realistic' depiction of story events; they were watching those events unfold in a highly mediated visual environment evocative of the dark forces eruptive in the films. (Luhr 2012: 204).

While lyrics by Bishop, Roberts, Townsend Warner or Auden will not include the superficially familiar tropes of *film noir*, like the character of a hard-boiled detective or a fatefully seductive *femme fatale*, the threat of death from air that inspired these poems unfolds 'in a highly mediated' linguistic environment characteristic of lyric poetry, further foregrounded through the figurative confusion of birds and planes that draws attention to the transformative capabilities of poetic imagery. These lyric environments are also 'evocative of the dark forces eruptive' in war poetry: the *avian noir* of Bishop's poem – its use of the image of the bird to evoke sexuality and aggression, a dream-like atmosphere and a sense of moral ambiguity where the sun that rises could either be an 'enemy, or friend' (Bishop 2011: 40) – is part of the texture of the poem and its mechanisms for achieving its effects.

What is more important than a cross-over of tropes from *film noir* into the *avian noir* of 1940s poetry is the implication of lyric aesthetics in the fears and fantasies of aerial destruction these poems express. Moreover, although poets used bird imagery widely to describe bomber planes in the 1940s, what is specific about queer women's writing of *avian noir*, as in 'Death of Miss Green's Cottage' or 'Roosters', is the gendered dichotomy of sexuality and violence – the contrast between female intimacy and male military aggression – and the layered social, moral and personal threat that war's violent exposure of the domestic space to the outside world represented. If *noir* films like *Double Indemnity* (1944) or *The Postman Always Rings Twice* (1946) include *femme fatale* characters with sexual desires and murderous intentions the domestic confines of their marriage are unable to contain, within *avian noir* it is the state-sanctioned violence of *hommes fatales* that threaten the protective walls of women's homes and their bedrooms. While entangled with *noir* themes of sexuality and violence, as well as its dark, heightened aesthetics, the avian thus manages to access elements of otherness – female, rural, queer – in *noir* poetry that are mostly absent from accounts of *noir* cinema.

However, this gendered dichotomy between intimate interiors and the external violence of aerial assault is ambivalent and complex; women's domestic space can be equally threatening and shadowy. Townsend Warner and Ackland had already experienced aerial warfare serving in the Red Cross during the Spanish Civil War. But back home in 1938, before Britain's declaration of war against Germany, Townsend Warner described the fears that could attend their frequently pained partnership in the lead-up to the Second World War: 'In Madrid, I never felt a flutter of fear; and yet, sitting in our own kind house, under the shadow of your black moods I become an abject coward' (Bingham 2021: 127–8). Living under a sky with planes dropping bombs did not inspire as much fear as sitting 'under the shadow of your black moods'; the distinction between the threat of intimate pain and distant violence is as disturbingly unstable as the distinction between animal and mechanical shapes in *avian noir* imagery. Meanwhile, if the 'kind house' of women could be a frightening environment, the American soldiers arriving in the rural Home Front in Maiden Newton – where men had been absent for so long – appear to Townsend Warner 'intensely fragile': 'In this accumulation of metal, soldiers seemed intensely fragile, *objets du luxe*. One stared at the craftmanship of their eyelashes and fingernails, their eyelids like flower-petals' (Harman 2015 [1989]: 200). In contrast to the 'accumulation of metal', the bodies of men are intricate and delicate – vulnerable to breaking, rather than agents of violence. The flower image also appears in Muriel Rukeyser's poem 'One Soldier', which opens her 1944 collection *Beast in View* and refers to and addresses Otto Boch, a German athlete who died in the Spanish Civil War; in the poem, 'the moral flesh' of the man inspires 'poems' that 'flower from the bone' (Rukeyser 2005: 207). The flesh of soldiers, like the bodies of birds, is organic, both standing out from and blurring into the violence of mechanical warfare, obscuring the distinction between the human and the nonhuman. The avian and floral imagery in these poems allows a more complex interplay of death and danger: the *fatale* is not simply masculine or feminine, internal or external, human or nonhuman. but a permeable element – a variable x.

However, the rapid movement of birds in the sky enables a cinematic and animated evocation of these permeable locations of violence. Employing an avian allegory to explore the ambivalent and unstable boundaries between internal and external violence, Rukeyser's poem 'Mortal Girl', also from *Beast in View* (1944), retells the myth of Zeus's rape of Leda in the shape of a swan. Throughout the poem, the speaker eroticises the god's destructive descent from the air, confusing sex and violence in its avian imagery. Alluding to aerial warfare, which Rukeyser (like Townsend Warner and Ackland) had witnessed during the Spanish Civil War, the swan descends from the sky as a 'flame' and 'unthinkable light', but also as 'a shower of gold'. The moment of assault is also a moment of consummation, as the body of the female speaker assumes the fire from the sky: 'When you took me as a flame, I turned to flame . . . Within me your city burning' (Rukeyser 2005: 211–12). The following poem in the collection, 'Child in the Great Wood', builds on many of the themes and images from 'Mortal Girl', but with a changed tone around its avian imagery. Instead of the swan and its flame, both violent and erotic, external and internal, 'the mechanical birds' in the next poem appear with '[w]ing, claw and sharpened eye' (Rukeyser 2005: 213), confusing the natural and the engineered. The poem's mood is one of midnight 'anxiety', its wartime setting 'not unlike the dream' (Rukeyser 2005: 212). Rukeyser's wartime poems in *Beast in View*, like those by other women poets, display a sinister combination of aggression and sexuality, vulnerability and violence, intimacy and warfare, with shifting moral combinations and dream-like atmospheres in the night-time settings characteristic of *film noir*. At the same time, the poems' speakers destabilise the gendered nature of wartime violence by representing female interiors as dangerous, threatening and shadowy. Aerial attacks from the sky may be less frightening than the 'black moods' of a woman lover, or the flames of war internalised as a 'city burning inside' the speaker's own body: the total destruction of a city conceived inside the womb which resulted from the original bird-shaped, male assault. Thus, 1940s *avian noir* is a means of exploring the continuities and discontinuities between female intimacy and the violence of war, between sexuality and aggression, while activating women's and queer voices otherwise decentred in urban *noir* films.

Coda: The Hostile Imagination

Rukeyser's wartime lectures on lyric poetry, collected together in her 1949 *The Life of Poetry*, reveal more about her understanding of the relationship between poetry, war and the visual language of cinema in the 1940s. Alluding to the malign psychological forces of war, Rukeyser argued that poetry may be seen 'as an image of the kind of fullness that can best meet the evening, the hostile imagination – which restricts, denies, and proclaims death – and the inner clouds which mask our fears' (1996: 21). As in *film noir*, with its flirtation with the darker undercurrents of the human mind, Rukeyser explains the role of poetry in the 1940s by reflecting on its relationship to darker psychological forces: a new lyric poetry emerges from an encounter with a sinister, death-proclaiming imagination, 'inner clouds' and 'fears'. These overlapping thematic and aesthetic interests in *film noir* and Rukeyser's lyric theory are not a coincidence; she specifically exemplifies the centrality of the image to lyric poetry in cinematic terms. In the same 1940s lecture series, she identifies similarities between Hitchcock's films and lyric poetry by focusing on scenes of violence familiar from the Second World War: the explosion of a bomb and an aeroplane crash. In *Foreign Correspondent* (1940), Hitchcock conveys the crashing of a plane, according to Rukeyser, 'in the speed and economy of image that is to be found in concentrated poems' (Rukeyser 1996: 144). Meanwhile, describing the bomb explosion in Hitchcock's *Sabotage* (1936), Rukeyser is interested in distortions of everyday stable structures that 'shudder and seem to lean'; she considers how the cinematic and poetic image can convey explosion as a distortion, which 'is maximum derangement from the human being's point of view' and 'a warping of reality that becomes more unbearable as you see it more clearly' (Rukeyser 1996: 143–4). For Rukeyser, violent film scenes familiar from the Second World War exemplify the speed and the perceptual distortions of the modern poetic image.

To explain the role of imagery in poetry in the 1940s, Rukeyser thus draws on moments of cinematic suspense that recall the violence of aerial warfare, while also evoking the surrealism and deceptions of *film noir*, underpinned by an interest in aberrant psychology, with its 'warping of reality' and perceptual 'derangement'. In 1936, Elizabeth Bowen also anticipated some of these cross-media influences between films, short stories and lyric poetry. Bowen described the 'affinities' between the new forms of the short story and cinema 'accelerating together' in 'the disoriented romanticism of the age' (Bowen 1950: 38). To shape this discourse on the two new media – or 'young art[s]', as Bowen calls them – she explains their formal similarities through the aesthetics of poetry: '[p]oetic tautness and clarity' are 'essential' for both (Bowen 1950: 38). A poeticised aesthetic was also part of the *film noir* as a genre. Borde and Chaumenton, for example, considered Orson Welles's *Othello* (1952) a *film noir* not just for its 'criminal psychology of the most modern kind', but also for its 'visual poetry', both of which culminate in the murder of Desdemona (Borde and Chaumenton 2002: 81) (indeed, to describe the *noir* essence of her death scene, Borde and Chaumenton quote the French symbolist poet Stéphane Mallarmé). The contemporary film scholar Winston Wheeler Dixon also identifies *noir* through its lyrical visual aesthetics, where *noir* functions 'as a literal and figurative zone of darkness' (Dixon 2009: 3). The affinities between lyric poetry and *film noir* therefore do not lie only in their interest in distant and intimate violence and the continuities between sexuality and aggression. Their cross-influences also emerge in a distinct engagement with a style of imagery that draws on the visual language of both poetry and cinema.

However, while using the metaphorical element of darkness to provide a capacious interpretation of *noir*, which 'persists in many forms, within many genres' (Dixon 2009: 2), Dixon establishes clear limits for what the setting of *noir* can be, arguing that 'the inescapable terrain of *noir* is the city' (Dixon 2009: 3). By contrast, 1940s *avian noir* shows how *noir* aesthetics and themes are present in rural settings; indeed, they become an essential lyric environment for exploiting a confusion of categories between planes and birds. As the poems use metaphor to blur the noise of engines and the cries of birds, these poems explore the contrast and continuity between aggression and eroticism in their representations of war, with wider implications for the understanding of the power and place of metaphor and other visual mechanisms of poetry in the 1940s late modernist lyric. The avian poems of the Second World War thus also open up questions about the limitations and possibilities of *noir* and the types of voices and settings they may include. Birds, the natural inhabitants of the sky, embody the oneiric and strange elements of *noir* in these poems, assuming qualities of bombs and planes, and unlocking affinities between lyric poetry and film in 'the disoriented romanticism of the age' (Bowen 1950: 38). 1940s *avian noir* does not betray an interest in 'literal and figurative zone[s] of darkness' (Dixon 2009: 3); indeed, in Rukeyser's wartime lyric theory, poetry is matched against the 'evening', the 'hostile imagination' and its dark psychological undercurrents. The *avian noir* of women war poets, from Townsend Warner and Bishop to Roberts and Rukeyser, in Rukeyser's terms, 'meet' the 'inner clouds which mask our fears' and the 'hostile imagination' by restating ambivalent moments of intimacy and vulnerability to distant aerial aggression in rural *noir* settings. The poets are thus capable of mobilising bird images 'of the kind of fullness' that can both delve into and 'meet' the fears and fantasies of the wartime imagination, both exploit and expand the visual mechanisms of lyric poetry to reflect on the place and power of the poetic at times of war.

Works Cited

Auden, W. H. 2007. *Collected Poems*. Ed. Edward Mendelson. London: Faber and Faber.
Bingham, Frances. 2021. *Valentine Ackland: A Transgressive Life*. Bath: Handheld Press.
Bishop, Elizabeth. 2011. *Poems*. London: Chatto & Windus.
Blasing, Mutlu Konuk. 1995. *Politics and Form in Postmodern Poetry: O'Hara, Bishop, Ashbery, and Merrill*. Cambridge: Cambridge University Press.
Borde, Raymond and Étienne Chaumeton. 2002. *A Panorama of American Film Noir 1941–1953*. Trans. Paul Hammond. San Francisco: City Lights Books.

Bowen, Elizabeth. 1950 [1936]. 'The Faber Book of Modern Short Stories'. In *Collected Impressions*. Ed. Elizabeth Bowen, 38–46. New York: Alfred A. Knopf.
Dimendberg, Edward. 2004. *Film Noir and the Spaces of Modernity*. Cambridge, MA: Harvard University Press.
Dixon, Winston Wheeler. 2009. *Film Noir and the Cinema of Paranoia*. Edinburgh: Edinburgh University Press.
Finkelstein, Haim, ed. and trans. 1998. *The Collected Writings of Salvador Dalí*. Cambridge: Cambridge University Press.
Frank, Nino. 1946. 'Un nouveau genre policier: l'aventure criminelle'. *L'Ecran français*, 61 (28 August).
Harman, Claire. 2015 [1989]. *Sylvia Townsend Warner: A Biography*. London and New York: Penguin Random House.
Haughton, Hugh, ed. 2004. *Second World War Poems*. London: Faber & Faber.
Hitchcock, Alfred, dir. 1945. *Spellbound*. New York: Selznick International Pictures.
Homer. 2014. *Iliad*, Volume 1. Trans A. T. Murray. Cambridge, MA: Harvard University Press.
Keaney, Michael F. 2011. *British Film Noir Guide*. Jefferson, NC, and London: McFarland.
Keery, James, ed. 2020. *Apocalypse: An Anthology*. Manchester: Carcanet.
Leach, Jim. 2014. 'British Noir'. In *International Noir*. Ed. Homer B. Pettey, 14–35. Edinburgh: Edinburgh University Press.
Lee, Hermione. 1997. *Virginia Woolf*. London: Vintage.
Luhr, William. 2012. *Film Noir*. Chichester: Blackwell-Wiley.
MacKay, Marina. 2010. *Modernism and World War II*. Cambridge: Cambridge University Press.
Marcus, Laura. 2007. *The Tenth Muse: Writing about Cinema in the Modernist Period*. Oxford: Oxford University Press.
Mellor, Leo. 2011. *Reading the Ruins: Modernism, Bombsites and British Culture*. Cambridge: Cambridge University Press.
Miller, Laurence. 1991–2. 'Evidence for a British "Film Noir" Cycle'. *Film Criticism* 16.1–2: 42–51.
Naremore, James. 2008 [1998]. *More Than Night: Film Noir in Its Contexts*. Berkeley, Los Angeles and London: University of California Press.
Reilly, Catherine, ed. 1984. *Chaos of the Night: Women's Poetry and Verse of the Second World War*. London: Virago.
Roberts, Lynette. 2005. *Collected Poems*. Ed. Patrick McGuinness. Manchester: Carcanet.
Rukeyser, Muriel. 1996 [1949]. *The Life of Poetry*. Middletown, CT: Wesleyan University Press.
Rukeyser, Muriel. 2005. *The Collected Poems of Muriel Rukeyser*. Ed. Janet E. Kaufman and Anne F. Herzog. Pittsburgh: University of Pittsburgh Press.
Sitwell, Edith. 1940. 'Lullaby'. *The Times Literary Supplement*, 1989 (16 March): 13.
Spender, Stephen. 1942. *Ruins and Visions: Poems, 1934–1942*. New York: Random House.
Stanford, Peter. 2004. *C Day Lewis: A Life*. New York and London: Continuum.
Stewart, Susan. 2002. *Poetry and the Fate of the Senses*. Chicago and London: University of Chicago Press.

Stewart, Susan. 2011. *Poet's Freedom: A Notebook on Making*. Chicago: Chicago University Press.
Townsend Warner, Sylvia. 2008. *New Collected Poems*. Ed. Claire Harman. Manchester: Carcanet.
Woolf, Virginia. 2000 [1941]. *Between the Acts*. London: Vintage.

NOTES

1. For accounts of the development of British *film noir*, see Laurence Miller (1991–2), 'Evidence for a British "Film Noir" Cycle'; Michael F. Keaney (2011), *British Film Noir Guide*, pp.1–6; and Jim Leach (2014), 'British Noir', pp.14–35.
2. See, for example, Raymond Borde and Étienne Chaumeton (2002), *A Panorama of American Film Noir 1941–1953*, p. 2; Edward Dimendberg (2004), *Film Noir and the Spaces of Modernity*, p. 11; or Naremore (2008 [1998]: 9).

14

UNHOMING THE PIGEON: AHMED ALI'S *TWILIGHT IN DELHI*

Caroline Hovanec

Perhaps no animal cuts a more modern figure than the pigeon. The consummate city dweller, at home amid concrete and metal, able to navigate by neighbourhood landmarks, the pigeon might be seen as a *flâneur* of the skies or a cosmopolitan of the gutters. While the encroachments of human development have been a death warrant for many other wild animals, the pigeon thrives in proximity to people. It is also, however, a victim of its own success. Around the middle of the twentieth century, people began to see feral pigeons as trespassers, vagrants and squatters in urban spaces. Critics called them 'rats with wings', city officials placed bans on pigeon feeding and pest controllers used spikes, nets and poisons to deter them. They became, to quote the sociologist Colin Jerolmack, 'a "homeless" species' (2008: 89). If, as Edward Said says, 'We have become accustomed to thinking of the modern period itself as spiritually orphaned and alienated, the age of anxiety and estrangement' (1984: n.p.), the pigeon is modern in that sense too.

Like their feral cousins, domestic pigeons have also faced a decline in stature in recent decades. Once, they were the messengers of kings and generals, the pride of pigeon racers and the trophies of fanciers (Allen 2009: 102–3, 110–15). They lived in elaborate dovecotes in the medieval and early modern periods, when keeping them was a special privilege of the nobility. Then they lived in rooftop coops in the nineteenth and twentieth centuries, from which their working-class guardians entered them in homing races or flew them simply for the beauty of it (Soth 2020; Allen 2009: 122–4). Today, the few remaining enthusiasts say that these human–pigeon cultures are on the verge of extinction. Once-popular pigeon clubs have dwindled to just a few members or disappeared entirely, and the rooftops that used to hold coops are now largely empty. The remaining old guard lament that 'Where once thousands of pigeon wings filled the air . . . now silent skies reign' (Jerolmack 2013: 89). Pigeon-keeping communities are not yet entirely dead, but they are now suffused with nostalgia and melancholy.

The fate of pigeons is a complicated one. They have been remarkably successful in adapting to environments built by and for humans, but they are also remarkably vulnerable, both to a modern spatial regime whose exclusions and enclosures make them homeless, and to a modern temporal regime whose ravages upon tradition make them endangered. Because they speak to both the promise and the inhospitality of urban modernity, pigeon iconography is widespread in modernist literature, art and film. They appear in poems by Marianne Moore, Gertrude Stein and Mina Loy, and in novels by Henry Green (Pong 2019); Picasso often painted them and named his daughter Paloma, Spanish for 'dove' (Bottinelli 2004); they are recorded in Joseph Cornell's experimental films *The Aviary* (1954) and *Nymphlight* (1957), and in Elia Kazan's Hollywood film *On the Waterfront* (1954). Pigeons are also a crucial motif in Ahmed Ali's 1940 novel *Twilight in Delhi*, the subject of this chapter.

Twilight in Delhi is a family saga that narrates the decline and fall of the Nihal clan, and of Delhi's Muslim culture more generally, under British occupation. Written in English and published by Virginia and Leonard Woolf's Hogarth Press, the novel blends the modernist aesthetics of ruin (readers will hear echoes of T. S. Eliot's *The Waste Land* (1922) and the 'Time Passes' section of Woolf's *To the Lighthouse* (1927)) with an Urdu poetics of loss. It is a work about colonialism, the experience of alienation in one's own home and the threat of cultural extinction. It is also a city novel peopled by pigeons. Its protagonist, the patriarch Mir Nihal, raises domestic pigeons and takes great pride in their flying. Ali also portrays Delhi's cracks and margins as tenanted by wild pigeons, other stray animals and beggars who have nowhere else to go. *Twilight in Delhi*'s pigeon imagery channels memories of a lost precolonial past, lamentation for the waning fortunes of Delhi's Muslim gentry and a fine thread of hope for survival through the British occupation into a new, changed future.

In this chapter, I want to trace two figures through *Twilight in Delhi*, using them to draw together Ali's moment with our own, and Ali's anticolonial concerns with the environmentalist concerns of today. The first figure is 'extinction', a term which, in the novel's historical context, describes colonialism's destruction of traditions and communities, and which has become a keyword for environmentalism today, where it refers to the death of species. The second figure is 'unhoming', a word I use to evoke the material displacements imposed by colonial modernity, as well as the psychic alienation that Freud called the unhomely (*Unheimlich*) (2003 [1919]: 124). These forces of unhoming, unleashed by imperial powers, distinctly shaped twentieth-century modernity, but they are no less powerful in our current century, as climate change displaces thousands and mass extinction makes the earth unrecognisable.

Pigeons are guides for both of these figures: as they have been made out of place or obsolete in the increasing rationalisation of urban modernity, they have become symbols of homelessness and endangered ways of life in the literary imagination. Yet just as real pigeons have proven harder to eradicate than many city officials bargained for, so the symbolic pigeon is a Janus-faced bird. One is the face of intense vulnerability, the other of stubborn survival.

Extinction

The word 'extinction' comes from the verb 'to extinguish', meaning to put out, as in a fire. It has long been a synonym for death, envisioned as the extinguishing of life. Its use 'with reference to a race, family, species, etc.' to describe 'a coming to an end or dying out' appears to have come later ('Extinction, n.' 2021: n.p.). The idea of family lineages going extinct predates the idea of biological species extinction; the latter was not widely accepted as even a possibility until the discoveries of Georges Cuvier at the turn of the nineteenth century (Kolbert 2014: 23–5). The term's history leads to two observations. 'Extinction' once described an active process – someone putting something out – but that volitional thrust has largely vanished in favour of uses which imply a natural or passive dying out. And to speak of 'cultural extinction' is no more metaphorical than to speak of 'biological extinction'. In fact, both may be regarded as metaphors based on the extinguishing of a light.

In the current age of the sixth mass extinction, recovering the connotation of agency in 'extinction' is important. 'Anthropogenic extinction' is the usual term for this purpose, and it is not wrong so far as it goes. But, following the work of scholars including Kathryn Yusoff (2018), Andreas Malm and Alf Hornborg (2014), and Joanna Zylinska (2018), I take the subject which extinguishes to be not 'man' or 'the human' as a species, but specific groups of white imperialists and capitalists who orchestrate and benefit from the exploitation of the planet and its inhabitants. There is, of course, a certain level on which 'man' as species does bear responsibility for the extinction of other species; Pleistocene hunters probably wiped out some species of megafauna long before the modern age. Yet the systematic destruction of the forests and wetlands, acidification of the seas and heating of the atmosphere beyond a point compatible with survival is, as these scholars and others have shown, a project of imperial capitalism. And that project has considered Indigenous peoples, colonised peoples and the global poor just as disposable as the nonhuman animals whose habitats have been sacrificed to it.

Understanding the sixth mass extinction as one face of imperial capitalism also casts the object which is being extinguished in a different light. It is not enough to think only of species or populations being lost; rather, it is ways of life. As Thom van Dooren argues, extinction is not a singular event which happens when the last member of a species dies. It is 'a slow unraveling' of 'complex ways of life that have been co-produced and delicately interwoven through patterns of sequential and synchronous multispecies relationship' (van Dooren 2014: 58). Van Dooren uses the term 'flight ways' to describe the 'unique, evolved, and evolving way[s] of life whose passing disrupts real lived relations' (van Dooren 2014: 58). Deborah Bird Rose shows that these ways of life draw humans into their orbit too; her book *Wild Dog Dreaming* (2011) studies an Aboriginal Australian community with a long history of kinship with dingoes. Both the humans and their dogs have been threatened with extermination by white settlers, and Rose's research makes it clear that what is at stake in the dingo's possible extinction is the destruction of an entire Aboriginal cosmos. Cases such as these support the idea that 'extinction is an inherently and inextricably *biocultural* phenomenon' (Rose et al. 2017: 5).

For Ahmed Ali and his cohort of Indian anticolonial writers, extinction would have been understood predominantly as a cultural threat facing peoples under colonial occupation. The 'anglicisation' of culture which would 'convert Indians to brown Englishmen' by destroying their languages, religious institutions and cultural practices was an explicit policy of British colonial rule (Ali 1994 [1940]: xiii). Resistance to this policy was pathologised; after the 1857 anticolonial rebellion in Delhi and subsequent British retaliation, the British began to speak of the 'Backward Muslim', a figure intransigently attached to the religion and traditions of his or her ancestors (Padamsee 2011: 32). The idea that Indian Muslims were trapped in the past, unable to adapt to modern times, and therefore bound for cultural extinction, was a common trope in the colonial period (Padamsee 2011: 32). Urdu literature of the post-1857 period (though significantly more complicated in its relationship to time and history) also developed a poetics of 'memorialisation' and 'loss' (Padamsee 2011: 33). And anticolonial activists, including the future Prime Minister Jawaharlal Nehru, made references to the temporal dislocation and gradual extinction of Indo-Muslim culture during the 1930s (Padamsee 2011: 27–9). Ali echoed these extinction tropes when he wrote, in the 1993 introduction to *Twilight in Delhi*, 'my purpose was to depict a phase of our national life and the decay of a whole culture, a particular mode of thought and living, now dead and gone already right before our eyes' (Ali 1994: xix). The characters and the narrator in the novel frequently lament the diminished state of their city's culture, contrasting it with the past glories of the Mughal Empire.

However, Alex Padamsee argues that there is more than meets the eye to this rhetoric of cultural extinction. He shows that Ali and other nationalist writers used the trope of Muslim moribundity not simply in a descriptive or predictive way, nor even in a nostalgic way. Rather, Ali figured extinction as a 'means of passage', and mourning as a way of 'opening up' to a 'postnational South Asian future' (Padamsee 2011: 29, 30). Padamsee reads Ali's poetics of extinction as fashioning forms for rebirth, rather than just mimetically representing a longing for the past. It is a reading that helps to make sense of the metaphor of rebirth Ali used to conclude his 1993 introduction to the novel: 'Life, like the phoenix, must collect the spices for its nest and set fire to it, and arise resurrected out of the flames' (Ali 1994: xx).

Twilight in Delhi's pigeons are part of the rhetoric of Muslim cultural decadence within the novel, yet they also contribute to the new subjectivities which Padamsee sees as emerging from the novel's mourning. The novel's protagonist, Mir Nihal, is an avid pigeon-keeper, and his birds serve an important social function: they make him feel accomplished and important among other men of his class. He competes with his neighbours in 'the pigeon game', the object of which is to get your flock to collect and bring home more of your opponents' birds. In one such scene, Mir Nihal succeeds in capturing some of his neighbour's dappled pigeons, and then he 'smile[s] to himself, a smile of satisfaction and victory' (Ali 1994: 16). This moment, which occurs early in the novel, shows Mir Nihal at the top of his game, taking pride in his flock's performance. Later, when he goes to buy some more pigeons, he participates again in a community of fliers who tell stories and debate over bird breeds as a way to socialise with each other and to jostle for status. Flying his pigeons gives Mir Nihal a sense of dignity and social embeddedness, and his hobby marks him as 'a typical feudal gentleman' who tries to keep the old traditions alive (Ali 1994: 28). In the sixteenth-century court of the Emperor Akbar, the 'breeding and training' of pigeons was regarded as an 'art form' and, until the fall of the Mughal Empire in 1857, pigeon-keeping was a 'prestigious pastime of the gentry in Delhi' (Frembgen and Rollier 2014: 55).

The literary critic Judith Brown echoes this notion of pigeon-keeping as an art, comparing it to the ghazal, qawwali and other poetic forms within the novel. Mir Nihal's pigeons, she writes, 'function as a living reminder of a Mughal pastime and passion raised to the heights of art, at once animal and art form' (Brown 2018: 840). Ali's painterly description of the birds supports her claim: 'They were ever so many, black ones and white ones, red ones and blue ones, dappled and grey, beautiful wings stretched out in flight' (Ali 1994: 15). There is more to this description than its stylised language, though. Its syntax is a curious echo of two other points in the novel – first when Ali is describing beggars, and again when he is describing kites:

> They were ever so many, young ones and old ones, fair ones and dark ones, beggars with white flowing beards and beggars with shaved chins . . . there

were beggars in tattered rags and beggars in long robes reaching down to their knees. There were beggars in patched clothes and beggars in white ones. (Ali 1994: 14)

The sky was full of kites, black kites and white kites, purple kites and blue. They were green and lemon-coloured, red and peacock blue and yellow, jade and vermilion . . . (Ali 1994: 22)

Why this repetition? For some readers, it might seem like a moment of (quite literal) local colour, in keeping with the novel's function as 'a guide to Delhi for Englishmen' (Askari 1998/9 [1949]: 245). Alternatively, we might follow Padamsee in seeing these moments as drawing on, and ultimately emptying out, the Urdu poetic genre of the *sharh-ashob*, in which 'linguistic wordplay' is of higher priority than 'literal referents' (Padamsee 2011: 39). My own reading of this triptych falls somewhere in between the ethnographic and deconstructive interpretations. The repetitions draw a connection between three cultural practices that, the novel suggests, defined the old Delhi – pigeon-keeping, kite-flying and generosity to beggars. Yet while these descriptions still, in my view, have some referential function, Padamsee is not wrong to see a Derridean absence within them as well (2011: 40–1). Their syntax creates a sense of plenitude and variety – so many colours, so many kinds! – yet the images also carry an undercurrent of poverty. The beggars in their tatters come first, and their lack haunts the subsequent two descriptions of pigeons and kites. Even the moment of apparent fullness is also already a moment of emptying out.

Mir Nihal's flock is riven with this sense of loss, and the birds' fate mirrors the fate of Delhi and of the family in its waning days. From their very first appearance in the first chapter of the novel, the pigeons are vulnerable. The novel's initial action occurs in the Nihal home, late at night. The family hears 'a sudden fluttering of wings' from the pigeon house, and when Mir Nihal goes to investigate, he finds a snake in the loft and grabs it and kills it (Ali 1994: 9). Only one bird is killed – a loss that Mir Nihal grieves, but not nearly as disastrous as it might have been. But the early signs of corruption are already present. The snake is already in the home. It does not seem much of a stretch to read this serpentine invader as a symbol for the British occupiers, who, at the novel's outset, are already in India. Indeed, the chapter juxtaposes the discovery of the snake with a moment in which Mir Nihal scolds his son for wearing English boots – the implication being that decadent forms of Anglicisation have already infiltrated his own house.

Throughout the rest of the novel, the pigeons continue to be menaced, first by a heat wave, then by a cat and finally by the First World War, which drives up the price of grain and makes pigeon-keeping prohibitively expensive for many residents. Ali writes of this last event, 'And one of the most outstanding characteristics of Delhi was threatened with extinction and death. But still there were enough people who flew the pigeons and kicked up their usual tapage' (Ali 1994: 155). One day, Mir Nihal hears that his mistress is sick; he rushes out of his house to visit her, only to arrive, too late, at her deathbed, and accidentally leaves the door of his pigeon loft open. When he returns home the next morning, he finds that a cat has decimated his birds. All at once, in his sorrow, he decides to retire from work and quit pigeon-keeping. Mir Nihal's depression here is both personal and cultural. To give up his pigeons is to give up on a tradition that was a source of pride and one of his few remaining connections to the past.

Note, though, the strange contradiction in the sentences quoted above. Pigeon-keeping is almost dead, and yet, 'still there were enough people who flew the pigeons and kicked up their usual tapage'. This formulation – the culture is dying, yet some tradition or person still lives – pervades the novel and is, I would argue, its signature expression. Judith Brown claims that *Twilight in Delhi*'s dominant aesthetic is that of the *afterlife*, 'a realm of persistence and in persistence, survival, even as that survival depends upon a prior death' (Brown 2018: 826). The people, traditions, art forms and animals of the novel have, she argues, a strange power of survival which is marked by their 'failure to die even when death has made its claim' (Brown 2018: 826). Brown suggests that these hesitant images of persistence are a way for the novel to point to, even if it cannot yet describe, what happens 'after the apocalypse of empire is complete' (Brown 2018: 826).

The last pigeon of the novel, a grey bird glimpsed on its final page, flies at twilight, '[plying] its lonely way across the unending vastness of the sky' (Ali 1994: 200). Twilight would seem, on the surface, to be an image of extinction – the extinguishing of the sun's light, the end of the day, the end of a culture. Yet Ulka Anjaria offers a very different interpretation of the meaning of twilights in Ali's oeuvre. Bringing Ali's 1931 play *The Land of Twilight* into conversation with *Twilight in Delhi*, Anjaria uncovers a 'powerful resignification of the concept of twilight' in his work, where it becomes not a symbol of death but rather 'the topos for a utopic, future land' (Anjaria 2011: 202). For Ali, she suggests, the dusk is a surrealistic image but also a political one, signalling a kind of liberation. One suspects it might also be Ali's rejoinder to the old imperial slogan. The sun does indeed set on the British Empire, and when it does, it will be left to the survivors to build something new.

Unhoming

Domestic pigeons like Mir Nihal's are bred for their homing ability, a remarkable capacity for navigation that uses sun position, olfactory stimuli and landmark recognition to allow pigeons to steer their way home. Homing is also a rich and evocative aesthetic symbol, and it is the central figure, and title, of writer and pigeon-keeper Jon Day's (2019) recent memoir. The chapters of *Homing* meditate on how people and pigeons make homes of their dwelling places, and Day revisits the contradictory forms that homeland politics took in the twentieth century, from the fascists' blood-and-soil ideology to Simone Weil's defence of rootedness. Day is also interested in modern and contemporary forces of unhoming, including exile, gentrification and housing scarcity. Cycling along the River Lea for a pigeon release, he witnesses houseboats, encampments and graffiti reading 'Give us Homes!' – all signs of 'London's housing crisis', a movement of evictions, pricing out and redevelopment that has made the city a speculator's dream while pushing its poor to the margins (Day 2019: 174).

In his exploration of unhoming as the hidden underbelly of dwelling, Day turns to Freud. Freud was, he points out, quite literally exiled from his homeland at the end of his life, as he moved to Britain in flight from the Nazis. Freud was also eternally interested in psychic alienation; as Day puts it, 'One of his most radical ideas was to acknowledge that people could become unhomed within themselves: that they could be unmoored from the familiarity of their own minds without ever going anywhere' (Day 2019: 20). The aesthetic expression of this, for Freud, was the *Unheimlich*, or unhomely, more commonly translated as the uncanny. Freud describes the unhomely as 'that species of the frightening that goes back to what was once well known and had long been familiar' (Freud 2003: 124). For Freud, the homely and the unhomely (*Heimlich* and *Unheimlich*) converge in meaning until they are no longer distinguishable: the home, the domestic and the familial are the sources of unhomely experience.

One of Freud's key examples of unhomely phenomena is 'repetition of the same thing' (Freud 2003: 143). He writes that under certain circumstances, repetition creates a sense of 'helplessness we experience in certain dream states' (Freud 2003: 144). In a passage that has become famous, Freud describes walking around an unfamiliar town in Italy, finding himself in a red-light district, hurrying away and getting lost, only to find himself returning to that same district over and over again. This inadvertent return disturbs him with its uncanniness. Freud proposes that the unhomely quality of such repetitions can be traced back to the unconscious '*compulsion to repeat*' (Freud 2003: 145; emphasis in original). We can see this compulsion not just in *Twilight in Delhi*'s characters, but in the narrative itself, which, like a melancholic patient, rehashes its losses over and over. The novel is structured on a 'principle of repetition, or a series of repetitions that amounts to a narrative aesthetic' (Padamsee 2011: 38), and Freud's work sheds light on how these repetitions evoke a sense of unhomeliness.

The unhomely is also an environmental atmosphere to which ecocritical theorists have recently turned to describe the experience of dwelling on an earth irrevocably changed by global warming and mass extinction. Amitav Ghosh identifies this critical trend and ties the uncanniness of climate change – the bizarre weather events, the pervasive sense of dread – to humans' remembrance of the nonhuman presences with which we share the world. He writes that the observable changes in the earth 'are not merely strange in the sense of being unknown or alien; their uncanniness lies precisely in the fact that in these encounters we recognize something we had turned away from [in the Enlightenment]: that is to say, the presence and proximity of nonhuman interlocutors' (Ghosh 2016: 30). Jennifer Fay, meanwhile, writes that under global warming, the changed earth

> raises to a new level of disorientation what the uncanny for Freud summons forth: the feeling that home, homeliness, and all that is familiar have been transformed into their dreadful opposites, that the home has been replaced with an artificial substitute that resembles it. (Fay 2018: 3)

Twilight in Delhi's urban and domestic spaces are deeply unhomely, reflecting Mir Nihal's experience of dwelling under British colonialism. It is not that he has been geographically exiled (although Indian Muslims were temporarily removed from Delhi following the 1857 rebellions) – he remains in the city and in the old family compound for the entirety of the novel. Rather, the city around him has changed until it is barely recognisable. As Padamsee points out, Ali was writing in a moment in which Indo-Muslims felt their position in India was increasingly liminal and unstable; if a sense of existential homelessness suffuses the novel, 'Homelessness, in this context, might well be the point' (Padamsee 2011: 36). The novel's unhomeliness speaks both to its 1930s political context and to the twenty-first-century context from which I read it today. Its eerie depictions of Delhi during a heat wave and in the aftermath of the First World War and the 1918 influenza pandemic resonate particularly strongly for readers today, who have witnessed the world made uncanny by colonialism, climate change and Covid-19.

Consider, first, the novel's description of the summer of 1911. The city is preparing for King George V's coronation ('a new and foreign king'; Ali 1994: 65), while it is also experiencing an extreme heat wave that kills and sickens people, plants and animals, including the aforementioned pigeons. Ali's prose connects this heat wave not only to the 1911 imperial ceremony, but also back to 1857, the year of the rebellion that was eventually crushed by the British colonial army:

> It was the terrible summer of nineteen hundred and eleven. No one had experienced such heat for many years. Begam Jamal complained that she had never known such heat in all her life. Begam Nihal said she had never experienced such a summer ever since 1857, the year of the 'Mutiny'. The temperature rose higher and higher until it reached one hundred

> fifteen in the shade. From seven in the morning the loo began to moan, blowing drearily through the hopeless streets. The leaves of the henna tree became sered and wan, and the branches of the date palm became coated with sand. The dust blew through the unending noon; and men went out with their heads well-covered and protected. The pigeons flew for a while and opened their beaks for heat. The crows cawed and the kites cried and their voices sounded so dull.
>
> . . .
>
> Fires broke out every now and then. At such times the sky was made red with the flames that shot up from the burning earth. Men died of sunstroke; and even birds were not immune from the destructive influence of the sun, and many pigeons died. (Ali 1994: 65)

This passage, though firmly located in history, reads as uncanny in its prescience today, as India faces more and more extreme heat, drought and other (un)natural disasters due to climate change. It also introduces several images of what Ghosh calls 'nonhuman interlocutors' – the wailing wind, the dried-up date palm, the lamenting birds – which Ali will repeat at later moments in the novel, evoking uncanniness through repetition as well as through inhuman presences.

Twilight in Delhi's surreal city is a place in which nature itself has become unnatural. In the passage quoted above, this making-unhomely is connected metonymically to colonial despoliation, through the references to the 1857 mutiny and the 1911 coronation. When Ali repeats these images later in the book, the connection to imperialism is figured more forcefully as a causal one. In 1918, the year of world war and global pandemic, unnatural disasters hit Delhi once again, turning it into a 'city of the dead' (Ali 1994: 171). Once again, Ali writes of a 'terrible' summer:

> The summer of 1918 was more terrible than the summers of the previous years. The sky was of a coppery hue throughout the day, and at night the stars were hidden behind the sand which rained down from the sky, and the loo did not stop. It howled more fiercely than before as the City Walls had been demolished and the wind could now blow free from the mountainous wastes outside the city. It howled through the empty streets and in the narrow by-lanes and bazars. The dogs moaned and wept at night as if afraid of death, and the cats, whose numbers had surprisingly decreased, were quiet and subdued. (Ali 1994: 169)

Many of the uncanny images of the 1911 passage recur here – the wind and sand, the moaning animals, the wrong-coloured sky, the atmosphere of death. This time, the city environment has been made unhomely not just by 'nature', but by the British forces which destroyed the walls in the period after 1857, leaving the streets unprotected. Like the 1911 passage, this one presages the sort of unseasonal disasters that regularly happen today, this time with a stronger sense of causality. Climate change, too, is an environmental unhoming driven by imperial capitalism.

This unhomely atmosphere becomes more and more oppressive as the novel progresses, and it reaches an apex in the last scene. These final paragraphs return, for the last time, to the images of dust, a hostile sky and crying animals. They clearly show a conjunction of deathliness, exile and unnatural nature that crushes Mir Nihal within his own house:

> Mir Nihal lay on his bed more dead than alive, too broken to think even of the past. The sky was overcast with a cloud of dust, and one grey pigeon, strayed from its flock, plied its lonely way across the unending vastness of the sky. The oven which had been built in the morning to boil the water for the dead was full of ashes and dust. On the bare top of the date palm sat a kite and shrilly cried for a while and flew away, leaving the trunk, ugly and dark, standing all alone against the sky.
>
> His days were done and beauty had vanished from the earth. [. . .] Yet he was still alive to mope like an owl, and count his days, at the mercy of Time and Fate.
>
> He lay on the bed in a state of coma, too feelingless to sit up or think. The sun went down and hid his face. The rooks cawed and flew away. The sparrows found their nest. And night came striding fast, bringing silence in its train, and covered up the empires of the world in its blanket of darkness and gloom . . . . (Ali 1994: 200)

Mir Nihal is consumed by the loneliness of being exiled in his own home, in his own city, even in his own mind. Yet he, like the birds which return here – the pigeon, the rooks, the kite – is somehow 'still alive'. They are all marked for death, but the life has not quite been extinguished from them; they hold on by a thread to the inhospitable world. As Brown says, Mir Nihal is 'kin to that lonely pigeon – vulnerable, doomed, yet persistent – against the vast reach of the sky' (Brown 2018: 842).

What exactly is ending here? Night blots out 'the empires of the world', not just the extinct Mughal Empire but, one must suppose, the British Empire as well. In 1940, in the ferment of Indian nationalism, this must have been a politically charged statement, yet the question of what comes after imperial occupation was not yet resolved. There is a sad irony to the author's personal history here. Seven years after *Twilight in Delhi*'s publication, India became independent, but at a terrible cost to Ali. After Partition, which divided British India into a majority-Hindu India and a majority-Muslim Pakistan, he was exiled from the former, 'and for no other reason than because I was Muslim' (Ali 1994: xviii). He spent the rest of his life based in Pakistan, where *Twilight in Delhi* was banned (Ali 1994: xix). In his 1993 introduction to the novel (penned just weeks before his death), Ali compared his own banishment to that of his grandparents, who were driven out of Delhi in 1857 when the British commandeered the city. 'Yet while their exile was temporary,' he wrote, 'mine was permanent, and the loss not only of home and whatever I possessed, but also my birthright, when I had no hatred of any caste or creed in my heart' (Ali 1994: xviii).

Ali's biography places him among the millions of people displaced from their homes in the mid-twentieth century. It is an important reminder that unhoming is not only a psychic or metaphorical experience, but a literal and political one. As Said wrote, 'to think of the exile informing [modernist] literature as beneficially humanistic is to banalize its mutilations, the losses it inflicts on those who suffer them, the muteness with which it responds to any attempt to recognize it as "good for us"' (1984: n.p.). The material dimensions of unhoming are especially crucial to recognise now that we are, in the twenty-first century, on the brink of another massive wave of unhoming, this time due to climate change. Sea level rise alone may displace as many as 50 million Indians who live on islands and along coasts (Ghosh 2016: 89), not to speak of the millions of potential climate refugees distributed throughout the rest of the world. It is not only humans whose homes are being destroyed, but also wild animals, at least those species that have managed to survive the past several centuries of habitat destruction wrought by mining, deforestation and plantation agriculture. The challenge for the environmental justice movement is how to imagine, and then materialise, something better than bare survival for those who are among these numbers of the vulnerable.

Politics, Ecology, Literary Modes

When Ali brought the manuscript of *Twilight in Delhi* to Britain in 1939, he ran into difficulties. He had managed to line up a publisher – the Hogarth Press – but the printers refused to print the novel because they were concerned about its potentially subversive (that is, anticolonial) content. Ali found support in E. M. Forster, who used his Bloomsbury connections to persuade Harold Nicholson, the official censor (and husband of Vita Sackville-West), to approve the book, and it finally came out in 1940 (Brown 2018: 829). The novel that was almost too radical for the British printers, however, was not radical enough for Ali's colleagues in India. In the 1930s, Ali had belonged to the All-India Progressive Writers Association (AIPWA), a group of young writers involved with leftist and anticolonial causes. The preferred literary mode of the AIPWA was social realism (Anjaria 2011: 186–9). Its members rejected art-for-art's-sake forms of aestheticism in favour of activist, socially engaged writing, which they believed would help in the project of Indian independence (Brown 2018: 828). When

Twilight in Delhi came out, many of these writers were disappointed by its apparent nostalgia for the Mughal past, regarding it as 'not befitting a committed Marxist' (Anjaria 2011: 189). Ali defended himself from these charges of political quietism, saying, 'They called it a reactionary thing, nostalgia of the past, a glorification of feudalism, forgetting that, as a writer, I had my technique, that I had evolved my own symbols, my own methodology' (qtd in Brown 2018: 829–30).

This critical debate over the novel's politics is caught up with questions of reading and of literary modes. Should it be read as a work of realism, mimetically describing a particular class located in a particular historical moment? Or is it better understood as a symbolist text (as Ali suggests in the quote above), a theatrical performance (as Anjaria argues), or a meta-literary translation and reframing of Urdu poetic forms (as Padamsee and Brown read it)? To whom does *Twilight in Delhi*'s nostalgia belong – the characters, the narrator or the author? And is nostalgia necessarily reactionary?

My intent here is less to resolve these questions than to note their remarkable similarity to the questions driving debate within ecological writing and ecocriticism today. Specifically, there is the problem of how to conceptualise and write about the sixth extinction and the destruction of wild animals' habitats. Some critics defend the public mourning of lost species and lost ecologies, as a way of insisting on the value of nonhuman life (Heise 2016: 32–5) or as a rhetorical act which uses the pathos of loss to bring together a political collective (Taylor 2019: 58–9). Others argue that a turn to the emotions of sadness and anxiety amounts to a passive form of resignation or an individualised retreat from politics. Anna Kornbluh, for instance, warns against mistaking 'the sylvan beatification of extinction rites' for political action, arguing that 'the dispersive poetics of attunement to the material world, romancing precarity, and dissolving binaries entice us to lie down' when, in fact, we need to 'stand up' (2020: 771, 775). Rithika Ramamurthy (2021), meanwhile, critiques the inward turn of recent climate anxiety novels. She proposes that the 'polyvocal' perspective of big, collective climate change novels (Kim Stanley Robinson's 2020 *Ministry for the Future* being her key example) is more befitting of the ecological politics we need.

There can be little doubt that the sixth extinction, global warming and climate displacement are problems of power, not of individual feelings, and many others have written persuasively of the need to attack these problems at their root, which is a system of imperial capitalism that extracts profits from nature and people while leaving them vulnerable to an increasingly unstable planetary climate. A more difficult question to answer is what these insights mean for literature and literary criticism. It might be that Ali's critics were right, that *Twilight in Delhi* gives too much space to a dying aristocracy and not enough space to an emerging revolutionary movement, that it is too in love with nostalgia and grief and languorous beauty to be of any use for leftist politics. It might be that social realism, big casts of characters and utopian imaginaries, not romantic elegy or modernist interiority, are the literary properties best suited to Ali's political moment and to our own.

Yet *Twilight in Delhi* has at least one lesson that is vital for ecological, anticolonial and anticapitalist politics today. That is, the end is not the end, and 'too late' is the only place left to begin. If two degrees of warming is catastrophic, four degrees is far worse and six worse still. If a thousand species lost is a tragedy, perhaps another thousand extinctions can still be averted. If 20 million people lose their homes to climate disaster, that is no reason to become resigned to the displacement of 200 million. 'And life went on . . .', Ali tells us again and again (Ali 1994: 31, 147, 159). That last 'grey pigeon' that 'plied its lonely way across the unending vastness of the sky' might well be the Angel of History, the winds of progress 'caught in his wings', watching as the on-going catastrophe 'keeps piling wreckage and hurls it in front of his feet' (Benjamin 1968 [1940]: 257). History just keeps happening; the sun keeps rising every morning and, as Ali shows, being marked for death is no escape. The only choice left, once you accept that life goes on, is to keep fighting for more life.

Works Cited

Ali, Ahmed. 1994 [1940]. *Twilight in Delhi*. New York: New Directions.
Allen, Barbara. 2009. *Pigeon*. London: Reaktion Books.
Anjaria, Ulka. 2011. 'Staging Realism and the Ambivalence of Nationalism in the Colonial Novel'. *NOVEL: A Forum on Fiction* 44.2 (Summer): 186–207.
Askari, Mohamed Hasan. 1998/9 [1949]. 'A Novel by Ahmed Ali'. Trans. Carlo Coppola. *Journal of South Asian Literature* 33/4.1–2: 243–54.
Benjamin, Walter. 1968 [1940]. 'Theses on the Philosophy of History'. In *Illuminations: Essays and Reflections*. Trans. Harry Zohn, ed. Hannah Arendt, 253–64. New York: Schocken Books.
Bottinelli, Giorgia. 2004. 'Pablo Picasso: Dove'. *Tate*, February. Available at: <www.tate.org.uk/art/artworks/picasso-dove-p11366> (last accessed 15 July 2022).
Brown, Judith. 2018. 'Ahmed Ali and the Art of Languishing'. *ELH* 85.3 (Fall): 823–46.
Day, Jon. 2019. *Homing: On Pigeons, Dwellings and Why We Return*. London: John Murray.
'Extinction, n.'. 2021. *OED Online*. Oxford University Press.
Fay, Jennifer. 2018. *Inhospitable World: Cinema in the Time of the Anthropocene*. New York: Oxford University Press.
Frembgen, Jurgen Wasim and Paul Rollier. 2014. *Wrestlers, Pigeon Fanciers, and Kite Flyers: Traditional Sports and Pastimes in Lahore*. Karachi: Oxford University Press.
Freud, Sigmund. 2003 [1919]. *The Uncanny*. Trans. David McLintock. New York: Penguin Books.
Ghosh, Amitav. 2016. *The Great Derangement: Climate Change and the Unthinkable*. Chicago: University of Chicago Press.

Heise, Ursula K. 2016. *Imagining Extinction: The Cultural Meanings of Endangered Species*. Chicago: University of Chicago Press.

Jerolmack, Colin. 2008. 'How Pigeons Became Rats: The Cultural–Spatial Logic of Problem Animals'. *Social Problems* 55.1 (February): 72–94.

Jerolmack, Colin. 2013. *The Global Pigeon*. Chicago: University of Chicago Press.

Kolbert, Elizabeth. 2014. *The Sixth Extinction: An Unnatural History*. New York: Henry Holt.

Kornbluh, Anna. 2020. 'Extinct Critique'. *The South Atlantic Quarterly* 119.4: 767–77.

Malm, Andreas and Alf Hornborg. 2014. 'The Geology of Mankind? A Critique of the Anthropocene Narrative'. *The Anthropocene Review* 1.1: 62–9.

Padamsee, Alex. 2011. 'Postnational Aesthetics and the Work of Mourning in Ahmed Ali's *Twilight in Delhi*'. *Journal of Commonwealth Literature* 46.1: 27–44.

Pong, Beryl. 2019. 'Henry Green's Pigeons'. *Modernism/Modernity PrintPlus* 4.3 (6 December). Available at: <modernismmodernity.org/articles/pong-henry-greens-pigeons> (last accessed 15 July 2022).

Ramamurthy, Rithika. 2021. 'Personal Hell: The Climate Anxiety Novel'. *The Drift* 4 (6 May). Available at: <www.thedriftmag.com/climate-anxiety> (last accessed 15 July 2022).

Rose, Deborah Bird. 2011. *Wild Dog Dreaming: Love and Extinction*. Charlottesville: University of Virginia Press.

Rose, Deborah Bird, Thom van Dooren and Matthew Chrulew. 2017. *Extinction Studies: Stories of Time, Death, and Generations*. New York: Columbia University Press.

Said, Edward. 1984. 'Reflections on Exile'. *Granta* (1 September). Available at: <granta.com/reflections-on-exile> (last accessed 15 July 2022).

Soth, Amelia. 2020. 'Our Long-Running Love Affair with Pigeons'. *JSTOR Daily* (19 November). Available at: <daily.jstor.org/our-long-running-love-affair-with-pigeons/> (last accessed 15 July 2022).

Taylor, Jesse Oak. 2019. 'Mourning Species: In Memoriam in an Age of Extinction'. In *Ecological Form: System and Aesthetics in the Age of Empire*. Ed. Nathan Hensley and Philip Steer, 42–62. New York: Fordham University Press.

van Dooren, Thom. 2014. *Flight Ways: Life and Loss at the Edge of Extinction*. New York: Columbia University Press.

Yusoff, Kathryn. 2018. *A Billion Black Anthropocenes or None*. Minneapolis: University of Minnesota Press.

Zylinska, Joanna. 2018. *The End of Man: A Feminist Counterapocalypse*. Minneapolis: University of Minnesota Press.

15

THE MODERNIST JELLYFISH

Rachel Murray

In December 1999, the Filipino island of Luzon, home to 40 million people, was suddenly plunged into darkness. As the hours passed, many began to suspect that a military coup was under way against the then President, Joseph Estrada, whose sharp decline in popularity during his first year in office had resulted in a tense and uncertain political atmosphere. Others blamed the blackout on an early outbreak of the millennium bug, an anticipated computer system flaw that caused widespread global panic in the final months of 1999. In actual fact, the power cut was caused by another bug in the system – namely, an influx of creatures dubbed the cockroaches of the sea (Stone 2011). With rumours of sabotage swirling, the government issued a statement explaining that a swarm of jellyfish had been sucked into the cooling system of a major power station north of Manila, causing the island's entire electricity grid to shut down. Seven hours and fifty truckloads of jellyfish later, power was finally restored.

This act of industrial vandalism will be familiar to anyone acquainted with reports of the so-called jellyfish apocalypse, or 'jellygeddon'. In recent years, jellyfish have frequently been cast as the 'durable and opportunistic inheritors' (Giggs 2018: n.p.) of marine ecosystems that are suffering from the effects of overfishing, eutrophication, acidification, habitat modification and species translocation (Richardson et al. 2009; Gershwin 2013). Vast blooms of jellyfish – such as those that immobilised the nuclear aircraft carrier the USS *Ronald Reagan* in 2006 – have been interpreted by some scientists as a sign of impending ecological collapse, prompting visions of future seas teeming with gelatinous life forms and very little else. As Rebecca Giggs notes, images of a sea gummed up with the bodies of jellyfish ('transformed into something like an aspic terrine') appear to signal a return to 'the ocean of pre-history' – a reversion of life to the 'primordial soup' (Giggs 2018: n.p.).

We might read these jellyfish blooms as a form of atavistic symptom, the resurfacing of the slimy evolutionary past that modern society had sought to expunge from itself, but which returns once more to clog up its inner workings. We might even be tempted to celebrate these cnidarian invaders as a force capable of arresting the industrial systems that have manufactured the present environmental crisis. Yet this narrative is complicated by the fact that these blooms are a by-product, as well as a beneficiary, of these very same systems: 'jellyfish and human industrialization', writes Eva Hayward, work 'hand in tentacle to alter and destroy ocean ecosystems' (Hayward 2012: 180). The problem, in other words, is that their environmental destructiveness is inextricably tied up with ours; there can be no clean separation between us and them. There is even a suggestion that '"we" – or, at least the excrement of twenty-first century civilization – are becoming jellyfish' (Johnson 2016: 65).

The uncertain status of jellyfish blooms as 'tangled objects' (Latour 2004: 24), which trouble the distinction between human and nonhuman, subject and object, nature and culture, has posed a particular challenge for blue humanities scholarship. Surveying recent work in this area, Brandon Jones notes that the jellyfish appears to have generated an 'antagonistic split [. . .] between arguments for the posthumanist ethics its radically inhuman body and perceptual apparatus afford, and arguments against its destructive agency in league with human industry, pollution, and extraction' (Jones 2019: 485).[1] In this chapter, I argue that the concept of trauma may offer a way out of this impasse, enabling us to think of jellyfish in ways that are neither wholly negative nor positive, but which instead foregrounds their capacity to disrupt our categories of sensemaking in ways that are at once destructive and potentially useful. Trauma, as the literary scholar Roger Luckhurst notes, violently opens up passageways 'between systems that were once discrete', making 'unforeseen connections that distress or confound' (Luckhurst 2008: 3). Dominic LaCapra has also written of trauma's ability to 'disarticulate relations', deconstructing binary oppositions and confusing self and other (LaCapra 2001: 21), while fellow trauma theorist Cathy Caruth has spoken of its 'peculiar temporality', the sense 'that the past it foists upon one is not one's own' (Caruth 1996: 171).

Modernist literature, it has often been noted, is particularly well suited to representing the effects of trauma: its epistemic ruptures, its techniques of fragmentation, its recursive rhythms and unruly temporality (Armstrong 2005: 92–5; Henke 2010). Modernist writing also exhibits a response to jellyfish that bears many of the hallmarks of trauma. In the interwar prose of Wyndham Lewis and H.D., images of jellyfish are suggestive of an encounter with the world that ruptures the boundaries of the human subject, unsettling the distinction between self and other, inside and outside, human and nonhuman. This chapter proposes that such encounters, while distressing, open up passageways between systems that were thought to be discrete, establishing points of contact between human subjects and seemingly distant or 'alien' forms of life (Alaimo 2013: 154).

The first part of this chapter focuses on the novelist and critic Tom McCarthy's essay collection *Typewriters, Bombs, Jellyfish* (2017), which uncovers surprising threads of connection between modernist aesthetics, trauma and the figure of the jellyfish. The second part examines the work of Wyndham Lewis, arguing that jellyfish in his writing appear representative of an 'authentic shock' (Lewis 1937: 85), which, in puncturing the subject's psychic defences, also serves to galvanise their aesthetic procedures, resulting in significant moments of textual rupture. The final part of the chapter examines H.D.'s interwar prose, contending that jellyfish are bound up in her thinking about the enabling possibilities of trauma, which, in breaking the mind apart, also brings it into contact with parts of the world – as well as aspects of the self – that would otherwise remain out of reach.

McCarthy, Jellyfish and the 'Traumatic Real'

Tom McCarthy's modernist proclivities have been well documented, including by the author himself. In a 2010 interview, he argued that 'the task for the contemporary novelist is to deal with the legacy of modernism', adding: 'I'm not trying to be modernist, but to navigate the wreckage of that project' (McCarthy qtd in Purdon 2010: n.p.). McCarthy's novels repeatedly circle back to the central themes and preoccupations of high modernism, including the impact of new media technologies on subject formation, the imbrication of humans and machines, the importance of recovered memory, and the materiality of language. Examining the influence of modernist aesthetics on his writing, Justus Nieland has even gone as far as describing McCarthy's response to modernism as a form of traumatic re-enactment, arguing that his work 'linger[s] in the remains of [modernism's] most fecund catastrophes, which are also those of the twentieth century itself' (Nieland 2012: 570).

McCarthy's critical writing is also marked by a tendency to linger in the wreckage of modernism. Written between 2002 and 2016, his essay collection *Typewriters, Bombs, Jellyfish* covers a range of modernist authors and themes, from Joycean scatology to dodgem jockeys as modern-day 'Angels of History' (McCarthy 2017: 207). The essays tend to proceed 'associatively, digressing, jolting, looping' (61): 'Semi Connected Thoughts', for instance, moves at breakneck speed from Japanese conceptual art to fly-fishing to exploding windowsills, while 'Nothing Will Have Taken Place' takes us from Stéphane Mallarmé to Don DeLillo to the virtuosic footwork of Zinedine Zidane. Reading the collection in its entirety, however, it is possible to identify a recurring preoccupation with the relationship between trauma and aesthetic innovation. This is particularly evident in an essay entitled 'Get Real, or What Jellyfish Have to Teach Us About Literature'. Drawing on Jacques Lacan's account of 'the Real' as that which is 'unassimilable by any system of representation' and which 'always returns to the same place' (Lacan qtd in McCarthy 2017: 69), McCarthy defines the 'real' in literature as an event which '*happens*, or forever threatens to do so, not as a result of the artist "getting it right" or overcoming inauthenticity', but rather through a sudden mishap or accident, a 'radical and disastrous eruption within the always-and-irremediably inauthentic' (69; emphasis in original). To illustrate this idea, McCarthy borrows a beastly analogy from the French surrealist writer Michel Leiris, who compares the writer to a toreador:

> Imagine a bullfight without the bull: it would comprise a set of aesthetic manoeuvres, pretty twills and pirouettes and so forth – but there'd be no danger. The bull, crucially, brings this to the party; and for Leiris, *that's* the real: the tip of the bull's horn. [. . .] If a matador is gored, the bullfight, its entire spectacle, suddenly shudders to an appalled halt; what the bull's horn brings to the party is not just danger but also the very thing that would catastrophically interrupt the party, plunging craft into chaos. (1984: 68–9; emphasis in original)

Here, the force of the 'real' is located in a violent encounter with a nonhuman creature – an encounter that may be orchestrated by the bullfighter-cum-writer, but which remains, to a large extent, out of their control. The threat posed to art by the 'real' is presented as a form of traumatic interruption or break in proceedings, a sudden intercession that 'would involve the violent rupture of the very form and procedure of the artwork itself' (68). Yet crucially, this threat of collapse is also what galvanises the artwork, prompting a set of thrilling aesthetic manoeuvres as the writer dallies dangerously with the point – the sharp tip – 'at which the writing's entire project crumples and implodes' (70).

Leiris's bullfight analogy draws on his experiences of attending corridas during the 1930s and 1940s, where he was captivated by the way that the matador 'reveals the whole quality of his style just when he is most threatened' (Leiris 1984: 155). For McCarthy, however, the 'real' is exemplified by a more recent form of creaturely interruption. Recalling a 2013 article in the *New York Review of Books* that reported that jellyfish 'were taking over the planet' (1), McCarthy suggests that these 'giant agglomerations' (1) of medusae threaten the emergence of something akin to the 'real' insofar as they resemble a kind of traumatic material that remains unassimilable within any system: 'there's a critical mass of goo in circulation; and it's coming back, lodging, sticking' (2). McCarthy's reading may help to explain why the phenomenon of jellyfish blooms appears so anxiety-inducing. To recall Lacan on the 'Real', the sight of these gooey masses seems to terrorise us with the prospect of returning 'to the same place', or rather a place of evolutionary and ontological sameness, in which there is no longer any distinction between self and other, or between primordial origins and apocalyptic endings.

Significantly, though, McCarthy goes on to suggest that jellyfish, as well as representing something akin to the 'traumatic real', may also provide a 'decisive model' (74) for how this 'real' might be registered by the literary text. This idea is suggested to him by an image from Sigmund Freud's *Beyond the Pleasure Principle* (1920), which contains one of the most influential early theories of trauma. In it, Freud envisages the mental apparatus, in its most basic form, as 'an undifferentiated vesicle of living substance that is susceptible to stimulation' (Freud 1961a: 20). In order to protect itself from the 'enormous energies at work in the external world', Freud writes, the mind has been forced to evolve a 'protective shield against stimuli' (21). Trauma constitutes a breach in this protective shield that floods the mind with large amounts of stimulus, preventing it from 'mastering [. . .] them, so that they can be disposed of' (24). McCarthy is struck by Freud's description of this mental apparatus as, at its core, 'an organ for receiving stimuli' (20), observing how his account of the psyche draws on 'earliest marine life, germ-plasms and protozoa' (McCarthy 2017: 73). At one point in *Beyond the Pleasure Principle*, Freud describes how 'the unconscious stretches out feelers [. . .] towards the external world and hastily withdraws them as soon as they have sampled the excitations coming from it' (Freud 1961a: 22). Responding to this tentacular image, McCarthy argues that the mental apparatus appears 'jellyfish-like', equipped as it is with 'feelers' that stretch out into the surrounding world (73).

Identifying the recurrence of this image in another of Freud's essays, written five years later, McCarthy goes on to note:

> What's most astonishing for me, about these medusozoan images, is the fact that Freud houses them in a longer meditation on a reusable notepad . . . [on which] inscriptions may be both kept and erased. This is his decisive model for consciousness and, ultimately, for life. (74)

McCarthy is referring to Freud's account of the mental apparatus as a form of 'mystic writing pad' or slab of dark resin (the unconscious) covered with a sheet of wax paper and celluloid (the perceptual system) on which messages can be written (Freud 1961b: 230–1). Though the writing on these surface layers can easily be erased, most notably by trauma, Freud suggests that 'the permanent trace of what was written is retained upon the wax slab and is legible in suitable lights' (Freud 1961b: 230). What McCarthy finds remarkable about this analogy is the suggestion that the formation of consciousness and the act of writing originate in a primal experience of trauma which remains unavailable to the conscious mind, yet which the subject is compelled to return to and repeat. 'We are all writing machines,' McCarthy concludes, 'jellyfish included. In fact, jellyfish especially' (74).

In order to illustrate this notion, McCarthy turns to a passage from Alexander Trocchi's late modernist novel, *Cain's Book* (1960), which combines images of plasmic receptiveness, trauma, and the act of writing. In a 'strangely Proustian sequence of perception' (74), the narrator watches a man urinating in an alley and suddenly feels 'like a piece of sensitive photographic paper, waiting passively to feel the shock of impression', a 'mute hunk of appetitional plasm . . . run through by a series of external stimuli' (Trocchi qtd in McCarthy 2017: 74–5). This urinary stream-of-consciousness is suggestive of a modernist experience of trauma ('the shock of impression', 'run through by stimuli') that returns the mind to its original, primordial function as an organ for receiving stimuli. It is also suggestive of an experience of trauma that is realised – or 'hypostatized' (75) – through the act of writing, with McCarthy proposing that the artwork is capable of bearing the traces of what the conscious mind cannot, acting as an 'organ for receiving stimuli' (Freud 1961a: 20). Crucially, however, this act of inscription is one that renders the human subject 'passive', reducing the artist to a mere receiver of impressions – a 'mute hunk of appetitional plasm' (Trocchi qtd in McCarthy 2017: 74–5). Though he does not press the point, McCarthy's reading aligns modernist experimentation with a state of relinquished mastery, in which the mind, run through by stimuli, finds itself jolted back to a state of primal receptiveness, which is also the scene of writing.

For McCarthy, then, the jellyfish represents the force of 'the real', understood as a traumatic impact from without, as well as a form of writing that is capable of registering and giving shape to its deleterious effects. McCarthy identifies a similar tendency at work in the writing of the American avant-garde novelist Kathy Acker, whose writing – like H.D.'s and Lewis's – is 'awash' (255) with jellyfish. McCarthy proposes that her cnidarian figures are associated with the recursive force of trauma that breaks in, nightmarishly, to the subject's consciousness in the form of an actual nightmare of 'huge jellyfish glop' (Acker qtd in McCarthy 2017: 256) chasing her down the street. At the same time, Acker's bodies are also '*like* jellyfish quivering as pulse signals reach them through a viscous sea', channelling and acting as 'hubs or mainstays in a world of viscerally connected continuity' (257; emphasis in original). Her jellyfish, he notes, '*both* anchor this world *and* serve as its disjecta' (257; emphasis in original). McCarthy's reading provides a crucial insight into the dual function of the jellyfish in modernist writing. In the work of Lewis and H.D., images of jellyfish are representative of a trauma from without, be it the volatile energies of the masses in Lewis's 'The War-Crowds' (1937), who resemble a 'jellyfish' in the eyes of his protagonist (Lewis 1937: 89), or the 'jelly-fish like' spectacle of 'modernity' (H.D. 1968: 174) that obstructs the subject's thought processes in

H.D.'s *Palimpsest* (written 1926, published 1968). At the same time, jellyfish also signify a mode of consciousness, as well as a mode of writing, that is capable of registering the impact of these traumatic incursions on its quivering surface, transforming trauma's deleterious effects into a form of creative energy.

To examine the gelatinous imagery of Lewis and that of H.D. alongside one another may appear somewhat perverse. After all, the jellyfish in Lewis is generally understood by critics to be a derided figure of aesthetic over-refinement, feminine fluidity and a chaotic melting of the self into others, representing all that is antithetical to the 'dry, hard' classicism (Hulme 2003: 75) of the men of 1914. The writing of H.D., by contrast, is thought to celebrate 'precisely those "jellyfish attributes" that Lewis attacks'; her gelatinous imagery aspires towards an extension rather than a reinforcement of the self through art, reaching out tentacularly towards networked 'forms of sensation distributed between persons rather than owned' (Armstrong 2005: 94; Crown 1995: 229–31). Re-examining their work in relation to McCarthy's account of the 'traumatic real', however, it becomes possible to identify important similarities, as well as key differences, between their medusozoan figures, which threaten the breakdown of the self at the same time as they promise to extend it in new directions.

Beyond jelly[f]ish diffuseness: Wyndham Lewis

Towards the end of Lewis's novel *Tarr* (1918), the titular protagonist finds himself suddenly 'overwhelmed' by powerful feelings of lust for the Russian–German aristocrat Anastasya Vasek. Fearing the loss of autonomy that might come with submitting to his desire (he has already spent much of the novel unsuccessfully attempting to wrest himself free from another romantic attachment), Tarr attempts to rationalise his feelings:

> He was a man. = A woman was a lower form of life. Everything was female to begin with. A jellyish diffuseness spread itself and gaped on the beds and in the bas-fonds of everything. Above a certain level of life sex disappeared, just as in highly organised sensualism sex vanishes. And, on the other hand, *everything* beneath that line was female. = Bard, Simpson, Mackenzie, Townsend, Annandale – he enumerated acquaintances below the absolute line and who displayed a lack of energy, permanently mesmeric state, and almost purely emotional reactions. He knew that everything on the superior side of that line was not purged of jellyish attributes; also that Anastasya's flaccid and fundamental charms were formidable, although the line had been crossed by her.[2] (Lewis 1996: 313–14)

The misogyny in this passage is palpable: there is little room for ambiguity in statements such as 'A woman was a lower form of life,' which seem designed to provoke 'almost purely emotional reactions' in the reader. ('On a first reading of *Tarr*,' notes Min Wild with commendable restraint, 'occasionally one gasps a little'; 2004: 25.) But what is often overlooked about these lines, and what might become clearer upon subsequent readings, is the way that Anastasya's 'jellyish' presence quickly confounds Tarr's 'absolute line', collapsing the binary distinctions that he has sought to erect (with obvious phallic implications) between himself and his soon-to-be lover. 'He *knew*', the narrator concedes, 'that everything on the superior side of that line *was not* purged of jellyish attributes' (314; emphasis added). The repetition of 'everything' over the course of this passage suggests that no one, including Tarr, is safe from this sensual spread; amid the ooze, categories meld and blur as the 'jellyish' other becomes indistinguishable from the 'jellyish' self.

Tarr's psychic disintegration is compounded by the form of the text, which highlights the growing 'diffuseness' of his thought processes in the face of his 'mentally outsize[d]' (Lewis 2010: 278) adversary. Definitive statements – 'He was a man' – give way to run-on sentences formed of increasingly unstable clauses that qualify and contradict themselves ('on the other hand', 'although'). The description of Anastasya's charms first as 'flaccid', then conversely 'fundamental' and finally 'formidable' gives the impression of someone leafing desperately through a thesaurus in search of the right adjective. Tarr's efforts to categorise and thus impose a degree of control over his amorphous rival appear destined to fail, leaving him with a sense of 'personal defeat' (314). The end of narrative – which leaves Tarr flip-flopping back and forth between Anastasya and his previous lover, Bertha, unable to escape the clutches of either – might be read as the ultimate triumph of these 'jellyish attributes' over Tarr's aesthetics of the 'armoured hide' (299).

I want to suggest that this sense of being thwarted by a jellyish adversary is something that Lewis's writing at some level invites, though it is hardly welcomed by his male subjects. Time and time again, Lewis's protagonists hit up against a gelatinous entity that serves to breach their psychic defences, throwing the author's 'externalist' (Lewis 1964: 121) vision of self and art into disarray.[3] At the same time, however, Lewis's writing appears to be galvanised by this force of disruption, repeatedly returning to that which threatens to implode the rigid systems of thought that he has sought to put in place. This is particularly apparent in a story entitled 'The War-Crowds', which appeared in his memoir *Blasting and Bombardiering* (1937). In the story, Lewis hands over the controls of the narrative to a fictional avatar named Cantleman, who, after hearing news of the outbreak of the First World War, travels down to London to witness the fervour of the wartime masses surging in waves of 'excited violence' (Lewis 1937: 94) through the city streets. Cantleman decides to undertake a series of 'crowd-experiments' (84), immersing himself within this sea of bodies before withdrawing to a nearby café to make notes on what he has experienced. In an image that recalls Freud's analogy of the mystic writing pad, Cantleman presents himself as a kind of medium, or *'planchette'* (85), who is able to receive messages from the crowd: 'he was inviting [them] to inscribe their ideas on the tabula rasa he offered them' (86).

Cantleman's desire to 'express the meaning of this crowd' (83) suggests that his agenda is ultimately one of mastery. Indeed, an earlier version of this text, which appeared in the second issue of Lewis's short-lived periodical *Blast*, was entitled 'The Crowd Master' (Lewis 1915). Like the Baudelairean figure of the dandy, who seeks to immerse himself in the urban masses before rushing off to record the impressions that assail him, Cantleman aspires to a kind of 'cold detachment' (Baudelaire 2010: 10) as he embarks on his crowd experiments, exhibiting an unshakeable determination to remain unmoved. Yet something happens that is not part of his plan. After sinking 'like a diver' into the depths of the crowd, Cantleman receives an unexpected jolt:

> Suddenly he experienced a distinct and he believed *authentic shock*. It could only come from the crowd! Evidently he had penetrated its mind – the cerebration of this jelly-fish! Hence the sting! He had received his first novel sensation. What was it exactly – could he define it? (85; emphasis in original)

The passage suggests an inversion of the power dynamics that Cantleman has sought to establish in relation to this amorphous mass of bodies: though he is eager to convince himself that he is the one doing the penetrating, really it is he who is on the receiving end of the crowd. Rather than emerging victorious from this conquest, Cantleman is left with the nagging sense that he has 'lost ground, even', finding himself unable 'to obtain a valuable note' from the mass of 'confusing' (85) messages that are pressing in upon him. As is often the case in Lewis's writing, Cantleman's internal conflict is presented in gendered terms as a struggle to assert one's masculinity against the threat of feminine fluidity. At one point he likens the crowd to suffragettes, before wondering: 'Are the crowds then female? . . . Is this opposition correct?' (82). As the modernist scholar Tom Holland points out, it becomes increasingly clear over the course of the text that it is not simply a mastery of the male over the female, but rather 'a weird cnidarian androgyny holds sway' (Holland 2007: 160).

Lewis's jellyfish imagery, then, seems designed to thwart the oppositional structures that his male subjects have put in place to obtain a degree of mastery over their surroundings. The presence of these gelatinous figures also hints at an experience of trauma, in which the overwhelming of the individual's psychic defences by the 'enormous energies' at work in the outer world results in a confusion of subject and object, self and other, inside and outside. Significantly, though, Lewis's writing indicates that this sense of shock also serves to galvanise his protagonist's thought processes, resulting in an unsettling but potentially generative state of confusion. Following his 'jellyish' encounter with Anastasya, the narrator of *Tarr* remarks: 'an entirely different world was revealed, that demanded completely new arguments' (Lewis 1996: 315). Similarly, after receiving his 'first novel sensation' from the jellyfish crowds, Cantleman rushes to a local bar to record his impressions in his notebook. His initial excitement is, admittedly, short-lived. After jotting down a series of disjointed thoughts, the narrator remarks flatly: 'He read [them] through. He was disappointed. He returned to the crowd' (Lewis 1937: 86). Cantleman repeats this process several times without success, with his notes resembling a mass of incoherent ideas, snatches of quotation and polyglot fragments. Yet while Cantleman may not be able to recognise the significance of these disconnected fragments, as readers we can begin to piece together a narrative about an ailing heroic figure, Lord Nelson, whose former glories fade from his mind as he lies face down in the mud: 'The wild ass stamps o'er his head' (88). What resembles an incoherent mass of words to Cantleman ('it had no meaning'; 84) may provide a source of insight into the puncturing of his controlling narrative, as well as the heroic fictions that preside over the conflict.

The fragments (or 'disjecta', to recall McCarthy) that Cantleman produces following his encounter with the 'cerebration of this jelly-fish' (85) suggest a characteristically modernist recognition of the potential of trauma to release the world from known categories. It is also indicative of an experience of shock that threatens to collapse the self, as well as the artwork, as an autonomous entity. Here and elsewhere in Lewis, the jellyfish appears to signify an encounter with the 'traumatic real' that results in moments of productive textual rupture, in which readers are afforded a glimpse of that which cannot be accommodated into the subject's oppositional systems, and which threatens instead to overwhelm them.

Jellyfish Consciousness: H.D.

In H.D.'s interwar writing, images of jellyfish are also bound up with an experience of trauma. In her novella *Kora and Ka* (1934), the shell-shocked businessman John Helforth describes a sensation of having a 'monster' in his brain known as Ka, 'who is a jellyfish, who is a microbe, who is (a specialist all but told me) a disease' (H.D. 1996: 29). While experiencing a mental breakdown, the protagonist of H.D.'s novel *Her* (written 1927, published 1984) likens the splitting of her psyche to the image of jellyfish giving birth by 'breaking apart, separating themselves from themselves' (H.D. 1984: 118). These two examples are suggestive of the ways in which trauma in H.D.'s writing tends to resemble a destructive force from without – a form an invasive entity or 'disease' – as well as a more generative phenomenon that serves to expand and multiply the self in unforeseen ways. For H.D., the jellyfish seems to offer a way of bringing together these two aspects of trauma – the destructive and the generative – without resolving the split between them.

This is particularly evident in 'Murex: War and Postwar London (circa A.D. 1916–1926)', which forms the middle section of H.D.'s novel *Palimpsest* (1926). The narrative focuses on the resurfacing of American poet Raymonde Ransome's traumatic recollections of the First World War following her return to London almost a decade later. Early on in the text, Raymonde receives a surprise visit from an old acquaintance, known as Ermy, whose unannounced arrival results in an 'unexpected breach in her armour' (H.D. 1968: 122) as her suppressed memories of the conflict come flooding back. The distant beat of soldiers marching towards the troop trains at Waterloo begins to echo through her mind ('Feet – feet – feet'; 175) as Raymonde recalls:

> face upon face, impression upon impression, and all of modernity (as she viewed it) was as the jellied and sickly substance of a collection of old colourless photographic negatives through which gleamed the reality . . . Antiquity showed through the semi-transparence of shallow modernity like blue flame through the texture of some jelly-fish-like deep-sea creature. Modernity was unfamiliar and semi-transparent and it obscured antiquity while it let a little show through, falsified by the nervous movement of its transparent surface. (179)

There are echoes here of Cantleman's encounter with the 'cerebration of this jelly fish' in 'The War-Crowds', with the mass of faces generating a multitude of impressions that threaten to overwhelm the onlooker. This 'jellied and sickly substance' also resembles a form of 'disjecta' (McCarthy 2017: 257), with H.D. likening this psychic phenomenon to a material substance that returns to jam up the workings of Raymonde's consciousness, obscuring and falsifying her reality. At the same time, H.D. hints that this obstruction – or viscous 'overlayer' – may also be what permits access to a deeper reality: the 'texture' of this 'jellyfish-like creature' serves to 'let a little show through'. What initially appears to be a barrier becomes the medium *'through which* gleamed the reality' (179; emphasis added). Consequently, while the jellyfish body may function as a creative obstruction, hindering Raymonde's efforts to gain access to the 'defined and clarid' (122) medium of verse, it also enables a fuller apprehension of her wartime experiences by allowing glimmers of something akin to the 'real' to show through.

The figure of the jellyfish, then, helps H.D. to imagine a form of consciousness, as well as a mode of writing, that is capable of registering, and giving shape to, trauma's belated effects. This idea is explored at length in *Notes on*

Thought and Vision (written 1919, published 1982), an experimental essay which H.D. wrote shortly after experiencing a series of traumatic wartime events, including the birth of her stillborn child during an air raid, as well as the deaths of her father and brother. The text was inspired by a hallucinatory episode that H.D. underwent while visiting the Scilly Isles with her partner Bryher in the summer of 1919. During this episode, her mind took on 'an almost physical character', resembling 'a jellyfish, placed over and about the brain . . . fluid yet with definite body':

> I should say – to continue this jelly-fish metaphor – that long feelers reached down and through the body, that these stood in the same relation to the nervous system as the over-mind to the brain or intellect.
>   There is, then, a set of super-feelings. These feelings extend out and about us; as the long, floating tentacles of the jelly-fish reach out and about him. They are not different material, extraneous, as the physical arms and legs are extraneous to the gray matter of the directing brain. The super-feelers are part of the super-mind, as the jelly-fish feelers are the jelly-fish itself, elongated in fine threads. (H.D. 1982: 18–19)

The striking similarity between H.D.'s jellyfish metaphor and Freud's medusoid image of the psyche is all the more surprising given that H.D. wrote this text prior to the publication of *Beyond the Pleasure Principle* in 1920. For both writers, the idea of the jellyfish seems to have offered a way of describing and giving shape to the effects of trauma in the immediate aftermath of the First World War. In contrast to Freud's, however, H.D.'s jellyfish analogy suggests a more enabling understanding of trauma, which, in breaching the subject's psychic defences, establishes new connections between mind and body, self and world, human and nonhuman.

In the above passage, H.D. is describing a form of aesthetic experience in which no form of sensory information is deemed 'extraneous' to any other, with mental and physical experience standing 'in the same relation' to one another. Significantly, however, this state of expanded consciousness is one that remains largely confined to the realm of possibility. 'If we had the right sort of brains,' she writes, 'we would receive a definite message from that figure, like dots and lines [. . .] received and translated into definite thought by another telegraphic centre' (26). The conditional nature of this statement – '*if* we had' – combined with the modal auxiliary 'would' is consistent with the speculative tone of her essay more generally. Here, as in 'The War-Crowds', the jellyfish appears to represent a message which may be 'received' but not 'translated' into something 'definite', holding out the promise of meaning even as it defies writerly attempts to grasp its significance. For both H.D. and Lewis, the jellyfish provides a means of registering the deleterious effects of trauma at the same time as it exposes the limitations of the human mind as an apparatus for receiving and translating its pulse signals into legible signs.

In contrast to Lewis, however, H.D.'s writing appears much more invested in the notion that by embracing the destructive effects of trauma, rather than attempting to remain shielded from them, it may be possible to gain access to a deeper layer of consciousness, as well as a heightened connectedness to the surrounding world. In a story set shortly after the First World War, the protagonist likens her mind to 'platinum sheet-metal over jelly-fish', adding: 'The inside could get out that way, only when the top was broken' (H.D. 2011: 39). This is a far cry from Tarr's efforts to conceal 'the naked pulsing and moving of the soft inside of life' behind 'the armoured hide' (Lewis 1996: 299). Here and elsewhere in H.D.'s writing, the jellyfish appears central to the notion that while trauma may expose the mind to harm, it also puts the subject in touch with parts of the self, as well as parts of the world, that would otherwise remain out of reach. Insofar as it threatens to disarticulate the self, it also promises to reconfigure it anew.

By paying close attention to the jellyfish, it becomes possible to develop a new awareness of the value of trauma for modernist writers, which, in breaching the modern subject's psychic defences, also serves to pierce the boundary separating inside from outside, self from other, human from nonhuman. The medusoid imagery of H.D. and Lewis may also enable us to recognise the significance of traumatic experience more generally: from Lewis's 'jellyish diffuseness' to H.D.'s 'super-feelers', these texts hint at trauma's capacity productively to undermine ideas of human separation and exceptionalism, presenting significant moments of slippage between human subjects and medusoid entities. With this in mind, the writing examined by this chapter may help us to think differently about our present environmental crisis, in which jellyfish have come to stand once more as a disturbing manifestation of the psychic and physical trauma wrought by capitalist modernity. By gathering together these gelatinous examples from H.D and Lewis, as well as from McCarthy and Freud, it becomes possible to envisage a response to jellyfish blooms that moves beyond narratives of invasion or apocalyptic endings, and which recognises the potential of these life forms to jolt, or sting, us into a new awareness of ourselves in relation to others. If, as Johnson suggests, the fear is that '"we" – or, at least the excrement of twenty-first century civilization – are becoming jellyfish', then the disruptive power of these blooms may also be ours to draw on.

Works Cited

Alaimo, Stacy. 2013. 'Jellyfish Science, Jellyfish Aesthetics: Posthuman Reconfigurations of the Sensible'. In *Thinking With Water*. Ed. Cecilia Chen, Janine McLeod and Astrida Neimanis, 139–64. Montreal and Kingston: McGill-Queen's University Press.

Armstrong, Tim. 2005. *Modernism: A Cultural History*. Cambridge and Malden, MA: Polity Press.

Baudelaire, Charles. 2010. *The Painter of Modern Life*. Trans. P. E. Charvet. London: Penguin.

Berwald, Juli. 2017. *Spineless: The Science of Jellyfish and the Art of Growing a Backbone*. New York: Riverhead Books.

Caruth, Cathy. 1996. *Unclaimed Experience: Trauma, Narrative and History*. Baltimore: Johns Hopkins University Press.

Crown, Kathleen. 1995. 'H.D.'s Jellyfish Manifesto and the Visible Body of Modernism'. *Sagetrieb* 14.1–2: 217–41.

Farrier, David. 2019. 'Swerve: The Poetics of Kin-Making'. In *Anthropocene Poetics: Deep Time, Sacrifice Zones and Extinction*, 89–124. Minneapolis: University of Minnesota Press.

Freud, Sigmund. 1961a. *Beyond the Pleasure Principle*. Trans. James Strachey. New York and London: W. W. Norton.

Freud, Sigmund. 1961b. 'A Note upon the "Mystic Writing Pad"'. In *The Ego and the Id and Other Works*. Trans. James Strachey, 227–32. London: Hogarth Press.

Gershwin, Lisa-Ann. 2013. *Stung! On Jellyfish Blooms and the Future of the Ocean*. Chicago: Chicago University Press.

Giggs, Rebecca. 2018. 'Imagining the Jellyfish Apocalypse'. *The Atlantic* (January/February). Available at: <https://www.theatlantic.com/magazine/archive/2018/01/listening-to-jellyfish/546542/> (last accessed 15 July 2022).

Hayward, Eva. 2012. 'Sensational Jellyfish: Aquarium Affects and the Matter of Immersion'. *differences: A Journal of Feminist Cultural Studies* 23.3: 161–96. DOI:10.1215/10407391-1892925

H.D. 1968. *Palimpsest*. Carbondale and Edwardsville. Southern Illinois University Press.

H.D. 1982. *Notes on Thought and Vision and The Wise Sappho*. San Francisco: City Lights.

H.D. 1984. *Her*. London: Virago.

H.D. 1996. *Kora and Ka*. New York: New Directions.

H.D. 2011. 'Pontikonisi (Mouse Island)'. In *Narthex and Other Stories*, 29–40. Toronto: Bookthug.

Henke, Suzette. 2010. 'Modernism and Trauma'. In *The Cambridge Companion to Modernist Women Writers*. Ed. Maren Tova Linett, 160–71. Cambridge: Cambridge University Press.

Holland, Tom. 2007. *Ezra Pound, Wyndham Lewis, and the Crowd*. Doctoral Thesis, University of York.

Hulme, T. E. 2003. 'Romanticism and Classicism'. In *T. E. Hulme: Selected Writings*. Ed. Patrick McGuinness, 68–83. New York: Routledge.

Johnson, Elizabeth. 2016. 'Governing Jellyfish: Eco-Security and Planetary "Life" in the Anthropocene'. In *Animals, Biopolitics, Law: Lively Legalities*. Ed. Irus Braverman, 59–78. Abingdon and New York: Routledge.

Jones, Brandon. 2019. 'Bloom/Split/Dissolve: Jellyfish, H.D., and Multispecies Justice in Anthropocene Seas'. *Configurations* 27.4 (Fall): 483–99. Available at: <https://doi.org/10.1353/con.2019.0032> (last accessed 15 July 2022).

Kime Scott, Bonnie. 1989. 'Jellyfish and Treacle: Lewis, Joyce, Gender and Modernism'. In *Coping with Joyce: Essays from the Copenhagen Symposium*. Ed. Morris Beja and Shari Benstock, 168–79. Columbus: Ohio State University Press.
LaCapra, Dominic. 2001. *Writing History, Writing Trauma*. Baltimore: Johns Hopkins University Press.
Latour, Bruno. 2004. *Politics of Nature: How to Bring the Sciences into Democracy*. Trans. Catherine Porter. Cambridge, MA: Harvard University Press.
Leiris, Michel. 1984. *Manhood: A Journey from Childhood into the Fierce Order of Virility*. Trans. Richard Howard. Chicago and London: University of Chicago Press.
Lewis, Wyndham. 1915. 'The Crowd-Master'. *Blast* 2 (July): 94–102.
Lewis, Wyndham. 1930. *Satire and Fiction*. London: Arthur Press.
Lewis, Wyndham. 1937. *Blasting and Bombardiering*. London: Eyre & Spottiswoode.
Lewis, Wyndham. 1964. *Men Without Art*. New York: Russell & Russell.
Lewis, Wyndham. 1996. *Tarr: The 1918 Version*. Ed. Paul O'Keeffe. Santa Rosa, CA: Black Sparrow Press.
Lewis, Wyndham. 2010. *Tarr*. Ed. Scott Klein. Oxford: Oxford University Press.
Luckhurst, Roger. 2008. *The Trauma Question*. Abingdon: Routledge.
McCarthy, Tom. 2017. *Typewriters, Bombs, Jellyfish: Essays*. New York: New York Review of Books.
Monroe, Melissa. 2020. *Medusa Beach*. New York: New York Review of Books.
Nieland, Justus. 2012. 'Dirty Media: Tom McCarthy and the Afterlife of Modernism'. *MFS: Modern Fiction Studies* 58.3 (Fall): 569–99. Available at: <https://doi.org/10.1353/mfs.2012.0058> (last accessed 15 July 2022).
Purdon, James. 2010. 'To Ignore the Avant-Garde is Akin to Ignoring Darwin'. *The Guardian* (1 August). Available at: <https://www.theguardian.com/books/2010/aug/01/tom-mccarthy-c-james-purdon> (last accessed 15 July 2022).
Richardson, Anthony J., Andrew Bakun, Graeme C. Hays and Mark J. Gibbons. 2009. 'The Jellyfish Joyride: Causes, Consequences and Management Responses to a More Gelatinous Future'. *Trends in Ecology and Evolution* 24.6: 312–22. Available at: <https://doi.org/10.1016/j.tree.2009.01.010> (last accessed 15 July 2022).
Stone, Richard. 2011. 'Massive Outbreak of Jellyfish Could Spell Trouble for Fisheries'. *Yale Environment 360* (13 January). Available at: <https://e360.yale.edu/features/massive_outbreak_of_jellyfish_could_spell_trouble_for_fisheries> (last accessed 15 July 2022).
Wild, Min. 2004. 'The Elation of Objects: Adorno and Wyndham Lewis's *Tarr*'. *Wyndham Lewis Annual* 11: 18–31.

Notes

1. For recent critical examinations of jellyfish blooms see Alaimo (2013); Berwald (2017); Farrier (2019); Gershwin (2013); Giggs (2018); Hayward (2012); Johnson (2016); Jones (2019); and Richardson et al. (2009).
2. As Melissa Monroe points out in her recent poem-essay *Medusa Beach*, 'many recent scholars' have mistakenly replaced the word 'jellyish', which appears twice in this passage, with the word 'jellyfish' (Monroe 2020: 165). This 'simple transcription error', which appeared in Bonnie Kime Scott's essay 'Jellyfish and Treacle'

(1989), has since been widely reproduced by critics 'in a process that one might call "textual selection"' (165).

3. Responding to what he saw as an undue emphasis on interiority in the work of writers such as James Joyce, Virginia Woolf and D. H. Lawrence, Lewis called for an externalist approach to art, which sought to pay 'more attention' to 'the outside of people', their 'shells, or pelts', the 'language of their bodily movements' (Lewis 1930: 46).

AFTERWORD:
THE ANIMAL IN THE MIRROR

Kari Weil

Mirror Recognition/Anthropocentric Vision

Towards the beginning of her memoir, 'A Sketch of the Past', Virginia Woolf gives an account of 'the incident of the looking-glass', when she attempts to understand why, at a young age, she already seemed ashamed of her own face and would look in a mirror only if alone. She recalls the memory of a dream – or perhaps of a real-life incident, she is not really sure – in which 'I was looking in a glass when a horrible face – the face of an animal – suddenly showed over my shoulder' (Woolf 1985: 69). And she adds, 'I have always remembered that other face in the glass, whether it was a dream or a fact, and that it frightened me' (69).

Who or what is this animal in the mirror? We can assume it is a beast in that 'debased' sense referenced by Djuna Barnes, given the fear it provokes, but who, where? Is Woolf seeing herself or another as beast? Perhaps what is frightening is the indeterminate slippage between what/who I see in the mirror and what/who I am, a slippage that, as so many essays in this volume point to, pushed modernist writers to look through the taxonomies and the 'logics of optical and literary realism' (see Fagan in this volume, p. 110) in order to uncover the forces and sensations of an animal/human or human/animal hidden, if also disavowed, within. In this regard we might be reminded of Kafka's protagonist, Red Peter, the ape turned human who admits in his lecture to the academy that he had to 'whip' the animal outside of himself to be accepted as such (Kafka 1993: 203). But every night as he returns from his work, that beastly, if humane, nature returns to allow him to find sympathy with his untrained, female ape-companion. Such sympathy is linked to the creaturely at the core of 'beastly modernisms', a function of the vulnerability shared between human and nonhuman animal and especially by those excluded from, othered or abused by the anthropological machine.

In Kafka's fiction, Red Peter is able to put the anthropological machine to work in his favour in order to free himself from his animal cage and be included in the community of humans, however debased that community appears. In Woolf's autobiographical account, on the contrary, Giorgio Agamben's 'ontological hiatus' is not a risk that is freely assumed, but rather, as we come to understand, a threat imposed by the memory of a shameful and traumatic past she did not choose and cannot erase. To write of this beastly image, however, might also be a means to allow for that past to be, in Derek Ryan's terms outlined in Chapter 1 of this volume, 'repurposed' or 'reimagined' (see p. 25). Such is also Rachel Murray's insightful argument, in the final chapter of this volume, about 'the enabling possibilities of trauma', which brings the mind and body into contact with aspects of the self and the world 'which would otherwise remain out of reach' (see Murray, p. 265). The animal in the mirror might then be like those hybrid figures that, for Leonora Carrington, according to Karen Eckersley in Chapter 11, 'function as a feminist catalyst for change' (see p. 199), or at least for creative innovation. This, moreover, can offer another way to understand the 'bio' that Carrie Rohman perceptively situates at the origin of aesthetic creativity in her chapter on bioaesthetics. The 'bio' here is not the blossoming of the erotic, but rather the blossoming of creative resistance to the abuse experienced as a passive, erotic object. In other words, as we will see below, creaturely vulnerability gives rise to an authorial urge as a means of aesthetic healing through a reimagined beastly entanglement and/or opening to the more than human world.

At a first level, the animal in the mirror might be associated with what Peter Adkins, in Chapter 5, refers to as a 'beastly masculinity', here seen in the face of Virginia's half-brother, Gerald Duckworth. Woolf writes of this mirror scene just after describing an incident when, in the same hall near the looking glass, Gerald picked her up and placed her on a ledge, where he began to explore and touch her 'private parts' (Woolf 1985: 69). This moment, she then understands, is the origin of her shame – 'I must have been ashamed or afraid of my own body' (68) – leading us to question whether that horrible, animal face might also be her own, a past image that has persisted into the present, whether through her dreams or in her memory. The point is not to insist that animals also feel shame – the emotion whose expression Darwin identified as most human – although I could offer that Woolf's dog protagonist, Flush, felt some 'version' of shame after biting Robert Barrett Browning.[1] I want, rather, to consider the animal face here as Woolf's insistence on an unspecified but persistent animality at the foundation of life and of the self, whether we recognise it or not; that animality is the felt foundation of our physical and emotional vulnerability to others, one we share with other animals. It is, moreover, this animal being that comes closest to figuring the person 'to whom things happen', and who, Woolf claims, is so often left out of memoirs (Woolf 1985: 69). If that is so, it may be because we so rarely see this person in a mirror, or if we do, we do not recognise the face as our own.

One might wonder, then, why the so-called mirror recognition test has become so important for proving that some species of nonhuman animals have self-awareness. It was fifty years ago that Gordon Gallup first showed a mirror to four chimpanzees, each alone in a cage (Gallup 1970). The chimps immediately reacted to the mirror image with fear or threatening sounds as if it were another, strange creature. But little by little they appeared to understand that the image was a reflection, one they could use to clean food from their teeth or examine their behinds and genitals. In order to prove their understanding of the mirror image, Gallup had the chimps anaesthetised and marked with red dye on their eyebrows or ears. When they awoke, the chimps noticed something amiss in the mirror as they then touched their fingers to the red spots upon their face (Preston 2018). The test has since been used on a wide range of species, from primates to chickens and elephants, and most recently on dolphins and some fish, but only a few species have passed the test. Unsurprisingly, those are the species who are regarded as highly intelligent and with an intellect closest to that of humans. But what does the test really prove? Who or what is the self that we see in a mirror?

Already around the age of six months, at a time when, according to Jacques Lacan, monkeys have 'mastered' the image and found it 'empty', human children will begin to play with their image in a mirror (Lacan 1977: 1). This 'specular image', as Lacan calls it, appears to compensate for, or at least mask, the 'motor incapacity and nursling dependence' of the child, offering in its place the image of a mobile and independent subject. The image, in other words, is a fiction, one whose assumption inaugurates the fundamental misrecognitions (*méconnaissances*) that 'constitute the ego, the illusion of autonomy to which it entrusts itself' (Lacan 1977: 6). If the image is a fiction, should we be so quick to think less of those animals who abandon the image? We might turn again to Flush, 'the philosopher', as Jane Goldman also quotes in the second chapter of this volume, 'meditating the difference between appearance and reality' (see p. 41). Held by his mistress before a mirror, Flush rejects the 'misrecognitions' of the mirror stage and instead asks what exactly it is he sees in the mirror. 'Was not the little brown dog himself? But what is oneself? Is it the thing people see or is it the thing one is?' (Woolf 2009: 32). According to Alexandra Horowitz, a canine cognition specialist, dogs are notorious for not recognising themselves in mirrors, but that is because their sense of self as of others comes largely through smell (Horowitz 2017). And smell, as Woolf emphasises, is a sense of which we humans have taken little notice. As she puts it in *Flush: A Biography*, 'The greatest poets in the world have smelt nothing but roses on the one hand and dung on the other. The infinite gradations that lie between are unrecorded' (Woolf 2009: 86).

In its prioritising of the visual, the mirror test reaffirms an anthropocentric hierarchy of the senses, since vision has been our primary means of recognition, not to mention the sense most associated with rationality and intellect. Most humans have difficulty entering into the *Umwelten* or phenomenological worlds of others who navigate their surroundings in different ways and through other senses.[2] We may, moreover, have been skewing the representations of our own human *Umwelt* through a long literary tradition that has privileged the visual and dismissed the fine gradations of such senses as smell, taste and touch. Woolf and other modernists, I would argue, sought to change this and to give a new importance, if not presence, to these other senses and to what is not visually confirmed. We need only think of Proust and the taste of the madeleine (Proust 2003). Returning to Lacan, we see also that the mirror registers what I can do – how I can move my leg or arm, play with a piece of clothing or change my facial expression. But it does not necessarily register what has been done to me and so give insight into the person 'to whom things happen' (Woolf 1985: 69). Can it in any way reveal the memories that are otherwise released by the taste of the dipped madeleine?

Visual Image or Felt Sensation: Oneself and the Cotton Wool

In her short story 'The Lady in the Looking Glass' (1972), Woolf emphasises the dangers and distortions of mirrors that can give only false impressions of life as it erases the movements of time and the environment. Her narrator contrasts the myriad of nocturnal creatures seen 'pirouetting across the floor', along with a flurry of changing light, colour and emotions with the absolute stillness seen within the reflection of (another) hallway looking glass.

> And there were obscure flushes and darkenings too, as if a cuttlefish had suddenly suffused the air with purple; and the room had its passions and rages and envies and sorrows coming over it and clouding it, like a human being. Nothing stayed the same for two seconds together.
> But, outside, the looking-glass reflected the hall table, the sunflowers, the garden path so accurately and so fixedly that they seemed held there in their reality unescapably. It was a strange contrast – all changing here, all stillness there. (Woolf 1972: 88)

A naturalist, Woolf suggests, would find little to explore in a mirror which is better used as a primary instrument for ladies and girls to confirm that their appearance conforms to the demands of convention. More importantly, as she writes in *A Room of One's Own* (1929), the convention is a patriarchal one, such that women themselves 'have served all these centuries as looking glasses possessing the magic and delicious power of reflecting the figure of man at twice its natural size' (Woolf 1929: 37). The same might be said of 'the animal', a word that has been used to reflect and guarantee human superiority by opposition. 'The animal', explains Jacques Derrida, 'is a word that men have given themselves the right to give' (Derrida 2008: 23). It is a word men use to separate themselves from other living beings and to identify them as objects for our own use and consumption (Derrida 2008: 23). This is why the modernist writer must find ways of uncovering the truth of an animal or the lady other than holding up the mirror in the fashion of realists. Rather, 'one must prize her open with the first tool that came to hand – the imagination' (Woolf 1972: 91).

That is not to say that our sense of self can ever be independent from the ways we see ourselves seen by another. For the purposes of autobiography and in a possible response to Lacan, Derrida thus asks 'cannot this cat also be . . . my primary mirror?' and ponders what it might mean to see oneself in the face of an animal (Derrida 2008: 51). Could it be a way of catching a glimpse, on one level, of the animal 'I follow' (*je suis*) in the evolutionary, Darwinian sense, whose articulations have allowed humans to hold on to our place at the top or the end of history? More importantly, and in a manner that might dismantle both gender and species hierarchies, could looking at myself in the eyes of an animal provoke me to see the animal I am (*je suis*)? It is interesting that, for both Derrida and Woolf, this animal in the mirror elicits an immediate sense of shame, as if the animal reflection has stripped each of the clothes and fictive bodily armour that glass mirrors allow us to assume, along with an autonomous or separate sense of self. As Derrida puts it, 'It is as if I were ashamed, therefore, naked in front of this cat, but also ashamed for being ashamed . . . A reflected shame' (Derrida 2008: 11). Derrida goes on to elaborate upon this shame as a feeling of nudity, a term he also questions since animals are said to be naked even as they have no consciousness of it. Rather than argue that animals do have this capacity, Derrida subverts the active/passive dichotomy that is implicated in the hierarchical human/animal binary and redefines nudity as 'that passivity, the involuntary exhibition of the self' (Derrida 2008: 11). A form of passive and imposed exposure, nudity is related to a 'passion of the animal' and, as such, opposed to a 'power or capability', a 'being-able'. What Derrida experiences in nudity, then, is a response in the form of a passivity that 'testifies to a sufferance, a passion, a "not-being-able"' (Derrida 2008: 27), one moreover that is shared between human and animal.

It is this sense of exposure, this vulnerability to an other that is both evoked and shared by the animal face in the looking glass, whether seen or dreamt by the young Virginia Woolf, and which helps explain her fear of mirrors more generally. At one level we have her vulnerability to her memory, not as what she can recall, but as what she is subjected to and cannot forget. In words that might bring to mind Proust's involuntary memory, Woolf insists that 'the things one does not remember are as important, perhaps more important' (Woolf 1985: 69) than the moments one does remember. Indeed, they are fundamentally connected to each other because 'the separate moments were however embedded in many more moments of non-being, [. . .] embedded in a kind of non-descript cotton-wool' (Woolf 1985: 70).

In her notion of the cotton wool, Woolf elaborates upon her philosophy of life and of art in a way that might shed light on modernism more generally. On the one hand there is the idea, influenced by Freud among others, that this cotton wool has something to do not only with the persistence of memory in the unconscious, but with the persistence of the past in the material world: '[i]s it not possible, I often wonder, that the things we have felt with great intensity have an existence independent of our minds; are in fact still in existence' (Woolf 1985: 67). Her philosophy of art and life is thus prescient for contemporary ecological thinking, for she expresses the fundamental connectedness of artists and all humans to the more-than-human world in which they too are embedded.[3]

> From this I reach what I might call a philosophy; at any rate it is a constant idea of mine; that behind the cotton wool is a pattern; that we – I mean all human beings – are connected with this; that the whole world is a work of art; that we are parts of the work of art. (Woolf 1985: 72)

Readers of Woolf will find this 'cotton wool' akin to what, in her essay on 'Modern Fiction' ([1919] 1984), she refers to as a 'semi-transparent envelope' that surrounds the living but is also of it:

> life is a luminous halo, a semi-transparent envelope surrounding us from the beginning of consciousness to the end. Is it not the task of the novelist to convey this varying, this unknown and uncircumcised spirit, whatever aberration or complexity it may display, with as little mixture of the alien and external as possible? (Woolf 1984: 160)

Lying somewhere between the material and spiritual, between what can be touched and what can be seen even as it enfolds one within the other, this envelope is very much like what Maurice Merleau-Ponty calls the 'flesh' of the world, and which is not 'a thing, but a possibility and a latency' – indeed, a 'kinship' between seer and seen, for we can only touch and see that of which we are a part (Merleau-Ponty 2004: 3). It is especially the folding of the seeing and touching body within what is visible and tangible that Merleau-Ponty explores in his chapter on 'The Intertwining – the Chiasm', which has particular relevance for the animal in Woolf's mirror. Provoked by the memory of the sensation of touch, that vision is the image of her own 'animality', the word Merleau-Ponty uses to refer to 'the logos of the sensible world: an incorporated meaning' (Merleau-Ponty 2003: 166). Woolf writes:

> His hand explored my private parts too. I remember resenting, disliking it – what is the word for so dumb and mixed a feeling? It must have been strong, since I still recall it. This seems to show that a feeling about certain parts of the body; how they must not be touched; how it is wrong to allow them to be touched; must be instinctive. (Woolf 1985: 69)

While Woolf elaborates here on this notion of instinct as a persistence of what 'thousands of ancestresses in the past' (69) had acquired, we understand that even if it escapes words, this feeling is not opposed to intellect or thought, but rather in continuity with it. In a letter to Vita Sackville-West on March 1926 she writes:

> A sight, an emotion, creates this wave in the mind, long before it makes words to fit it; and in writing (such is my present belief) one has to recapture this, and set this working (which has nothing apparently to do with words) and then, as it breaks and tumbles in the mind, it makes words to fit it. (Woolf 1975–80, III: 247)

Woolf here sets out even more dynamically that forcefield of communication that Merleau-Ponty describes within and between bodies: 'secreting a sense, projecting this sense about material surroundings and communicating it' (Merleau-Ponty 2012: 203).

Already, in a diary entry of 1922, Woolf admits that 'when I write I'm merely a sensibility' (cited in Howard 2007: 51), and in 'A Sketch of the Past' she insists on the centrality of this sensibility to her life and her work, explaining how the most painful and shocking sensations, those which most expose and remind her of her vulnerable animality and her woundedness, are also those which excite and move her to capture them in words, and in so doing, to turn her passivity into creative agency:

> And so I go on to suppose that the shock-receiving capacity is what makes me a writer. I hazard the explanation that a shock is at once in my case followed by the desire to explain it. I feel that I have had a blow; but it is not, as I thought as a child, simply a blow from an enemy hidden behind the cotton wool of daily life; it is or will become a revelation of some order; it is a token of some real thing behind appearances; and I make it real by putting it into words. (Woolf 1985: 72)

Of course, words may themselves lose their hard reality and merge into sensation. Writing of an experience when, lying in the grass and reading a poem she understood for the first time, she writes 'I had a feeling of transparency in words when they cease to be words and become so intensified that one seems to experience them'. And at that point, like a dog, 'the pen gets on the scent' (Woolf 1985: 93).

The point, then, Woolf intimates in a manner that is similar to what Peter Adkins finds in Djuna Barnes in Chapter 5, is not to abject the animal in the mirror, no matter how horrible its face might be and how much we want to disown it. Writing on 'Animal Abjects', Kelly Oliver notes that Julia Kristeva, like Derrida, finds an animal lurking behind the very origin of humanity, 'a darker more frightening beast, our dependence on which we disavow and abject' (Oliver 2009: 282). Abjection is the very process of that disavowal and, for much of Western culture, the beast has figured the abject other of civilisation – a fact Kafka's Red Peter knew only too well. Elsewhere I have written of certain protagonists of Edgar Allan Poe and Thomas Mann, who are themselves regarded as abject because of their own identification with other animals – whether cats or dogs – and who destroy themselves and/or their animal kin in an effort to conform to the upright image of the fully human (Weil 2012). Woolf offers another path, if an avowedly difficult one, as she hints at in her memoir and explores more fully in her novel *The Waves* (1931). Rather than focus on our relations with pets or other individualised animals, the novel explores our own animality and, consequently, our relations to that sometimes 'frightening' beast who is also an aspect of ourselves – whether or not we choose to see it in the mirror.

Beastly Waves and Ways

In *A Room of One's Own* (1929), written just three years before *The Waves*, Woolf discussed differences between men and women's writing and admitted to a certain delight in reading a man whose prose 'indicated such freedom of mind, such liberty of person, such confidence in himself'. His writing gave the sense of 'one who had never been thwarted or opposed' (Woolf 1929: 98). But then, she finds she grows tired of this hardened ego which, like the letter 'I', hid what might lie in the landscape behind it, whether woman or tree: 'the worst of it is that in the shadow of the letter "I" all is shapeless as mist', if indeed anything can grow at all (Woolf 1929: 98). Woolf admits her desire to renounce or seek beyond this self-contained 'I' and so to explore, if not give shape to, the world of which both self and the writing must be a part. *The Waves* is just such a novel about the fluid and transparent interconnectedness of humans with each other and of humans with the 'more than human world', as David Abram calls it (Abram 2017). 'We melt into each other with phrases,' says Bernard, the most writerly of the six characters of the novel whose lives are intertwined, even as each lives life with a style of their own, a particular attunement to light or sound or touch (Woolf 1931: 16). Readers are alerted to the texture of the melting matter in which they are immersed in the very opening pages, where sea and sky, initially indistinguishable, are slowly divided into woollen wrinkles by the light of the rising sun, even as these 'fibres', subject to the movements of time and light, are also 'fused into one candescence' and turned into a 'million atoms of soft blue' (Woolf 1931: 7). At the end of the novel, Bernard admits, 'We grew; we changed; for, of course, we are animals. We are not always aware by any means; we breathe, eat, sleep automatically. We exist not only separately but in undifferentiated blobs of matter' (Woolf 1931: 246). Bernard embraces animality as both cause and effect of our existence within the fluid and fleshy envelope of the world.

Accepting our transparency, however, and living with the constant sensation of one's own fluid and flimsy boundaries, is not always easy and can be threatening, as we witness in the character of Rhoda. It is Rhoda, moreover, who brings us back to the animal in the mirror, or a version of it. When she sees her face 'in the looking-glass behind Susan's shoulder', she ducks to hide it because 'I have no face . . . Other people have faces . . . their world is the real world. The things they lift are heavy. They say Yes they say No; whereas I shift and change and am seen through in a second' (Woolf 1985: 43). Having a face, according to Emmanuel Levinas, is the proper signifier of being human and, significantly, what initiates an ethical relation between humans (Levinas 1998: 114). Thus, for Rhoda to be without a face is, as Vicki Tromanhauser claims, 'to fall outside the sanctuary of ethical regard and to join the ranks of the abject, the flesh, the edible' (Tromanhauser 2014: 86). Building on the work of Shari Benstock (1988), Stephen Howard has written of Rhoda as caught within the semiotic or prelinguistic self, such that her difficulties stem from her 'lack of Lacan's imago' or mirror image (Howard 2007: 50). With no visual assurance of a self, Rhoda looks for physical boundaries, something she can touch, to feel the limits of her physical extension. Trying several times to cross a puddle, she says, 'Unless I can stretch and touch something hard, I shall be blown down the eternal corridors forever. What then can I touch? What brick, what stone? and so draw myself across the enormous gulf into my body safely?' (Woolf 1931: 159). Rhoda desires or needs precisely what she also fears, for there is, as Merleau-Ponty explains, no touching without being touched. She risks the very 'shock of sensation' that she so tries to avoid: 'I am afraid of the shock of sensation that leaps upon me, because I cannot deal with it as you do – I cannot make one moment merge in the next. To me they are all violent, all separate' (Woolf 1931: 130).[4]

Rhoda is unable to turn the 'shock of sensation' into words, and so make it both productive and protective, as Woolf claims to do in her own writing, by making it unable to hurt her. Bernard is the one who turns things into 'phrases and phrases' with which to 'interpose something hard between myself and the stare of housemaids, the stare of clocks, staring faces, indifferent faces' (Woolf 1931: 30). Yet it seems that the effectiveness of phrases also breaks down for him as he increasingly senses not only the vulnerability of the faces around him, but also their power to inflict pain. 'It is strange that we who are capable of so much suffering, should inflict so much suffering. Strange that the face of a person whom I scarcely know . . . should have power to inflict this insult' (Woolf 1931: 293). The realisation, moreover, follows from that of the 'corruption' in which he too is implicated, a corruption linked to what Caroline Hovanec, in Chapter 14 of this volume, describes as the 'inhospitality of urban modernity' (see p. 249). 'Disorder, sordidity and corruption surround us. We have been taking into our mouths the bodies of dead birds. It is with these greasy crumbs, slobbered over napkins, and little corpses that we have to build' (Woolf 1931: 292). Indeed, at the end of the novel Bernard drops his book to the floor for the charwoman to sweep up, admitting 'I have done with phrases.' 'What is the phrase for the moon? And the phrase for love? By what name are we to call death [. . .] I need a howl; a cry' (Woolf 1931: 295).

Phrases are insufficient for expressing the animal we are; words cannot heal the wounds, even as they may work to explain them. Unlike the howl or the cry, words and phrases are always incommensurate with the animal body, temporally separated from what they seek to explain, much as the mirror image is visually separate from the seeing body. In each case, we might say, the 'I' is always, if ever so slightly, out of touch with the body, with the flesh, even as it is animated by it. And this may also be because, as Judith Butler explains, the I can never fully know the touch or the look of the other who affects us and so animates us into being. Reflecting on the role of 'touch' in Merleau-Ponty and Nicholas Malebranche, she writes:

> But if feeling becomes mine on the condition of an autobiographical report in language, and if feeling follows from a touch that is not mine, then I am, as it were, grounded in, animated by a touch that I can know only on the condition that I cover over that primary impression as I give an account of myself. (Butler 2015: 43)

Touch is like the waves that swell within and without us and which, as Bernard concludes, we must ride like the 'proud horse' (Woolf 1931: 297). We may ride and spur them forward or, like Rhoda, try to pull back so as not to face the shock of sensation. For if that touch is felt as harmful and abusive, it threatens not only my sense of self, but also the very wave and rhythm and flesh of the world that must sustain it, rendering all hideous and horrible. A howl or a cry may thus be the only adequate expression of wounded animality, or of an animal face in the mirror.

As the varied chapters in this volume illustrate, riding the waves and exploring by experiencing the untamed and often overpowering sensations of the wounded, excluded and abject animal is a risk that so many modernist authors took on, a risk that gives rise to the intense vibrancy of their writing. In their attention to a seemingly ineffable, if fleshy vulnerability, moreover, these writers opened new pathways for acknowledging, and possibly healing, the fragile interconnectedness of mind and body, self and other, past and present, and especially, of the human and more-than-human world.

Writing about modernist art, Steve Baker claims that 'there was no modern or modernist animal because pictures had to be about the act of picturing before they were anything else' (Baker 2000: 20). If we take *The Waves* as an example of modernist literature, we might similarly say that it is about the act of expression, about the language of sensation before it is about anything else. But that act is also about animals, and even more so, it is *of* them, it is of and about the animals we are and with whom we engage; it is of and about the animality that feels and sees and smells and hears and desires, and without which there would be no expression, even as it may have no singular face or image that we recognise as animal. It aims to capture what lies beneath the metaphors and similes, 'beneath the like and like and like . . . beneath the semblance of the thing' (Woolf 1931: 163), and so beneath the mirror image.

Works Cited

Abram, David. 2017 [1997]. *The Spell of the Sensuous: Perception and Language in a More-than-Human-World.* New York: Vintage.
Baker, Steve. 2000. *The Postmodern Animal.* London: Reaktion Books.
Benstock, Shari. 1988. 'Authorizing the Autobiographical'. In *The Private Self: Theory and Practice of Women's Autobiographical Writings.* Ed. Shari Benstock, 10–33. Chapel Hill: University of North Carolina Press.
Bergson, Henri. 2008. *Time and Free Will: An Essay on the Immediate Data of Consciousness.* New York: Cosimo.
Butler, Judith. 2015. *Senses of the Subject.* New York: Fordham University Press.
Derrida, Jacques. 2008. *The Animal that Therefore I am.* Ed. Marie-Louise Mallet, trans. David Wills. New York: Fordham University Press.
Despret, Vinciane. 2014. *Que diraient les animaux si on leur posait de bonnes questions?* Paris: Poche.
Gallup, G. G., Jr. 1970. 'Chimpanzees: Self-Recognition'. *Science* 167: 86–7.
Horowitz, Alexandra. 2017. 'Smelling Themselves: Dogs Investigate Their Own Odors Longer When Modified in an "Olfactory Mirror Test"'. *Behavioral Processes* 143 (October): 17–24.

Howard, Stephen. 2007. 'The Lady in the Looking Glass: Reflections on the Self in Virginia Woolf'. *Journal of International Women's Studies* 8.2: 44–54.
Kafka, Franz. 1993. 'A Report to the Academy'. In *Collected Stories*. Ed. Gabriel Josipovici, 195–205. New York: Knopf.
Lacan, Jacques. 1977. 'The Mirror Stage as Formative of the Function of the I as Revealed in Psychoanalytic Experience'. In *Écrits: A Selection*. Trans. Alan Sheridan, 502–9. New York: Norton.
Levinas, Emmanuel. 1998. *Otherwise than Being or Beyond Essence*. Trans. Alphonso Lingis. Pittsburgh: Duquesne University Press.
Merleau-Ponty, Maurice. 2003. *Nature: Course Notes from the Collège de France*. Trans. Robert Vallier. Evanston, IL: Northwestern University Press.
Merleau-Ponty, Maurice. 2004. '*The Visible and the Invisible:* The Intertwining, the Chiasm'. In *Maurice Merleau-Ponty: Basic Writings*. Ed. Thomas Baldwin. New York: Routledge.
Merleau-Ponty, Maurice. 2012. *The Phenomenology of Perception*. Trans. Donald A. Landes. New York and London: Taylor and Francis.
Oliver, Kelly. 2009. *Animal Lessons: How They Teach Us to be Human*. New York: Columbia University Press.
Preston, Elizabeth. 2018. 'A "Self-Aware" Fish Raises Doubts About a Cognitive Test'. *Quanta Magazine* (12 December). Available at: <https://www.quantamagazine.org/a-self-aware-fish-raises-doubts-about-a-cognitive-test-20181212/> (last accessed 15 July 2022).
Proust, Marcel. 2003. *Swan's Way*. Trans. Lydia Davis. New York: Viking Press.
Ryan, Derek. 2013. *Virginia Woolf and the Materiality of Theory: Sex, Animal, Life*. Edinburgh: Edinburgh University Press.
Tromanhauser, Vicki. 2014. 'Eating Animals and Becoming Meat in Virginia Woolf's *The Waves*'. *Journal of Modern Literature* 38.1: 73–93.
Von Uexküll, Jacob. 2010. *A Foray into the Worlds of Animals and Men*. Trans. Joseph D. O'Neil. Minnesota: University of Minnesota Press.
Weil, Kari. 2012. *Thinking Animals: Why Animal Studies Now*. New York: Columbia University Press.
Westling, Louise. 1999. 'Virginia Woolf and the Flesh of the World'. *New Literary History* 30.4: 855–75.
Woolf, Virginia. 1929. *A Room of One's Own*. New York: Fountain Press.
Woolf, Virginia. 1931. *The Waves*. New York and London: Harcourt, Brace, Jovanovich.
Woolf, Virginia. 1972. 'The Lady in the Looking Glass'. In *A Haunted House and Other Short Stories*. New York: Harcourt, Brace and World.
Woolf, Virginia. 1975–80. *The Letters of Virginia Woolf*. Ed. Nigel Nicolson and Joanne Trautmann, 6 vols. New York: Harcourt Brace Jovanovich.
Woolf, Virginia. 1984. 'Modern Fiction'. In *The Essays of Virginia Woolf*, Vol. 4. Ed. Andrew McNeillie. London: Hogarth Press.
Woolf, Virginia. 1985. 'A Sketch of the Past'. In *Moments of Being*. Ed. Jeanne Schulkind. San Diego, New York and London: Harcourt.
Woolf, Virginia. 2009. *Flush: A Biography*. Oxford: Oxford University Press.
Woolf, *The Waves*. 1931. New York and London: Harcourt, Brace Jovanovich.

NOTES

1. Vincianne Despret suggests that nonhuman animals may experience versions of human emotions, implying that they may not be exactly equivalent but are similar enough to expand the meaning of the term. See Despret (2014: 231–42).
2. On *Umwelten* see von Uexküll 2010.
3. For more on this see, for instance, the work of Louise Westling (1999) and Derek Ryan (2013).
4. Rhoda's sense of self – or lack thereof – might also be said to exist between Bergson's iteration of a 'self with well-defined states' and 'a self in which succeeding each other means melting into one another and forming an organic whole'. See Bergson (2008: 128).

NOTES ON CONTRIBUTORS

Peter Adkins is an Early Career Teaching and Research Fellow at the University of Edinburgh. He is the author of *The Modernist Anthropocene: Nonhuman Life and Planetary Change in James Joyce, Virginia Woolf and Djuna Barnes* (2022) and co-editor of *Virginia Woolf, Europe and Peace: Aesthetics and Theory* (2020). He has also co-edited a special issue of *Comparative Critical Studies* on Rosi Braidotti and Virginia Woolf (2022) and an issue of *19: Interdisciplinary Studies in the Long Nineteenth Century* on 'Victorian Ecology'.

Katharina Alsen is a Research Associate at Hamburg University of Music and Theatre. She has been a doctoral fellow at the international research training group InterArt and a Global Humanities Junior Fellow at the research network Principles of Cultural Dynamics, both at Freie Universität Berlin, and held visiting scholarships in Copenhagen, Stockholm and Hong Kong. Her research interests concern intimacy in theatre and performance art, postcolonialism in the Nordics and cultural animal studies with a special focus on insects and parasitism. She is the co-author of the book *Nordic Painting: The Rise of Modernity* (2016).

Laura Blomvall is a Research Associate at the University of York and Product Specialist at Adam Matthew Digital. Her work on different aspects of twentieth-century lyric poetry, from Blitz poetics to the work of Ted Hughes, has previously been published by Cambridge University Press, Palgrave Macmillan and *Journal of Modern Literature*. In 2019, she was the research lead in the Digital Humanities

NOTES ON CONTRIBUTORS

project 'Bombing Britain: An Air Raid Map', a collaboration between Routledge, Taylor & Francis, the National Archives and the University of York, which was covered widely in the press.

Lauren Cullen completed her PhD in English at the University of Oxford, where she was also a Social Sciences and Humanities Research Council (SSHRC) Doctoral Fellow. Her thesis traces the relationship between literary culture, animal characters and nineteenth-century animal welfare discourse. She specialises in nineteenth-century British literature and animal studies, with further research interests across literature and science, Canadian fiction, and ecocriticism.

Elizabeth Curry completed a PhD in English at the University of Oregon, concentrating on multiethnic modernisms and representations of animals as not so radically other. Her chapter in this volume developed as part of her dissertation project, *Refiguring the Animal: Race, Posthumanism, and Modernism*. She is Associate Faculty at Cascadia College and Adjunct Faculty at Portland State University.

Karen Eckersley is the recipient of a funded PhD studentship at Nottingham Trent University and is conducting a project that investigates the intersections between feminism and posthumanist theory in women's surrealist praxis. Her research focuses, in particular, on the ways in which women surrealist artists and writers anticipate and confront environmental debates of today. Her research has been published in peer-reviewed journals including *Gothic Nature*, the *Journal for Intermedial Crossings* and *Transpositiones*.

Paul Fagan is an IRC Postdoctoral Fellow at Maynooth University. The research for, and composition of, his contribution to this collection was undertaken during his position as a Senior Scientist at Salzburg University. He is a co-founder of the International Flann O'Brien Society and a founding general editor of the open access journals *The Parish Review: Journal of Flann O'Brien Studies* and *Production Archives* (Open Library of Humanities). Paul is the co-editor of *Irish Modernisms: Gaps, Conjectures, Possibilities* and *Stage Irish: Performance, Identity, Cultural Circulation*, as well as four well-received edited collections on Flann O'Brien. He is currently finalising a monograph on Irish literary hoaxes and developing research projects on 'Representations of Nonhuman Skin in Modernist Writing' and 'Celibacy in Irish Women's Writing, 1860s–1950s'.

Jane Goldman is Reader in English at the University of Glasgow and a General Editor of the Cambridge University Press edition of the works of Virginia

Woolf. Her books include *The Feminist Aesthetics of Virginia Woolf* (1998), *The Cambridge Introduction to Virginia Woolf* (2006), *With You in the Hebrides: Virginia Woolf and Scotland* (2013) and *Modernism, 1910–1945: Image to Apocalypse* (2004). A co-editor of *Flush: A Biography*, forthcoming for Cambridge (2022), she is currently writing a book, *Virginia Woolf and the Signifying Dog*. She is also a poet. Her first collection, SEKXPHRASTIKS, was published by Dostoevsky Wannabe in 2021.

Alex Goody is Professor of Twentieth-Century Literature and Culture at Oxford Brookes University. She is the author of *Gender, Leisure Technology and Modernist Poetry: Machine Amusements* (2019), *Technology, Literature and Culture* (2011) and *Modernist Articulations: A Cultural Study of Djuna Barnes, Mina Loy and Gertrude Stein* (2007), and co-editor of *The Edinburgh Companion to Modernism and Technology* (2022), *Reading Westworld* (2019) and *American Modernism: Cultural Transactions* (2009).

Caroline Hovanec is Associate Teaching Professor in English and Writing at the University of Tampa and the author of *Animal Subjects: Literature, Zoology, and British Modernism* (Cambridge University Press, 2018). With Rachel Murray, she is the editor of 'Reading Modernism in the Sixth Extinction', a special issue of *Modernism/Modernity PrintPlus*. Her current research focuses on vermin in literature.

Gabriela Jarzębowska is an Assistant Professor at the Faculty of Artes Liberales, University of Warsaw. She was a Fulbright Fellow at the Wesleyan University, the Seedbox network at the Linköping University grantee and a short-time visiting scholar at the University of California (Santa Cruz). Her interdisciplinary work, bridging the gap between cultural studies, history and sociology, is focused on critical animal studies and environmental humanities. Her main research interests include rhetoric of environmental conflicts, representations of animals in popular discourse and entanglements between environment, socialism and modernity. She has published in *Journal for Critical Animal Studies* and *Society & Animals*.

Saskia McCracken completed her PhD on Virginia Woolf's Darwinian animal tropes at the University of Glasgow. Her research has been published in *Virginia Woolf, Europe, and Peace: Aesthetics and Theory* (2020), *Matraga: Modernist Prose in Contemporaneity* (UERJ 2020), *The Modern Short Story and Magazine Culture: 1880–1950* (2021), *Modernism/Modernity: Reading Modernism in the Sixth Extinction* (2022) and *Crossing Borders: Transnational Modernism Beyond the Human* (2022). Her forthcoming research will be published in *Flush: A Biography* (Cambridge University Press), *Animal Satire* (Palgrave Macmillan) and *Virginia Woolf and the Anthropocene* (Edinburgh University Press).

NOTES ON CONTRIBUTORS

Rachel Murray is a Lecturer in English at the University of Northumbria who specialises in modernist literature, science and animal studies. She has published articles on a range of authors and topics, including James Joyce and apiculture and Samuel Beckett's worms – the latter of which won the 2016 BSLS Early Career Essay Prize. Her book *The Modernist Exoskeleton: Insects, War, Literary Form* was published by Edinburgh University Press in 2020.

Beerendra Pandey, Professor of English and Dean at the School of Language and Literature, KIIT-Deemed University (Bhubaneswar), has a Fulbright PhD from the State University of New York at Stony Brook. His research and teaching focus on Partition Studies, Trauma Studies, Human Rights Literature, hum-Animal Studies, Cultural Studies, Affect Theory, and the Poetics and Politics of Irony. His current research interest includes a comprehensive study of the metaphysics at work in the folk art of Mithila Painting, practised in the Mithila region straddling the Bihar State of India and Madhesh Province of Nepal. He can be reached at birunepali@gmail.com

Carrie Rohman is Professor of English at Lafayette College. She has published widely in animal studies, modernism, posthumanism and performance in such journals as *Deleuze Studies*, *Modernism/modernity*, *American Literature*, *Modern Fiction Studies* and *Hypatia*, and in a number of edited volumes. She is author of *Stalking the Subject: Modernism and the Animal* (2009) and *Choreographies of the Living: Bioaesthetics in Literature, Art, and Performance* (2018), and co-editor with Kristin Czarnecki of *Virginia Woolf and the Natural World* (2011). Rohman is on the editorial board of the Palgrave Studies in Animals and Literature series and serves as Associate Editor for *Contemporary Women's Writing*.

Derek Ryan is Senior Lecturer in Modernist Literature at the University of Kent and author of *Animal Theory: A Critical Introduction* (2015) and *Virginia Woolf and the Materiality of Theory: Sex, Animal, Life* (2013). He has co-edited several volumes encompassing historical and theoretical research on modernism and animal studies, including *Reading Literary Animals: Medieval to Modern* (2020), *Cross-Channel Modernisms* (2020) and *The Handbook to the Bloomsbury Group* (2018). Currently, he is completing two projects relating to 'beastly modernism': a co-edited scholarly edition of *Flush: A Biography* for the Cambridge Edition of Virginia Woolf, and a new monograph titled *Bloomsbury, Beasts and British Modernism*.

Kari Weil is University Professor of Letters, College of the Environment and Feminist, Gender and Sexuality Studies at Wesleyan University. She is the author of *Precarious Partners: Horses and their Humans in Nineteenth-Century France*

(2020), *Thinking Animals: Why Animal Studies Now* (2012), *Androgyny and the Denial of Difference* (1992), and numerous essays dealing with animal studies, gender and feminist theory. Her current research explores the legacies of animal magnetism in nineteenth- and twentieth-century theories of affective influence, tactility and traumatic healing.

Juanjuan Wu is currently a postdoctoral fellow at the Department of Foreign Languages and Literatures at Tsinghua University, Beijing, China. She earned her MA in English Literature from Fudan University, China, in 2016 and her PhD from the University of Melbourne, Australia, in 2021. Her main fields of interest include twentieth-century Anglophone modernism and China, women's travel writing, animal studies, and the history of emotions and literature. Her research has been published in peer-reviewed journals including *Women's Studies, an Interdisciplinary Journal*, *Studies in Travel Writing* and *Women's Writing*.

INDEX

1851 Great Exhibition (Hyde Park), 109

abject, 64, 96, 97, 111, 114, 120, 286, 287, 289
Acker, Kathy, 268
Adair, William, 116–17
aeroplane, 230, 233, 235, 238, 239, 241, 242, 244, 245
affect, 10, 56–7, 60–2, 64, 222
Africa, 59, 115–16; see also South Africa
Agamben, Giorgio, 3, 10, 129, 146, 280
agency, 3, 16, 56–7, 60–1, 66, 69, 77, 83, 84, 96, 129, 143, 148, 154, 156, 160, 162, 163, 165, 172–3, 174 182, 193, 205, 250, 264, 285
Akhmatova, Anna, 'The Wind of War', 232
Akeley Hall of African Mammals, 115–17
Akeley, Carl, 115–17, 118
Alaimo, Stacy, 10, 265
Ali, Ahmed, 8, 13, 16, 249–54, 255, 256–61
  Twilight in Delhi, 249–61
Ahmed, Sara, 64–5, 70

All-India Progressive Writers Association (AIPWA), 259
American Museum of Natural History (New York), 115
American Red Cross Museum (Washington, D.C.), 116
Anand, Mulk Raj, 143, 144, 148–9, 156
  'The Parrot of the Cage', 148–9
animacy, 5
animal agency, 77, 83, 162, 172, 173, 182
animal authority, 75–7, 81
animal authorship, 76
animal, commodification of, 47, 114
animal consciousness, 37, 187, 225
animal cruelty, 8
animal and domestication *see* domestication
animal epistemologies, 175
animal protection, 219–21, 223
animal psychology, 16, 185, 187
animal slaughter, 98, 99
animal suffering *see* animal cruelty
animal sentience *see* animal consciousness
animal welfare, 7, 129, 121

INDEX

Anthropocene, 182, 201, 202
anthropocentrism, 11, 26, 165, 185, 186
  ontological anthropocentrism, 165
  epistemological anthropocentrism, 165, 172
anthropological machine, 3, 146, 280
anthropomorphism, 26, 27, 28, 57–8, 63, 66, 69, 81, 130, 131
anthropos, 11, 198, 213
anthroposophy, 2
ape, 279
Aragon, Louis, 234–35
Atlantic Monthly, 183
Atwood, Margaret, *Survival,* 184
Auden, W. H., 'Hymn to St. Cecelia', 240
Audubon, John James, *The Birds of America*, 108
Australia, 8, 59, 151
autobiography, 24, 30 56–7, 59, 62, 68, 69, 94, 283
avant-garde, 166, 181, 268
Ayscough, Florence, 15, 56–62, 66–71

Barad, Karen, 10, 209
Barnes, Djuna, 1–5, 91–106, 217, 279, 286
  Ann Portugeuise, 105
  The Antiphon, 105, 92–100
  Biography of Julie van Bartmann, 91–9
  Creatures in an Alphabet, 6
  Ladies Almanack, 6
  'A Portrait of a Man Who Is, At present, One of the More Significant Figures in Literature', 1
  Nightwood, 4, 96, 217
  'The Rabbit', 105
  Ryder, 15, 91–103
Barnum, P. T., 112, 115
Barrett, Laura, 218
Barrett Browning, Elizabeth, 23, 25, 26, 29, 36, 38–55, 56
  'Flush, or Faunus', 23, 49–50, 52
  'To Flush, My Dog', 23

Barthes, Roland, 76, 85–6, 112
Bartlett, Abraham Dee, 112
bat, 27, 204, 205, 209
bear, 188, 193
bestiary, 6–7, 216
Beastly Modernisms conference, ix, 10
Beckett, Samuel, 2, 3, 9, 113
beetle dress, 110
becoming-animal, 11, 107, 119, 199, 204, 208, 210–13
becoming-with, 11, 12
Benjamin, Walter, 261
Bennett, Jane, 10, 18, 58, 69, 70, 88, 90, 219, 222, 223, 224, 226, 227
Bennett, Joshua, 222, 223
Bergson, Henri, 11, 291n
Berridge, Elizabeth, 'Bombed Church', 233
bioaesthetics, 75, 280
biofiction, 25, 35
bird
  auk (great), 112
  The Birds of America see Audubon, John James
  bird hats, 110
  A Century of Birds from the Himalaya Mountains see Gould, John
  chicken, 215, 216, 226, 21
  The Death and Burial of Cock Robin see Potter, Walter
  dodo, 112
  dove, 237, 238, 248, 249, 261
  eagle, 101, 133, 189, 190, 192, 212
  flamingo, 111
  goose, 188, 189
  humming-bird, 86
  macaw, 79, 80
  moa, 112
  nightingale, 204, 205, 233, 239, 240
  owl, 191, 192, 233
  peacock, 118, 253
  pigeon, 8, 13, 16–17, 94, 248–62 ;
    pigeon-feather screens, 110
  raven, 111
  swan, 118, 241, 243

Bishop, Elizabeth, 16, 231, 240, 241, 245
    'Roosters' 238–40
Black labour, 217, 224
    domestic servitude, 225
    subjugation, 220, 223, 225
Black modernism, 216, 217
Blackness
    race and animality, 217
    and animalisation, 222
    and bodily vulnerability, 220, 223
    and speculative interiority, 225–6
Bloomsbury, 14, 15, 23–37, 113, 259
blue humanities, 264
boar, 204, 205, 209
bodies, 64–6, 108–11, 114, 115, 118–20, 127, 131, 160, 199, 209, 242, 264, 268, 270, 288
Boni and Liveright, 91
Boisseron, Bénédicte, 12, 221, 222, 225
Borges, Jorge Luis, 6
Bowen, Elizabeth, 244
Braidotti, Rosi, 11, 199, 200, 203, 207, 208, 211, 213
Brecht, Bertold, 'This Summer Sky', 232
bred, 28, 41, 254
breed, breeding, 23, 28, 41, 42, 53, 59, 62, 66, 67, 98, 102, 252
Breton, André, 202
British Empire, 8, 19, 110, 254, 258
Browning, Robert, 23, 49, 55, 280
bull, 97, 117, 118, 151, 152, 266
bullfighting, 117, 266
Burton, Antoinette and Renisa Mawani, *Animalia: An Anti-Imperial Bestiary for Our Times*, 7, 8, 18
Butler, Judith, 188

Canada, 56–7, 68, 183–5, 195, 196
canine, 11, 15, 24, 28, 34, 35, 38–53, 56–71, 105, 145–55, 281
capitalism, 3, 17, 18, 30, 88, 127, 184, 199, 213, 250, 251, 258, 260, 261, 275
captivity, 29, 189, 192, 217, 225
carnivalesque, 111

Carrington, Leonora, 3, 8, 16, 198–214, 280
    'As They Rode Along the Edge', 199, 202, 204, 207, 208, 213
    'The Cabbage in a Rose', 203, 213
    'Jemima and the Wolf', 16, 199, 208, 214
    Self-Portrait (Inn of the Dawn Horse), 202
    'What is a Woman?', 198, 199, 201, 206, 213
Carroll, Lewis, *Alice's Adventures in Wonderland*, 111
Cassell's Household Guide, 110
cat
    and authenticity, 225
    'Bob', 114
    cat-paw letter-opener, 114, 122
    domestic cat, 225
    feral cat, 225, 253, 254
    house-cat, 12, 224–6, 283
    kitten, 110
Catullus, 38, 48, 49, 53, 55
Césaire, Aimé, 216, 222
Chen, Mel Y., 5, 13, 222, 223
chimpanzee, 281, 289
China, 14, 15, 58–9, 61–71
Chineseness, 62–3
cinema, 115, 231–47, 261
class, 8, 24, 40, 56, 59, 63, 68, 69, 108, 110, 115, 118, 158, 189, 202, 208, 248, 252, 260
climate change, 10, 17, 161, 195, 250 255, 256, 258, 261, 260
clothing, 105, 120, 170, 177, 282
Coetzee, J. M., 27, 34, 89
Coleman Anita Scott, 215–28
    'The Dark Horse,' 215, 216
    'The Dust of the Streets', 224
    'Idle Wonder,' 16, 217, 224–7
    'Respective Flight', 224
    'She Was Not Wise', 224
    'Three Dogs and a Rabbit', 217–23, 226
    Western Echoes of the Harlem Renaissance, 216, 227

299

colonialism, 8, 13, 19, 63, 70, 108, 114, 118, 120, 158, 161, 164, 176, 183, 222, 227, 249, 256
companion species, 2, 11, 12, 14, 15, 23, 24, 28–30, 32, 33, 38–52, 59–61, 65, 69, 77, 78, 114, 116, 145–9, 155, 184, 192–4, 209, 224, 225, 280
comparative psychology, 24, 181, 183
Confucius, 66–7
Cornell, Joseph, 249
Cornford, Frances, 'Daybreak', 239
cosmopolitanism, 66, 248
creatural, 5, 19, 75, 76, 78, 79, 83, 85, 88, 89, 104, 148, 149, 206, 209
Crisis, The, 217
critical animal studies (CAS), 13
critical race studies *see critical race theory*
critical race theory, 12, 13, 164
critical whiteness studies, 164
critters, 5, 9
crocodile, 119
cruelty, 8, 18, 28, 69, 83, 102, 191

Dalí, Salvador, 234, 246
Dante, 106
Darwin, Charles, 9, 19, 35, 58, 104, 183, 195, 277, 280
Darwinian evolution, 7, 9, 94, 95, 98, 283
Da Silva, Denise, 226, 227
Dalziel, Hugh, 23, 41, 53
Day, Jon, *Homing*, 255
Day-Lewis, Cecil, 232
Decka, Maneesha, 8, 12, 18
decolonial theory, 164, 175
Deleuze, Gilles and Félix Guattari, 78, 79
 becoming animal *see* becoming-animal
 Kafka: Toward a Minor Literature, 199
 A Thousand Plateaus, 11, 199
 Thus Spoke Zarathustra, 11
Delhi, 249, 251–4, 256–62

Derrida, Jacques, 12, 15, 18, 38, 39, 44, 47, 49, 53, 76, 95, 100, 103, 104, 152, 155, 157, 214, 225, 227, 283, 286, 289
 The Animal That Therefore I Am, 12
 animot, 12, 76
Descartes, René, 62, 201
de Ville, Jacques, 100, 103
Dickens, Charles, 107, *Our Mutual Friend*, 111, 121
dingo, 251
diorama, 107, 115–22
disability studies, 14
doe, 1, 2
dog, 56–63, 65–9
 Australian Shepherd, 52
 Bismarck, 77, 78, 80–8
 Blenheim, 41
 Buster, 60, 68
 Cayenne, 11, 52
 cocker, 23, 25, 39, 40, 41, 56
 Flush, 15, 23–37, 38–55, 56–71, 280–2
 Hans, 42
 James Buchanan, 57, 59, 60, 61, 63–6, 68, 69
 King Charles, 41
 Looloo, 77, 78, 80, 88
 Lo-sze, 59, 66, 67
 Pekinese, 77
 'Sergeant Stubby', 116
 Seleuchi [saluki] hound, 118
 Spaniel, 3, 23–37, 38–55, 70
 Yo Fei, 56–60, 66–9
domestication, 161, 163, 168, 188
domesticity, 224–6
Donne, John, 92
Dovey, Ceridwen, 15, 23–37, 70
dragon, 85, 88
Dufresne, Louis, 108, 115

ecology, 9, 13, 18, 20, 34, 70, 76, 88, 89, 90, 103, 126–7, 130, 132, 139, 141, 176, 177, 199, 202, 213, 227, 233, 259–63, 277, 284
ecosystem, 129, 201, 204

marine, 263, 264
eggs, 112
elephant, 116, 281
Eliot, T. S., 92, 102, 103–5, 184
  The Waste Land, 144, 157, 249
embroidery, 15, 110, 160
emotion, 31, 58, 61, 64–6, 70, 71, 100, 134, 260, 282, 291, 296
environmental concerns, 10, 125, 126, 129, 138, 139, 140, 177, 185, 199, 249, 255, 259
environmental destruction, 17, 161, 189, 195, 264, 275
Epstein, Jean, 234
Ernst, Max, 202, 234
ethics, 12, 13, 19, 35, 37, 69, 89, 92, 107, 128, 130, 147, 152–4, 158, 176, 207, 264
eugenics, 24, 35, 40, 115
evolution, theories of *see* Darwinian evolution
extinction, 7, 10, 11, 14, 16, 17, 112, 113, 195, 249–55, 260–2, 276, 294

Faber and Faber, 92, 104
familial relations, 92, 93, 101, 106, 255
fascism, fascist, 24, 30, 31, 35, 138, 255
feathers, 8, 41, 109, 110, 190, 196, 233, 237, 238, 239
feminism, 4, 8, 11, 12, 58, 59, 61, 77, 198, 199, 200, 201, 202, 205, 207, 208, 213, 280
Field Museum of Natural History (Chicago), 115, 116
film noir, 236, 237, 239, 241, 243–7
First World War, 59, 62, 238, 253, 256, 270, 273, 274, 275
fish, 29, 79, 112, 290
fish-scale embroidery, 110
flaying, 110, 120
fly (insect), 111, 214
fly (verb), 82, 85, 186, 188, 232, 234, 249, 252, 261
forest, 193, 194, 202, 204, 207, 208, 212, 250, 259; *see also* woods

forgery, 112
Foucualt, Michel, 15, 18, 76, 77, 86, 88
  biopolitics, 10
  The Order of Things, 6, 7, 18
fox, 2, 119, 184, 189, 212, 233
Freud, Sigmund, 83, 105, 268, 271, 274–6, 284
  Beyond the Pleasure Principle, 267
  Unheimlich, 250, 255–6, 261
frog, 45, 110, 111

Gallup, Gordon, 281
Gaunt, Mary, 57, 58, 59–66, 69
  A Broken Journey, 56, 59–61, 62, 63–4, 65
  A Woman in China, 62, 64, 65
genealogy, 96, 97, 201
gender, 3, 8, 10, 13, 14, 24, 56–7, 84, 95, 96, 108, 110, 115–18, 168, 202, 205, 210, 212, 218–20, 242, 243, 271, 283
geostories, 199, 201, 203
Ghosh, Amitav, 255, 256, 257, 259, 261
giraffe, 119
global warming *see* climate change
Gould, John, *A Century of Birds from the Himalaya Mountains*, 108

H. D., 17, 264–5, 268, 275, 276
  Her, 272
  Kora and Ka, 272
  Notes on Thought and Vision, 274
  Palimpsest, 269, 273
  'R.A.F.', 132, 232
Haldane, J. B. S., 9, 54
Haraway, Donna, 5, 10, 14, 42, 66, 69, 110, 112, 115, 116, 186, 199, 203, 204, 207, 208, 212, 218
  The Companion Species Manifesto, 11, 52
  'A Cyborg Manifesto', 11
  Staying with the Trouble: Making Kin in the Chthulucene, 201
  When Species Meet, 11
Harlem Renaissance, 215

Harper's Weekly, 187
Hatt, Emilie Demant, 166, 169
hedgehog, 111
Hegel, 39, 54
Hemingway, Ernest, 10, 107, 120
  The Sun Also Rises, 116–17
Hemingway Sanford, Marcelline, 116
Hitler, Adolf, 31
hoax, 115, 120
  Bloomsbury Dreadnought hoax, 113
  Feejee mermaid hoax, 112
  Ossian hoax, 113
  Spectrist hoax, 113
Hobbes, Thomas, 100
Hogarth Press, 36, 45, 54, 249, 259, 276
Holland, Sharon, 217, 218
Höller, Carsten, *Soma,* 168
horse, 43, 69, 202, 212, 215, 216, 288
  horse-hoof inkwell, 110
Hughes, Langston, 3
humanism, 3, 10, 108, 112, 114, 120, 144–9, 156, 182, 198–201, 205, 208, 211
Hurston, Zora Neale, 3, 217
Huxley, Julian, 9
hybrid, 2, 16, 51, 113, 198–213, 234, 235, 280
hygiene, 108, 115, 129–32, 136–40

India, 8, 14, 143–58, 248–62
Italy, 41, 56, 57, 255
imperialism, 8, 14, 57–8, 114, 257
In Brightest Africa, 116
indexicality, 109, 112
Indigenous people, 161, 164, 165, 177, 250
Indigenous resistance, 165
Indigenous studies, 164, 165
  and 'critical care', 164
  and cross-disciplinary scholarship, 163–5
  and decentralisation, 165–6
  and heterogeneity, 6, 161, 165
industrialisation, 68, 108, 138, 160

Influenza pandemic (1918), 256
insect, 9 108, 130, 209
intersectionality, 13
interspecies, 12, 42, 50, 51, 52, 126, 161, 173, 199, 216, 223, 226
interspecies empathy, 219, 223, 226

Jackson, Zakiyyah, 226
jellyfish, 14, 17, 263–78
'jellygeddon', 263
Joyce, James, 1–4, 9, 113, 265
  'The Dead', 2
  Finnegan's Wake, 4
  Ulysses, 1, 2
Jungle, The (Piccadilly shop), 110

Kafka, Franz, 9, 26, 104, 217, 279–80, 286, 290
  The Metamorphosis, 217
Keats, John, 'Ode to a Nightingale,' 239, 240
Kim, Claire Jean, 217, 225
Kipling, Rudyard, 62, 70, 181, 184, 197
kitsch, 109, 120

Lacan, Jacques, 44, 53, 266, 281, 282, 283, 287, 290
Laika, 32
Latour, Bruno, 173, 264
Lawrence, D. H., 3, 9, 15, 37, 75–89, 104, 278
Lee, Laurie, 'The Edge of Day', 235
Leiris, Michel, 266
Levinas, Emmanuel, 287
Lévi-Strauss, Claude, 105
Lewis, Wyndham, 9, 17, 264, 265, 269
  Blast!, 271
  Tarr, 269, 270, 272
  'The War-Crowds', 268, 270, 273, 274
lion, 101
literacy, 42, 51, 83, 84
literary realism, 109, 110, 111, 279
Locke, Alain, 215
lobster, 3

London, 23, 29, 30, 32, 56, 59, 77, 184, 189, 197, 232, 233, 236, 240, 270, 273
Lowell, Amy, 58
Luciano, Dana and Mel Y. Chen, 222, 223
Luzon (Phillippines), 263

McCarthy, Tom, 265–9, 272, 273, 275
  Typewriters, Bombs, Jellyfish, 265
  traumatic real, 265, 267, 269, 272
Macpherson, James, 113
manhood *see* masculinity
marten, 110
Manto, Saadat Hasan, 143–58
Marakatt-Labba, Britta, 15, 160–2, 166, 172, 174
  Historjá, 160, 161, 177
marmoset, 14, 15, 23–37
masculinity, 10, 84, 94, 100, 116–18, 271, 280
Mauritius, 112
Mbembe, Achille, 218, 220
meat, 29, 44, 103, 105, 187, 193, 194, 196, 206, 214, 290
Merleau-Ponty, Maurice, 284–8
mermaid, 112, 120
metamodernist, metamodernism 14, 25, 33, 34–6
metamorphosis, 16, 118, 206, 210, 211, 212
metaphor, 2, 3, 78, 100, 101, 125, 132, 136–40, 161, 164, 172, 173, 174, 210, 235, 238, 239, 245, 250, 252, 259, 274, 289
  material metaphor, 164, 172–4
military technology, 232
mirror image, 26, 40, 41, 70, 99, 279–91
Mitford, Mary Russell, 23, 38, 39, 42, 47, 52
Mitz, 15, 23–37
mobility, 59, 69, 161, 170, 190
monkey, 29, 35, 112, 281
Moore, Marianne, 17, 249

moose, 182, 194
moth, 204, 205
Muir, Edwin, 105
Munch, Edvard, 168

Nagel, Thomas, 27
na Gopaleen, Myles (Flann O'Brien), 107, 119, 120
  'Two in One', 119
naming practice, 63, 67
Narayanan, Yamini, 13, 143, 145
Naturalism, 120, 195, 197
Nature Fakers debate, 183
Nazi, 30, 32, 132–42
new materialism, 90, 164
New Mexico, 215, 216
New York, 94, 97, 140, 215, 266
New York Times, 183
New Zealand, 8, 112
Nietzsche, Friedrich, 11
Nordic countries, 161, 163, 164, 168, 171, 178
  and colonial entanglements, 164
Norris, Margot, 4, 92
nostalgia, 115, 117, 118, 249, 260–1
Nunez, Sigrid, 15, 23–37

O'Brien, Flann *see* na Gopaleen, Myles
Opportunity, 215, 217, 224
optical realism, 279, 109, 110, 111, 279
orca, 186
Orwell, George, 25, 32

Pakistan, 8, 145, 147, 149, 150, 152, 153, 258–9
Pall Mall Gazette, 112, 113
panther, 187–93
Paris, 1, 93, 106, 116, 236
Partition, 143–58, 258
pastoral, 105, 161, 232, 233, 235
patriarchy, 13
Peking, 59, 65, 68
personhood
  constructions of, 220–1
  human rights, 222

303

pet *see* companion species
Picasso, Pablo, 249, 261
Plautus, 23–37
Ploucquet, Hermann, 109, 110
poetry, lyric, 38, 231–45
Poland, 15, 125–42
pollution, 264
polygamy, 94
postcolonial, 12, 162, 164, 216
posthuman figures, 227
posthumanism, 9, 10, 11, 186, 201, 207, 264
Potter, Walter, *The Death and Burial of Cock Robin*, 110, 111, 129
primal, 3, 50, 51, 52, 206, 267, 268
Proust, Marcel, 268, 282, 284
Psycho, 120

queer, 4, 5, 13, 14, 83, 84, 118, 221, 231, 237, 242, 243

rabbit, 26, 76, 77–88, 110, 119, 191, 218–23, 226
race, 3, 8, 12, 13, 57–8, 57–71, 87, 108, 115, 164, 189, 216–28, 250
racism, 57, 58, 62, 64, 114, 216
  scientific racism, 114
racial oppression, 12
racial imaginary, 216
Rakesh, Mohan, 8, 15, 143–58
rat, 14, 15, 125–42
realism, 109, 110–20, 134, 162, 181, 186, 195, 259, 260, 261
reindeer, 8, 14, 15, 159–78
  antlers, 159–61, 169, 170, 175
  herding, 161, 178
relics, 112
religion, 28, 54, 67, 144, 186, 203, 204, 206, 251
Reynolds, Michael S., 116
Roberts, Charles G. D., 16, 181–97
  'Black Swamp', 193
  'The Boy and Hushwing', 191
  'Do Seek their Meat from God', 187, 193

'The Homesickness of Kehonka', 187–9
'The Haunter of the Pine Gloom', 192
Kindred of the Wild, 196
'The King of the Mamozekel', 182
'The Moonlight Trails', 191
'Savoury Meats', 193
'Strayed', 187
'The Tiger of the Sea', 185
'The Treason of Nature', 190
'The Watchers of the Campfire', 193
Watchers of the Trails, 196
'When Twilight Falls in the Stump Lot', 190
'Wild Motherhood', 193, 194
Roberts, Lynette, 'Crossed and Uncrossed', 240
Robeson, Paul, 215
Rohman, Carrie, *Stalking the Subject,* 4, 9
Ronald Reagan (USS aircraft carrier), 263
Roosevelt, Teddy (U.S. president), 116, 184
Rose, Deborah Bird, *Wild Dog Dreaming*, 251
Royal Museum of Stuttgart, 109–10
Royal Society for the Protection of Animals (RSPCA), 7
Royal Society for the 33 Protection of Birds (RSPB), 7
Rukeyser, Muriel, 16, 242–5
  'Child in the Great Wood', 243
  The Life of Poetry, 243
  'Mortal Girl', 243
  'One Soldier', 242
Russell, Bertrand, 9

Sackville-West, Vita, 36, 40, 46, 54, 259, 285
Said, Edward, 248
Sámi, 159–78
  art, 8, 160, 162, 163, 164, 166, 168, 169, 172, 174, 175
  and assimilation policies, 161, 163, 168

cosmology, 153, 166
cultural self-appropriation, 162, 171, 172, 175
culture, 162, 165
lifestyle, 160, 161, 162, 168, 172
and non-human animals *see* nonhuman
regional fauna, 162
and reindeer *see* reindeer
settlement areas, 163
shamanism, 166
traditions, 15, 172
Sámi Dáiddajoavku (Sámi Artist Group), 160
Sápmi region, 171, 177, 178
Savio, John, 162, 163, 168
  Alene, 171, 172
  Gutter med lasso, 175
  Man with Bull Reindeer, 169
  Sleighride, 170
Scandinavia, 162, 163
science, 7, 9, 14, 28, 44, 51, 57, 108, 109, 115, 120, 127, 140, 178, 182, 185, 186, 187, 196–7, 257
scientific realism, 108
Scott, Bonnie Kime, 2, 92, 106, 277
Second World War, 16, 32, 127, 139, 231, 232, 235, 238, 241, 242, 244, 245
semiotics, 110
Sewell, Anna, 32, 69, 70, 182
sexuality, 13, 14, 94, 95, 96, 98, 105, 206, 208, 239, 241, 242, 243, 245
Shanghai, 56, 58, 68
Shetland pony, 119
short story, 16, 25, 113, 119, 144, 181–95, 202, 205, 211, 217, 222, 244, 282
Shukin, Nicole, *Animal Capital*, 184–5
Skum, Nils Nilsson, 162, 163, 168, 172
  Same sita (Sámi Village), 168
Singer, Peter, *Animal Liberation*, 13
Sitwell, Edith, 'Lullaby', 232
skin, 108, 109, 114, 115, 120, 177, 184, 211

slavery, 12, 24, 63, 64, 219–21
snake, 3, 80, 150, 191, 253
soldier, 118, 145–8, 231, 242, 273
South Africa, 8, 24
Spanish Civil War, 242, 243
speciesism, 10, 13, 57, 58, 114, 207
Spellbound, 233
Spender, Stephen, 'To Poets and Airmen', 232
Spengler, Birgitte and Babette Tischleder, *An Eclectic Bestiary*, 7
spider, 119
Spillers, Hortense, 12
squirrel, 110, 205
Strachey, Lytton, 46
stuffed animals *see* taxidermy
Steiner, Rudolf, 2
subjectivity, 9, 24, 56–8, 61, 66, 69, 80, 83, 92, 183, 156, 183, 191, 200, 202, 214, 225
suffragette movement, 117, 271
surrealism, 231, 233, 234
Sylvanian Families, 110

taxidermy, 107–22
  anthropomorphic taxidermy, 107, 109–11, 115
  commercial taxidermy, 108, 110, 111, 119
  diorama, 117
  human taxidermy, 114
  museal taxidermy, 107, 109, 110, 112, 115, 116
  naturalist taxidermy, 109, 116, 117
  Victorian taxidermy, 107–11, 120
  trophy taxidermy, 109, 110 117, 118
testimony, 152, 219–23
Texas Chainsaw Massacre, The, 120
Toomer, Jean, 215, 217
tortoise, 14, 15, 23–37, 89
transcendentalism, 94, 95
travel, 56–60, 69
trauma, 65, 98, 99, 102, 127, 143, 144, 149, 150, 151, 152, 153, 156, 264, 265–9, 271, 272–5

Trocchi, Alexander, *Cain's Book*, 268
trophy hunting *see* hunting
trope, 56, 60, 69, 117, 118, 122, 150, 217, 231, 251, 252
Turi, Johan, 162, 163, 166–8
   Muittalus samid birra, 166, 168
   'Reindeer Corral in Autumn', 166, 167

Uexküll, Jakob von, 11
   Umwelten, 11, 282
unhoming, 8, 13, 16, 17, 248–59

Van Vechten, Carl, 215
vegetarianism, 105n
Victorian, 15, 23, 24, 25, 52, 56, 57, 61, 107–11, 120, 122, 182, 183, 189, 195
violence, 5, 10, 24, 28, 29, 38, 83, 88, 102, 109, 114, 118, 119, 143, 144, 150, 151, 156, 159, 161, 168, 170, 185, 188, 192, 193, 195, 218–23, 231, 232, 237–45, 270
   chattel slavery, 12, 24, 63, 64, 219–21
   assault, 99, 117, 219–21, 242, 243
   military state, 220
   and white brutality, 218, 222, 223
   police, 30, 148, 158, 218, 219, 221–3
   predation, 223
vital materialism, 10, 11, 58, 87

Ward, Henry Augustus, 115
Ward, James Rowland, 110
Ward, John, 108
Wardian furniture, 110, 111, 114, 115, 118, 119
Warner, Sylvia Townsend, 231, 237–8
   'Death of Miss Green's Cottage', 237, 238
Weheliye, Alexander, 12, 220

Wells, H. G., 116, 228n
   'The Triumphs of a Taxidermist', 112–14, 119, 120
Weil, Kari, *Thinking About Animals*, 9
whiteness, 62, 16, 216, 226
white violence *see* violence and white brutality
wilderness, 182, 183, 185, 186, 189, 190, 194
wildness, 7, 200, 208, 209
wolf, 45, 192, 194, 209, 210, 211–12
Wolfe, Cary, 9, 10, 20, 83, 89, 90, 157, 192, 196, 214
woods, 189, 193, 194, 204, 205, 212
   see also forest
Woolf, Leonard, 15, 24, 28–32, 36, 54, 249
Woolf, Virginia
   Between the Acts, 232, 233
   Flush: A Biography, 18, 23–37, 38–55, 56–7, 71, 282, 290, 294, 295
   Jacob's Room, 47
   'The Lady in the Looking Glass', 282
   'Modern Fiction', 284, 290
   Mrs Dalloway, 55
   Orlando: A Biography, 25, 40, 45, 54, 55, 117, 118
   'Oxford Street Tide', 30, 36
   A Room of One's Own, 33, 54, 283, 286, 290
   'A Sketch of the Past', 279, 285, 290
   To the Lighthouse, 46, 55, 249
   The Waves, 45, 47, 286, 289, 290
   The Years, 55
Wynter, Sylvia, 12, 223

Yeats, W. B., 92

zoo, 29
zoomorphism, 111, 130
zoopoetics, 76, 88, 89
Zoological Gallery (Oxford Street), 43, 109
Zoological Society of London, 42, 108